THE WAR TRUMPET

Iberian Epic Poetry, 1543–1639

EDITED BY EMIRO MARTÍNEZ-OSORIO
AND MERCEDES BLANCO

The War Trumpet

Iberian Epic Poetry, 1543–1639

UNIVERSITY OF TORONTO PRESS
Toronto Buffalo London

© University of Toronto Press 2023
Toronto Buffalo London
utorontopress.com
Printed in the USA

ISBN 978-1-4875-4632-8 (cloth)   ISBN 978-1-4875-4633-5 (EPUB)
                                   ISBN 978-1-4875-4635-9 (PDF)

Library and Archives Canada Cataloguing in Publication

Title: The war trumpet : Iberian epic poetry, 1543–1639 / edited by Emiro
   Martínez-Osorio and Mercedes Blanco.
Names: Martinez-Osorio, Emiro, editor. | Blanco, Mercedes, 1953– editor.
Series: Toronto Iberic ; 79.
Description: Series statement: Toronto Iberic ; 79 | Includes bibliographical
   references and index.
Identifiers: Canadiana (print) 2022046121X | Canadiana (ebook)
   20220461309 | ISBN 9781487546328 (cloth) | ISBN 9781487546359
   (PDF) | ISBN 9781487546335 (EPUB)
Subjects: LCSH: Epic poetry, Spanish – Iberian Peninsula – History and
   criticism. | LCSH: Spanish poetry – Classical period, 1500–1700 – History
   and criticism. | LCGFT: Literary criticism.
Classification: LCC PQ6088 .W37 2023 | DDC 861/.0320903–dc23

We wish to acknowledge the land on which the University of Toronto Press
operates. This land is the traditional territory of the Wendat, the Anishnaabeg,
the Haudenosaunee, the Métis, and the Mississaugas of the Credit First
Nation.

University of Toronto Press acknowledges the financial support of the
Government of Canada, the Canada Council for the Arts, and the Ontario Arts
Council, an agency of the Government of Ontario, for its publishing activities.

Contents

Part Three: Gendered Epics

Part Four: New Historiographic and Cartographic Boundaries

Illustrations

Acknowledgments

A collaborative endeavour, such as this volume, is the result of the effort of numerous people and institutions. Some of the chapters in this book were first presented at panels organized for the biannual meeting of the Society for Renaissance and Baroque Hispanic Poetry or sponsored by SRBHP for the annual meeting of the Renaissance Society of America. The quality of those essays benefited from the intellectual community and the stimulating dialogues that have become a trademark of SR-BHP. Other chapters were first presented at the symposium *Epic New Worlds: Alonso de Ercilla's* La Araucana *(1569–2019)* held at the Centre for Renaissance and Reformation Studies at the University of Toronto in October 2019. The symposium was made possible with contributions from the Centre for Comparative Literature and the Department of Spanish and Portuguese at the University of Toronto, the Canadian Association of Hispanists, *Revista Canadiense de Estudios Hispánicos*, the Thomas Fisher Rare Book Library, the Department of Spanish and Portuguese at Princeton University, the Department of Romance Languages at the University of Georgia at Athens, the Department of Languages, Literatures, and Linguistics and the Office of the Provost at York University. It is my pleasure to record my debt of gratitude to the group of scholars who participated in the symposium: Mercedes Blanco, Imogen Choi, Nicole Delia Legnani, Jason McCloskey, Matthew da Mota, Aude Plagnard, Cory A. Reed, Luis Fernando Restrepo, María Gracia Ríos, Shaun Ross, Felipe Valencia, and Elizabeth R. Wright; I also would like to thank Ettan Matt Kavaler, Natalie Oeltjen, Sanda Munjic, David Fernandez, Miguel Torrens, Odile Cisneros, Susan Ehrlich, Maria João Dodman, Susan Antebi, Laura Colantoni, Mario Boido, Yolanda Iglesias, Alan Durston, Tamara Walker, Felipe Ruan, Enriqueta Zafra, and Antonio Ricci. The success of the symposium was made possible thanks to their support and collegiality.

I am profoundly indebted to the anonymous readers for their thoughtful comments and suggestions and to all the contributors for revising their chapters with eagerness and professionalism. Financial support for publication has come from the Faculty of Liberal Arts & Professional Studies at York University, a SSHRC Exchange – KMb Grant, and Sorbonne Université. I owe a great debt of gratitude to Janet Friskney, Timothy Lytle, and copy editor Charles Stuart for their careful attention to the manuscript and many suggestions for improvement, and to Sean Manning for his excellent English rendition of the original Spanish version of chapters 5 and 9. I thank Suzanne Rancourt, Barbara Porter, and the editorial team at University of Toronto Press for their unwavering support for this volume and for their guidance throughout the different stages of the publication process. Here too, I am indebted to Professor Mercedes Blanco, who embraced this project from day one. Her advice, friendship, intellect, and wit enriched immeasurably the process of assembling this collection of essays. My deepest gratitude goes to my partner, Heather Nicole White, and to our children, Amelia Rose and Elías Joaquín, who fill my days with joy. As usual, Heather generously read every word I wrote and our conversations helped me find unexpected connections and fine-tune many ideas. The friendship and love we share has shaped everything I have written for more than twenty years.

THE WAR TRUMPET

Introduction: The Age of Iberian Epic

EMIRO MARTÍNEZ-OSORIO

The War Trumpet: Iberian Epic Poetry, 1543–1639 addresses a range of pressing issues key to understanding early modernity in the realms of Spain and Portugal, the first maritime empires. Specific objectives animating this collection include the following. First, to examine the transformation of epic topoi in the works of poets like Jerónimo Corte-Real who wrote outstanding epic poems in Portuguese and Spanish, and sought patronage, respectively, from King Sebastião of Portugal and King Philip II of Spain.[1] Second, to feature essays that elucidate long-standing interpretative conundrums present in canonical works such as Luis de Camões's *Os Lusíadas* (1572) and Alonso de Ercilla's *La Araucana* (1569, 1578, 1589). And third, to draw critical attention to long-neglected poems such as Luis Zapata de Chaves's *Carlo famoso* (1566), Juan de Castellanos's *Elegías de varones ilustres de Indias* (1589), and Bernardo de Balbuena's *El Bernardo, o victoria de Roncesvalles* (1624). In its entirety, this collection fosters greater appreciation of the intersection between poetry, war, and exploration, and encourages more critical understanding of the transformative changes that took place on the shores of the Mediterranean Sea and the Atlantic, the Pacific, and the Indian Oceans during the period of Iberian expansion.

The War Trumpet expands understanding of epic poetry by posing questions seldom previously raised in relation to these poems, particularly those concerned with early modern understandings of the natural world, the discipline of cartography, the practice of poetic imitation, or the reception of Petrarchism in the newly established viceroyalties of the New World. In addition, this collection, whose essays are authored by emerging and leading scholars, addresses topics as diverse as material culture, the ethical implications of violence in warfare, and the politico-theological underpinnings of Spain's incorporation, in 1580, of the Kingdom of Portugal and its overseas territories. Since the production of epic and heroic poetry in the domains of Spain and Portugal was versatile, enduring, and widespread, the authors featured in this collection do not abide by a single methodology; instead, they pursue innovative theoretical frameworks designed to illuminate the pivotal role of epic poetry in the cultural, political, and social milieux of Spain and Portugal.

Although issues pertaining to imperialism and colonialism are undoubtedly central to the epic genre, this collection proposes the following: in the Iberian Peninsula during the sixteenth and seventeenth centuries, individuals from different social and economic backgrounds found appeal in the prestige of epic for a variety of reasons. These motivations cannot be fully apprehended through the constricted dichotomy of "epics of the imperial victors and epics of the defeated," or solely through a lens such as "Iberian satanic epics."[2] Instead, as stated by Rodrigo Cacho Casal and as the essays in this volume confirm, Iberian epic poetry was a "varied, rich, marvellous and exemplary" genre; in other words, "a *multigenre* able to encompass all of them, including tragedy, thus demonstrating that it is superior to it."[3] When tracing the trajectory of the theorizations that informed the production of epic poems in Portugal, a similar understanding of epic emerges from Hélio Alves's commentary of the prologue by Aquiles Estaço:

> What Estaço is effectively proposing across these two prefaces (the dedication to the prince and the prologue) is a treatise on the art of narrative and heroic poetry, in which certain elements of dramatic art as well as the whole of rhetorical art have determining roles. This classification of rhetorical practices becomes decisive in the effort to identify the theory of epic poetry that was being formulated at that time, since by requiring not only a knowledge of the Aristotelian theory of tragedy, but also of oratorical theory, Estaço postulated that, in essence, during that period both could be combined harmoniously.[4]

Similarly, Aude Plagnard reminds us that "the epic is, of all literary genres, the most varied, both by its long history and by its presence in a multitude of geographical and cultural areas."[5] That writers gravitated towards epic poetry during the Renaissance and Baroque periods is not at all surprising. The impulse to experiment, or to offer a synthesis, informs numerous Iberian texts of this time. These range in diversity from Garcilaso de la Vega's "Eclogue II" to Luis de Góngora's *Soledades*. Among the poems studied in this volume, Bernardo de Balbuena's *El Bernardo, o victoria de Roncesvalles* (1624) announces most forcefully to its readers the all-encompassing objectives of the poem. In the frontispiece to the first edition, Balbuena states that his ambitious poem is "a work woven with an impressive variety of elements: Spanish antiquities, Spanish noble houses and lineages, the customs of different peoples, geographic descriptions of the lushest parts of the world, the architecture of buildings and sumptuous palaces, gardens, objects and novelties, transformations and new enchantments and outlandish artifice, all filled with judgments and moralities" (obra tejida con una admirable variedad de cosas: antigüedades de España, casas y linajes nobles de ella, costumbres de gentes, geográficas descripciones de las más floridas partes del mundo, fábricas de edificios y suntuosos palacios, jardines, cosas y frescuras, transformaciones y encantamientos de nuevo y peregrino artificio llenos de sentencias y moralidades).

However, indebted with to the classical literary tradition, the narrative poems written during Portugal's and Spain's rise on the global stage often dealt with topics quite unimaginable to the likes of Virgil or Homer. They reveal the astounding opportunities for upward social mobility and self-promotion afforded by broader access to print, and the vast amount of knowledge and material wealth accrued through maritime exploration. Iberian poets of the period were quite cognizant about their ventures into uncharted territory, and that awareness informed their literary journeys.[6] The essays in this volume contribute to recovering the sense of awe invoked by the epic poems from this period. The authors of these poems inspired such reaction with new strategies of authorial self-fashioning and self-assertion at a time in which the redeployment of well-known material was still entrenched in the literary culture.

When Frank Pierce called for the re-evaluation of epic poetry in Spanish Golden Age literature more than six decades ago, he lamented the lack of a definite critical assessment on the language and structure of poems such as Diego de Hojeda's *La Christiada* (1611) and Bernardo de Balbuena's *El Bernardo, o victoria de Roncesvalles*; he also asserted that crucial aspects of Alonso de Ercilla's *La Araucana* merited further critical attention.[7] Pierce's observations remain true today to some extent. Among the changes that could be noticed, contemporary scholars hold

Figure 0.1. Frontispiece to Bernardo de Balbuena *El Bernardo, o victoria de Roncesvalles* (1624). Image courtesy of the Thomas Fisher Rare Book Library, University of Toronto. Toronto. *El Bernardo* narrates Roland's defeat at the hands of Bernardo del Carpio at the Battle of Roncevaux. Balbuena completed his poem by 1600 and dedicated it to don Pedro Fernández de Castro, the great Count of Lemos, president of the Royal Council of the Indies and Viceroy of Naples. The publication of the poem was delayed for more than two decades and the seventh Count of Lemos died before the poem appeared in print. In the frontispiece of the princeps edition, Balbuena dedicates his poem to don Pedro's brother, Francisco Fernández de Castro. Antonio Mira de Amescua approved the publication of *El Bernardo* by stating: "learned Spaniards, attentive to the lessons of the Poets, have no Poem like this in their language. Because in the variety of events and episodes, it emulates Ludovico Ariosto, and in the unity of action and the composition of the fabula, Torquato Tasso."

greater appreciation for the value of studying epic and heroic poetry beyond linguistic boundaries, and outside the limits imposed by national literary traditions. Similarly, scholars today are more eager to explore the constitutive relationships among the poems themselves as they engage in dialogue with each other, or emulate not only prestigious literary models, but also works written by their contemporaries. A prime example of the advantages of this approach is found in James Nicolopulos's *The Poetics of Empire in the Indies: Prophecy and Imitation in "La Araucana" and "Os Lusíadas"* (2000). Nicolopulos examines the more ambitious literary agenda embraced by Alonso de Ercilla in the second and third instalments of his poem after the publication of *Os Lusíadas*. Rather than digressive or irrelevant, Nicolopulos argues, the narration of events that take place far from the theatre of war in Chile, and particularly the global vision offered by the wizard Fitón, form part of an intricate web of imperial prophecy that runs through parts 2 and 3 of *La Araucana* and is imbued with poetic, ideological, and dynastic rivalries. In turn, Hélio Alves points out that Camões's reading of Jerónimo Corte-Real's *Sucesso do Segundo Cerco de Diu* played a decisive role in the writing of key portions of *Os Lusíadas*, referring to elements of the work not yet completed prior to Camões's return to Portugal in 1570. In addition, Alves's study reveals that in poems such as *Felicísima Victoria concedida del Cielo al señor Don Juan de Austria* (1578) and *Naufrágio y perdição de Sepulveda* (1594), Corte-Real offers a contending view of epic poetry and Portuguese history when compared to the one offered by Camões.[8] More recently, Aude Plagnard examines the poems by Ercilla and Corte-Real, and persuasively argues for the emergence of a common and original genre of Iberian epics between 1569 and 1589. While *The War Trumpet* exceeds the scope of Plagnard's work by offering a broader chronological and geographic range, and by devoting attention to poems written in the viceroyalties across the Atlantic, from its conception the volume was acutely informed by Plagnard's pluralistic understanding of Iberian epics, particularly her view that the genre was "confronted with a territory and writing practices under construction."[9]

From a literary perspective, the essays in this collection use epic poetry as a vantage point from which to capture the dynamic shifts that took place in the literary field from the publication of *Las obras de Boscán y algunas de Garcilaso de la Vega, repartidas en quatro libros* in 1543 to the appearance of Manuel de Faria e Sousa's annotated edition of *Os Lusíadas* in 1639. As an erudite poet with a "long and so intimate connection with the actual workings of imperial warfare and diplomacy," and as a soldier "who received many signs of imperial favor and performed many acts of imperial service,"[10] Garcilaso de la Vega was well positioned to produce a superb epic poem, but he died before attempting to do so. The closest Garcilaso ever came to such an endeavour was Nemoroso's historical narrative in the second half of "Eclogue II," an encomiastic section celebrating the House of Alba.[11] However, as several essays in this book attest, many authors who chose to write epics looked back to Garcilaso de la Vega, engaging in a productive dialogue with his work. In addition, without establishing any direct connection, it is worth noting that in pivotal sections of "Eclogue II," Garcilaso anticipates one of the vital challenges faced by subsequent poets endeavouring to write epic poems about recent historical events: the imbrication in the fabric of the text of the poet's personal experience and the narration of recent history. Moreover, for a poet like Alonso de Ercilla in particular, Garcilaso de la Vega served as the paradigm of imitative practice, while the ekphrastic prophecy displayed in the crystal urn in "Eclogue II" is also a crucial subtext to grasp fully the aesthetically encoded messages of Luis de Camões's poem.[12]

The publication in 1639 of Manuel de Faria e Sousa's annotated edition *Lusíadas de Luis de Camoens, Principe de los poetas de España* represents a high point of *Os Lusíadas*'s rise to canonical status, a process facilitated in no small part by the translation of the poem into Spanish, and the attention it received in Spain. As Hélio Alves reminds us, Faria e Sousa's edition of *Os Lusíadas* represents "the most thorough literary commentary of the work of any poet since medieval times."[13] In this sense, Faria e Sousa's edition of *Os Lusíadas* embodies the productive intercultural exchange that serves as one of the distinguishing features of Spain's and Portugal's contributions to the international "Republic of Letters" (*respublica litterarum*).

The phrase "The War Trumpet" included in the title serves both as a metaphor for the epic poems studied here, and as a reminder of the shared literary culture that flourished in the Iberian Peninsula and their territories abroad during the sixteenth and seventeenth centuries. The phrase comes from the first line of the *canción* that the nineteen-year-old Luis de Góngora wrote to celebrate Luis Gómez de Tapia's translation of *Os Lusíadas* into Spanish in 1580: "Suene la trompa bélica."[14] At the time Góngora wrote his celebratory poem, Spanish authors were starting to read "Camões as the new Virgil of the new Augustus's Spanish Empire."[15] In closing, by offering a transatlantic and broader vision, this collection of essays turns away from terminology such as "Spanish Golden Age," "The Age of Cervantes," or "The Age of Góngora" and proposes instead to refer to the period between 1543 and 1639 as the Age of Iberian Epics. Without disputing the merits of the former labels, the periodization I propose takes seriously not only Hélio Alves's invitation to reassess the literary history of the Iberian Peninsula, but also Garcilaso de la Vega's creative rewriting of passages from classical epics as well as Miguel de Cervantes claim that his most important work, *Los trabajos de Persiles y Sigismunda* (1617), was an "epic in prose" that emulated not Virgil, but Heliodorus. Certainly, "[i]n its engagement with epic as an encyclopedic form, the *Persiles* explores a paradoxical reconciliation of the opposing values and ideals that shape the epic tradition."[16]

The image on the cover of this volume reproduces an illustration that poet and painter Jerónimo Corte-Real prepared for canto XV of *Sucesso do Segundo Cerco de Diu* (ca. 1568–9), a poem about the siege in 1546 of the Portuguese fortress at Diu near the Gulf of Cambay, India (see fig. 0.2).[17] The drawing depicts a fleet of heavily armed Portuguese vessels at sea. The majority of the ships in the upper section are slightly tilted by powerful winds. As they sail towards the horizon, these ships proudly display on their sails the Order of Christ Cross, a symbol of Portuguese maritime expansion that frames the dangerous voyage as a knightly crusade. The vessel in the centre displays a banner from the royal coat of arms of the Kingdom of Portugal and other colourful military insignias. In the lower half of the composition, a group of mythological sea creatures sing and play musical instruments, including a harp, flute, seashell horn, viola da braccio, and chirimía. Above them, on the left side, Neptune sits in his horse-drawn chariot, a trident in hand, while enjoying their performance. In its original setting, the image, and the corresponding portion of the poem, serve to shift the action from the fortress at Diu to Goa, the seat of Viceroy Dom João de Castro (1500–48), whose assistance proved crucial for the Portuguese victory.[18] We highlight this illustration because it also directs the attention of its viewers to crucial aspects of the period under study, among them the centrality of the ocean and the process of mastering wind systems in the early phase of exploration, as well as some of the technological improvements that cemented military and commercial advantages (superior ships, heavy artillery). In addition, the prominence given to the mass of anonymous sailors pushing the oars in the largest vessel in the centre conveys the human cost of expansion and serves as a remnant of the violence that accompanied forced enslavement. Moreover, Corte-Real's illustration renders eloquently the interplay between

Figure 0.2. Illustration prepared by Jerónimo Corte-Real for canto XV of his poem *Sucesso do Segundo Cerco de Diu* (ca. 1568–9). Casa de Cadaval, n.º 31 PT/TT/CCDV/31 Arquivo Nacional da Torre do Tombo, Lisbon. Reproduced by permission.

The first edition of Corte Real's poem appeared in Lisbon in 1574 without the twenty illustrations carefully prepared by the poet. *Sucesso do Segundo Cerco de Diu* was translated into Spanish by Pedro de Padilla, who was a prolific poet in his own right. The Spanish translation received approval for publication by Alonso de Ercilla in 1594 and was printed in Alcalá de Henares in 1597.

history and fantasy, as well as the tension between Judaeo-Christian elements and the pagan mythological apparatus evident in some of the epic poems produced during this period.

Two of the three essays included in part 1 of *The War Trumpet* ("Of Gods and Textual Models") focus precisely on the significance of pagan gods and other classical mythological figures like the ones depicted in the illustration. The volume opens with an examination of the relationship between *Os Lusíadas* and Corte-Real's *Felicissima victoria* (1578), a fifteen-canto poem in Spanish that sings the triumph of the Christian coalition over Ottoman naval forces at the Battle of Lepanto (1571). Taking the lukewarm reception of *Sucesso do Segundo Cerco de Diu* in the court of King Sebastião as his point of departure, Hélio Alves in chapter 1 argues that Corte-Real wrote his second epic poem "not only as a way of recovering political and poetic initiative, but also as a tight neo-Virgilian response to the challenge raised by divine action in *Os Lusíadas*." Although until recently scholars have failed to grasp fully Corte-Real's poetic talent and contributions to Iberian epic, Alves's analysis shows how allusion and verbal and episodic reminiscences turn *Felicissima victoria* into a poetic triumph, one that creatively corrects narrative inconsistencies in *Os Lusíadas*, including the roles assigned to Venus and Bacchus in Camões's account of Vasco da Gama's first journey to India. Similarly, Alves's study demonstrates how Corte-Real marginalizes Camões's poem by signalling *Sucesso do Segundo Cerco de Diu*, rather than *Os Lusíadas*, as the immediate predecessor for his poem about the victory of Don Juan de Austria (1547–78) at Lepanto.

The pagan gods inhabiting the epyllions of Silvestre de Balboa (1563–ca. 1647) and Bento Teixeira (ca.1560–1600) have long marvelled critics for their merger of American nature with European artistic models derived from Greco-Roman antiquity. In chapter 2, Luis Rodríguez-Rincón argues that the Greco-Roman gods constituted not a simple aesthetic convention, but rather a charged symbolic language located at the intersection of nature and art. As ciphers through whom the secrets of nature were conveyed to mortals in the mythographic tradition, the pagan gods could merge with the natural world to constitute a syncretic order, a "Pagan Nature" that asserted a designed and hierarchical structure to the world. Through a comparative study of the poems of Teixeira, Balboa, and Camões, Rodríguez-Rincón's essay ties Pagan Nature to Iberian colonial ideology. It is in opposition to Camões's Triton from *Os Lusíadas* that the pagan gods of Teixeira and Balboa assert a naturalized colonial hierarchy in Brazil and Cuba. In a world in which the pagan gods speak for the environment, and assert a concord between colonial power and nature, colonialism itself is naturalized. The nascent criollo consciousness and crypto-Jewish resistance that critics read in Balboa and Teixeira's epyllions, respectively, must also account for the role of Pagan Nature in making Iberian imperialism a part of American nature. Here again, the drawing by Jerónimo Corte-Real is useful for grasping two of the central functions of what Rodríguez-Rincón labels "Pagan Nature" in early modern poetry and artwork. First, the horizontal row of musicians in the bottom half of the image transforms the advance of the Portuguese galleys into a scene of oceanic triumph. Much like nymphs and satyrs celebrate the freedom of Bishop Altamirano in Balboa's *Espejo de paciencia*, as well as the triumph of Catholic settlers over French Huguenot pirates, the tritons and mermaids in Corte-Real's illustration accompany and celebrate the Portuguese fleet in Asia. Second, the figure of Neptune riding his horse-drawn chariot signals a direct association between natural phenomena and the pagan gods. Neptune's horses are turning in the direction of the wind that is propelling the caravels in the upper half of the image. The winds propelling the Portuguese fleet are thus associated with divine providence by their visual relation to Neptune's turning chariot. In short, Corte-Real's illustration conveys forcefully the centrality of the pagan gods to a conceptual nexus between divine providence, the representation of nature, and colonial overseas ventures in the early modern period.

Masterfully interlacing two separate literary historiographies, in chapter 3 Mercedes Blanco takes us beyond the geographic contours of the Iberian Peninsula to establish the grounds for comparing Torquato Tasso's *Gerusalemme liberata* and Alonso de Ercilla's *La Araucana*, two long narrative epic poems, both of which had a laborious gestation process. While the impact of Ariosto on these poems by Tasso and Ercilla has long been acknowledged, Blanco further identifies points of contact between Tasso and Ercilla in relation to their efforts to reconcile ostensibly diverging poetic requirements. More precisely, Blanco argues that, as they aimed to surpass the appeal and success of *Orlando furioso*, Tasso and Ercilla "were ultimately doomed to give a prominent place in their works to the mood and ethos of lyric poetry, through intertextual connections with the foremost lyric poets in their respective traditions: Petrarch and Garcilaso de la Vega." In her analysis of how each poet produced a fragmented and ambiguous poem quite distinct from the coherent work they initially set out to write, Blanco gives special attention to the story of Tancredi and the warrior woman Clorinda, as well as the episode describing the amorous interlude between Lautaro and Guacolda in the *Gerusalemme liberata* and *La Araucana*, respectively. Blanco's comparison of an epic by one of the most emblematic figures from the Italian Republic of Letters with the work of a Spanish courtier

cons of the appropriation of hendecasyllable.[23] However, just as important to assess in Castellanos's writings are the intense debates about the nature of Indigenous people, the rights of those individuals who carried out the enterprise of conquest, and the effects of the implementations of the reformist project inherent in the New Laws (1542). After all, Castellanos's *Elegías* represents one of the most unapologetic examples of pro-*encomendero* writing, a project which, in turn, included the "bold transmutation of dominant poetic discourses typically associated with the nobility."[24] The analysis of how Castellanos's "Elegy 14" conveys the message that certain kinds of poetry relate to certain types of men also explores two pivotal sections of the poem in which Castellanos abandons the male-centred priorities of his poetic discourse to focus his attention on female characters. First, when he praises the Spanish women residing on the island of Margarita, and then when he memorializes Inés de Atienza, the unfortunate lover of Pedro de Ursúa, who died at the hands of the rebel Lope de Aguirre and his followers.

In chapter 7, Nicole Legnani digs deeper into questions regarding gender in Colonial Spanish American society. Legnani compares the depiction of the relationship between Fresia and Caupolicán in Pedro de Oña's *Arauco domado* (1596) and its immediate predecessor, Ercilla's *La Araucana*. In her essay, she pays acute attention to the potency of Fresia's curse of Caupolicán, considering the subtexts provided by Dido's curse of Aeneas from Virgil's *Aeneid* and the Council of Trent's reforms to the sacrament of marriage. For Legnani, Fresia's public disavowal of her marriage and her son carries implications for future generations of Indigenous people, and, although *La Araucana* does denounce some forms of colonial violence, "it performs others, and even has the native Other perform [them]." From this vantage point, Legnani then juxtaposes the crises of succession in the Arauco region to Philip II's claim of the throne left vacant by the death of King Sebastião and the subsequent integration of Portugal in 1581. On the other hand, Legnani explains, in Oña's *Arauco domado*, the depiction of the love scene between Caupolicán and Fresia erases the horrors of the impalement of Caupolicán while, at the same time, revealing a "criollo ambivalence on indigeneity in the Spanish empire, one that both exalts the virtues of the land of his birth, while advocating for its cultivation and settlement by Hispanic mores and people." Through the analysis of the imbrication between marriage and indigeneity on both sides of the Atlantic, Legnani leads us to reconsider the corpus of female characters that appears in Colonial Spanish American epics, giving them consideration well beyond the critical attention already bestowed on Indigenous characters such as Tegualda, Guacolda, Glaura, and Lauca. Legnani previously paved the way to pursue this line of analysis through her recent article about the anonymous pregnant Mapuche women who are noted in *La Araucana* for joining their male counterparts in defending their territory.[25]

Part 4 ("New Historiographic and Cartographic Boundaries") includes two essays about poems published roughly at the opposite ends of the spectrum considered by *The War Trumpet*: Luis Zapata de Chaves's *Carlo famoso* (1566) and Bernardo de Balbuena's *El Bernardo, o victoria de Roncesvalles* (1624). While these two poems both offer ample evidence of the lasting impact in Spain of Ariosto's *Orlando furioso*, they are grouped together in a section that explores epic poetry's engagement with contemporary developments in the fields of history and cartography. Prior to the first Atlantic crossing, Christopher Columbus lived in Portugal for several years, and unsuccessfully sought support from King Dom João II (1455–95) for an expedition to reach Asia by sailing westward. Most historians today agree that Columbus "was familiar with the cartographic tradition flourishing in Portugal at the time,"[26] and that he acquired his "navigational knowledge and skills" in Portugal.[27] However, in the wake of the first Atlantic crossing, there emerged a legend attributing to an anonymous Spanish pilot the knowledge of an entire new continent and the maritime route to reach it. In chapter 8, Jason McCloskey examines the version of that legend included in Luis Zapata de Chaves's *Carlo famoso*, a sprawling, fifty-canto poem about the deeds of Charles V (1500–58) in Europe. McCloskey situates Zapata's version of the legend in the context of the emerging historiographic tradition about the New World, chiefly the works by Francisco López de Gómara (1511–66), Gonzalo Fernández de Oviedo (1478–1557), and the humanitarian friar Bartolomé de las Casas (1484–1566). According to McCloskey, the inclusion of the anonymous pilot in Zapata's rendition of Columbus's navigational feats conjures Fray Bartolomé de las Casas's criticism against the excesses of the conquistadors but at the same time "symbolically releases ... Columbus from any assignment of guilt for the ravages of conquest and colonization."

The volume closes with Martín Zulaica López's chapter 9 study of the reliance of Bernardo de Balbuena (1563–1627) on maps from Abraham Ortelius's *Theatrum Orbis Terratum* (1570) to write the stanzas that describe Alcina's journey to the palace of Morgana in the first canto of *El Bernardo, o victoria de Roncesvalles* (1624), a twenty-four-canto poem about Bernardo del Carpio's victory over Roland at the Battle of Roncevaux Pass (778). As indicated earlier in this introduction, in the frontispiece of *El Bernardo*, Balbuena announces that his poem will include "geographic descriptions of the lushest parts of the world." Indeed, relying on *kataskopia* (the view from above) and other topoi with a long provenance in the epic tradition, the poem includes extensive descriptions of different regions from around the globe that merit comparison with the ones readers grasp through Tethys's globe in *Os Lusíadas*, the world map in *La Araucana*, and the aerial journeys described in Ariosto´s *Orlando furioso*. Through the close analysis of its sources, Zulaica López argues that *El Bernardo* offers evidence of the emergence of a new cartographic mentality (cartodoxy), and of the impact of the generic innovation represented by the geographical charting of fantasy. In doing so, if the hero of Balbuena's poem (as well as the soldier-poets of the previous generation) had shown dexterity in handling the sword and the pen, Zulaica López's analysis shows how Bernardo de Balbuena distinguishes himself by showing his skill with "the pen and with maps."

In closing, the nine essays included in this volume are divided into four sections that reflect the state of the discipline and seek to spark further comparative dialogues: part 1: "Of Gods and Textual Models"; part 2: "The Poet as Hero"; part 3: "Gendered Epics"; and part 4: "New Historiographic and Cartographic Boundaries."[28] The volume is enhanced by an afterword by Mercedes Blanco in which she reflects on the opportunities afforded by reading epic poetry in our times and illuminates the critical path that brought us to this point. From the outset, I acknowledge that this collection of essays is not comprehensive: it would require several volumes to encompass fully the dozens of poems published during this period, or to bring into full critical view other poems that were censored or that received approval for publication but never appeared in print.[29] In addition, while the collection is quite diverse, it is left to future scholars to examine the impact made by the vibrant theatre culture on poets like Alonso de Ercilla, or to study epic poems in relation to emerging categories of racial difference.[30] It is worth noting that the period encompassed by these poems coincided with the intensification of the slave trade. Here again, Corte Real's image offers ample food for thought. In particular, the noticeably darker skin complexion of the "*cautivos galeotes*" at the centre and the image of the guard whipping them beckons us to interrogate the racial underpinnings of the poetic evocations of "este mundo de extrema violencia y crueldad."[31]

NOTES

1 Jerónimo Corte-Real published in 1574 *Sucesso do segundo cerco de Diu* [MS ca. 1568], a poem about a 1546 Portuguese victory in India and in 1578 *Felicísima Victoria concedida del Cielo al señor Don Juan de Austria* [MS 1575], a poem about the Battle of Lepanto in 1571.

2 For an examination of the epic tradition in terms of epics of the winners and epics of the defeated, see Quint, *Epic and Empire*, 8. For an approach to Iberian epic poetry from the perspective of satanic epics, see Cañizares-Esguerra, *Puritan Conquistadors*, 35–81.

3 Quotes in the original language are "vario, rico, maravilloso y ejemplar" and "un *multigénero* capaz de englobarlos a todos, incluso a la tragedia, demostrando de este modo que es superior a ella." See Cacho Casal, "Volver a un género olvidado," 5.

4 "Lo que Estaço efectivamente nos propone en el conjunto de estos dos prefacios (dedicatoria al príncipe y proemio general) es un tratado sobre el arte del poema narrativo y heroico, en el que tanto una parte del arte teatral como la globalidad del arte retórico tienen papeles determinantes. Esta clasificación de las ciencias del discurso se vuelve decisiva para el propósito de identificar la teoría de la épica que entonces se iba formulando, puesto que, al obligar no sólo al conocimiento simultáneo de la teoría aristotélica de la tragedia, sino también al de la teoría oratoria, Estaço postulaba, en el fondo, que una y otra, en esa época, se podían conjugar armoniosamente." Alves, "Teoría de la épica en el renacimiento portugués," 146.

5 "que l'épopée est, de tous les genres littéraires, le plus varié, tant par sa longue histoire que par sa présence dans une multitude d'aires géographiques et culturelles." Plagnard, *Une épopée ibérique*, 6.

6 In this regard, I agree with Jorge Cañizares-Esguerra's assessment that in his remarkable study of Ercilla's and Camões's poems, Quint "overlooks the self-confident modernity of the sixteenth-century Iberians as a critical configuring factor of their poetry." See "The Colonial Iberian Roots of the Scientific Revolution," 170.

7 Pierce, *La poesía épica del siglo de oro*, 10.

8 Alves, "Teoría de la épica en el renacimiento portugués" and "Corte Real, Jerónimo." See also Alves's "Design Ingeniously Corrected: Corte-Real, *Os Lusíadas* and the Gods in the *Felicissima*" in the present volume, *The War Trumpet*.

9 "confronté à un territoire et à des pratiques d'écriture en construction." Plagnard, *Une épopée ibérique*, 4.

10 Helgerson, *A Sonnet from Carthage*, 6.

11 For a study of Eclogue II as "an encyclopedic work of poetry" that contains "the first classical epic to be written in Renaissance Spanish," see Rivers, "Nymphs, Shepherds, and Heroes."

12 Nicolopulos, *The Poetics of Empire in the Indies*. For the connection between Garcilaso de la Vega and Ercilla, see also the first chapter in Felipe Valencia's *The Melancholy Void*.

13 "los más extensos comentarios literarios jamás realizados a la obra de un poeta post-medieval." Alves, "Teoría de la épica en el renacimiento portugués."

14 On Góngora's poem, see Micó, "Góngora a los diecinueve años" and
   Alonso, "La recepción de *Os Lusíadas* en España (1579–1650)."

15 Martínez, "A Poet of Our Own," 75.

16 Rupp, *Heroic Forms*, 18. For a comprehensive analysis of Cervantes's exploration of classical epic in *Persiles*, see Armstrong-Roche's *Cervantes' Epic
   Novel*.

17 Corte-Real prepared twenty handsome illustrations for his poem, but his
   drawings were excluded from the 1574 edition of *Sucesso do Segundo Cerco de
   Diu*. The illustrated manuscript of the poem is at Arquivo Nacional da Torre
   do Tombo, Casa de Cadaval. Reproductions of the illustrations are included
   in Plagnard, *Une Épopée Ibérique* and in Padilla, *La Verdadera Historia y admirable suceso del segundo cerco de Diu*, edited by Herraiz and DiFranco.

18 The shift from Diu to Goa is highlighted earlier in canto XIV, and the corresponding illustration depicting the viceroy receiving news of the Portuguese resistance (Plagnard, *Une Épopée Ibérique*, 172–9). See also Plagnard,
   "Épica e imagen: un análisis sociopoético de los manuscritos de Jerónimo
   Corte-Real."

19 On the genre of *relaciones de méritos y servicios* in Colonial Spanish America
   and its connection to the economy of *mercedes* (royal rewards), see Folger,
   Writing as Poaching.

20 In her article, Uribe Bracho refers mainly to sixteenth-century Spanish
   lyric poets. See "Orphans of Orpheus," 196.

21 Navarrete, *Orphans of Petrarch*, 2.

22 Middlebrook, *Imperial Lyric*, 7.

23 See Castellanos, *Elegías*, volume IV, 350–1.

24 Martínez-Osorio, *Authority, Piracy and Captivity*, xi–xviii.

25 See Legnani, "La minoría insurgente,"

26 Wey Gómez, *The Tropics of Empire*, 11.

27 Newitt, *Portugal in European and World History*, 49.

28 As I was finishing this introduction, I realized the extent to which I had
   returned to the questions about Iberian Studies or epic poetry I was introduced to in graduate seminars under the direction of Jorge Cañizares-
   Esguerra and the late James Nicolopulos. I benefited immeasurably from
   their intellectual generosity and I hope this volume renews those questions and presents them to *públicos amplios y diversos*.

29 I am referring to poems such as *Alteraciones del Ariel* by Juan Francisco
   de Páramo y Cepeda and *Discurso del Capitán Francisco Draque* by Juan
   de Castellanos. The latter was censored by Pedro Sarmiento de Gamboa,
   official censor of the third volume of Castellanos's *Elegías*. The poems by
   Páramo Cepeda and Castellanos appeared in print for the first time in 1994
   and 1921, respectively.

30 In regards to *La Araucana*'s connection to drama and the emerging theatre
   culture in Spain, the forthcoming essays by Felipe Valencia, Imogen Choi,

and Mercedes Blanco offer valuable contributions. See *La Araucana (1569–2019)*, a special issue of *Revista Canadiense de Estudios Hispánicos* edited by Paul Firbas and Emiro Martínez-Osorio. For an exploration of the intersection between race, religion, and Renaissance epic poetry, see Elizabeth Wright, *The Epic of Juan Latino*.

31   Alves, "Góngora y Corte-Real," 38.

WORKS CITED

Printed Sources

Alonso, Dámaso. "La recepción de *Os Lusíadas* en España (1579–1650)." In *Obras completas*, 9–40. Vol. 3. Madrid: Gredos, 1974.

Alves, Hélio. "Corte-Real, Jerónimo." In *Dicionário de Luís de Camões*, edited by Vítor Aguiar e Silva, 298–303. Sao Paulo: Leya, 2011.

–   "Góngora y Corte-Real a la luz de dos intuiciones de Eugenio Ascencio." In *Hilaré tu memoria entre las gentes. Estudios de literatura aurea*, edited by Alain Bègue and Antonio Pérez Lasheras, 25–53. Zaragoza: Prensas de la Universidad de Zaragoza, 2014.

–   "Teoría de la épica en el renacimiento portugués." In *La teoría de la épica en el siglo XVI (España, Francia, Italia, Portugal)*, edited by María José Vega and Lara Vilá, 137–73. Vigo: Editorial Academia del Hispanismo, 2010.

Armstrong-Roche, Michael. *Cervantes' Epic Novel: Empire, Religion, and the Dream Life of Heroes in "Persiles."* Toronto: University of Toronto Press, 2009.

Balbuena, Bernardo de. *El Bernardo, o victoria de Roncesvalles*. Madrid: Diego Flamenco, 1624.

Boscán, Juan. *Las obras de Boscán y algunas de Garcilasso de la Vega, repartidas en quatro libros*. Barcelona: Carles Amorós, 1543.

Cacho Casal, Rodrigo. "Volver a un género olvidado: la poesía épica del Siglo de Oro." *Criticón* 115 (2012): 5–10.

Camões, Luís de. *Lusíadas de Luis de Camões comentadas por Manuel de Faria i Sousa*. Madrid: Ivan Sanchez a costa de Pedro Coello, 1639.

–   *Os Lusíadas*. Lisbon: Antonio Gõçalvez, 1572.

Cañizares-Esguerra, Jorge. "The Colonial Iberian Roots of the Scientific Revolution." In *Nature, Empire, and Nation. Explorations of the History of Science in the Iberian World*, 14–45. Stanford, CA: Stanford University Press, 2006.

–   *Puritan Conquistadors: Iberianizing the Atlantic, 1550–1700*. Stanford, CA: Stanford University Press, 2006.

Castellanos, Juan de. *Discurso del capitán Francisco Draque*. Edited by Angel Gonzalez Palencia. Madrid: Instituto de Valencia de Don Juan, 1921.

–   *Elegías de varones ilustres de Indias*. Vol. 4. Bogotá: Editorial A.B.C., 1955.

– *Primera parte de las elegías de varones ilustres de Indias*. Madrid: En casa de la viuda de Alonso Gómez, 1589.

Cervantes, Miguel de. *Don Quixote*. Translated by Edith Grossman. New York: HarperCollins, 2003.

Corte-Real, Jerónimo. *A Felicíssima Vitoria concedida del cielo al señor don Iuan de Austria en el Golfo de Lepanto de la poderosa armada othomana*. Lisbon: Antonio Ribeiro, 1578.

– *Naufrágio e lastimoso sucesso da perdiçam de Mnoel de Sousa de Sepúlveda e Dona Lianor de Sá...* Lisbon: Simão Lopez, 1594.

– *Sucesso do Segundo Cerco de Diu Estando D. João Mascarenhas por Capitão da Fortaleza. Año de 1546*. Lisbon: Antonio Gonçalvez, 1574.

Ercilla, Alonso de. *La Araucana*. Edited by Isaías Lerner. Madrid: Cátedra, 2002.

Folger, Robert A. *Writing as Poaching. Interpellation and Self-Fashioning in Colonial relaciones de méritos y servicios*. Leiden: Brill, 2011.

Helgerson, Richard. *A Sonnet from Carthage. Garcilaso de la Vega and the New Poetry of Sixteenth Century Europe*. Philadelphia: University of Pennsylvania Press, 2007.

Legnani, Nicole D. "La minoría insurgente: Secuelas de las madres guerreras en *La Araucana*." In *La Araucana (1569–2019)*, a special issue of *Revista Canadiense de Estudios Hispánicos* 45, no. 1 (2020): 161–80.

Martínez, Miguel. "A Poet of Our Own: The Struggle for *Os Lusíadas* in the Afterlife of Camões." *The Journal for Early Modern Cultural Studies* 10, no. 1 (2010): 71–94.

Martínez-Osorio, Emiro. *Authority, Piracy and Captivity in Colonial Spanish American Writing: Juan de Castellanos' Elegies of Illustrious Men of the Indies*. Lewisburg, PA: Bucknell University Press, 2016.

Martínez-Osorio, Emiro, and Paul Firbas. *La Araucana (1569–2019)*, a special issue of *Revista Canadiense de Estudios Hispánicos* 45, no. 1. Forthcoming.

Micó, José María. "Góngora a los diecinueve años: modelo y significación de la canción esdrújula." *Criticón* 49 (1990): 21–30.

Middlebrook, Leah. *Imperial Lyric: New Poetry and New Subjects in Early Modern Spain*. University Park: The Pennsylvania State University Press, 2009.

Navarrete, Ignacio. *Orphans of Petrarch: Poetry and Theory in the Spanish Renaissance*. Berkeley: University of California Press, 1994.

Newitt, Malyn. *Portugal in European and World History*. London: Reaktion Books, 2009.

Nicolopulos, James. *The Poetics of Empire in the Indies: Prophecy and Imitation in "La Araucana" and "Os Lusíadas."* University Park: The Pennsylvania State University Press, 2000.

Padilla, Pedro de. *La Verdadera Historia y admirable suceso del segundo cerco de Diu*. Edited by José Labrador Herraiz and Ralph DiFranco. Mexico: Frente de Afirmación Hispanista, 2011.

Páramo y Cepeda, Juan Francisco. *Alteraciones del Dariel*. Edited by Héctor H. Orjuela. Bogotá: Editorial Kelly, 1994.

Pierce, Frank. *La poesía épica del siglo de oro*. Madrid: Editorial Gredos, 1968.

Plagnard, Aude. "Épica e imagen: un análisis sociopoético de los manuscritos de Jerónimo Corte-Real (ca. 1569–1575)." *Hipogrifo: Revista de literatura y cultura del Siglo de Oro* 5, no. 2 (2017): 215–39.

– *Une épopée ibérique: Alonso de Ercilla et Jerónimo Corte-Real (1569–1589)*. Madrid: Casa de Velázquez, 2019.

Quint, David. *Epic and Empire: Politics and Generic Form from Virgil to Milton*. Princeton, NJ: Princeton University Press, 1993.

Rivers, Elías. "Nymphs, Shepherds, and Heroes: Garcilaso's Second Eclogue." *Philological Quarterly* 51, no. 1 (1972): 123–34.

Rupp, Stephen. *Heroic Forms: Cervantes and the Literature of War*. Toronto: University of Toronto Press, 2014.

Uribe Bracho, Lorena. "Orphans of Orpheus: Music Lost and Regained in Spanish Golden Age Poetry." *Hispanic Review* 89, no. 2 (2021): 193–216.

Valencia, Felipe. *The Melancholy Void: Lyric and Masculinity in the Age of Góngora*. Lincoln: University of Nebraska Press, 2021.

Virgil. *The Aeneid*. New York: Vintage Classics, 1990.

Wey Gómez, Nicolás. *The Tropics of Empire. Why Columbus Sailed South to the Indies*. Cambridge, MA: MIT Press, 2008.

Wright, Elizabeth. *The Epic of Juan Latino: Dilemmas of Race and Religion in Renaissance Spain*. Toronto: University of Toronto Press, 2016.

PART ONE

Of Gods and Textual Models

1 Design Ingeniously Corrected: Corte-Real, *Os Lusíadas*, and the Gods in the *Felicissima*

HÉLIO J.S. ALVES

Men like me should not be offered gold; paper would suffice.[1]

Jerónimo Corte-Real certainly had his eyes on Luís de Camões's *Os Lusíadas* when he began writing his own *Felicissima Victoria de Lepanto* around 1572.[2] Camões's poem was too close for comfort. It had been printed quickly during the late autumn and early winter of 1571–2, before Corte-Real was able to print his own earlier work the *Segundo Cerco de Diu* (1574), which he had offered to King Sebastião of Portugal in a manuscript version that had been finished with splendid calligraphy and lavish colour images by 1568. Given the small world of Portuguese typography and its difficulties in handling large numbers of original images, Corte-Real found the endeavour of printing his earlier twenty-one-canto illustrated epic costly and problematic. At the same time, the teenage king who was the manuscript's recipient did not show any signs of favouring the poet-painter, or of demonstrating support for his artistic competence. So when Camões's *Os Lusíadas* first appeared in print, Corte-Real saw in it and its author everything that he himself lacked: the king's early and favourable response to Camões's direct request for the Crown's permission to print the book; a yearly allowance for poetic talent; and an official show of interest for the continuation of his literary activity in the monarch's favour.[3] On top of all of those issues, it quickly became obvious to him that Camões had imitated the *Segundo Cerco* to finish off his own poem. The most glaring element in this imitation (from the point of view of the epic's design) had been the addition of the Isle of Love, a mega-episode that had little to do with the narrative course of *Os Lusíadas*, but which was modelled structurally on the *Segundo Cerco*'s own apotheosis, the dream of the Temple of Victory.[4]

We can only guess how Corte-Real reacted to all of these circumstances. Even in 1574, when he finally obtained permission to print the *Segundo Cerco*, there was no praise for poet or poem. The king's licence came only after all the other permissions; it was evidently shorter and drier in content and tone; and it did not include hopes for further verse in the monarch's honour (see figs. 1.1 and 1.2).[5] In fact, no document exists to suggest the Crown's favourable disposition towards the poet-painter and his *Segundo Cerco* – in salary, privilege, or any other means. The *mercê* that he received from King Sebastião in this period – the post of commander (*capitão-mor*), for one year only, of a fleet travelling to and from India – has been shown to be rather meagre, if not disparaging.[6] The gift of the poem to the king and, later, its appearance in printed form did not provide Corte-Real with any palpable social, economic, or political advantage. The poet was unfortunate enough to experience personally the royal disregard that he denounced in the poem.[7]

The two epics also suffered this difference in fate at the hands of the censor. Friar Bertolameu Ferreira, a Dominican, was charged with reading the texts, passing general judgment on their moral and religious nature, and changing them whenever required by the criteria of the Inquisition. His reports had to appear alongside the poems when published. The friar certainly did not censor *Os Lusíadas* for erotic content.[8] It is also clear that he did not amend any of Camões's verses, in spite of concerns about the significance of certain words.[9] His report for the *Segundo Cerco* is similar in size, form, and nature to the one he wrote for *Os Lusíadas*. It also includes praise for the author, an identical concern for the religious meaning of some words, and a defence of their pertinence in the context of poetry. This time, however, the Dominican declares that he personally "corrected" Corte-Real's text.[10] This is the one major difference between the two authorizations. Less tolerance was extended to the ethics and poetics of the *Segundo Cerco* than had been the case for Camões's work.

It is highly improbable, of course, that any of this reflects the king's, the royal family's, the government's, or the Inquisition's opinions about poetry in general, or either of the epics in particular. What it does suggest quite evidently is that Camões had powerful sponsors and benefactors close to King Sebastião, before and after the publication of *Os Lusíadas*, while Corte-Real did not.[11] The paratextual apparatus of the editions, barren for *Os Lusíadas* while rich and varied for the *Segundo Cerco*,[12] does not explain anything about the position of their authors vis-à-vis the Crown.[13] The relevant documents are unequivocal: Camões's and Corte-Real's fates as poets, in the view of the political powers of the land, were then almost exactly opposed.

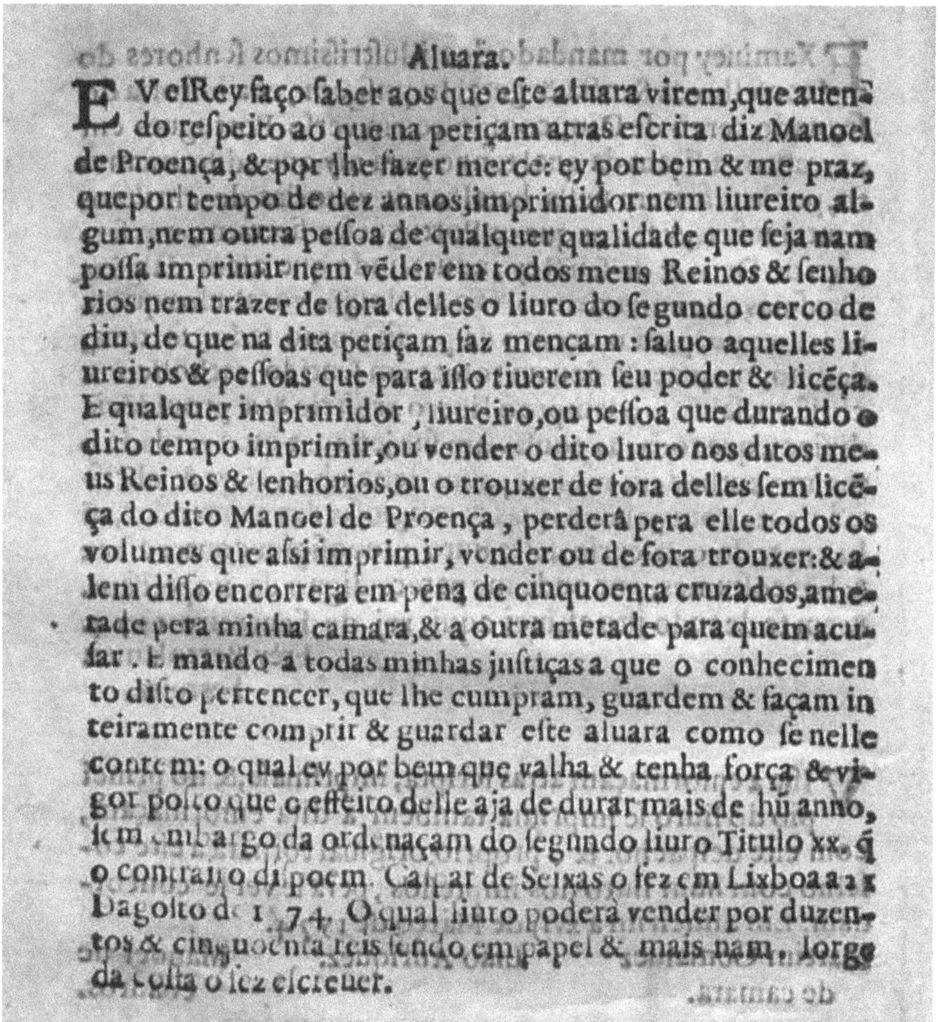

Aluara.

EV elRey faço ſaber aos que eſte aluara virem, que auendo reſpeito ao que na petiçam atras eſcrita diz Manoel
de Proença, & por lhe fazer merce: ey por bem & me praz,
que por tempo de dez annos, imprimidor nem liureiro algum, nem outra peſſoa de qualquer qualidade que ſeja nam
poſſa imprimir nem vēder em todos meus Reinos & ſenho
rios nem trazer de fora delles o liuro do ſegundo cerco de
diu, de que na dita petiçam faz mençam: ſaluo aquelles li-
ureiros & peſſoas que para iſſo tiuerem ſeu poder & licēça.
E qualquer imprimidor, liureiro, ou peſſoa que durando o
dito tempo imprimir, ou vender o dito liuro nos ditos meus Reinos & ſenhorios, ou o trouxer de fora delles ſem licēça do dito Manoel de Proença, perderà pera elle todos os
volumes que aſsi imprimir, vender ou de fora trouxer: & a-
lem diſſo encorrera em pena de cinquoenta cruzados, ame-
tade pera minha camara, & a outra metade para quem acu-
ſar. E mando a todas minhas juſtiças a que o conhecimen
to diſto pertencer, que lhe cumpram, guardem & façam in
teiramente comprir & guardar eſte aluara como ſe nelle
contem: o qual ey por bem que valha & tenha força & vigor poſto que o effeito delle aja de durar mais de hũ anno,
ſem embargo da ordenaçam do ſegundo liuro Titulo xx. q̃
o contrario diſpoem. Gaſpar de Seixas o fez em Lixboa a 21
Dagoſto de 1574. O qual liuro podera vender por duzen-
tos & cinquoenta reis ſendo em papel & mais nam. Iorge
da coſta o fez eſcreuer.

Figure 1.1. *Alvará* for Jerónimo Corte Real's *Segundo Cerco de Diu* (1574). Image courtesy of the Thomas Fisher Rare Book Library, University of Toronto.

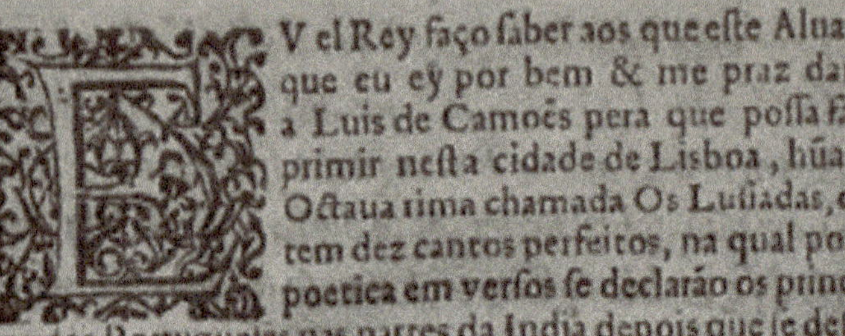

EV el Rey faço saber aos que este Aluara virem que eu ey por bem & me praz dar licença a Luis de Camões pera que possa fazer imprimir nesta cidade de Lisboa, húa obra em Octaua rima chamada Os Lusíadas, que contem dez cantos perfeitos, na qual por ordem poetica em versos se declarão os principaes feitos dos Portugueses nas partes da India depois que se descobrio a nauegação pera ellas por mādado del Rey dom Manoel meu visauo que sāncta gloria aja, & isto com priuilegio pera que em tempo de dez anos que se começarão do dia que se a dita obra acabar de empremir em diāte, se não possa imprimir nē vender em meus reinos & senhorios nem trazer a elles de fora, nem leuar aas ditas partes da India pera se vender sem licēça do dito Luis de Camões ou da pessoa que pera isso seu poder tiuer, sob pena de quē o contrario fizer pagar cinquoenta cruzados & perder os volmes que imprimir, ou vender, a metade pera o dito Luis de Camões, & a outra metade pera quem os acusar. E antes de se a dita obra vender lhe sera posto o preço na mesa do despacho dos meus Desembargadores do paço, o qual se declarará & porá impresso na primeira folha da dita obra pera ser a todos notorio, & antes de se imprimir sera vista & examinada na mesa do conselho geral do santo officio da Inquisição pera cō sua licença se auer de imprimir, & se o dito Luis de Camões tiuer acrecentados mais algūs Cantos, tambem se imprimirão auendo pera isso licença do santo officio, como acima he dito. E este meu Aluara se imprimirà outrosi no principio da dita obra, o qual ey por bem que valha & tenha força & vigor, como se fosse carta feita em meu nome por mim asinada & passada por minha Chancellaria sem embargo da Ordenação do segundo liuro, tit. xx. que diz que as cousas cujo effeito ouuer de durar mais que hum ano passem per cartas, & passando por aluaras não valhão. Gaspar de Seixas o fiz em Lisboa, a. xxiiij. de Setembro, de M.D.LXXI. Iorge da Costa o fiz escreuer.

Figure 1.2. *Alvará* for Luis de Camões's *Os Lusíadas* (1572). Image courtesy of the National Library of France.

Meanwhile, the naval battle of Lepanto had occurred in October 1571, and the first reports, chronicles, and poems about it started to be released by European presses soon after. From late 1572 to early 1573, Corte-Real would have had access to all the textual materials he needed to write the *Felicissima*. The poem was completed by 1575, and this time he turned to Philip II of Spain for support. He addressed to him a manuscript of an epic, written in Spanish, whose main hero was the king's half-brother, John of Austria. This cost the poet some censure in Portugal.[14] But he proceeded nevertheless to finish a luxurious personal copy for the Spanish king that was dispatched from Lisbon in the beginning of October 1576.[15] Philip II took little time to reply; in early November, he sent the poet a letter of thanks, praise, and goodwill for the future. Corte-Real's glee over this is manifest in the fact that he arranged to get Philip's letter printed alongside the poem. It represented a very different response from what the poet-painter received in Portugal, and he made sure it showed. He then campaigned intensively to get the epic as finely printed and well known as possible. He arranged to get it published in Lisbon as fast as he could, but also requested a licence for its sale and distribution in the neighbouring kingdom.[16] When it came out in January 1578, the *Felicissima* became the first Iberian poem ever published with woodcuts, the closest form of illustration the author could achieve in print relative to the artistic quality of the manuscript. The greatest military disaster in Portuguese history – the defeat of King Sebastião's army in North Africa – was only a few months away.

In the final octave of *Os Lusíadas*, Camões had promised the Portuguese king that he would write a new poem to celebrate him as a reborn Alexander if he attacked the Moors in Morocco. The traditional notion that he was intent on writing another epic when Sebastião was effectively preparing the African war cannot be confirmed,[17] but Camões did write a short panegyric in 1574, in the same stanzaic form as *Os Lusíadas*, praising the king and expressing again the hope (*esperança*) that he would invade Muslim North Africa.[18] This text is consistent with other lines of poetry where his wish for new Portuguese military intervention in Morocco is clear.[19] Corte-Real thought differently: the *Segundo Cerco* did not encourage the king to attack Morocco, and its rhetoric about Sebastião emphasized the need for peace.[20] The epic went so far as to warn against the nefarious consequences of a ruler who does not heed good advice and wages war, thinking victory is certain.[21] The message was repeated in 1574 when the work finally appeared in print.[22] This was unlikely to have brought about the king's enthusiasm for the *Segundo Cerco*. War in Africa served his own desires, some young nobles' hopes for promotion through military prowess, and the widely held bellicose opinion of the townspeople. Only an apparent minority did not think in the same way.[23]

In the meantime, the Turkish threat to the Catholic powers continued. The Battle of Lepanto was a tremendous victory for the Christian (Holy) League, but it was not a decisive one: Cyprus was definitively lost (the Venetian Republic tacitly accepted the fact by 1573), and the Ottoman Empire quickly recovered from the naval defeat, continuing to pose a menace even as Corte-Real was writing the *Felicissima*. Considering the author's lack of success with the Portuguese king regarding the previous poem, and the urgency of a united defence of Christian powers against the Turks, it made sense personally and politically to celebrate a victorious act of war that was supposed to protect Christian nations from Ottoman aggression. The subject was so pressing during those years that Sebastião attempted to justify the African project before the Pope and other Catholic powers as a way of fighting Turkish ambitions. The poet, however, gives another explanation for Portugal's absence from the naval League, arguing diplomatically that the young monarch was too busy with the wars in Asia (*Felicissima*, fol. 5v).

The true story was not quite this one. Sebastião was increasingly dedicated to his own project of invading Africa, independently from what happened at Lepanto, the Ottoman threats in the Mediterranean, conflicts in the Indian subcontinent, or his uncle Philip's plans. Camões was at the forefront of his king's and people's belligerence, and he supported it explicitly.[24] Corte-Real looked elsewhere. While the *Segundo Cerco* related a past that was exclusively Portuguese, the *Felicissima*, through several instances of ekphrastic narrative, showed the conjoined efforts and common bloodlines of Spaniards and Lusitanians.[25] But it did not propose a joint military policy of the two nations and, as in the *Segundo Cerco*, no new wars were encouraged.[26] In this rendering, Corte-Real could be seen as adhering to the policies of Philip II, who wanted to avoid any Iberian military interventions in Africa. Nevertheless, he was being consistent with his own previously expressed views, views he apparently shared with other cultivated minds that were not suspected of special sympathies for Philip, like António Pinheiro[27] and Jerónimo Osório.[28]

Even though Corte-Real's qualities as heroic poet and blazoner may have been better regarded near the reign's end,[29] in an unfinished piece written after Sebastião's death, called *Lamentable pérdida*, he denounced the monarch's misguidedness in lines where political correctives come together with poetic ones. By then, with Philip II already turned into Philip I of Portugal, Corte-Real recalled his own version of Portuguese history construed in the *Segundo Cerco* to show how Sebastião's actions covered it with ignominy,[30] while alluding to Camões as one poet who incited the king to lead the catastrophic invasion.[31]

Some Inconsistencies of Narrative Design in *Os Lusíadas*

"Camões is not a great storyteller."[32] This statement, made by renowned literary historian and critic António José Saraiva, was destined to become the predictable object of rebuttal among Lusitanists. *Os Lusíadas*, as the great narrative poem in the language, telling the story of one of the most momentous occasions in human history, surely must show the qualities of great narrative. And yet, Saraiva's statement is not without precedent: the poem's reception history suggests that the defect has been perceived for a long time. "The conformity of parts" is how a respected critic of late neoclassical persuasion, Francisco Alexandre Lobo, expressed one of *Os Lusíadas*'s faults.[33] Yet these criticisms have usually been understood to result from a desire to deprecate the name of Camões, and serve obscurely motivated hostilities.[34]

The narrative design of *Os Lusíadas* has rarely been studied in its entirety. To name but the two honourable modern attempts, one by Jorge de Sena, the other by Fernando Gil, the results have been mixed and inconclusive. Sena's work, which was meant as a response to unnamed critics of the epic, is, unfortunately, full of misconceptions and lacunae.[35] By contrast, Gil's is a sound attempt at comprehending the "parts" of *Os Lusíadas* as they could be expected to function multidimensionally, but his conclusions point to the poem's structural failings on several counts.[36]

The narrative weaknesses of *Os Lusíadas* are not hard to come by. Take Venus and the Nereids. These sea nymphs appear for the first time in the poem accompanying Vasco da Gama's fleet as it leaves Mozambique (I.96). By the time the fleet reaches the next seaport, Kilwa, Venus prevents the ships from entering the harbour by using opposing winds (I.100). Two stanzas later (I.102–3), Gama arrives at Mombasa, but Venus, again, does not let the caravels enter at port, only this time the reader does not know how she stops them. Gama eventually tells the ruler of Mombasa that his ships will enter the next day because it is becoming dark (II.5). In the morning, as the fleet tries to move into the harbour, Venus flies "from the sky to the sea" and calls the Nereids. After explaining to them why she came down from the gods' abode, they depart together to reach the caravels' site (II.18–19). Once arrived, the Nereids circle the ships and block their advance, forcing them to change course (II.21–2). Later in the voyage, Venus and the sea nymphs join forces again to tame the winds (VI.86–91), and to welcome Gama and his sailors to an island (the Isle of Love) located on the men's voyage back from India (IX.36–50).

There are many inconsistencies in this narrative. If the Nereids accompanied Gama's ships since Mozambique, Venus should not have had to call them and take them with her to the point where the fleet was: the nymphs were already there. On the other hand, the reader is not informed about the means used by Venus the first time to prevent the ships from entering the harbour at Mombasa, nor how she got to the fleet. Yet the second time we are told that she had to fly towards the sea to get the Nereids' help. If Venus had already managed to prevent the fleet from entering the ports of Kilwa and Mombasa, why should she need, the second time in Mombasa, to do a quick flight for that purpose? And why should she call the sea nymphs, if Venus did not need their help on the previous occasions?

An issue that complicates things further is that of the means available to Venus to exert her powers. At Kilwa (I.100), she uses contrary winds. If she has powers over the winds, the reader is not informed about how she came to have them. In canto VI, however, Venus requires the Nereids' help to tame them. Her powers over the winds remain, therefore, unclear, to say the least.[37]

A more structural concern is her control over the Nereids themselves. It has been noticed that no reasons are given in the poem for the powers of Venus over the sea nymphs, powers that mythology does not seem to authorize.[38] But it is the very internal probability, or narrative coherence, of the poem that is contradicted here. In canto VI, the Nereids save the Portuguese even after all the sea gods (including the nymphs) had been persuaded by Bacchus to destroy Gama's fleet.[39] In canto IX, the Nereids are heavily persuaded, by the joint effort of Cupid, Fame, and Credulity, to welcome the ships' men to Venus's island.[40] They later become their lovers and wives. At the end of the same canto, with Venus apparently forgotten, the Nereids are allegorized as honours and glories (IX.89). And the contradictions seem to increase tenfold in the final, tenth canto. Even if one argues that Camões, as poet, was free to make use of mythology as he saw fit, there is no consistency in his narrative regarding the actions attributed to Venus and the Nereids.

Os Lusíadas was famously criticized for the incongruity of having Vasco da Gama pray to God for help in a sea storm while Venus comes to his rescue.[41] The mix of classical mythology with Christian references was a relatively common phenomenon in the first phases of early modern epic and other genres, sometimes in more radical ways than Camões ever conceived.[42] But the poetic rules of consistency of character and stance ensured that there was a barrier in perception and mode of existence between humans and supernatural beings. Therefore, situations are frequently found in which the same action is understood simultaneously from at least two unconnected points of view, human and divine.[43] This seems to be the case in *Os Lusíadas* when Gama thanks God for salvaging him although, at another level of the poem's narrative, it is Venus and the Nereids who do so. This narrative mechanism, however, does not always work in Camões's epic. Was it Venus who prevented the ships from entering the harbour at Mombasa (I.102), or was it Vasco da Gama who decided to wait until the next day because night was closing in (II.5)? These are not two versions of the same action; they are two ideas narratively incompatible with each other. To argue that one of the speakers (the narrator or the fleet's commander) is lying is surely beside the point.

These are major narrative fault lines. Perhaps one can explain them partly because of the problems created by the poem's choice of making mythology essential to action; this has been argued by several critics. There is also the question of interpretation: Venus and the sea nymphs in *Os Lusíadas* may require critical perspectives that have not been successfully attempted yet.[44] However, not everything can be sorted out through interpretation, and the classical gods should not be an obstacle to writing an articulate story. The relationship between the Nereids and the Portuguese seamen goes from canto I, 96 to canto X, 143, covering most of the poem. Yet, if one were to select and isolate the tale of Venus, the sea nymphs, and Vasco da Gama – in a sense, the main storyline of *Os Lusíadas* – it would easily be perceived as nonsensical. The narrator seems to have simply forgotten what he had told the reader earlier, or what he intended to write later. When the actions themselves become so inconsistent with one another, one has to raise the possibility of either a high disregard for narrative logic or, more probably, a case of writing and publishing in haste.

Corte-Real's Response to Camões's Inconsistencies – Introduction

In the *Segundo Cerco*, the Classical gods are deployed in a comparatively sparse way. Supernatural actions are carefully put in place in order to build a kind of geometrically disposed hall of mirrors.[45] Even though no inconsistencies are to be found in the deployment of mythology, there is no sense in which one can talk about a "story" of the gods in the *Segundo Cerco*. *Os Lusíadas*, however, attempts to imitate the divine narrative of Virgil's *Aeneid*, from Venus and her allies favouring the heroes, to Bacchus opposing them. Even if the mythological plot of *Os Lusíadas* has nothing to do with the poem taking first place in contemporary royal and public regard, the epic's creative imitation of the *Aeneid*'s narrative design contributed strongly to the assertion of Camões's poetic authority. Plot, causality, the way in which the gods interact as agents throughout the narrative – collectively, they represent one issue of Virgilian epic that the *Segundo Cerco* had no response for. But it came. Corte-Real wrote the new poem, the *Felicissima*, not only as a way of recovering political and poetic initiative, but also as a tight neo-Virgilian response to the challenge raised by divine action in *Os Lusíadas*.

Allusion is the means by which a re-establishment of lost poetic authority becomes possible.[46] It works at least as a double in the second of Corte-Real's epics: it forges an alliance between the *Aeneid* and the poet-painter's own tried and tested practice. It consists mainly of reinstallments of structural motifs from the *Segundo Cerco*, reinforced by a now fuller and tighter imitation of the Virgilian narrative model. Camões's epic appears occasionally between the lines of this sturdy poetic framework, emerging at the surface through verbal or episodic reminiscence in ways that reveal the first deeply critical readings of *Os Lusíadas* ever written. Allusion can only happen when its object is important, meaningful, and highly influential. Because *Os Lusíadas* had a profound impact on Corte-Real as reader and witness to its early reception, the *Felicissima* exhibits, whenever deemed relevant, his genuine admiration for the rival's verse. At the same time, however, Corte-Real's imitations, by recognizing the subtext, indicate how a better poet should have done it instead. The *Felicissima* becomes then a corrective, sometimes a pitiless corrective, of Camões's literary designs.

The Portrait of Venus Recast

In the new epic, Venus is introduced as the protectress of Cyprus.[47] This is both relevant to an important part of the *Felicissima*'s subject (the conquest of the Mediterranean isle by the Ottomans) and in agreement with classical mythology.[48] Before the goddess herself is directly introduced into the epic, Cyprus is described as the fertile place where Venus used to be worshipped.[49] Despite the past tense, it looks like myth is still in force in the present, since it does not take long before Cyprus reveals its magic bucolic wonder. In canto II, Mostafà, the Turkish commander who has just taken Nicosia from the Venetians, enters a *locus amoenus* where little Cupids throw arrows around and four beautiful nymphs sing and embroider tapestries. These nymphs are not Nereids or goddesses of any plants or rivers; they are local deities and wear garlands made of myrtle, Venus's preferred flower (*Felicissima*, fol. 25r). They know why the Ottoman commander is in Cyprus and wish to take their revenge on him (*Felicissima*, fol. 28v). In a sense, they do retaliate, because, later on, the woman Mostafà loves is killed by another man's act of jealousy.

Cyprus's divine protectress is introduced a second time, again indirectly, as an ekphrastic motif. The first tapestry the nymphs are working on pictures the tale of Venus and Mars, the lovers caught by Vulcan's net and mocked by the other gods, a well-known mythological theme (*Felicissima*, fols. 28v–29r). This second appearance of Venus is directly relevant to the supernatural plot of the *Felicissima* as it will develop later. Venus, Mars, and Vulcan will interact across much of the poem.

Finally, in canto VI, Venus appears for the first time as an agent, at a moment when the Ottomans are besieging Famagusta, the last stronghold in Cyprus to have resisted thus far. She appears because she wants to give a suit of armour (*armadura*) to the commander of the only force that can protect her isle from all the pain and suffering. For that purpose, she needs to convince the god of metalwork, Vulcan, who happens also to be her husband, to forge that armour. The *Felicissima* enters then very clearly into neo-Virgilian mode, imitating the corresponding episode in *Aeneid* 8.[50]

But within the overall imitation of Virgil's episode, Corte-Real alludes explicitly to his Portuguese contemporary. He introduces the portrait of Venus with a Camonian hyperbole originally placed near the end of Venus's description in *Os Lusíadas*:

Felicissima, canto VI, fol. 80r	*Os Lusíadas*, canto II, fol. 26r (stanza 42)
Ella se para tal, que a Hyrcanos Tigres,	E destas brandas mostras comovido,
Y a peñascos durissimos, moviera.	Que moveram de hum Tigre o peito duro ...
[She dresses up in such a way	[And moved by these tender appearances
that she would move Hyrcanian tigers	that would move the hard heart of a tiger ...]
and very hard crags.]	

At this detailed level, one can already observe how allusion to Camões is elaborated in the *Felicissima*. As Corte-Real initiates literal reference to the cluster of textual materials on Venus in *Os Lusíadas*, the choice is to affirm correction by identifying, singularizing, and reversing the original. *Moveram* and *Tigre* in the beginnings of one line by one poet become *Tigres* and *moviera* at the end of two lines by the other poet. Camões's alliterative play on the soft *mm* (*mostras, comovido, moveram*) and *dd* (*destas, brandas, comovido, de, duro*) almost disappears in Corte-Real under a barrage of harsher *pp, tt, ss,* and *qq,* taken over and multiplied from the verse alluded to. *Duro* becomes *durissimos, Tigre* turns into *Tigres* (from Hyrcania, where the most ferocious tigers were supposed to reside), and tenderness, suggested by the adjective *brandas,* is exchanged for suggestions of violence. In the end, Corte-Real's *moviera* means as much the opposite of Camões's *moveram* as their relative position in the lines reflects, in a kind of syllepsis straight out of Riffaterre.[51] Moreover, Jupiter is so aroused by the goddess in *Os Lusíadas* that a new Cupid could have been conceived there and then. In the *Felicissima,* Venus kills. This is confirmed four lines down, when the goddess's eyes are described as sending murderous (*homicidas*) beams of light. The *Venus vulgivaga* of Camões is corrected into an anti-Neoplatonic and anti-Epicurean *Venus homicida.* Corte-Real recognizes the high poetic value of his contemporary's effigy;[52] despite this, he scraps Camões's concept of the goddess of love.[53]

The correction, however, is not made only at the level of ideology; it is perhaps deeper at the level of narrative. Camões included the seduction and trickery of Venus in an interview with Jupiter, sending the reader a message on the necessary comparison of the scene in *Os Lusíadas* with the equivalent tableau in *Aeneid* 1. Since no feminine charms were present in the *Aeneid*'s interview of Venus and Jove, the original strength of Camões's representation stood forth brightly. One could say that *Os Lusíadas* added to Virgil an erotic portrait of a young woman, in the manner of Apuleius or Ariosto, an imitative juxtaposition that could have been appreciated as highly vivid. However, narrative logic implied that the goddess's efforts were directed towards obtaining something palpable from Jupiter. That does not happen in *Os Lusíadas.* The two things she gets from him are of dubious relevance to the action: a prophecy and a repetition of Jupiter's decision at the council of the gods.[54]

Corte-Real shows that the provocative tableau in canto II of *Os Lusíadas,* more than creatively imitating *Aeneid* 1, depended really on Venus as shown in the much later scene of *Aeneid* 8, in which she overpowers Vulcan through deception and sexual arousal. As in Virgil and unlike Camões, her intervention in the *Felicissima* is motivated by a special request, the making of a new suit of armour and shield to support her hero's immunity in battle. To create this extraordinary piece of craftsmanship, Vulcan really needed some persuading. By imitating Venus's erotic wiles in a glaringly neo-Virgilian scene with Vulcan, Corte-Real returns the representation of the goddess to its rightful place in epic.

Allusion to *Os Lusíadas* has here the function of showing why and how the position of Venus's portrait in the narrative ought to be corrected.

How to Clear a Sea Storm: Solving a Story of Navigation with the Gods

The next appearances of Venus in the *Felicissima* happen, for purposes of navigation, in canto VIII. Venus visits Neptune's kingdom to plead with him to stop the constant stormy weather preventing John of Austria's fleet from progressing. The episode is a reworking of the meeting between Venus and Neptune, followed by a pageant of sea gods, in *Aeneid* 5. Later in the same canto, she goes to see Aeolus, the god of all winds, for identical reasons, recalling Juno's conversation with him in *Aeneid* 1.

After his maritime court, including Nereids, is introduced to the reader, Neptune condescends and orders the waves to settle down and help John of Austria. Neptune reappears in canto XII, remembering the promise he made Venus to keep the sea calm for the League's fleet, and takes his court with him to watch the battle. In canto XIV, he participates in the naval conflict, throwing Turks against coastal rocks and burying them there, while rewarding their dead galley slaves with freedom in the vast sea and the company of the sea nymphs. Finally, Neptune and all his court joyfully congratulate the victors in canto XV; the celebration even includes a song of praise by three Nereids.[55] The contrast with respect to Venus, Neptune, and the other sea gods in *Os Lusíadas* could not be greater. As opposed to them, the sea gods in the *Felicissima* are characters with narrative memory. The conspicuous absence of a ruler-subject bond between Venus and the Nereids as well as the way the *Felicissima* builds a coherent narrative for the alliance between Venus and the sea results in a kind of non-allusional allusion to *Os Lusíadas*, where those relationships objectively fail.

The same can be said of the Winds, and the way to deal supernaturally with sea storms. In *Aeneid* 1, the storm is created by Aeolus after persuasion by Juno. When Neptune finds out about it, he angrily appears at the water's surface and tells the Winds that they should never have created havoc at sea without his permission. The sea storm in canto VI of *Os Lusíadas* was raised instead by Neptune himself calling on Aeolus to release the Winds (VI.35 and 37). For a while, it looks like the tempest was provoked by wind only; but, of course, there is no sea storm without the sea. Neptune is furious (*furibundo*); so much so that he now shows more power and terrifying violence than Vulcan and even Jupiter (*Os Lusíadas*, VI.76–8). However, even though wind and water together make up the storm (*Os Lusíadas*, VI.79), Neptune's subjects, the Nereids, directed, as we saw, by Venus, end it by calming down the Winds. Technically, this is a case of false denouement. The narrative complication (or knot) of the storm is not entirely solved (or untied) since the reader is not informed about why, how, or even if Neptune changed his mind. The fact that the Nereids act without his supervision, and even against his wishes, adds to the narrative confusion.

Air and sea water are different elements, ruled by different gods. This is why stormy weather at sea is only partially appeased in the *Felicissima* after Venus's interview with Neptune: the Winds, especially Boreas and Eurus, are still going wild, and the ships need to bring down the sails and use oars to move, and even then with great difficulty. Corte-Real emphasizes the point succinctly:

> El mar inchado estava, y muy furioso
> Por Neptuno mandar que se aplacasse,
> Dexando Eolo alla tan desmandados,
> Volando aca y alla sueltos los vientos. (*Felicissima*, canto VIII, fol. 114v)

(The sea was swollen, and furious / For Neptune commanded that it placate itself, / Leaving Aeolus there, so unruly / The winds flying freely here and there.)

The personified Sea is angry, and hence agitated, because Aeolus did not control and remove the Winds. Perhaps Neptune should have informed Aeolus before sending orders to the waves. Whatever the case, the fact is that Venus, scared about what is happening to Cyprus, takes charge of the matter and visits Aeolus herself. He will accept her request, collect the stormy winds, and imprison them in the Aeolian caves, leaving Zephyrus to fill gently the League's sails (*Felicissima*, fols. 115v–116r). The storm is truly over only after meetings with both gods, Neptune and Aeolus. In a sense, canto VIII of the *Felicissima* is a lesson in how to articulate coherently a story of real navigation and natural sea storms with the classical gods as agents.

The Shield of Corte-Real, Emblem of Divine Epic Craftsmanship

Venus, Vulcan, and Mars, the triad first introduced in the nymph's tapestry of canto II, are the original source for the main structural emblem of the *Felicissima*, the shield of John of Austria. This is quite possibly the most Virgilian of all the narrative and symbolic structures in the poem. The shield of Aeneas represents the climax of the *Aeneid*, and it is the most encompassing icon to what Virgil's epic represents.[56] Through systematic allusion to the shield, why it was made, how it was forged by Vulcan, how it was delivered by Venus, and how it was received by the hero – always in close parallel with *Aeneid* 8 – Corte-Real reinforces greatly his Virgilian affiliation. Narratively speaking, however, the *Felicissima* uses the shield quite differently from the *Aeneid*. While the shield of Aeneas appears complete in one single book of the Roman epic (it is mentioned later, but only as a calling sign for Aeneas's troops), John of Austria's piece of armour stretches narratively to no less than four different cantos of the *Felicissima* (IV, VI, IX, and XII), making its conception, production, and destiny a narrative axis for much of the epic.

The temple of Mars in Ali Pascha's premonitory dream of canto IV is the first place where the reader hears about, and "sees," the shield. It is the second of a total of four times when Mars has an action of sorts in the narrative progress of the poem. First, as we saw in canto II, he is represented in tapestry with Venus and Vulcan; now he is shown sculpted (with an added woodcut drawing of the god as a statue);[57] and later he appears as a living character, interacting with Venus in canto XIII, and intervening in the battle in canto XIV.[58] In this way, Mars's progress along the narrative is like Venus's: they both begin as figures but evolve into agents. Within the temple itself, there is already progress in artistic representation since Mars appears first as notched relief on a temple gate, and afterwards, in the building's main hall, as a shining sculpture (*Felicissima*, fols. 53v–54v). Right next to his statue (but much further down in the narrative), there is a sculpture of a young man towards whom the figure of Mars shows special affection. This is John of Austria (*Felicissima*, fol. 64). Like Venus and Mars, the main hero of the poem is gradually introduced to the narrative: first mentioned indirectly (as a son of Charles V; *Felicissima*, canto IV, fol. 59), and now represented in art, a statue rendered in magnificent armour. In its hand the sculpture carries a shield on whose central section someone has painted a sea full of corpses, with a royal eagle rising to the clouds while carrying a crown of laurel and palm. In the *Aeneid*, Vulcan carved the battle of Actium in the middle of the shield;[59] in the *Felicissima*, the centre is taken by the Battle of Lepanto.[60]

When Venus turns up as a supernatural agent for the first time in the poem, she asks Vulcan to make the suit of armour for John of Austria. Vulcan agrees and orders his blacksmiths to start work immediately on it. In the newly forged shield, Vulcan engraves heroic feats performed by Charles V, and some of the victories (*parte de los successos*) of his son Philip II (*Felicissima*, canto VI, fol. 84v.), described at length during the rest of the canto. Later on, in canto IX, Venus delivers the arms to John of Austria in a dream (*Felicissima*, fol. 124v–125r) and, when he awakes, he sees the representations on the shield, and feels filled with desire to emulate his father's triumphs (*Felicissima*, fol. 130v). Finally, in canto XII, just before the great naval battle begins, John of Austria looks again at the engravings on Vulcan's shield, and renews his desire for military glory (*Felicissima*, fol. 166v).

The disposition of the *Felicissima*'s narrative ensures that the "paintings" on the hero's shield will only be completed once the battle is also finished, at the end of the poem. The finished work is the one we read about first, the image of Lepanto at the centre of the shield in the temple of Mars. The shield appears earlier in the poem (*Felicissima*, canto IV) as the artistic result of the naval battle, but it later becomes (*Felicissima*, cantos VI, IX, and XII), through the scenes carved all around it, the artistic means to inspire John of Austria to victory. This is metalepsis (*transumptio*), the trope in which the effect or consequence is presented as the cause or precedent. The shield becomes not only an artistic product resulting from the naval victory, but also the artwork which inspires that victory. It is as if Corte-Real did not write because John of Austria won the battle, but rather that John of Austria won because he read Corte-Real. The poet renders unto Caesar the things that are Caesar's, but unto art the things that belong to art. When the narrator says, just before the naval encounter, that his hero's decisions were "moved by divine inspiration more than by knowledge of naval warfare," the words ring true way beyond their original historiographical sense.[61] Through metalepsis, Vulcan's shield – the figure for Corte-Real's poem – prophesies its ability to inspire virtue and success.

This instance was not the first occasion the author of the *Felicissima* used a shield as emblem of his own poetic work. When Corte-Real's *Segundo Cerco* was printed for the first time in 1574, there appeared on the title page an engraving of the goddess Pallas bearing her shield. As in Greek mythology, the centre of the shield had the head of the Medusa, the Gorgon. Nothing is known about the reasons for the choice of this image to open the *Segundo Cerco*, but this goddess was already present in the frontispiece of the manuscript version of the work offered to King Sebastião, identifiable by the Gorgon on her shield. The shield of Pallas does not appear as an image in the *Felicissima*, but it returns during the representation of Vulcan's forges in the text of canto VI. *Aeneid* 8 described what the fire god's blacksmiths were working on: a thunderbolt for Jupiter, a chariot for Mars, a breastplate for Pallas (ll. 426–38). Compared with Virgil, Corte-Real reduces to a minimum the reference to Jupiter's arms (only two lines for the Latin's seven), chooses a helmet rather than the *Aeneid*'s chariot for Mars (but keeping the same two lines of the original), and a shield rather than the *petto* for Pallas. In the latter case, the four lines for the *Aeneid*'s breastplate become twelve for the *Felicissima*'s shield (fol. 83v). It is right after Pallas's shield is fully described that Vulcan interrupts the blacksmiths' work and orders them to concentrate instead on making the new armour (and shield) for John of Austria.

The shield of John of Austria is therefore the successor of the shield of Pallas in Vulcan's forge. Both shields are formidable in battle, but they are, most of all, great artworks created by the same subtle and ingenious craftsman.[62] If Pallas's shield functions as an emblem of Corte-Real's epic poetry, then its twelve-line description in the *Felicissima* intensifies the narrative metalepsis associated with Vulcan's labour. The shield inspiring kings and princes is itself preceded by another shield; an artwork by another artwork; a poem by another poem. The original of the *Felicissima*, the inspiration of the inspiration, is none other than the *Segundo Cerco de Diu*.

Correcting the Antagonist: Bacchus's Loss is the Furies' Gain

Corte-Real constructs his own poetic precedence and the comparative marginality of Camões's *Os Lusíadas* in Portuguese and Iberian epic right from the beginning of the *Felicissima*'s story, in canto I.

Where the *Segundo Cerco* opened the narrative with a gerund (*reinando*) followed by the name of the Portuguese king, the new epic opens it with an almost synonymous gerund (*imperando*) before the Ottoman emperor's name. In both cases, the prince who will be the enemy of the Christian heroes is soon introduced, delving deep in thought. Then, Morpheus, or Sleep, arrives with his tools, in a manner reminiscent of Palinuro's in *Aeneid* 5, and the monarch falls asleep. The *Segundo Cerco* is shown as the one and only predecessor of the *Felicissima*'s narrative form; Camões and his work certainly have no part in it.

The very close similarities, however, make the differences shine forth. In the *Felicissima*, Morpheus substitutes the canonical bough filled with Lethe's dew and bathed in the Styx (Virgil, *Aeneid* 5, 854–5; Corte-Real, *Segundo Cerco*, canto XX, 387) for a branch of vine bathed in wine. The poet emphasizes his departure from the subtexts through a *recusatio*:

Morpheo ...
Ramo de verde vid trae en la mano
Reçumando por el precioso vino
No tocado en las aguas del Letheo,
Ni en la estigie laguna oscura y triste,
mas en su licor proprio. (Corte-Real, *Felicissima*, fol. 3v)

(Morpheus ... / A branch of green vine he brings in his hand / Oozing through the precious vine / Not steeped in the waters of the Lethe, / Nor in the Stygian pool, dark and sad, / but in its own liquor.)

Corte-Real has a field day at the expense of Emperor Selim II. The portrait of the leading villain as a drunkard who is delighted with the sight of the vine seems to come out of burlesque comedy rather than epic. In the whole portrait of Selim, alcohol is made responsible for the emperor's loss of heroic spirit and lack of willpower. The only action he is capable of is motivated by drunkenness.[63] Not deserving of any respect, Selim II is literally laughable.

With drunken sleep, however, there begins a dream. Imitating the *Segundo Cerco*'s opening nightmare, Selim sees an armed creature emerging from a horrendous mouth in the ground; it speaks, inciting him to war. Corte-Real uses similar figures, and often the same words, for both poems: the creatures are Furies from the classical underworld: Discord, Allecto, War. Apart from the different historical circumstances described by the Furies in each epic, the content is pretty much the same. In the case of the *Felicissima*, this dream awakens Selim to action; it changes his attitude. In the end, as the Fury says, the emperor will follow Mars and leave behind "useless Bacchus" (*Bacho inutil*) (*Felicissima*, fol. 7r). Selim will engage in a war of conquest. The vine will never return to the poem again.

Such opposition between a Fury and Bacchus contradicts classical models. Corte-Real is most likely imitating here Allecto's actions in *Aeneid* 7 where she enrages Queen Amata, Turnus, and Ascanius's hounds. There, however, the Fury and Bacchus work together: Amata becomes a sort of Bacchante in her choleric frenzy (*Aeneid* 7, ll. 385–91). It is true that Bacchus in the *Aeneid* is really a fiction produced by Allecto's almost limitless capacity to impersonate and pretend; still, Virgil places the desire for war as a Fury on the same side of the fence as Bacchic madness. Selim II, however, is already under the power of Bacchus when the Fury comes to him in a dream. In the *Felicissima*, her appearance is designed as a corrective.[64]

But the Ottoman emperor is not the only one corrected here. Allusion ensures the message travels in other ways too. The Fury begins her invective like this: "Emperador, indigno del estado / Y del ceptro Othomano, que descuido / Es el en que aora vives ...?" (*Felicissima*, I, fol. 4v) (Emperor, unworthy of the state / And of the Ottoman scepter, what carelessness / Is that in which you now live ...?).

Corte-Real's choice of words indicates that the Bacchus he is thinking about is also the main supernatural antagonist in *Os Lusíadas*, for the

Fury's address to Selim echoes distinctly Bacchus's speech to the gods
of the sea in Camões's epic:

> Princepe que de juro senhoreas
> D'um Polo, ao outro Polo o mar irado
> [...]
> E vós, Deoses do mar [...]
> Que descuido foy este em que viveis?
>
> (*Os Lusíadas*, VI, fol. 101r [stanza 28])

(Prince [Neptune], who by right, rules / From one Pole to the other, the
angry sea / [...] / And you, Gods of the sea [...] / What carelessness was
this in which you live?)

Raising censure against the Ottoman emperor because of his depend-
ence on Bacchus, which makes Selim unable to be reckoned with, while
at the same time recalling the god's largest and most important address in *Os Lusíadas*, amounts to a dismissal both of the Bacchus who
motivates Selim's actions and the Bacchus who acts oppositionally in
Camões's narrative. At this point, where none of the models (*Aeneid*
and the *Segundo Cerco*) make their presence felt, and history has no part
in the story, Bacchus is selected for criticism as a weak and ineffective
source for a workable epic plot.

One could say that Corte-Real's view of the antagonist in *Os Lusíadas* is terribly partial, and therefore of very limited relevance: in Camões,
Bacchus is above all a mythical ancestor of the Portuguese, and the conqueror of India; he appears only once or twice as the god of wine. But it
is also true that, in *Os Lusíadas*, Bacchus does not bear arms, and there is
no army of Maenads to support him. He is incapable of any of his mythical bloodletting violence. None of his actions in the poem depend on
strength or valour, only on cunning and deceit. He struggles knowingly
and from the beginning against Fate itself, signalling the hopeless nature
of his behaviour. He solicits and receives the help of Neptune and the sea
gods, but only provisionally, and with no success whatsoever, since Vasco
da Gama apparently does not lose a single man or ship, and the fleet does
not even go off course. The other gods either detest him (namely, Mars
and Venus), or ignore him. In the end, he just disappears, still rebellious,
but largely inconsequential.[65] In this context, Corte-Real's belittlement of
Bacchus represents a valuable contemporary reading of Camões.

The *Felicissima* marginalizes *Os Lusíadas* through imitation and development of antagonistic action, as realized in the *Segundo Cerco*. The
Furies take on the active role that Camões's Bacchus is too weak to

perform: they personify a ferocious challenge to the heroic course of action that is essential to the narrative's main structural organization:

Canto I – in a dream, War incites Selim II to initiate a war of conquest against Christian powers and invade Cyprus.

Canto II – as Pielí (naval commander) and Mostafà (army leader) travel to besiege Nicosia, the three Furies sit on the stern of Pielí's ship, with Allecto at the helm. Allecto inflames Mostafà too.

Canto III – Jealousy, transformed by Love into a Fury, admonishes Mostafà.[66] Allecto drives Pielí into murderous frenzy.

Canto XI – the secondary narrator finds Mostafà incensed by hell-inspired anger, suggesting that the Furies' influence has never left him.[67]

The end result is that the entire action of the Turks in or around Cyprus is inspired by the Furies.[68] The Furies are so closely associated with the invasion and conquest of the isle by the Ottoman Empire that, with one exception,[69] they never reappear in the other parts of the poem.

Felicissima's Well-wrought Design at the Expense of *Os Lusíadas*

Even though Selim's commanders who fight at Lepanto continue to play a decisive role in the *Felicissima*, their actions are not impelled by the underworld. On the contrary, as the poem's action leads towards the clash of the two armadas, the reader discovers for the first time the Olympic and sea gods favouring the Christian heroes. Venus, Vulcan, Mars, Neptune, Aeolus, and others turn up and intervene only in the actions leading towards Lepanto. There are no Olympic gods for the actions in Cyprus, and no underworld gods for the war in the Mediterranean. Corte-Real underlines in this way basic differences between the two stories: the conquest of Cyprus; and the conflict of Christian and Ottoman forces at sea. We are faced with a double plot based on principles of contrast. The characters and actions are deliberately differentiated, even opposed, obscuring the relationship between both plots. In a kind of resistance to completed form, the poet creates a narrative fault line that prevents convergence. The two plots never become one.

The first plot has a beginning (Selim's dream and the decision to wage war), a middle (the conquest of Nicosia), and an end (the loss of Famagusta and, with it, the triumph of the Ottomans over all of Cyprus). Its unity is emphasized by tableaux such as the flaying of Christians before the departure of the invading armada (*Felicissima*, canto II), and the flaying of Marcantonio Bragadino as the symbol of Cypriot defeat at the end (*Felicissima*, canto XI). The second plot begins with the preparation and departure of Ali Pascha's fleet from Constantinople at the end of canto III, after Pielí had returned there to tell Selim II the news about Cyprus.[70] The complex of events in the following cantos leads inexorably to the Battle of Lepanto, the victory of the "Holy" League, and its celebration. This action has also a beginning, a (complex) middle, and an end. Two different actions with different characters, both human and supernatural, ensure the bisected nature of the poem.

But the two plots also establish causal relations that interweave them, creating bonds of action and event. If it were not for his dream and change of personality in canto I, Selim II would not have ordered Ali Pascha to conquer Christian strongholds in the Mediterranean, and destroy the League's armada (*Felicissima*, cantos III, VI, and X). The loss of Cyprus to Fury-frenzied Mostafà in canto XI serves to incite the League's men in canto XII to vanquish Ali Pascha's fleet. And, of course, only the invasion of Cyprus caused Venus to favour John of Austria and hurt the Turks.

In general narrative design, the *Felicissima* works as an ingeniously balanced whole. The Ottomans are the protagonists in the first six cantos (I–VI), the Christians in the next six (VII–XII). The hinge of this diptych lies in the mirroring of canto VI, in which Vulcan's shield is engraved, and canto VII, in which John of Austria is given ceremonially the Leagues's blazoned standard, also described as a work of art.[71] Ottomans and Christians share protagonism in the two cantos of the naval battle (XIII–XIV), beginning with a mirrored pairing of the two fleets.[72] The last canto, XV, is the crowning piece of the whole design, with the celebration of the League's victory and the engraving of letters, heroes' names, and the poem itself in the Temple of Immortality.

The *Felicissima*'s well-wrought design, supported by the central model, the *Aeneid*, and Corte-Real's inaugural epic, the *Segundo Cerco*, responds to political neglect with poetic authority. It presents itself as a triumph of artistic ability, in plot, shape, and composition. It performs a self-conscious celebration of art as inspired and inspirational. Along the way, it corrects Camões. The two main supernatural agents of *Os Lusíadas*, Venus and Bacchus, are rectified by direct allusion. The goddess is denounced both for the ideology of love she advertises and, above all, for her lack of an adequate narrative role in epic form. The god of wine is comically debunked as a useless antagonist. Neptune, the Nereids, and the Winds are made to fit a coherent narrative plot, with deployment of the kind of logical chain of actions they entirely lack in *Os Lusíadas*. In short, Corte-Real reconstructs the classical gods' motives, agency, and kinships, and thus affirms his principal position in Portuguese, if not Iberian, epic poetry, while taking some notable sideswipes at Camões. It is therefore highly ironic that the *Felicissima* came to be read, if at all, as merely "a dull historical account of the war," or a slavish imitation of *Os Lusíadas*.[73]

NOTES

1   Words attributed to Jerónimo Corte-Real by Cristóvão de Moura in a letter to Gabriel de Zayas, secretary to Philip II, dated 3 September 1579. Quoted in Plagnard, *Une Épopée Ibérique*, 293; my translation.
2   The first word of the poem's title page, *felicissima* (old Spanish spelling), is printed in the largest upper-case type. The word is also used to indicate the poem indirectly in the epilogue (*felicissima memoria*, fol. 216v). Other than these occurrences, it is only attributed consistently to John of Austria, the epic's main hero. I find these reasons justify calling Corte-Real's poem by this word from now on. My citations in this chapter are from the edition published in Lisbon in 1578. With respect to *Os Lusíadas*, I cite from the poem's original Portuguese first edition of 1572.
3   The *alvará* (permit), dated 24 September 1571, granting the publication of *Os Lusíadas* was made in direct response to Camões's own petition. As the text states, the licence was granted even before the censors had a look at the poem, something contrary to normal practice. The other *alvará* conceding an allowance, the famous *tença* of 15,000 *reis* to be paid from 12 March 1572, specifically mentions Camões's abilities as a writer and his rank as the royal household's *cavaleiro-fidalgo*. In both *alvarás*, the king praises the poem and its subject, and says that he expects further services from Camões, including literary ones.
4   It is a commonplace in Camões criticism, past and present, to say that the Isle of Love, forming most of canto IX and almost all of X, represents a strange addition to *Os Lusíadas*. Even in this aspect, however, the poem imitated Corte-Real with some exactness: the Temple of Victory in cantos XX and XXI represents a real excrescence within the *Segundo Cerco* (see Costa e Silva, *Ensaio Biographico-Critico sobre os Melhores Poetas Portuguezes*, 17).
5   The *alvará* of the *Segundo Cerco de Diu* is dated 21 August 1574. Corte-Real's name is not mentioned at any time in this licence, which was explicitly granted only to a certain Manoel de Proença.
6   The *alvará* for this privilege is dated 22 February 1571, certainly long after King Sebastião received the illustrated manuscript of the *Segundo Cerco*. The text emphasizes the services of Corte-Real's wife rather than his own, and puts the poet, quite literally, in the queue to have the privilege bestowed. See Almeida, "Introdução," xvii.

7 Criticism of the Portuguese Crown's injustices towards its deserving
subjects frames the *Segundo Cerco*, from canto I, where the Indian court of
Cambay is vehemently praised for the way the sultans reward their best
subjects, to the apotheosis of the Temple of Victory, where an old man
called Merit (*Merecimento*) speaks about the predominance of this type of
royal injustice in the present. Ironically, perhaps, the latter is one of the
tracts from the *Segundo Cerco* that Camões imitated verbally in *Os Lusíadas*
(see Alves, "Teoría de la épica en el Renacimiento portugués," 162).

8 Lines from *Os Lusíadas* in which eroticism was supposedly intolerable to the
Dominican, like 2:34, 1–4 (see Ribeiro, *Luís de Camões*, 2:132), were imitations
of verses by António Ferreira (see Rodrigues, *Fontes dos Lusíadas*, 170) that
were never censored. On Friar Bertolameu's censorship of licentiousness,
see Pinho, "Critérios e métodos de censura na 'edição dos piscos' d'*Os Lusíadas* de Camões e no poema *De Senectute* de Lopo Serrão, de 1579."

9 A short digression in canto X, 82–4 may have been included by Camões in
response to the friar's concerns about the words "god," "divine," etc. applied to Graeco-Roman mythology.

10 Friar Bertolameu admits having changed sentences in the poem (... alem
dalgũas clausulas que emendamos ..."). Beyond this, there is at least one
case in the *Segundo Cerco* of the word "god" (*deos*) applied to mythology
(tolerated in the 1572 *Os Lusíadas*) being erased from the printed version
and exchanged for "king" (*rey*). Compare Corte-Real s.d., MS, fol. 156v
and Corte-Real, *Sucesso do Segundo Cerco de Diu*, 248.

11 The long-standing notion that Manuel de Portugal and his close family,
the Vimioso, were the source of some kind of palace coup to publish *Os
Lusíadas* is based on the feeblest of evidence. The thesis was pleasing to
nationalist intellectuals who wished to associate Camões with the aris-
tocrat who was known to have refused support for Philip II's ambitions
towards the Portuguese throne. The ode that Camões dedicated to him
is not known to have drawn any response. It should perhaps be noted
that, when Manuel de Portugal married for the second time, he became
Corte-Real's brother-in-law. The two men shared a deep interest in poetry,
and Corte-Real wrote a rather moving tribute to Manuel de Portugal and
two of the children from his first marriage, seven rhymed octaves in the
long poem *Naufrágio de Sepúlveda e Lianor*, canto XIV.

12 Camões was published with only the king's *alvará* and Friar Ferreira's
report as prefatory material. The *Segundo Cerco* included, apart from the li-
cences, an engraving for the title, eulogies by several contemporary poets,
the author's prologue to the general reader, another one to King Sebastião,
and a list of contents.

13 There is nothing to support the multiple statements in criticism
that consider the 1572 edition of *Os Lusíadas* an exceptional event in

contemporary editorial practice. Jerónimo Osório's *De rebus Emmanuelis gestis* and *De regis institutione*, for instance, printed almost at the same time as Camões's epic in 1571–2, also lack paratextual elements beyond the *alvará* and Friar Ferreira's report, and the Dominican praises both works more eloquently than he does *Os Lusíadas*. Osório's volumes, each comprised of several "books," lack a list of contents as do the ten cantos of Camões's poem. As for poetry, one need only look at Diogo Bernardes's *Varias Rimas* of 1594 and *Rimas Varias Flores do Lima* of 1597 to find, in the first, a eulogizing report by Friar Bertolameu and, in both, no extra prefatory material. Both volumes by Bernardes and, for example, the epic *Elegíada* by Luís Pereira (1588) were printed in smaller octavos than *Os Lusíadas*. One could go on.

14 "La lengua y frasis castellano escogi, aunque murmurado y arguido de algunos de mi patria," writes the poet in the *prologo* (Corte-Real, *Felicissima*, fols. s.n.).

15 The letter accompanying the gift is dated 2 October (see Alves, *Sepúlveda e Lianor*, 20–1; and Plagnard, *Une Épopée Ibérique*, 20–1). The discovery of this letter invalidates the hypothesis put forward by Martínez Torrejón (Ánimo, valor y miedo," 164 and "Víspera de la batalla," 209) that the poem was sent to Philip the previous summer with King Sebastião's embassy.

16 King Sebastião's *alvará* is dated 4 February, too late for most copies of the poem to include it. The Spanish authorization, or *cédula*, is dated 10 July (for details, see Plagnard, *Une Épopée Ibérique*, 22).

17 One of his first biographers says so (see Faria, "Vida de Luís de Camões," fol. 128). But there are no other corroborating sources for this information.

18 These are the rhymed octaves addressed to the king beginning with the line: "Mui alto Rei a quem os céus em sorte." Camões, *Rimas*, 1595, fol. 69r–70v.

19 In Camões's eclogue beginning "Que grão variedade vão fazendo" (Camões, *Rimas*, 1595, 71r–80v) it is prophesied that Sebastião will conquer "o largo pasto de Ampelusa / c'o monte que em mau ponto viu Medusa" ll. 371–2), i.e., Moroccan plains and mountains. This eclogue was composed some time after the death of King João III in 1557, but its disregard for Oriental affairs and its expression of a palpable sense of threat coming from North Africa suggest a date of completion after Camões's return from India in 1570. The death of Rui de Sousa Carvalho in Tangiers in July 1573, which made a deep impression on King Sebastião, could well be alluded to in the lines (53–4; 88ff) referring to a destroyed oak (*carvalho*) and "wolves from Tangiers." In my view, the presence of the eclogue in the early folios of the Luís Franco Correia manuscript is not incompatible with a composition dating from late 1573 or 1574 (but see Aguiar e Silva, "Camões e D. Sebastião," 128).

20 Despite the similarities of design in the references to the king, Corte-Real represents a contrast to Camões in this respect (compare Corte-Real s.d., MS: canto IX, fol. 83v and canto XI, fols. 315r–317v or Corte-Real, *Sucesso do Segundo Cerco de Diu*, 126–7 and 505–9 to Camões, *Os Lusíadas*, canto I, fols. 2r–3v and canto X, fols. 185r–186v).

21 Sultan Mahmud figuratively portrays King Sebastião in the *Segundo Cerco* (see Alves, *Camões, Corte-Real e o Sistema da Epopeia Quinhentista*, 375–9).

22 The poem was being printed exactly when the young king was in Morocco, August to October 1574, in a performance to show his hopes to fight the Moors.

23 King João III, Sebastião's grandfather and predecessor to the throne, decided to abandon gradually a series of military positions in Morocco during the 1540s and 1550s. This decision was received with disbelief (a mais viva repulsa do País," in the words of Loureiro, *Uma Jornada ao Alentejo e ao Algarve*, 40). In the Cortes of 1562, the town's representatives expressly advocated invading Africa. Sebastião's ideas about attacking Morocco were clear from early on, and some of the individuals who opposed them are known (see Buescu, *Catarina de Áustria (1507–1578)*, 404–7).

24 "Never has a king followed the recommendation of a poet with greater fidelity than King Sebastião followed that of Camões. But then the recommendation may itself have been made with a knowledge of the king's projects. [...] *The Lusiads* was written as a courtly poem in search of royal patronage, a poem that fit itself to the tastes of its dedicatee – who, in this case, was already bent on doing precisely what his poet told him to do" (Helgerson, *Forms of Nationhood*, 162).

25 This is especially true of cantos IV, VI and IX of the *Felicissima*, where names of great soldiers from both nations are each praised in short vignettes.

26 This represents a contrast to Francisco de Aldana's octaves to Philip II, a poem that insisted, in an almost panic-stricken tone, that the Spanish king ought to join forces with Sebastião and invade Morocco. For a different view, see Martínez Torrejón, "Ánimo, valor y miedo" and "Víspera de la batalla," 210–12.

27 Pinheiro, the royal preacher, suffered Sebastião's fury in 1574 for being publicly critical of the king's trip of that year to North Africa (see Buescu, *Catarina de Áustria (1507–1578)*, 415; see also Spaggiari, *Obras de André Falcão de Resende*, 1:427 for a poet's reference to this). Pinheiro is described as a direct interlocutor of Corte-Real's in a long letter by the poet-painter dated from Alenquer, 31 January 1581 (Archivo General of Simancas, *Estado*, 426; many thanks to Aude Plagnard for providing me with a complete transcript of this letter).

28 The bishop of Silves wrote Sebastião a letter in 1574, emphasizing the need to prefer a secure peace to an offensive war, while inviting the king to

desist from his wish to invade Morocco. Later on, during the crisis for succession of the throne, Osório was convinced that Philip II should become king of Portugal so as to avoid civil war (see Pinho, "D. Jerónimo Osório e a crise sucessória de 1580").

29 By late 1577 and/or 1578, Corte-Real was the apparent recipient of some "new good fortune" that allowed him to write about Sebastião (see Spaggiari, *Obras de André Falcão de Resende*, 1:369–74 for the relevant verse). He is also said to be one of three men who were charged in 1578 with designing the timbre (of arms) for the Moroccan expedition (see Braga, *História de Camões, Parte II*, 522–3; Barata, *Subsidios para a Biographia*, 14; and Martínez Torrejón, "La lamentable pérdida," 96n.8). These two pieces of information suggest that Corte-Real's artistic talents became recognized by the Crown at a late stage, but no official documents are known to corroborate them.

30 In lines 462–507 (Martínez Torrejón, "'La lamentable pérdida,'" 113–14), the *Lamentable pérdida* speaks of Sebastião degrading the glorious reputation of Afonso Henriques (the first king of Portugal), Portuguese feats in India, and the siege of Mazagão in North Africa. These exemplary moments are the three historic milestones that shape the *Segundo Cerco* narratively, from the prose prologue (Afonso I) and body of the verse (the second siege of Diu, India) to the last heroic action described in the poem (Mazagão). Furthermore, words and expressions from the *Segundo Cerco*'s prologue seem alluded to in the *Lamentable pérdida* – compare Corte-Real, s.d., MS, fol. 7v8r or Corte-Real, *Sucesso do Segundo Cerco de Diu*, 1–2 to Martínez Torrejón, "'La lamentable pérdida,'" 114.

31 Two lines of the *Lamentable pérdida* (530–1) echo with dismay the ending of *Os Lusíadas*, precisely where Camões encourages Sebastião to attack North Africa. Compare "Ou... / ou rompendo.../os muros de Marrocos e Trudante" (Camões, *Os Lusíadas*, fol. 186v) to "O que podría llegar fácilmente / a abrasar a Marruecos o a Turdante" (Martínez Torrejón, "'La lamentable pérdida,'" 115).

32 Saraiva, *Estudos sobre a arte d'Os Lusíadas*, 69. The essay in which this sentence appears was originally published in 1981.

33 Lobo, *Memoria Historica e Critica ácerca de Luiz de Camões, e das suas obras*, 122.

34 Lobo was accused by a French translator of *Os Lusíadas* of writing "in a too obvious system of bad faith and reaction against Camões," as well as of being "a sworn apologist for our poet's enemies" (quoted in Lobo, *Breves Reflexões*). Saraiva has been the object of not dissimilar accusations; see, for example, the subtitle of Silveira, *O Tejo é um rio controverso* (António José Saraiva against Luís de Camões).

35 Sena, *A Estrutura de "Os Lusíadas."* For some of the infelicities in Sena's book, see Alves, *Camões, Corte-Real e o Sistema da Epopeia Quinhentista*, 208 and 483; and Matos, *Camões*, 247–54.

36 A word Gil uses and repeats about the poem's coherence is "failure" (see *malogro* in Gil, *O Efeito-Lusíadas*, 47, 51, 57, 61).

37 "Não explica o poeta como Venus poude dispôr dos ventos sobre os quaes não tem poder algum; o que o mesmo poeta nos-faz sentir no Cant. VI, onde, para lhes-applacar a furia, e serenar a tempestade que haviam alevantado, é mister á Deosa impregar as seducções das Nymphas, que lhe-formam o cortejo" (The poet does not explain how Venus could dispose of the winds over which she has no power; as the poet himself makes us feel in canto VI, where, to placate their fury and calm down the storm they had raised, the goddess is forced to deploy the seductions of the nymphs). Leoni, *Camões e Os Lusíadas*, 190.

38 "Não sei que da fabula conste que a Venus tocasse o imperio do mar, o que era necessario para ella despoticamente convocar e mandar as Nereidas" (I ignore anything in myth that ascribes to Venus the rule over the sea, since that would be necessary for her to call on and order around the nymphs despotically). Barbosa, *Analyse*, 33.

39 In canto VI, before the episode in which the sea nymphs seduce the winds, Neptune and all of his court had been persuaded by Bacchus to punish the Portuguese with a sea storm. It is hard to understand how the Nereids could, shortly afterwards, help Venus end the storm.

40 It is not clear why the Nereids should need to be persuaded to favour the Portuguese in the isle of Venus when they actually favoured them until then.

41 Voltaire wrote in his *Essay on Epic Poetry* (first edition, in English, of 1727) that "Gama in a storm addresses his prayers to Christ, but 'tis Venus who comes to his relief; the heroes are Christians and the poet heathen [...] So incongruous a machinery casts a blemish upon the whole poem." White, *Voltaire's Essay on Epic Poetry*, 110.

42 For a study of one of these more radical cases of mixing classical mythology and Christianity, a short epic from the fifteenth century, in the context of other Renaissance examples, see Alves, *Tempo para Entender*, 85–96.

43 Among many instances that could be mentioned, the following is possibly the most relevant for the episodes under discussion: in Virgil's *Aeneid 1*, Ilioneus attributes to Orion (535–8) the sea storm the reader knows was ordered by Juno, provoked by Aeolus and quelled by Neptune.

44 A recent exception is the allegorization of the Nereids in cantos II and VI as sea foam (Murrin, *Trade and Romance*, 175–6).

45 See Segurado e Campos, "Crónica ou poema?"; Alves, *Camões, Corte-Real e o Sistema da Epopeia Quinhentista*, 575–80; and Plagnard, *Une Épopée Ibérique*, 376–9. The *Segundo Cerco de Diu* includes a considerable panoply of gods from Roman mythology: there are three characters from the Underworld (Pluto, Allecto, and Tisiphone), Neptune, and many other sea

gods and sea nymphs, and even an Olympic deity like Mars and his sister Bellona.

46 I take allusion to be intentional and purposive. It must also answer to criteria of documented evidence. Book-length essays that balance each other with respect to the working definitions of allusion, and have greatly informed my own work, are Guillory, *Poetic Authority*; Martindale, *John Milton and the Transformation of Ancient Epic*; and Quint, *Epic and Empire*.

47 For convenience, I shall quote the *Felicissima* from the printed version of 1578. All the allusions cited here are already present, however, in the 1575 autograph manuscript held by Spain's National Library.

48 By comparison, the motives for Venus to support the Portuguese in Camões, *Os Lusíadas* (I.33–4 and IX.38) have often looked obscure, inadequate, or trifling.

49 "Cipro fertilissima [...] la Isla fertil, / Do tuvo Venus hâra y sacrificio." Corte-Real, *Felicissima*, canto 2, fol. 15r.

50 For the details, see Pozuelo Calero, "Transmutando la historia contemporánea en epopeya virgiliana," 175–7.

51 Syllepsis, as the trope that produces simultaneously two meanings for one word and, differently from ambiguity, "forces us not to choose, compelling us to recognize the equal necessity and equal actualization of both alternatives," is explained by Michael Riffaterre via a scene from Proust that recalls the *Aeneid* and Venus-like beauty. Riffaterre, *Fictional Truth*, 77–83. The "same word" *movera(m)/moviera* in Corte-Real preserves Camões's meaning and substitutes it for an opposite one, simultaneously.

52 This admiration for Camões's poetic talent in the portrait of Venus is shown by Corte-Real's many verbal allusions to it throughout the episode of canto VI, and in the same order as they appear in *Os Lusíadas*, canto II: "crespos fios de ouro" becomes "crespas hebras de oro"; "lácteas tetas" are transformed into "encolmado pecho y niveas pomas"; "alva petrina" turns into "vientre de marfil"; "lisas colunas" becomes "columnas de alabastro"; "delgado cendal" is now "transparente cendal"; the effect of the *cendal* in "nem tudo esconde nem descobre" is transformed into "trasluzese y apparesce"; and, finally, the similes of the dewy rose and of the weeping child are recalled too. The corrective mode is hardly ever absent in these imitations, however. In the last of the similes, for example, both little boys cry the more coddled they are, but while Camões's began as a "menino ... castigado" (*Os Lusíadas*, II.43), a punished child, Corte-Real's is exposed from the beginning as a "niño regalado" (*Felicissima*, fol. 82v), a spoilt child.

53 Camões, however, is not without contradictions in this too; in *Os Lusíadas*, Venus can also be destructive (see IX.32–5). Corte-Real deals with the contradictory nature of these two conceptions of love in tercets sung by the nymphs of Cyprus. *Felicissima*, canto II, fols. 25v ff.

54 After his interview with Venus, Jupiter tells Mercury to show Vasco da
   Gama an East African port where his men could rest and find their way
   to India, in imitation of *Aeneid* 1 (297–304). However, Jupiter and the gods
   had already decided on sending Mercury much earlier (compare *Os Lusíadas*, II.56 to I.40–1). Venus's initiative does not, therefore, translate into any
   progress in the narrative. It is also doubtful that Jupiter's prophecy (*Os
   Lusíadas*, II.43–55), imitated from *Aeneid 1*, is of any material advantage
   because the reader has known since canto I that she is informed about the
   future awaiting the Portuguese.
55 This song is the equivalent, in the economy of the epic's design, to the
   anonymous Nereid's much longer song of celebration in canto X of *Os
   Lusíadas*. It is the only piece in the *Felicissima*'s narrative written in rhymed
   octaves.
56 On this subject, see especially Hardie, *Virgil's "Aeneid,"* 336ff.
57 Every canto of the *Felicissima*'s 1578 edition begins with a woodcut representing some action taking place in that canto (see Plagnard, *Une Épopée
   Ibérique*, 397–405). The woodcut for canto IV represents, among others, the
   statues of Mars and John of Austria in the temple's main hall.
58 Compare with the single appearance of Mars as agent in Camões's *Os
   Lusíadas* (fol. 7; I.36–41).
59 The long description of the battle of Actium, the centrepiece of Vulcan's
   shield, is set in the middle of it; see *Aeneid* 8, 671 (*haec inter*).
60 Corte-Real, *Felicissima*, canto IV, fol. 64r (*en medio del*). Vilà ('Historia verdadera' y propaganda política," n. 39) first noticed the parallel. As Murrin
   notes, Corte-Real "does not develop the comparison to Actium the way
   the other poets do to emphasize the newness of Lepanto and its importance." *History and Warfare in Renaissance Epic*, 142. Through imitation, he
   shows rather more than he tells.
61 John of Austria was by now "movido / por diva inspiracion, mas que por
   arte / de naval disciplina." Corte-Real, *Felicissima*, canto XII, fol. 154v. This
   sentence comes literally from Corte-Real's historical source: "por inspiracion divina, mas que por alguna razon de diciplina de mar." Herrera,
   Relacion, ch. 24, fol. s/n.
62 Note the similarities: "Era cosa de ver la subtil mano / Del ingenioso
   artifice" (shield of Pallas; Corte-Real, *Felicissima*, fol. 83v); "En el forjado
   escudo ingenioso, / Vulcano haze al buril, con subtil arte" (shield for John
   of Austria; Corte-Real, *Felicissima*, fol. 84v).
63 This represents an extremely negative view of the Ottoman emperor, but
   not one completely devoid of historical fact: Selim II became also known
   as Sarhoş Selim, Selim the Drunkard.
64 The emperor's dream commences because of his drunkenness and enters
   through the gate of ivory, explicitly conveyed as the gate of false dreams

(as in Virgil, *Aeneid* 6). These facts do not harm the dream's authority, however. Selim II's dream is false because it will lead him to wrong and unjust military action, but that does not prevent the dream from correctly inciting him to abandon the influence of Bacchus. There is, therefore, no real ambiguity to the meaning of Selim's dream.

65 Bacchus does not resolve the complication he creates, and does not participate in the denouement. This fact has been noticed at least since the early eighteenth century (the commentary by Garcez Ferreira, in Camões, *Lusiada Poema Epico*, is a good example). I am not considering interpretations that see Bacchus as hiding, or implicit, in the Isle of Love (Gil, *O Efeito-Lusíadas*; Alves, "Post-Imperial Bacchus"; Figueiredo, "Pais tiranos"; and Nóbrega, *No Reino da Água o Rei do Vinho*) because I wish to distinguish as clearly as possible narrative plot performed by agents from symbolic connections subject to interpretation.

66 In this extraordinary scene, Corte-Real alludes to Mercury's speech to Aeneas in Virgil's *Aeneid* 4. "Insensato," the exclamation beginning Jealousy's warnings (*Felicissima*, fol. 36v), comes from Mercury's "demens" (*Aeneid* 4, 562); the rhetorical questions that follow are drawn from the same model. The concept, of course, is entirely different: one of Cyprus's nymphs explains that Love generates Jealousy and transforms it afterwards into a Fury (*Felicissima*, fol. 36r).

67 The following expressions are the closest an unknowing human bystander can get to describing the hidden influence of a Fury in Mostafà's behaviour: "Mas luego rebentô la infernal peste / En las falsas entrañas escondida," "... iniquo hablar del Baxa fiero, / El cual como frenetico furioso ...," "El barbaro ministro del infierno: / Lleno de venenoso ardor" (canto XI, fols. 149v–151r).

68 War, Alecto, and the other two Eumenides are mentioned together in Virgil, *Aeneid* 6, 279–80; Jealousy has a more probable early modern origin.

69 This is Megaera, the Fury who appears in canto XIII to circle above Ali Pascha, predicting his death; but she does not determine or control the Turkish commander's actions.

70 Constantinople becomes, therefore, the focal point where the transition between the first to the second plot happens. It had earlier been the place where the first plot began.

71 Ignacio de Luzán noticed this reflexive structure in an acute reading of the *Felicissima:* "es una fantasía muy extravagante el mezclar el guión de la fe y el estoque dado por el Papa a D. Juan de Austria, con la armadura regalada al mismo héroe cristiano por la diosa Venus." *La poética*, 661.

72 On this pairing in canto 13, and its meaning in Corte-Real's concept of art, see Alves, "Cervantes' Portuguese Painter."

73 The quote comes from Ticknor, *History of Spanish Literature*, 2:492; this was standard opinion (see also, for example, Braga, *História de Camões, Parte*

II, 519). On the traditional notion that Corte-Real revered Camões in the
Felicissima, see Luzán, *La poética*, 661; and Pierce, *La Poesía Épica del Siglo de
Oro*, 290.

WORKS CITED

Manuscript Sources

Archivo General of Simancas, *Estado 426*
Corte-Real, Jerónimo s.d. *Sucesso do Segundo Cerco de Dio Estando Dom Ioham
Mazcarenhas, Por Capitam e Governador da Fortaleza. Anno de 1546*, MS,
National Archives at Torre do Tombo, cód. Cadaval 31, Lisbon.
Corte-Real, Jerónimo 1575 Espantosa, y *felicissima victoria cõncedida del cielo al
señor don Juan d'Austria en el golfo de Lepanto, de la poderosa armada Othomana,
en el año de nuestra salvación de M. D. Lxxii*, MS, National Library of Spain, n.
3693, Madrid.

Printed Sources

Aguiar e Silva, Vítor. "Camões e D. Sebastião." In *Dicionário de Luís de Camões*,
128–34. Lisbon: Caminho, 2011.
Almeida, M. Lopes de. "Introdução." In *Obras de Jerónimo Corte-Real*, v–xxxvi.
Porto: Lello & Irmão, 1979.
Alves, Hélio J.S. *Camões, Corte-Real e o Sistema da Epopeia Quinhentista*.
Coimbra: Por Ordem da Universidade, 2001.
– "Cervantes' Portuguese Painter." *Bulletin of Hispanic Studies* 96 no. 9 (2019):
905–17.
– "Post-Imperial Bacchus: The Politics of Literary Criticism in Camões Studies
1940–2001." *Portuguese Literary & Cultural Studies* 9 (2003): 95–106.
– ed. *Sepúlveda e Lianor. Canto Primeiro*. Coimbra: Centro Interuniversitário de
Estudos Camonianos, 2014.
– *Tempo para Entender. História comparada da literatura Portuguesa*. Casal de
Cambra, Sintra: Caleidoscópio, 2006.
– "Teoría de la épica en el Renacimiento portugués." In *La teoría de la épica en
el siglo XVI (España, Francia, Italia y Portugal)*, edited by María José Vega y
Lara Vilà, 137–73. Vigo: Editorial Academia del Hispanismo, 2010.
Barata, A.F. *Subsidios para a Biographia do Poeta Jeronymo Corte Real
Commemorando a vinda de Sua Magestade a Évora em 1899*. Évora: Minerva
Commercial de Ferreira, Irmão e C.ª, 1899.
Barbosa, Jerónimo Soares. *Analyse dos Lusíadas de Luiz de Camões dividida por
seus cantos com observações criticas sobre cada um d'eles*. 2nd ed. Coimbra:
Livraria Central de J. Diogo Pires, 1882.

Bernardes, Diogo. *Rimas Varias Flores do Lima*. Lisbon: Manoel de Lyra, 1597.

– *Varias Rimas ao Bom Jesus e a Virgem gloriosa sua May e a sanctos particulares*. Lisbon: Simão Lopez, 1594.

Braga, Teófilo. *História de Camões, Parte II: Eschola de Camões, Livro II os poetas épicos*. Porto: Imprensa Portuguesa Editora, 1875.

Buescu, Ana Isabel. *Catarina de Áustria (1507–1578). Infanta de Tordesilhas, Rainha de Portugal*. Lisbon: A Esfera dos Livros, 2007.

Camões, Luís de. *Lusiada Poema Epico [...] illustrado com varias, e breves notas, e com um precedente apparato do que lhe pertence, por Ignacio Garcez Ferreira*. Vol. 1. Naples: Officina Parriniana; Vol. 2. Rome: Officina de Antonio Rossi, 1731–2.

– *Os Lusíadas*. Lisbon: Antonio Gõçalvez, 1572.

– *Rhythmas*. Lisbon: Manoel de Lyra, 1595.

Corte-Real, Jerónimo. *Felicissima Victoria concedida del cielo al señor don Iuan d'Austria, en el golfo de Lepanto de la poderosa armada Othomana. En el año de nuestra salvacion de 1572*. Lisbon: Antonio Ribero, 1578.

– *Naufrágio e lastimoso sucesso da perdiçam de Mnoel de Sousa de Sepúlveda e Dona Lianor de Sá ...* Lisbon: Simão Lopez, 1594.

– *Sucesso do Segundo Cerco de Diu: Estando Dõ Ioham Mazcarenhas por Capitam da Fortaleza. Año de 1546*. Lisbon: Antonio Gonçalvez, 1574.

Costa e Silva, José Maria da. *Ensaio Biographico-Critico sobre os Melhores Poetas Portuguezes*. Volume 4. Lisbon: Na Imprensa Silviana, 1852.

Faria, Manuel Severim de. "Vida de Luís de Camões." In *Discursos Varios Políticos*, fols. 88–136. Évora: Manuel Carvalho, 1624.

Figueiredo, João R. "Pais tiranos: o Baco de *Os Lusíadas* e Camões." In *A Teoria do Programa. Uma homenagem a Maria de Lourdes Ferraz e a M. S. Lourenço*, edited by António M. Feijó e Miguel Tamen, 19–37. Lisbon: Programa em Teoria da Literatura, Universidade de Lisboa, 2007.

Gil, Fernando. *O Efeito-Lusíadas*. Lisbon: Edições João Sá da Costa, 1999.

Guillory, John. *Poetic Authority. Spenser, Milton and Literary History*. New York: Columbia University Press, 1983.

Hardie, Philip R. *Virgil's "Aeneid": Cosmos and Imperium*. Oxford: Clarendon Press, 1986.

Helgerson, Richard. *Forms of Nationhood. The Elizabethan Writing of England*. Chicago: University of Chicago Press, 1992.

Herrera, Fernando de. *Relacion de la Guerra de Cipre, y Sucesso de la batalla Naval de Lepanto*. Seville: Alonso Escrivano, 1572.

Leoni, Francisco Evaristo. *Camões e "Os Lusíadas." Ensaio historico-critico-litterario*. Lisbon: Livraria de A.M. Pereira, 1872.

Lobo, Francisco Alexandre. *Breves Reflexões sobre a vida de Luiz de Camões escrita por M. Charles Magnin, membro do Instituto, no principio da sua traducção dos Lusíadas*. Lisbon: Academia Real das Sciencias, 1842.

– *Memoria Historica e Critica ácerca de Luiz de Camões, e das suas obras*. Lisbon: Academia Real das Sciencias, 1820.

Loureiro, Francisco de Sales. *Uma Jornada ao Alentejo e ao Algarve. A alteração das linhas de força da política nacional. Texto do cronista João Cascão*. Lisbon: Livros Horizonte, 1984.

Luzán, Ignacio de. *La poética o reglas de la poesía en general, y de sus principales especies*. Edited by Russell P. Sebold. Madrid: Cátedra, 2008.

Martindale, Charles. *John Milton and the Transformation of Ancient Epic*. 2nd ed. London: Bristol Classical Press, 2002.

Martínez Torrejón, José Miguel. "Ánimo, valor y miedo. Don Sebastián, Corte Real y Aldana ante Felipe II." *Península: revista de estudos ibéricos* 2 (2005): 159–70.

– ed. "'La lamentable pérdida del rey don Sebastián y del reino de Portugal' de Jerónimo Corte-Real." *Colóquio-Letras* 201 (2019): 73–146.

– "Víspera de la batalla. El hervidero manuscrito portugués ante la invasión de Marruecos." *Românica: revista de literatura* 18 (2009): 195–216.

Matos, Maria Vitalina Leal de. *Camões: Sentido e Desconcerto*. Coimbra: Centro Interuniversitário de Estudos Camonianos, 2011.

Murrin, Michael. *History and Warfare in Renaissance Epic*. Chicago: University of Chicago Press, 1994.

– *Trade and Romance*. Chicago: University of Chicago Press, 2014.

Nóbrega, Luiza. *No Reino da Água o Rei do Vinho. Submersão dionisíaca e transfiguração trágico-lírica d' "Os Lusíadas."* Natal: Editora da Universidade Federal do Rio Grande do Norte, 2013.

Osório, Jerónimo. *De rebus Emmanuelis regis Lusitaniae invictissimi virtute et auspicio gestis*. Lisbon: Antonio Gonçalves, 1571.

– *De regis institutione et disciplina*. Lisbon: João de Espanha, 1572.

Pereira, Luís. *Elegíada*. Lisbon: Manoel de Lyra, 1588.

Pierce, Frank. *La Poesía Épica del Siglo de Oro*. 2nd ed. Madrid: Gredos, 1968.

Pinho, Sebastião Tavares de. "Critérios e métodos de censura na 'edição dos piscos' d'*Os Lusíadas* de Camões e no poema *De Senectute* de Lopo Serrão, de 1579." In *Decalogia Camoniana*, 37–51. Coimbra: Centro Interuniversitário de Estudos Camonianos, 2007.

– "D. Jerónimo Osório e a crise sucessória de 1580." *Humanitas* 43–4 (1991–2): 305–31.

Plagnard, Aude. *Une Épopée Ibérique. Alonso de Ercilla et Jerónimo Corte-Real (1569–1589)*. Madrid: Casa de Velázquez, 2019.

Pozuelo Calero, Bartolomé. "Transmutando la historia contemporánea en epopeya virgiliana: la 'Felicísima victoria' de Jerónimo Corte-Real." In *Matrizes Clássicas da Literatura Portuguesa*, edited by Paula Morão and Cristina Pimentel, 169–78. Lisbon: Campo da Comunicação, 2014.

Quint, David. *Epic and Empire. Politics and Generic Form from Virgil to Milton*. Princeton, NJ: Princeton University Press, 1993.

Ribeiro, Aquilino. *Luís de Camões. Fabuloso. Verdadeiro. Ensaio.* 2 vols. Lisbon: Bertrand, 1958.

Riffaterre, Michael. *Fictional Truth.* Baltimore: Johns Hopkins University Press, 1990.

Rodrigues. José Maria. *Fontes dos Lusíadas.* Lisbon: Academia das Ciências, 1979.

Saraiva, António José. *Estudos sobre a arte d'Os Lusíadas.* Lisbon: Gradiva, 1992.

Segurado e Campos, J.A. "Crónica ou poema? Observações sobre o 'Segundo Cerco de Diu' de Jerónimo Corte-Real." In VVAA, *Miscelânea de Estudos em Honra do Prof. A. Costa Ramalho.* Coimbra: INIC/Centro de Estudos Clássicos e Humanísticos da Universidade de Coimbra, 1992.

Sena, Jorge de. *A Estrutura de "Os Lusíadas" e outros estudos camonianos e de poesia peninsular do século XVI.* 2nd ed. Lisbon: Edições 70, 1980.

Silveira, Jorge Fernandes da. *O Tejo é um rio controverso: António José Saraiva contra Luís Vaz de Camões.* Rio de Janeiro: 7Letras, 2008.

Spaggiari, Barbara, ed. *Obras de André Falcão de Resende.* 2 vols. Lisbon: Edições Colibri, 2009.

Ticknor, George. *History of Spanish Literature.* Volume 2. New York: Harper and Brothers, 1849.

Virgil. *Aeneid.* Translated by H. Rushton Fairclough. Loeb Classical Library. 2 vols. London and Cambridge, MA: William Heinemann and Harvard University Press, 1953.

White, Florence Donnell. *Voltaire's Essay on Epic Poetry: A Study and an Edition.* 1915. Reprint, New York: Phaeton Press, 1970.

Electronic Sources

Vilà, Lara. "'Historia verdadera' y propaganda política: la 'Felicísima victoria' de Jerónimo Corte Real y el modelo épico de Virgilio." *Res Publica Litterarum: Documentos de trabajo del Grupo de Investigación "Nomos"* 5 (2005). https://dialnet.unirioja.es/servlet/articulo?codigo=2996741&orden=215593&info=lin.

2 Pagan Nature and the Naturalization of Empire in the New World Epyllions of Bento Teixeira and Silvestre de Balboa[1]

LUIS RODRÍGUEZ-RINCÓN

Since Columbus, Europeans contending with the challenge of explaining the novelty of American flora and fauna have turned back to the Old World for both learned and everyday points of reference for describing the new.[2] For the two poets at the centre of this study, it was by looking at American nature through the filter of pagan mythology that these early Iberian settlers transformed the novelty of the New World into a semblance of home. The epyllions, or short epic poems, by Bento Teixeira (ca. 1560–1600) and Silvestre de Balboa (1563–ca. 1647) have never been assessed from a comparative framework even though both authors and their poems share crucial defining characteristics. Both *Prosopopéia* (Lisbon, 1601) and *Espejo de paciencia* (Puerto Príncipe, Cuba, ca. 1608) share the same verse form – *octavas reales* in Castilian – composed of eight-line stanzas of hendecasyllables with the rhyme pattern ABABABCC typical of Iberian epic poetry of this period.[3] Though modelled off the full-fledged epics of Luís de Camões (d. 1580) and Alonso de Ercilla (1533–94), among others, both Teixeira's *Prosopopéia* and Balboa's *Espejo* are better labelled epyllions given their modest lengths (752 and 1,213 lines of verse, respectively) and idiosyncratic use of mythology. These epyllions were written by European settlers to the respective Portuguese and Spanish colonies that are today Brazil and Cuba and celebrate in an epic key local colonial histories. They furthermore represent the points of departure for the national literary histories of Brazil and Cuba. Finally, and most crucially for this essay, both poems incorporate pagan gods such as nymphs and tritons in their descriptions of the flora and fauna of the Americas. What this convergence of pagan mythology with American flora and fauna says about the nature of colonial ideology and epic poetic form at the turn of the seventeenth century is the focus of this essay.

From Pagan Gods to Pagan Nature

In order to better contextualize our assessment of pagan gods in the New World epyllions of Teixeira and Balboa, it is important to first address the links between early modern mythological art, allegorical representations of nature, and the mythographic tradition. Take for example the allegorical illustration of Columbus's Atlantic crossing done by the Flemish artist Johannes Stradanus (Jan van der Straet, 1523–1605) included as part of his series *America retectio* (Antwerp, 1589).[4] The engraving depicts the moment Columbus's fleet first caught sight of land in October 1492 accompanied by a retinue of pagan sea gods (fig. 2.1). To the left of Columbus is the goddess Diana – recognizable by the moon-shaped crescent on her brow and her quiver and arrows – who guides his ship by a rope towards the American land masses on the horizon. To the right of Columbus are two tritons blowing their horns and announcing his arrival while Neptune, identified by his trident, guides the fleet towards land on his seahorse-drawn chariot. The land masses of America are discernible on the horizon with shores guarded by sea monsters. Jorge Cañizares-Esguerra interprets this engraving by Stradanus, which was later reprinted by Theodore de Bry in his famous *Americae pars quarta* (1594), as emblematic of "a model of imperial science, popularized by early modern Spain, in which chivalric, gendered values colored the pursuit of knowledge."[5] Columbus in full armour, holding up a banner with the Cross in his right hand, represents "the cosmographer as knight," setting out to conquer the world through an uncovering of its secrets.[6] As I see it, the guiding hand of the goddess Diana recasts Columbus's voyage as part of a providential narrative. As European history transforms into prophecy, the ocean becomes inhabited by a retinue of pagan deities who represent a higher order governing the unfolding of human history and its perceived relation to the natural world. The question of why early modern poets and artists linked pagan gods to the representation of nature in an epic key – whether the ocean or American flora and fauna – merits attention.

While scholars generally recognize that early modern Christian readers and artists gleaned moral and political truths behind the veils of pagan mythological figures and stories, the relation between the pagan gods and conceptions of nature in the period is less widely understood. Artists like Stradanus inherited from the Middle Ages a hermeneutical tradition that reconciled the pagan gods with the Christian faith by interpreting them as fables conveying allegorical truths about history, morality, and nature. The hermeneutic rehabilitation of pagan mythology in the hands of the early church fathers divorced the classical forms

Figure 2.1. Johannes Stradanus, from *America retectio* (Antwerp, 1589). Image courtesy of the John Carter Brown Library.

of the pagan pantheon from their original significations. Following Jean Seznec, "form and subject survived in isolation, so to speak, each distinct from the other. As pagan ideas gradually became severed from expression in art, Christian ideas came forward to inhabit the forms thus abandoned, just as Christian cult took over the empty temples or the imperial baths."[7] The tradition of interpreting Christian moral truths behind the veil of pagan mythology is long, varied, and exemplified by the fourteenth-century *Ovid moralisé* and, in an Iberian context, by parts of Juan Pérez de Moya's (1514–96) *Philosophía secreta* (Madrid, 1585). Hand in hand with the moral lessons conveyed allegorically by pagan myths in the early modern period came a close association between political power and the gods of Graeco-Roman antiquity. "The prominence of the gods in the art of the Renaissance," as Gordon Teskey has argued, "reflects their role in the conjoining of political authority to spiritually resonant cultural forms."[8] For Teskey, "the classical gods were politically sacred, conferring an aura of mysterious power on the symbols of the state."[9] Part of what made the pagan gods such potent symbols of power and morality in the period was their polyvalent function as allegories through which artists conveyed nature's truth as well.

To understand nature through the medium of pagan mythological figures and art seems counterintuitive to readers today given our penchant for separating the study of nature from the study of antiquity and the practice of art. Yet the relation between Greco-Roman mythology and nature in the early modern period was grounded precisely in the permeability of the divide between nature and art. Horst Bredekamp describes the episteme of the sixteenth century in the following terms: "the idea that works of art, in particular the art of antiquity, could mediate between human beings and nature was a basic tenet of both the natural sciences and aesthetics."[10] Bredekamp's proposition can be understood in part as the endurance of the medieval hermeneutic practice of interpreting pagan poetry and artwork as fables conveying, alongside moral truths and political imperatives, allegorized natural history. Pérez de Moya's Spanish-language mythography exemplifies the conceptual range of allegories associated with pagan gods when he declares his intent to elucidate "el sentido histórico, y el físico y moral" of pagan "fábulas."[11] Pérez de Moya's interest in the "físico o natural" when interpreting pagan fables puts him squarely in line with the Christian mythographic tradition that extends from the *Etymologiae* of Isidore of Seville (560–636) through the *Genealogia deorum gentilium* of Giovanni Boccaccio (1313–75) to the *Mythologiae* (Venice, 1567) of Natale Conti (1520–82) and Francis Bacon's (1561–1626) *De sapientia veterum* (London, 1609).[12]

When attempting to explain nature, writers from the Middle Ages to the Renaissance used pagan poetry and artwork as primary data for writing accounts of natural history.[13] Prior to the advent of scientific methodologies, writers interested in understanding and representing nature "used pagan myths as essential data in the mapping of the cosmos."[14] Reading and interpretation were the privileged methodologies that uncovered God's hidden design in both natural and artistic signs.[15] This was certainly the case in early modern Europe under the banner of what William B. Ashworth calls an "emblematic natural history," which characterized the study of nature from 1560 to 1650.[16] Among the many threads that define the conceptual tapestry of emblematic natural history was pagan mythology and the mythographic tradition. Following Ashworth, "it is well known that classical mythology had an overwhelming impact on Renaissance art and literature, but it also left its mark on natural history."[17]

Given pagan mythology's role in early modern conceptions of nature, it is here argued that the Greco-Roman gods constituted not a simple aesthetic convention for artists, but rather a charged symbolic language at the intersection of nature with art. When functioning as ciphers through which nature's secrets were conveyed to mortals, the pagan gods formed an integral part of a syncretic order, a Pagan Nature, asserting a designed and hierarchical structure to the world that buttressed moral and political imperatives as well. Pagan Nature is syncretic in the sense of weaving together disparate strands of the intellectual history of the early modern period: from emblematic natural history to the mythographic tradition's moral and political currents in addition to the antiquarian interests of artists and patrons. While the pagan dimension to this vision of natural order is distinctive to the early modern period, the general structure of grounding social and political norms in understandings of nature is a more widespread phenomenon. As Lorraine Daston argues, "all human dreams of order, revolutionary or reactionary, local or global, are ultimately figures, made visible and alluring, in nature's *Wunderkammer* of possible orders."[18] The pagan gods as polyvalent fables at the blurred frontier between nature and art were one iteration of this dream of an order tying European political and moral imperatives to allegorized conceptions of nature that harked back to a bygone age of pagan imperial glory. As the poems of Teixeira and Balboa demonstrate, Pagan Nature was not exclusive to Europe but was extended to the Americas as well in the wake of European colonization.

Europeans made varied use of the Greco-Roman gods to understand the Indigenous peoples, flora, and fauna of the Americas. The gods of the Mexica and Inca were repeatedly compared to those of ancient Greece and Rome throughout the sixteenth and seventeenth centuries.[19] For example, the Franciscan Bernardino de Sahagún (1500–90) assigned to many Mexica deities an equivalent from the Greco-Roman pantheon to help explain their novelty.[20] Like in Stradanus's engraving of Columbus, pagan gods also appeared in European artistic representations of the colonial history of the Americas. On the surface, these gods appear as little more than a commonplace aesthetic of the early modern period. But when pagan mythology in early modern colonial poetry and artwork is discussed in relation to the intellectual history of the mythographic tradition in Europe, their aesthetic appeal becomes just one thread in a dense network of significations. Pagan Nature is the name given here to a point of conversion of nature with art where emblematic natural history couples with the political, moral, and aesthetic imperatives of European settlers in the Americas. In this vein, Pagan Nature represents an iteration of what Daston describes in general terms as "a kind of covert smuggling operation in which cultural values are transferred to nature, and nature's authority is then called upon to buttress those very same values."[21] At issue is the function of nature as the guarantor for human conceptions of order. For Daston, "the human impulse to make nature meaningful is rooted in a double insight about order: normativity demands order; and nature supplies exemplars of all conceivable orders."[22] The order at play in the engraving by Stradanus, that of Pagan Nature, is present as well in the New World epyllions of Bento Teixeira and Silvestre de Balboa. It will be argued that Pagan Nature in the epyllions of Teixeira and Balboa was the symbolic language through which a European colonial order was naturalized as part of the Americas.

A note about the use of the term "epyllion" to refer to the poems of Teixeira and Balboa is in order since this genre is not without controversy. The term "epyllion" refers to a short epic poem that adapts the verse forms and style of epic poetry to a more circumscribed length and at times subjective artistic sensibility. The scarcity of references to epyllions in the literature and criticism of Greco-Roman antiquity has led some scholars to decry the genre as a modern coinage.[23] It is true that "epyllion" entered the lexicon of classical scholarship in the nineteenth century and that "no consensus on what an 'epyllion' is emerges from the ancient material."[24] Nevertheless, classicists note the prevalence of the term in early-modern Neo-Latin poetry in reference to "short mythological hexameter narratives that either constitute a poem of their own or a clearly defined part of a larger poem."[25] The centrality of pagan mythology to the early modern conception of the epyllion is noteworthy. The syncretic merger of natural history with pagan mythology is prevalent in a range of Neo-Latin epyllions from Girolamo Fracastoro's (1478–1553) *Syphilis, sive morbus gallicus* (Verona, 1530) to René Rapin's (1621–87) mythological account of the origin of the tulip in his *Hortorum libri IV* (Paris, 1665). Another notable example is the final book of Nicolò Partenio Giannettasio's (1648–1715) *Nautica* (Naples, 1685), where Columbus ascends the Pico de Teide in Tenerife accompanied by his mother, the nymph Urania, who reveals a vision of the oceans and lands he is set to discover. In conjunction with Stradanus's allegorical engraving and the poems of Teixeira and Balboa, *Nautica* attest to the practice of recasting European colonial history in the Americas as a providential epic mission under the aegis of Pagan Nature.

While the history of the epyllion in Spain largely follows the history of the genre in early modern Europe more generally, there is something to be said of the distinctive iteration of the genre that emerged in and in reaction to the colonization of the Americas. Sofie Kluge has done the most in recent years to advance the study of the Spanish epyllion though her conclusions cannot be applied to New World epyllions wholesale. For Kluge, "the most fertile period of the early modern Spanish epyllion was undoubtedly the years following the turn of the [seventeenth] century."[26] Certainly, the poems of Balboa and Teixeira fit this chronology. The Spanish epyllion takes on distinctive characteristics for Kluge as a result of the Counter-Reformation critique of pagan mythology in epic poetry by Torquato Tasso (1544–95), Alonso López Pinciano (d. 1627), and Francisco Cascales (1564–1642). Out of this "Counter-Reformation purgation of the epic narrative arose the epyllion as a demonstratively fictitious genre, bluntly equaling myth and fiction and, on the surface at least, depriving the mythological tale of all ethical, moral, and religious significance."[27] Divorced from the mythographic tradition that linked allegorical meanings to pagan mythology, the Baroque epyllion as a short mythological poem in epic verse became a "poetic form whose main constituent was the disinterested and self-reflective narrative [...] a form apparently divested of all national, political, and religious significance."[28] Kluge's characterization of the Baroque epyllion as disinterested and politically divested does not describe well the epyllions of Teixeira and Balboa. Through its mythological imagery, the epyllions of Teixeira and Balboa naturalize an Iberian colonial presence in the Americas by merging European political, moral, and aesthetic imperatives with American flora and fauna.

Teixeira, Balboa, and New World Nature

The manner in which Teixeira and Balboa describe the natural marvels of their adopted homes of Brazil and Cuba has long fascinated critics, who see their poems as the points of departure for their respective national literary traditions. This essay proposes a reading of the pagan gods in *Espejo de paciencia* and *Prosopopéia* as fables through which a colonial order asserts itself to be divinely ordained and grounded in the natural order of the Americas. In a world where the pagan gods speak for the environment and assert a concord between colonial power and nature, colonialism itself is naturalized. Before discussing the function of Pagan Nature in naturalizing a colonial order, I will describe the poems in question, their authors, and the history of their reception since they reveal crucial similarities between Teixeira and Balboa that help ground this study's comparative framework.

Although published in 1601, *Prosopopéia* did not enter the Portuguese literary canon until 1741 as part of the celebrated *Biblioteca lusitana* by Diogo Barbosa Machado (1682–1772). There, the famed bibliophile and scholar listed the following information about the author of *Prosopopéia*: "Bento Teixeira Pinto was born in Pernambuco and was proficient in both poetry and history."[29] Machado goes on to attribute the authorship of several works to Teixeira, including the prose narration of the shipwreck experienced by Jorge de Albuquerque in 1565 as well as the famous *Diálogos das grandezas do Brasil*, both now recognized to be works of other writers. The subsequent history of Teixeira's reception is in no small part the gradual correction of these initial bibliographical and biographical errors. Putting to one side the history of erroneous attributions, the scholarly consensus regarding Teixeira's place of birth and religious beliefs has changed dramatically since the twentieth century. Decisive in catalyzing this change was the discovery of the Inquisition records of one Bento Teixeira taken into custody in 1595 in Olinda, Brazil. This Teixeira was not born in Pernambuco, Brazil, but rather in Porto, Portugal, to New Christian parents who migrated to Brazil when the poet was three years old.[30] After receiving a Jesuit education that left him "perhaps the individual with the highest level of education in both sacred and profane letters in the colony of Pernambuco," Teixeira made a living as a teacher for many years in Brazil.[31] Teixeira's life took a turn for the worse upon the arrival of the Inquisition to Brazil in 1594. Accused of practising Judaism, Teixeira was arrested and taken to Lisbon in 1596, where he was kept prisoner and interrogated until finally confessing to the charges. Teixeira made public penance for his apostasy in 1599 and released, only to die the year after.[32]

Teixeira's poem *Prosopopéia* is dedicated to Jorge de Albuquerque Coelho (1539–96), hereditary ruler of the Captaincy of Pernambuco. In the tradition of laudatory epic poetry, *Prosopopéia* celebrates the trials and tribulations of its hero-dedicatee and his family. Jorge de Albuquerque, in the words of C.R. Boxer, "came of solid *conquistador* stock on both sides" since his father, Duarte Coelho (1485–1554), was a celebrated Portuguese soldier and colonial administrator in both Asia and Brazil.[33] On his mother's side, Jorge was related to the celebrated Afonso de Albuquerque (1453–1515), conqueror of Ormuz, Goa, and Malacca. Teixeira's poem centres on the life and exploits of Jorge de Albuquerque: his bloody campaigns to pacify the Indigenous populations of Pernambuco in 1560 (stanzas 22–34); his harrowing shipwreck while crossing the Atlantic in 1565 (stanzas 35–68); and, in conclusion, his exploits at the Battle of Alcácer-Kibir fighting alongside King Sebastião in 1578 (stanzas 69–91). The poem forms part of the first printed source for the popular story of Jorge de Albuquerque dismounting from his horse so that a wounded Dom Sebastião could escape from the carnage of Alcácer-Kibir, thus contributing to the popular messianic belief in

Sebastianism.[34] In light of Teixeira's Inquisition records, scholars have argued for a hidden message of Jewish resistance in *Prosopopéia* discussed below. The controversy surrounding Teixeira's nationality and motivation for writing his poem parallels the debates over the authenticity of Silvestre de Balboa's *Espejo* and its account of the capture of the Bishop of Cuba, Juan de las Cabezas Altamirano (1565–1615), by French pirates in 1604.

The transatlantic life trajectory of Silvestre de Balboa mirrors that of Teixeira. Born in Las Palmas de Gran Canaria in 1563 to a family with extensive commercial interests in the Americas, Balboa began to criss-cross the Atlantic and Caribbean by the 1580s. Both poets are thus settler-colonizers in their respective regions. Balboa settled definitively in Eastern Cuba around the city of Bayamo by 1592.[35] Thanks to the archival records published by José María Chacón y Calvo and Leví Marrero, scholars can definitively identify Balboa as a prominent resident of the towns of Bayamo and Puerto Príncipe (Camaguey) due to his recorded employment as "escribano público" of Puerto Príncipe and his ties to prominent families of the area.[36] Such records document the presence not only of Balboa but also of many other characters that appear in *Espejo*, which helps put to rest the controversy surrounding the text's authenticity even if the whereabouts and history of the manuscript copies that form the basis for all modern editions of the poem remain in doubt.[37] The convoluted history of *Espejo*'s literary reception and manuscript history led to the charge, first levelled by Carolina Poncet in 1913, that the poem was a nineteenth-century forgery.[38] *Espejo* was never published in Balboa's lifetime, but was only rediscovered in 1836 by José Antonio Echevarría as part of a manuscript that was subsequently lost with only the handwritten copies made by Echevarría surviving and serving as the basis for all subsequent editions.[39] Poncet speculated that Echevarría forged the poem in order to promote his abolitionist cause at a time when Cuba was still a Spanish colony with a slave economy. Archival findings have since confirmed not only the accuracy of the events narrated by the poem, the capture by French pirates of Bishop Altamirano, but also corroborated the existence of many of the figures named in the poem, including Balboa and the sonneteers who celebrate his work.[40]

The story commemorated by Balboa's *Espejo* – one of pirates, contrabandists, and a local community forced to fend for itself – is emblematic of the history of Cuba over the course of the sixteenth and seventeenth centuries. After the first wave of European settlement ended around 1524, Cuba suffered a period of administrative neglect and depopulation as Spaniards turned their attention to the riches of mainland Mexico and Peru.[41] Spanish settlers outside of Havana and Santiago de Cuba were largely excluded from lucrative transatlantic trading networks by restrictive Crown policies that concentrated trade in certain ports. Left to fend for themselves beyond the view of colonial administrators, the residents of Bayamo and Puerto Príncipe participated in a lucrative transatlantic network of contraband trade with English, French, and Dutch smugglers. Given its strategic location, the Gulf of Guacanayabo and its port of Manzanillo became the centre of illicit trade in the Spanish Caribbean in the sixteenth and seventeenth centuries with the towns of Bayamo and Puerto Príncipe becoming the two largest settlements on the island after Havana and Santiago.[42]

Balboa's *Espejo* recounts in an epic key the events of the year 1604 when Spanish settlers around the town of Bayamo came into conflict with French Huguenot pirates moored in the port of Manzanillo. The first canto of the poem recounts the events that occurred as Bishop Altamirano – while passing through the village of Yara on a visitation to the outlying towns of his diocese – was taken captive by the French corsair Gilberto Girón and kept hostage on his ship. After his ransom is negotiated, the bishop is released. Responding to the events unfolding on shore, the local community bands together to exact revenge on the corsairs. Given the near universal implication of the region's inhabitants in the contraband trade, including Balboa and the bishop, it has been argued that their violent reprisal was a means of placating the Crown and drawing a line in the sand between the loyal, nominally Catholic inhabitants of Cuba and foreign, Protestant interlopers.[43] The second canto recounts the exploits of Gregorio Ramos, a known contrabandist, and his makeshift militia as they confront and kill Girón and his crew. Of note are the heroic exploits of Salvador, "criollo, negro honrado" (criollo and honourable black man), an African slave who fought alongside the Spanish and beheaded the French captain.[44] After their victory, Ramos and his band gather to celebrate with Bishop Altamirano, and the poem concludes with a celebratory motet sung in the church of Bayamo in 1604.

If not for the fact that these poems are considered the points of departure for the national literary canons of Brazil and Cuba, respectively, they would be little read today. Their prominence at the head of literary anthologies is tempered by a critical disdain that has characterized them as poorly executed imitations of Camões and Ercilla. Although Cintio Vitier assigned *Espejo* a prominent place at the head of his survey of Cuban literary history, he nevertheless concluded that "*Espejo*'s poetic value is in the end minimal."[45] Likewise, Bento Teixeira's reputation has suffered at the hands of critics who, like Wilson Martins, consider him a "sub-Camões."[46] Antônio Soares Amora summarizes this tradition of negative assessments of *Prosopopéia* when he writes that "though it contains moments of beautiful poetry, on the whole it demonstrates the author's inability to sustain his talent over a long and emotionally charged poem, qualities that his predecessor Camões had in excess."[47] What saves these poems from total obscurity is the supposed nativist sentiment of both writers that resulted in inspired celebrations of the flora, fauna, and geography of their adopted American homes.

For Brazilian and Cuban critics, it is the way Teixeira and Balboa describe and celebrate American nature that merits their inclusion in their respective literary canons. While Cintio Vitier questions the quality of the poem, he does identify a nascent criollo consciousness in *Espejo*: "But what one does find in Balboa is the rare desire to observe closely the flora and fauna of the island, and to enumerate with style and an almost infantile pleasure the fruits and animals of a land that already seemed to be a part of him."[48] Likewise, Teixeira forms part of what Afrânio Coutinho labelled the "successive waves of enchantment with the local land, which gave birth to the boastful lyricism of exaltation of local things and countryside" at the core of Brazilian letters.[49] In both cases, the germinating seeds of literary nationalism stem from a fascination with the natural marvels of their adopted American homes. According to this commonplace nationalist narrative, it was under the auspices of a distinctly American nature that there emerged the first signs of a distinctly American consciousness at odds with the aesthetic categories and political imperatives of the Iberian metropoles.[50] Nevertheless, Teixeira and Balboa both introduce readers to the marvels of American flora and fauna by means of the mediating influence of pagan mythological figures imported from the Mediterranean. As will be argued here, it is not just the novelty of the New World which is thus given a European frame of reference, but also the aesthetic and political hierarchies of Europe which are made a part of the Americas through the New World epyllion's depiction of an American Pagan Nature.

Pagan Nature and the Naturalization of Iberian Empire

When describing the natural marvels of their adopted American homes, both Teixeira and Balboa merged New World nature with the pagan gods. Seeing American nature through the filter of Old World textual models was commonplace in early colonial poetic texts such as Ercilla's *La Araucana*.[51] Pagan gods appear in both *Espejo* and *Prosopopéia* merged with a natural environment they allegorically encapsulate. Teixeira's poem is largely a prophetic narration of the exploits of Jorge de Albuquerque and his family given by the sea god Proteus on the shores of Pernambuco to an assembled pantheon of maritime deities. Balboa, likewise, celebrates Bishop Altamirano's freedom from captivity by having a retinue of nymphs, satyrs, and other pagan deities emerge from Cuban forests and streams carrying tributes of native flora and fauna. Balboa concludes his poem by personifying the River Bayamo as a river god in the tradition of Virgil's depiction of the Tiber in book 8 of the *Aeneid*. Such pagan figures in the epyllions by Balboa and Teixeira have been explained away by critics as either an aesthetic commonplace of the period or as signs of the importance of *imitatio* as a precept of poetic creation.[52] It is by foregrounding the function of the pagan gods in conveying a naturalized colonial order that their aesthetic appeal becomes but one of their many important characteristics.

River and sea gods were widely incorporated into the iconography of European rulers in the early modern period to display the extent of their authority. As Claudia Lazzaro writes, "in the sixteenth century, river gods, inspired by the ancient statues, became obligatory in ceremonial entries and festivities and acquired new roles, as references to place, territories ruled, and alliances between states."[53] For example, at the Imperial Coronation of Charles V at Bologna in 1530, "there was a triumph of Bacchus with nymphs, fauns and satyrs, and one of Neptune with tritons, sirens and sea-horses to show that Charles's sway extended over both land and sea."[54] As symbols for the extension of political authority over the natural world, river and sea gods were also a recurring component of triumphal processions in the Americas as testified by Sor Juana Inés de la Cruz's *Neptuno alegórico* (ca. 1680). The ubiquity of Pagan Nature to the expression of power in the early modern period demonstrates the syncretic mindset of a political authority that looked to nature through the mediating lens of art in order to justify itself.

In the colonial context of Cuba in the early 1600s, Balboa's pagan gods represent a mutually reinforcing network of political, ecclesiastic, and natural orders. In the prologue to the reader, the poet explains why he included the pagan gods: "Imitating Horace, I depicted the maritime gods surrounding Gilberto's ship to help the Bishop in order to make clear that even brute animals feel the slights against his anointed ones."[55] The pagan gods are explained as a rhetorical strategy whose aim is to convey the universality of Catholic ecclesiastical authority. Even nature exhibits an innate respect for the prelates of the Catholic Church, a sign, for Marrero-Fente, of Balboa's "subordination of pagan symbols to Christianity."[56] This interweaving of ecclesiastic with natural orders is represented in the first canto when the bishop is taken captive onboard the pirate's ship. In response to this transgression, the ocean exhibits signs of a violent upheaval:

> Embraveciose el mar en aquel punto,
> como sentido de la humana afrenta,
> y con el viento hizo contrapunto,
> tan triste como suele en gran tormenta. (106.I.XVIL.1–4)

> (The sea boiled in anger at the sight / As if feeling the human affront, / And with furious winds reacted, / tempestuous like in a great storm.)

The ocean's upheaval acts as a material counterpoint to the political and social crisis unfolding on land. The sea's tempestuous response to the bishop's capture foreshadows the reaction of the pagan gods themselves:

> Luego por todo el reino de Neptuno
> la fama publicó caso tan feo;
> el cual con Tetis, Palemón, Portuno,
> Glauco, Atamante, Doris y Nereo,
> y las demás deidades de consuno
> [...]
> llegaron a la nave de Gilberto. (106–7.I.XVIII.1–5, 8)

> (Later throughout Neptune's kingdom / Fame spread the sorry news; / Who alongside Thetis, Melicertes, Portunus, / Glaucus, Athamas, Doris, and Nereus, / And the other deities of the sea/ [...] / Gathered together at Gilberto's ship.)

The news of the bishop's capture spreads throughout the watery domains of Neptune's kingdom, and its denizens gather to witness the events unfolding in Cuba. The fate of one bishop on one island is magnified as the repercussions spread like shockwaves threatening the order of both land and sea.

Given the rhetorical functions of nature in the poetry of this period, it is not surprising that American nature would be called upon to naturalize Spanish colonial rule in *Espejo*. Following M.J. Woods, poets in the age of Góngora used nature for specific rhetorical functions: either to describe place and time, or as a means of "amplifying the expression of love and of suffering [...] a means of intensifying the main theme."[57] One of the rhetorical functions that Woods identifies as distinctive to the poetry of the seventeenth century is the topos of cornucopia, which consists of "the systematic listing in a more or less leisurely fashion of a multitude of different natural products and creatures, such as animals, flowers and fruits."[58] Balboa's description of the pagan gods who gather to celebrate the bishop's freedom are one such cornucopia of American flora and fauna: "All the hybrid creatures of the area, / satyrs, fauns, and sylvan beings" (todos los semicapros del cortijo, / los sátiros, los faunos y silvanos; 110.I.LX.3–4), "Napaeae" (las napeas; 110.I.LXI.1), and "Nayades" (náyades"; 111–12.I.LXIII.2). The pagan gods appear carrying American flora and fauna, for example, "corn and tobacco, / mamey, pineapples, prickly pear, and avocados, / plantains, genips, and tomatoes" (mehí y tabaco, / mameyes, piñas, tunas y aguacates, / plátanos y mamones y tomates; 111.I.LXI.6–8). For Woods, this spectacle of cornucopia seeks to exemplify the poet's knowledge and wit, but its function does not end with just an exposition of poetic *ingenio*. Moreno Fraginals notes how the presence of Indigenous names for Cuban fruits and flora in this scene – though a much commented on sign of *lo cubano* in the poem – circumscribes the Indigenous presence to a ceremony that honours the Catholic prelate: "El utilizar términos locales daba a su escrito un sabor de delidad y permitía entregar la imagen de la sujeción espiritual de la tierra al representante de Dios."[59] It is the facility with which such natural richness is presented to the bishop in *Espejo* that conveys a more general sense of a *locus amoenus incultus*, following Marrero-Fente, made amenable to European desires and open to transformations following European artistic and political models.[60]

At the end of the second canto of *Espejo*, once revenge is exacted on the treacherous pirates, the victorious Spanish settlers gather in the town of Bayamo where the river itself celebrates their victory. In Iberian vernacular literature, the personification of rivers as pagan gods began with Garcilaso de la Vega's (ca. 1500–36) "Eclogue II," which influenced Camões's *Os Lusíadas* (Lisbon, 1572), where the Ganges and the Indus appear to Dom Manuel in canto IV, as well as Frey Luis de León's (ca. 1527–91) Ode VII, "Profecía del Tajo." Balboa's River Bayamo forms part of this literary tradition, which had a homologue in visual art with two statues of the rivers Tiber and Nile discovered in 1512–13 that were displayed prominently at the Vatican.[61] After emerging from his watery home in *Espejo*, the personified River Bayamo explains the interlocking relation between colonial power and Cuban nature. The bishop's captivity threatened the natural order of the island since, according to the river god, "deep within my veins and cold caverns / I felt the pain of your absence; / as the most secluded streams dried up" (hasta en mis venas y cavernas frías / de vuestras gracias se sintió el ausencia; / secáronse las fuentes más sombrías"; 134.II.LXII.1–3). The bishop's capture disrupted the water cycle of the island and dried up sources of fresh water, threatening the land with starvation. Fortunately, the bishop's release from captivity ensured the renewed stability of the natural order. Altamirano's freedom thus ushered in an age of renewed fertility and prosperity for Cuba:

> Ahora brotarán todas las flores
> con que se matizaban mis orillas;
> cantarán sin dolor los ruiseñores,
> silgueros, pentasilbos y abobillos;
> abundaran los frutos en mejores;
> alegraranse todas estas villas. (135.II.LXVIII.1–6)

> (Now the flowers will bloom / Which once crowned my shores; / The nightingales will sing effortlessly, / Goldfinches, robins, and hoopoes too; / The best fruit will be abundant once more; / Pleasing all the inhabitants of this village.)

The re-establishment of Catholic colonial order in Cuba manifests itself in the land's renewed fertility. The message conveyed by the River Bayamo exemplifies how, "in the sixteenth century, river gods became vehicles for contemporary notions about natural science, artistic creativity, and political hegemony."[62] It is this convergence of colonial hierarchies, natural history, and the pagan gods that made river gods such resonant symbols of power in the period.

What Balboa's Pagan Nature exemplifies is the syncretic form favoured by colonial power in depicting itself in art geared towards baroque spectacle. Following Roberto González Echevarría, Balboa's syncretic mixture of pagan, natural, and Indigenous elements is characteristic of a colonial baroque in which "everything is spectacle, ostentation, and an exercise of power; first to impress the natives but also to maintain a strict social stratification."[63] Spectacles of river gods and cornucopias crystalized in an aestheticized form a colonial hierarchy. The stanzas describing the pagan inhabitants of Cuba and their offerings create a spectacle in which colonial power circumscribes the Indigenous population to the role of ornament:

> Después que la silvestre compañía
> hizo al santo pastor su acatamiento,
> y cada cual le dio lo que traía
> con amor, voluntad, gozo y contento,
> al son de una templada sinfonía,

flautas, zampoñas, y rabeles ciento
delante del pastor iban danzando. (113.I.LXVIII.1–7)

(After the sylvan company / Paid the bishop his due tribute, / Each offered what they brought / With love, open arms, joy, and happiness, / To
the sound of a tempered symphony / Of flutes, reed pipes, and rebecs, /
They danced before the prelate.)

This spectacle is one of colonial power naturalized on the island, with
the genocidal campaigns against the Indigenous inhabitants of Cuba
erased as the natives are merged with an abundant and pliant natural
world mediated by pagan mythological forms. In the words of Belén
Castro Morales, Indigenous people in *Espejo* appear "almost undif-
ferentiated from nature" in a spectacle that incorporates them into a
Spanish colonial order; "the fact that they prostrate themselves will-
ingly before the bishop suggests their cultural integration as well as
their capacity to participate, in their own way, within a social structure
that Balboa [...] was keen to represent as a unified organism against
the foreign threat."[64] If Balboa's text is the point of departure for a nativist sentiment in tension with the Iberian metropole, it is a nationalism that requires an a priori forgetting of the violence of early modern
colonization.

The Spanish conquest as a rupture in the history of Cuba is glossed
over in *Espejo* by means of a spectacle of Pagan Nature that offers an alternative historical genealogy, one that extends back to ancient Greece
and Rome, and makes Cuba an extension of the Arcadian dream of antiquity. Not all critics agree. For Juana Goergen, Balboa's inclusion of
native flora and fauna is a momentous sign of American differentiation from European aesthetic norms. Balboa exhibits "an undeniable
desire to characterize American nature – and by extension the whole
Americas – as an Arcadian cosmos, that is to say, as its own world, coherent, harmonious, and orderly."[65] Goergen's reading of Balboa's pagan gods carrying American fruits as demarcating a split between the
criollo consciousness of the naturalized Cuban and the Iberian metropole encapsulates a critical tradition that extends back through Vitier
to the very first critical assessments of *Espejo* by José Antonio Echevarría in 1836. What this nationalist discourse risks losing sight of is the
fact that Iberian colonialism is itself naturalized by means of Balboa's
syncretic depictions of the pagan gods dressed in Indigenous garbs
emerging from a Cuban forest. Consider Balboa's famous description
of nymphs descending from the trees dressed like Indigenous women
and carrying autochthonous flora and fauna:

Bajaron de los árboles en naguas
las bellas amadríades hermosas,
con frutas de siguapas y macaguas
y muchas pitajayas olorosas. (111.I.lxvi.1–4)

(They descended robed in native attire / the beautiful dryads / with fruits
and macaws / and with several fragrant pitayas.)

At a time when the visual personification of nature in Europe was favouring a nude female figure to represent the prelapsarian innocence
of the natural world, these clothed pagan deities indicate a valuation of
human art and reason as perfecting the raw stuff of nature.[66] As will be
seen with Teixeira, this valuation of nature through the mediating influence of art is part and parcel of a colonial ideology that saw Indigenous
peoples and American lands as inchoate and in need of the refining
influence of European colonization.

Balboa's naturalization of a colonial order in Cuba through his use of
Pagan Nature is the a priori substratum upon which the other rhetorical functions of the text play out. Whether the text honestly celebrates
the bishop, or merely constructs an idealized image of him to curry
royal favour for a prelate implicated in contraband trade networks, is
beyond the point.[67] The bishop in Balboa's poem stands at the centre of
a colonial order that includes the settlers of Bayamo and that, thanks to
the pagan gods, also encompasses the Indigenous people and natural
wonders of the island. In *Prosopopéia*, Bento Teixeira similarly depicts
the pagan maritime gods on the shores of Pernambuco, Brazil, in a way
that naturalizes a Portuguese colonial order. While the contours of Teixeira's ideals of empire remain a matter of debate at a time of violent
anti-Semitism and tense political union with the Habsburg monarchy
of Spain, the necessity and beauty of European colonization is established from the very beginning by means of *Prosopopéia*'s merger of pagan gods with Brazilian nature.

The pagan maritime gods are introduced early in *Prosopopéia* in conjunction with the setting of the natural scene on the shores of Pernambuco. There, Neptune's kingdom gathers to hear Proteus's prophetic
account of the life of Jorge de Albuquerque Coelho. The logic of recasting history as prophecy – discussed above in relation to the epic
portrayal of Columbus by Stradanus – lies at the heart of the appeal
of merging pagan mythology with New World natural wonders. Triton is the first sea god to appear, "along the beach, whose sand / covered with the tracks of seabirds, / with wrought shells scattered about"
(ao longo da praia, cuja area / É de Marinhas aves estampada, / E de

encrespadas Conchas mil se arrea; 25.X.1–3). The fact that these shores lie untouched, save for the fleeting footprints of birds and a sprinkling of colourful shells, implies an absence of human habitation. This blank natural slate contrasts with the wrought forms of the pagan gods who represent in their very forms the transformation of raw oceanic materials into objects of priceless beauty based on European models.

Triton is the first sea god to appear on the shore of Brazil identified by his distinctly amphibious body: "Cutting through the sea's silvery main, / Came Triton with his double tail" (Do mar cortando a prateada vea, / Vinha Tritão em cola duplicada; 25.X.5–6). It was not uncommon in Greco-Roman mosaics and statues to depict Triton with two tails rather than one. The relatively conventional appearance of Teixeira's Triton is quickly qualified: "I did not see on his head placed / as Camões describes, a lobster shell helmet" (Não lhe vi na cabeça casca posta / (Como Camões descreve) de Lagosta; 25.X.7–8). Camões's *Os Lusíadas*, a key influence on Teixeira's pagan mythology, is mentioned in order for the poet to assert his difference from his literary model. Rather than a repurposed shell, Teixeira's Triton sports a highly wrought helmet composed of carved oceanic materials:

> Concha lisa e bem lavrada
> De rica Madrepérola trazia,
> De fino Coral crespo marchetada,
> Cujo lavor o natural vencia. (25.XI.1–4)

(A smooth and decorated shell / of rich mother of pearl he had / decorated with fine coral, / whose artistry outdid nature's beauty.)

Triton's wrought helmet incorporates the raw materials of the ocean (mother of pearl, coral) into a visual regime based on European models derived from antiquity. The materials that compose this shell are themselves precious commodities transformed by artisans who outdo nature through their skill. Triton's helmet is distinctive not only for its beauty, but also for the story it conveys since

> Estava nela ao vivo debuxada
> A cruel a espantosa bataria,
> Que deu a temerária e cega gente
> Aos Deoses do Ceo puro e reluzente. (25.XI.5–8)

(There one could see depicted / the cruel and frightening battle, / between the horrible and misguided Titans / and the Olympian gods of heaven.)

Precious oceanic materials are transformed into a wrought helmet conveying the ideologically charged story of the Gigantomachy. As critics like Philip Hardie assert, the Gigantomachy "is a myth that concerns the struggle between cosmos and chaos at the most universal level."[68] The Gigantomachy stands ever in the shadows of European epic poetry as the latent threat of a return to a primordial chaos kept at bay by the exploits of heroes.[69] Like the shields of Achilles and Aeneas, Triton's lobster-shell helmet asserts an order tying together nature and art to empire. In colonial Brazil, the Gigantomachy furthermore references the conflicts between the Portuguese and the Indigenous Tupi-speaking inhabitants of Pernambuco.

The Indigenous inhabitants of Pernambuco appear in Teixeira's retelling of the colonization of Brazil by Duarte Coelho and his sons as part of the forces of chaos kept at bay by epic prowess. Having been granted the Captaincy of Pernambuco in 1534, Duarte Coelho and his sons, Duarte and Jorge de Albuquerque Coelho, gained control over their dominions by subjugating the region's Indigenous tribes.[70] When Proteus narrates this history of Portuguese colonization, the violence of conquest is first coupled with the potential for peaceful conversion:

A braço invicto vejo com que amansa
A dura cerviz bárbara insolente,
Instruindo na Fé, dando esperança
Do bem que sempre dura e é presente. (39.XXVIII.1–4)

(His victorious arms which tame / the thick heads of the insolent barbarians, / Instructing in the Faith, giving hope / of the Good that is eternal and everlasting.)

This initial ambivalence over the use of violence in the spreading of the Christian faith falls away as violence is identified in the poem as the necessary answer. For Proteus, Coelho and his descendants do not prefer violence towards "the cruel barbarians" (Os bárbaros cruéis; 39.XXX.3), but draw their swords only when they run out of peaceful options:

E primeiro que a espada lisa e fera
Arranquem, com mil meios d'amor brando,
Pretenderão tirá-la de seu êrro,
E senão porão tudo a fogo e ferro. (39.XXX.5–8)

(Before they draw their sharp swords / with friendly words and reasonable thoughts / they try to correct lovingly their errors, / if not the Portuguese burn and pillage everything.)

To pacify the Indigenous inhabitants of Pernambuco is to combat the chaos of an unrefined Brazilian nature and to transform those raw materials into a new order notable for its aesthetic beauty based on European models. Triton's shell helmet is emblematic of this process of artistic colonization as the product of an unrefined American nature transformed into a European form.

The refashioning of raw natural materials into beautiful forms as a figuration of the process of colonization as it intersected with the material world is central to Teixeira's poetic vision and colonial ideology. Teixeira's appreciation for the transformative labour of colonization in Brazil appears in his description of the port of Pernambuco. The port is first described as the fruit of nature's ingenuity:

> Junto da Nova Lusitânia ordena
> A natureza, mãe bem atentada,
> Um pôrto tão quieto e tão seguro,
> Que pera as curvas Naus serve de muro. (31.XVII.5–8)

> (Close by this New Lusitania / Nature, like an attentive mother, designed / a port so calm and secure, / That ships lie safe within its walls.)

It is thanks to the attentiveness of Nature that this natural port can serve the needs of Portuguese colonizers. The port is protected by a natural rock wall extending into the ocean that protects the harbour from the fury of the waves:

> É êste pôrto tal, por estar posta
> uma cinta de pedra, inculta e viva,
> Ao longo da soberba e larga costa,
> Onde quebra Neptuno a fúria esquiva. (31.XVIII.1–4)

> (This port is such due to its walls / of solid, unworked rock, / that stretch along the long coast, / And against which Neptune crashes his fury.)

The adjectives "inculta," meaning uncultivated, and "viva," which when referring to rocks means unquarried or uncarved, highlight the unrefined nature of the port. These natural features are reflected in the Tupi name of Pernambuco used to designate the port, suggesting once again a link between the Indigenous inhabitants and an untouched nature. The port opens up like

> uma bôca [...]
> Que, na língua dos bárbaros escura,

Paranambuco de todos é chamado
de Para'na, que é Mar; Puca, rotura. (33.XIX.2–5)

(a mouth [...] / Which in the native language, / Pernambuco is by all
called, / From *Para'na*, which is sea, and *Puca*, which means opening.)

The geography of the port is contained within the etymology of its Tupi
name. This initial state of nature, while favourable for the needs of the
Portuguese, could still benefit from further artistic intervention. In order to make the port safe from enemy ships, Teixeira suggests building
a defensive tower:

Pera entrada da barra, à parte esquerda,
Está ûa lajem grande e espaçosa,
Que de Piratas fôra total perda,
Se ûa tôrre tivera sumptuosa. (33.XX.1–4)

(Near the opening of the rock walk to the left, / there is a great promontory /
Which would be the bane of pirates, / If a tower were there placed.)

Attentive colonial builders can improve upon the raw materials of nature to produce a more perfect port much like the natural features of the
Bay of Havana were transformed and built up over the sixteenth and
seventeenth centuries until the city became a formidable fortress and
colonial entrepot.[71] This maritime opening on the shores of Pernambuco can thus be closed to pirates by diligent European builders.

When placed in dialogue with Camões, Teixeira's celebration of colonialism as the refinement of nature stands in tension with his model's equivocal assessment of Portuguese maritime empire. It is through
the competing ways in which Camões and Teixeira depicts the sea god
Triton that their disagreement over the moral and political imperatives
of Portuguese maritime empire come to the fore. Recall that Teixeira
rejected Camões's description of Triton. Camões lacks the aesthetic hierarchy of the later poet's sea god when he describes Triton in canto
VI of *Os Lusíadas* as a "huge, swarthy, ugly youth" (mancebo grande,
negro e feio"; VI.16.7).[72] The description that follows establishes Triton
as anthropomorphic but with unsettling signs of his oceanic origins:

Os cabelos da barba e os que decem
Da cabeça nos ombros, todos eram
Uns limos prenhes de água,
[...]
Nas pontas, pendurados, não falecem

> Os negros missilhões, que ali se geram.
> Na cabeça, por gorra tinha posta
> Hua mui grande casca de lagosta.
> O corpo nu e os membros genitais,
> Por não ter ao nadar impedimento,
> Mas porém de pequenos animais
> Do mar todos cobertos, cento e cento;
> Camarões e cangrejos y outros mais,
> Que recebem de Febe crecimento.
> Ostras e camarões, do musco sujos,
> Às costas co a casca, os caramujos. (VI.17–18)

(The hairs of his beard and the hair / Falling from his head to his shoulders / Were all one mass of mud, / [...] Each dangling dreadlock was a cluster / Of gleaming, blue-black mussels. / On his head, by way of coronet, he wore / The biggest lobster shell you ever saw. / His body naked, even his genitals, / So as not to impede his swimming, / But tiny creatures of the sea / Crawled over him by the hundreds; / Crabs and prawns and many others / Which wax with the growing moon, / Cockles and oysters, and slimy husks / Of convoluted whelks and other molluscs.)[73]

Triton's amphibious physique is striking. His hair and beard are long and filthy, a feature that connects the sea god to the giant Adamastor who threatens Vasco da Gama in canto V. The tips of Triton's green locks are likewise teeming with mussels in a striking merger of the human and the oceanic. Unlike Teixeira's Triton, whose body ends in a double fishtail, Camões's Triton's lower half is hidden beneath teaming multitudes of sea life. It is left for readers to decide whether there actually is a body underneath this mass of shrimp, crab, and other shellfish. Triton's body appears as an incubator for marine life and possesses an affinity with the sea that inscribes the anthropomorphic within the oceanic without asserting a clear anthropocentric hierarchy.

When compared to other images from the period that celebrate Portuguese oceanic conquest through an anthropomorphic aesthetic, Camões's Triton is distinctly wet. That is to say, the maritime god carries signs of immersion that convey the transformations wrought by the ocean on human-ship bodies.[74] As a product itself of shipwreck, *Os Lusíadas* exemplifies the discursive dynamics of the wet and the dry that Steve Mentz theorizes in relation to early modern shipwreck accounts. The wet portion of a shipwreck narrative is the account of going down, of the near total breakdown in the governing order of a ship; the dry part is the retrospective attempt to derive a providential narrative or moral lesson from this breakdown.[75] Shipwreck narratives, following Josiah Blackmore, are in part "a type of counter-historiography that troubles the hegemonic vision of empire evident in the accounts of the canonical authors of colonialism."[76] As a wet poem conscious of the perils of shipwreck, *Os Lusíadas* conveys a truth through Triton that the dry, imperial historiography seeks to keep out of sight.

As a counter example to Camões's Triton as an emblem for shipwreck, take the image of King Manuel I of Portugal (r. 1495–1521) riding a sea creature that appears in Martin Waldseemüller's (ca. 1470–ca. 1518) *Carta Marina* (1516). At the bottom of the map, adjacent to the southern tip of Africa, appears Dom Manuel of Portugal (see figs. 2.2 and 2.3), the king who tasked Vasco da Gama with his voyage to India. The king appears riding a sea monster, "indicating his nation's technical mastery and also political control of the seas."[77] The symbols of authority the king carries in his right and left hands assert a seamless continuation of terrestrial hierarchies into the ocean much like Stradanus's allegorical illustration of Columbus surrounded by a retinue of pagan gods. Mastery is conveyed symbolically by the king's bodily integrity, which asserts a triumph of the anthropomorphic over the oceanic. By contrast, Camões's Triton questions this anthropocentric hierarchy as swarming hordes of sea life reminds readers that shipwreck is a heavy price to pay for maritime empire.

When placed in this iconographic tradition, Teixeira's Triton seems more akin to Waldseemüller's triumphant Dom Manuel than to Camões's shipwrecked Triton. Rather than a chaotic mass of swarming sea life, Teixeira's Triton sports a neat "cola duplicada" (double-tail) (X.6). By contrast, Camões's Triton conveys what happens to bodies when they are submerged in the ocean for extended periods of time. In his commentaries on *Os Lusíadas* published in 1639, Manuel de Faria e Sousa's (1590–1649) explains the sea life encasing Triton's loins as a logical consequence of the known affinities between shellfish and human genitalia: "Let us recall what all the natural historians say, which is that shellfish awaken the venereal appetite by means of the secret sympathy that exists between those regions of the body and such creatures."[78] Faria e Sousa backs this claim with evidence derived from the experience of shipwrecked sailors forced to swim several days to reach land as well as the bloated bodies that wash ashore covered in such creatures. These contrasting depictions of Triton by Camões and Teixeira and their links to debates about the relative merits of overseas empire hark back to the Stoic condemnation of Imperial Rome that Mercedes Blanco sees as underlying conflicting valuations of overseas navigation in the early modern Iberian epic tradition.[79]

Figure 2.2. Martin Waldseemüller, *Carta Marina* (1516). Image courtesy of the Library of Congress.

Printed on twelve sheets in 1516 (each about 45.5 x 63 cm, total dimensions of the assembled wall map 128 x 233 cm), Martin Waldseemüller's *Carta marina* represents a milestone in the history of early modern geographical prints. When compared to his earlier 1507 world map – famous for being the first to apply the name "America" to the New World – the *Carta marina* is notable for abandoning a Ptolemaic model and adopting instead the style of portolan charts to convey the latest knowledge of world geography gleaned from print sources. For more on the *Carta marina*'s iconography and sources, see Chet Van Duzer, *Martin Waldseemüller's "Carta Marina" of 1516: Study and Transcription of the Long Legends* (Springer International Publishing, 2020).

Figure 2.2. (*Continued*)

Figure 2.3. Martin Waldseemüller, detail with image of King Manuel I of Portugal from *Carta Marina* (1516). Image courtesy of the Library of Congress.

The image of the Portuguese king, Manuel I, riding a sea monster off the coast of southern Africa in the bottom centre of Martin Waldseemüller's *Carta marina* evidences a shift in European understandings of the relation of humans to the ocean. In his 1507 map, the Indian Ocean is described as full of sea monsters in the printed legends. By contrast, the image of the Portuguese king astride a sea monster "boldly proclaims human control over the dangers of the sea" (Van Duzer 19). While Waldseemüller borrows from an established tradition of depicting Neptune riding sea monsters in early modern printed maps – for example, Jacopo de' Barbari's map of Venice from ca. 1500 – his *Carta marina* updates the classical type to foreground human maritime prowess. Rather than conveying the divine power of a sea god like Neptune, Waldseemüller's *Carta marina* foregrounds the temporal powers of a European monarch at sea.

By drawing attention to competing depictions of Triton, what becomes clear is Teixeira's understanding of the Portuguese colonial order as an American nature perfected by European artistic and political models. The wrought crown on Triton's head is like a colony because the final product surpasses the original in terms of beauty and worth to European eyes. The helmet as product is cut off from the history of its production, much how Molly Warsh describes the commodification of pearls in the period: "On a hem, around a neck, traded for food or wine or passage, pearls bore no trace of the lives altered and lost through enslavement or the submarine pillaging of the reefs that brought them to light. Pearls bore no mark of origin, leaving room for their consumers to imagine one as they saw fit."[80] Along the same lines, Robert González Echevarría notes the role of fruits in *Espejo* as representatives of Cuban nature: "nature in Balboa's poem is represented by its fruits, its final products, the end of a process that is not itself being represented."[81] In all these cases, the violence and extractivism of European early modern colonialism is glossed over by an aesthetic where the beauty of the product elides and justifies the violence of production. In the context of the Colonial Baroque reduction of colonial tensions and violence to "surface, festival, mask,"[82] a focus on Pagan Nature reveals the intertwined moral, political, and natural historical implications of the New World epyllions of Teixeira and Balboa.

Even if Teixeira himself was at odds in his religious beliefs with the rigidly orthodox and anti-Semitic Catholicism of Philip II (r. 1556–98), any crypto-Jewish readings of his poem do not negate the text's colonial ideology. When Pereira and Costigan assert a crypto-Jewish significance to the mythological figures in Teixeira's poem – whether Triton's twisted shell as a Shofar or Proteus's shifting form as emblematic of the plasticity of Jews forced to hide their beliefs – such meanings do not negate the fundamental relation of pagan figures to the naturalization of European colonial power in Brazil.[83] These other meanings are predicated on, and limited in their critical thrust by, Teixeira's acceptance of European colonial power as part of an American natural order. In this regard, the reading proposed by Sônia Aparecida Siqueira strikes the right balance between the subversive potential of Teixeira's Judaism and his thorough indoctrination in colonial ideology. Siqueira notes how religious and class differences were put aside in a Brazilian colonial context where survival depended upon cooperation: "Whatever their faith, all were required to discover ways to survive in an alien land."[84] Teixeira thus forms part of a group of "men interested in collaborating with the Throne in the maintenance of Order in the Overseas Empire."[85] Whatever criticism the poem might convey to its readers regarding the religious politics of Philip II is couched within the frameworks of a dialogue in which subjects petitioned the monarch. As Guilherme Amaral Luz argues: "It is not a matter of offending the monarchy; it is rather a legitimate means of negotiating more privileges for vassals who see themselves as unjustly lowered on the social hierarchy."[86] Though Teixeira arguably found the religious politics of the Iberian Union unbearable, the larger issue of an Iberian colonial order is tellingly reinforced by his poem's depiction of the pagan gods merged with a transformed natural world.

Conclusion

What is distinctive about Pagan Nature is its liminal status between the categories of nature and art. While at first glance Triton or a river god like the Bayamo might seem to belong exclusively to the realm of art, they also served as a conceptual bridge to the material world of nature. River gods encapsulated the natural phenomenon they represented and demonstrated the extent to which human ingenuity and knowledge had mastered it. In a colonial context, such mastery of the natural world was the grounds upon which social and political hierarchies were erected in the distant shores of America. The long tradition of allegorical interpretations made pagan gods into polyvalent allegories for conveying a range of moral, political, and natural historical truths. These conceptual channels in a colonial American context permitted European political and religious imperatives to be smuggled from one side of the nature-art dichotomy to the other as American nature was transformed in the image of European models. The Pagan Nature that appears in the New World epyllions of Teixeira and Balboa exemplify this conceptual smuggling operation. That a poet like Camões could manipulate symbols of triumph like Triton to convey the precarity of oceanic empire indicates a questioning in the early modern period of this anthropocentric, colonialist logic. In his classic study of nature and art in the Renaissance, Edward William Tayler explains how the variable meaning of both terms resulted from a shifting valuation of human reason. For Tayler, any "controversy over the relative values of Nature and Art is thus in effect a controversy over man's role in the order of nature."[87] If human reason was deemed corrupt, then art was considered a corruption of a divinely ordained natural order. By contrast, if nature was understood to be inchoate, then human reason was called upon to perfect and refine the raw stuff of the world.[88] While Camões can be seen to represent the first trend, Balboa and Teixeira exemplify the second. Rodrigo Cacho Casal has recently argued that "*Prosopopéia* announces the artistic shift between Renaissance and Baroque," but the discussion here raises questions about what these commonplace period labels might obscure about the shifting relation between nature and art in the context of the Colonial Baroque.[89] The danger lies in limiting the discussion of the pagan gods as art to the categories of aesthetics or rhetoric without also assessing the conceptual links between art, politics, and conceptions of nature in the early modern period. For both Balboa and Teixeira, New World nature was in need of the refining influence of European culture. Pagan Nature is this refined product, one that justifies the fashioning of a colonial order by comparing the value of the product against the supposed deficiencies of the unrefined original. Both convey a natural order given pagan form that reinforces their respective colonial hierarchies and allows Europeans to call the New World home. Ultimately, it is this desire to belong to the land and claim ownership over it that undergirds the spectacle of Pagan Nature in the New World epyllions of Balboa and Teixeira.

NOTES

1 An earlier version of this essay was awarded the inaugural Founder's Prize for best graduate student essay by the Society for Renaissance and Baroque Hispanic Poetry at its 2019 biennial conference at UC Irvine. Many thanks to the society for their recognition and support.

2 As Anthony Grafton reminds his readers, in the early modern period "ancient texts served as both tools and obstacles for the intellectual exploration of new worlds." Grafton, *New Worlds, Ancient Texts*, 6. This was certainly the case with a figure like Columbus, who "used his texts to make the new familiar, to locate it." Grafton, *New Worlds, Ancient Texts*, 84.

3 For this article, I have used as my reference the 1972 edition of Teixeira's *Prosopopéia*, edited by Celso Cunha and Carlos Duval, and the 2010 edition of Balboa's *Espejo de paciencia*, edited by Raúl Marrero-Fente. All translations are the author's unless otherwise indicated.

4 Details about the life and work of Jan van der Straet can be found in Baroni and Sellink, *Stradanus 1523–1605*. The most complete catalogue in English of his paintings, prints, and tapestries can be found in Leesberg, *Johannes Stradanus*, 3 vols.

5 Cañizares-Esguerra, *Nature, Empire, and Nation*, 10.

6 Cañizares-Esguerra, *Nature, Empire, and Nation*, 10.

7 Seznec, *The Survival of the Pagan Gods*, 212–13.

8 Teskey, *Allegory and Violence*, 79.

9 Teskey, *Allegory and Violence*, 79.

10 Bredekamp, *The Lure of Antiquity and the Cult of the Machine*, 12.

11 Pérez de Moya, *Philosophía secreta*, 70.

12 Pérez de Moya, *Philosophía secreta*, 69.

13 Barkan, *The Gods Made Flesh*, 117; Bredekamp, *The Lure of Antiquity and the Cult of the Machine*, 13; and Foucault, *The Order of Things*, 33.

14 Barkan, *The Gods Made Flesh*, 121.

15 Glacken, *Traces on the Rhodian Shore*, 203.

16 Ashworth, "Natural History and the Emblematic World View," 302.

17 Ashworth, "Natural History and the Emblematic World View," 309.

18 Daston, *Against Nature*, 61.

19 "Comparison between Inca and Aztec and Greco-Roman deities, between Greco-Roman architecture and religious celebrations and their counterparts in the American present, and between Greco-Roman and American burial customs and modes of sacrifice all multiplied in the course of the sixteenth and seventeenth centuries." MacCormack, "Perceptions of Greco-Roman and Amerindian Paganism," 87.

20 Pecci, "Images from the Codex," 16.

21 Daston, *Against Nature*, 4.

22 Daston, *Against Nature*, 60.

23 Allen, "The Epyllion: A Chapter in the History of Literary Criticism," 25.

24 Tilg, "On The Origins of The Modern Term 'Epyllion,'" 29.

25 Korenjak, "Short Mythological Epic in Neo-Latin Literature," 519.

26 Kluge, "Mirror of Myth: The Baroque Epyllion," 152.

27 Kluge, "Mirror of Myth: The Baroque Epyllion," 151.

28 Kluge, "Mirror of Myth: The Baroque Epyllion," 153.

29 "BENTO TEIXEIRA PINTO Natural de Pernambuco igualmente perito na Poetica que na Historia." Quoted in Sousa, *Em tôrno do poeta Bento Teixeira*, 5.

30 Mello, "Bento Teixeira, Autor da *Prosopopéia*," 15; and Sousa, *Em tôrno do poeta Bento Teixeira*, 10.

31 "na Capitania de Pernambuco, talvez o indivíduo que maior cultura possuia nas letras, tanto sagradas como profanes." Mello, "Bento Teixeira, Autor da *Prosopopéia*," 8.

32 Sousa, *Em tôrno do poeta Bento Teixeira*, 11–12.

33 Boxer, "Jorge d' Albuquerque Coelho," 3–4.

34 Boxer, "Jorge d' Albuquerque Coelho," 16–17; and Sousa, *Em tôrno do poeta Bento Teixeira*, 41.

35 Marrero-Fente, *Espejo de paciencia*, 11–12.

36 Marrero, *Cuba: economía y sociedad*, 134, 209–10; Wakefield, "Three Lives of a Cuban Epic," 392; Saínz, *Silvestre de Balboa y la literatura cubana*, 80.

37 Cruz-Taura, *Espejo de paciencia*, 91–3.

38 Marrero-Fente, *Espejo de paciencia*, 17.

39 Vitier, *Espejo de paciencia*, 7.

40 Debates over *Espejo* as a forgery – given its praise for the slave Salvador – mirrors the ambiguous place of race in Cuban nationalist discourse since this controversy "insinuates that the agency [the poem] gives a black slave is inconceivable in Cuba of the early seventeenth century." Lamas, "Race and the Critical Trajectory of *Espejo de paciencia*," 129.

41 García del Pino, "El Obispo Cabezas, Silvestre de Balboa, y los contrabandistas de Manzanilla," 13–14; De la Fuente, *Havana and the Atlantic in the Sixteenth Century*, 3; Saínz, *Silvestre de Balboa y la literatura cubana*, 9–10.

42 García del Pino, "El Obispo Cabezas," 32–3; Saínz, *Silvestre de Balboa y la literatura cubana*, 15; Cruz-Taura, *Espejo de paciencia*, 109.

43 García del Pino, "El Obispo Cabezas," 40–1; Moreno Fraginals, "Claves de una cultura de servicios," 3–4.

44 Balboa, *Espejo*, 130.

45 "el valor poético absoluto del *Espejo* resulta escaso." Vitier, *Lo cubano en la poesía*, 26.

46 Martins, *História da inteligência brasileira*, 109.

47 "se no poemato há passagens de boa poesia, o conjunto revela ter faltado ao Autor o talento para uma obra de largo fôlego e intensa emoção, qualidades que seu antecessor, Luís Vaz de Camões, possuíra em alta dose." Amora, *Panorama da poesia brasileira*, 5.

48 "Pero lo que sí hay en Balboa es el deseo, raro para la versificación de la época, de acercarse a la flora y fauna de la isla, de enumerar con cierta glosa y hasta infantil delectación, los frutos y animales de la tierra que ya siente como suya." Vitier, *Espejo de paciencia*, 17.

49 Coutinho, *An Introduction to Literature in Brazil*, 47.

50 Moreno Fraginals is the rare Cuban critic to reject the characterization of *Espejo* as a Cuban poem referring to the text rather as "un poema español compuesto por un canario de escasa residencia en Cuba." Moreno Fraginals, "Claves de una cultura de servicios," 5.

51 Attempting to explain the lack of realism in Ercilla's description of Chile, Rosa Perelmuter-Pérez concludes, "dichas descripciones por lo general no arrancan del plano real de lo natural, de la naturaleza observada, sino de una naturaleza estilizada, modelada en normas dictadas por la tradición." Perelmuter-Pérez, "El paisaje idealizado en *La Araucana*," 145.

52 Vitier, *Espejo de paciencia*, 10; Mota, *Naufragio & Prosopopea*, XL; Amora, *Panorama da poesia brasileira*, 5–6.

53 Lazzaro, "River Gods," 77.

54 Strong, *Art and Power*, 79.

55 "Fingí, imitando a Horacio, que los dioses marineros vinieron a la nave de Gilberto a favorecer al Obispo, para que entiendan los temerosos de Dios

que hasta los brutos animales sienten las injurias que se hacen a sus ungidos." Balboa, *Espejo*, 81.

56 Marrero-Fente, "Classical *Epyllion* and Tropical Cornucopia," 241.

57 Woods, *The Poet and the Natural World in the Age of Góngora*, 15.

58 Woods, *The Poet and the Natural World in the Age of Góngora*, 83.

59 Moreno Fraginals, "Claves de una cultura de servicios," 5.

60 Marrero-Fente, "Classical *Epyllion* and Tropical Cornucopia," 240.

61 Coffin, *The Villa in the Life of Renaissance Rome*, 85.

62 Lazzaro, "River Gods," 93–4.

63 "todo es espectáculo, boato, despliegue de poder; primero para impresionar a los aborígenes, luego para mantener una rígida estratificación social." González Echevarría, "Reflexiones sobre *Espejo de paciencia*," 587.

64 "casi indiferenciada con la naturaleza [...] el hecho de que se inclinen dadivosos y felices ante el obispo promete su integración cultural, así como su capacidad de participar, desde las nieblas de su barbarie, de una estructura social que Balboa [...] le interesó mostrar unida como un solo organismo frente a la amenaza extranjera." Morales, "La Arcadia caribe de 'Espejo de paciencia,'" 142.

65 "un innegable afán por caracterizar la naturaleza americana – y por ende el mundo americano – como un cosmos arcádico, es decir, como un mundo propio, coherente, armónico y ordenando." Goergen, *Literatura fundacional americana*, 47.

66 Katherine Park summarizes this iconographic shift in the representation of Nature as follows: "The new Renaissance depiction of nature, as largely or completely naked and defined by the anatomical attribute of breasts and the physiological attribute of lactation, dramatically reconfigured Nature's character in medieval allegorical texts and images." Park, "Nature in Person," 56–7.

67 Marrero-Fente, *Espejo de paciencia*, 24; Saínz, *Silvestre de Balboa y la literatura cubana*, 98.

68 Hardie, *Virgil's Aeneid*, 85.

69 Hardie, *Virgil's Aeneid*, 92.

70 Boxer, "Jorge d' Albuquerque Coelho," 3–5.

71 De la Fuente, *Havana and the Atlantic in the Sixteenth Century*, 6.

72 White, *The Lusiads*, 122.

73 White, *The Lusiads*, 122.

74 Fernando Gil describes Triton as a mirror for the Portuguese and their ships: "Triton, Neptune's messenger (VI.15), covered by mollusks and crustaceans, is the living image of the fusion of King Manuel's caravels with the elements." Gil, "*The Lusiads* Effect," 55.

75 Mentz, *Shipwreck Modernity*, 1, 4.

76 Blackmore, *Manifest Perdition*, xxi.

77 Van Duzer, *Sea Monsters on Medieval and Renaissance Maps*, 76.
78 "Acordemonos de que todos los naturales dizen, que el marisco despierta mucho el apetito venero, por secreta simpatia que ay entre los instrumentos de esse apetito, i estos animalejos." Faria e Sousa, *Lusíadas Comentadas*, vol. 2, 39.
79 Blanco, *Góngora heroico*, 303–4.
80 Warsh, *American Baroque*, 48.
81 González Echevarría, "Reflections on the *Espejo de paciencia*," 146.
82 González Echevarría, "Reflections on the *Espejo de paciencia*," 145–6.
83 Pereira, *A poética da resistência em Bento Teixeira*, 88; and Costigan, "Bento Teixeira," 113.
84 "Fôsse qual fôsse a antiguidade de sua crença, estavam todos constrangidos no descobrir técnicas que lhes permitisse viver no meio estranho." Siqueira, "O cristão-novo Bento Teixeira," 402.
85 "homens interessados em colaborar com o Trono na manutenção da ordem no Império Ultramarino." Siqueira, "O cristão-novo Bento Teixeira," 403.
86 "Não se trata, portanto, de uma ofensa à monarquia ou a um monarca em particular, mas de uma maneira legítima de negociar lugares mais privilegiados para súditos que se vêem rebaixados em determinada hierarquia social mediada pelo rei." Luz, "O canto de Proteu ou a corte na colônia em *Prosopopéia*," 208.
87 Tayler, *Nature and Art in Renaissance Literature*, 23.
88 Tayler, *Nature and Art in Renaissance Literature*, 36.
89 Cacho Casal, "Colonial Poetry," 12.

WORKS CITED

Allen, Walter, Jr. "The Epyllion: A Chapter in the History of Literary Criticism." *Transactions and Proceedings of the American Philological Association* 71 (1940): 1–26.

Amora, Antônio Soares, ed. *Panorama da poesia brasileira: era Luso-brasileira*. Vol. 1. Rio de Janeiro: Editôra Civilização Brasileira, 1959.

Ashworth, William B. "Natural History and the Emblematic World View." In *Reappraisals of the Scientific Revolution*, edited by David C. Lindberg and Robert S. Westman, 303–32. Cambridge: Cambridge University Press, 1990.

Balboa, Silvestre de. *Espejo de paciencia*. Edited by Raúl Marrero-Fente. Madrid: Cátedra, 2010.

Barkan, Leonard. *The Gods Made Flesh: Metamorphosis and the Pursuit of Paganism*. New Haven, CT: Yale University Press, 1986.

Baroni, Alessandra, and Manfred Sellink, eds. *Stradanus 1523–1605: Court Artist of the Medici*. Turnhout: Brepols, 2012.

Blackmore, Josiah. *Manifest Perdition: Shipwreck Narrative and the Disruption of Empire*. Minneapolis: University of Minnesota Press, 2002.

Blanco, Mercedes. *Góngora heroico: Las Soledades y la tradición épica*. Madrid: Centro de Estudios Europa Hispánica, 2012.

Boxer, C.R. "Jorge d'Albuquerque Coelho: A Luso-Brazilian Hero of the Sea, 1539–1602." *Luso-Brazilian Review* 6, no. 1 (1969): 3–17.

Bredekamp, Horst. *The Lure of Antiquity and the Cult of the Machine: The Kunstkammer and the Evolution of Nature, Art and Technology*. Translated by Allison Brown. Princeton, NJ: Markus Wiener Publishers, 1995.

Cacho Casal, Rodrigo. "Colonial Poetry." In *The Cambridge Companion to Latin American Poetry*, edited by Stephen Malcolm Hart, 3–17. Cambridge: Cambridge University Press, 2018.

Camões, Luís de. *Os Lusíadas*. Edited by Emanuel Paulo Ramos. Porto: Porto Editora, 2011.

Cañizares-Esguerra, Jorge. *Nature, Empire, and Nation: Explorations of the History of Science in the Iberian World*. Stanford, CA: Stanford University Press, 2006.

Coffin, David R. *The Villa in the Life of Renaissance Rome*. Princeton, NJ: Princeton University Press, 1979.

Columbus, Christopher. *Textos y documentos completos: relaciones de viaje, cartas y memorials*. Edited by Consuelo Varela. Madrid: Alianza, 1982.

Costigan, Lúcia Helena. "Bento Teixeira: A New Christian Caught by the First Visit of the Inquisition to Brazil." In *Through Cracks in the Wall: Modern Inquisitions and New Christian Letrados in the Iberian Atlantic World*, 79–124. Leiden: Brill, 2010.

Coutinho, Afrânio. *An Introduction to Literature in Brazil*. Translated by Gregory Rabassa. New York: Columbia University Press, 1969.

Cruz-Taura, Graciella. *"Espejo de paciencia" y Silvestre de Balboa en la historia de Cuba*. Madrid: Iberoamericana-Vervuert, 2009.

Daston, Lorraine. *Against Nature*. Cambridge, MA: MIT Press, 2019.

De la Fuente, Alejandro. *Havana and the Atlantic in the Sixteenth Century*. Chapel Hill: University of North Carolina Press, 2008.

Faria e Sousa, Manuel de. *Lusíadas de Luís de Camões Comentadas por Manuel de Faria e Sousa*. Lisbon: Imprensa Nacional, Casa de Moeda, 1972.

Foucault, Michel. *The Order of Things: An Archeology of the Human Sciences*. New York: Pantheon Books, 1970.

García del Pino, César. "El Obispo Cabezas, Silvestre de Balboa, y los contrabandistas de Manzanilla." *Revista de la Biblioteca Nacional José Martí* 66, no. 2 (1975): 13–54.

Gil, Fernando. "*The Lusiads* Effect." In *The Traveling Eye: Retrospection, Vision and Prophecy in the Portuguese Renaissance*, translated by K. David Jackson, 33–85. Dartmouth: University of Massachusetts Press, 2009.

Glacken, Clarence J. *Traces on the Rhodian Shore: Nature and Culture in Western Thought from Ancient Times to the End of the Eighteenth Century.* Berkeley: University of California Press, 1967.

Goergen, Juana. *Literatura fundacional americana: "El Espejo de paciencia."* Madrid: Editorial Pliegos, 1993.

González Echevarría, Roberto. "Reflections on the *Espejo de paciencia.*" In *Celestina's Brood: Continuities of the Baroque in Spanish and Latin American Literature,* 128–48. Durham, NC: Duke University Press, 1993.

– "Reflexiones sobre *Espejo de paciencia* de Silvestre de Balboa." *Nueva Revista de Filología Hispánica* 35, no. 2 (1987): 571–90.

Grafton, Anthony. *New Worlds, Ancient Texts: The Power of Tradition and the Shock of Discovery.* Edited by April Shelford and Nancy Siraisi. Cambridge, MA: Harvard University Press, 1992.

Hardie, Philip R. *Virgil's "Aeneid": Cosmos and Imperium.* Oxford: Oxford University Press, 1986.

Kluge, Sofie. "Mirror of Myth: The Baroque Epyllion." In *Diglossia: The Early Modern Reinvention of Mythological Discourse,* 138–55. Kassel, Germany: Edition Reichenberger, 2014.

Korenjak, Martin. "Short Mythological Epic in Neo-Latin Literature." In *Brill's Companion to Greek and Latin Epyllion and its Reception,* edited by Manuel Baumbach et al., 519–36. Leiden: Brill, 2012.

Lamas, Carmen S. "Race and the Critical Trajectory of *Espejo de paciencia.*" *Latin American Research Review* 47, no. 1 (2012): 115–35.

Lazzaro, Claudia. "River Gods: Personifying Nature in Sixteenth-Century Italy." *Renaissance Studies* 25, no. 1 (2011): 70–94.

Leesberg, Marjolein, comp. *Johannes Stradanus.* Edited by Huigen Leeflang. 3 vols. Ouderkerk aan den Ijssel: Sound and Vision Publishers, 2008.

Luz, Guilherme Amaral. "O canto de Proteu ou a corte na colônia em *Prosopopéia* (1601), de Bento Teixeira." *Tempo: Revista do Departamento de História da Universidade Federal Fluminense* 13, no. 25 (2008): 193–215.

MacCormack, Sabine. "Limits of Understanding: Perceptions of Greco-Roman and Amerindian Paganism in Early Modern Europe." In *America in European Consciousness, 1493–1750,* edited by Karen Ordahl Kupperman, 79–129. Chapel Hill: University of North Carolina Press, 1995.

Martins, Wilson. *História da inteligência brasileira.* Vol. 1. São Paulo: Editora da Universidade de São Paolo, 1976.

Marrero, Leví. *Cuba: economía y sociedad.* Vol. IV. Madrid: Playor, 1972.

Marrero-Fente, Raúl. "Classical *Epyllion* and Tropical Cornucopia in Silvestre de Balboa's *Espejo de paciencia.*" In *The Rise of Spanish American Poetry 1500–1700: Literary and Cultural Transmission in the New World,* edited by Rodrigo Cacho Casal and Imogen Choi, 239–52. Cambridge: Legenda, 2019.

Mello, José Antonio Gonsalves de. "Bento Teixeira, Autor da *Prosopopéia*."
In *Estudos Pernambucanos: crítica e problemas de algumas fontes da história de
Pernambuco*, 5–43. Recife: Universidade do Recife Imprensa Universitária, 1960.

Mentz, Steve. *Shipwreck Modernity: Ecologies of Globalization, 1550–1719*.
Minneapolis: University of Minnesota Press, 2015.

Morales, Belén Castro. "La Arcadia caribe de 'Espejo de paciencia': Ninfas,
sátiros y desculturación." *Revista de Crítica Literaria Latinoamericana* 50
(1999): 133–46.

Moreno Fraginals, Moreno. "Claves de una cultura de servicios," *La Gaceta de
Cuba* (July 1990), pp. 2–5, republished in *Archivo Rialta* (September 2020).
https://rialta.org/moreno-fraginals-cultura-servicios.

Mota, Fernando de Oliveira, ed. *Naufragio & Prosopopea*. Recife: Universidade
Federal de Pernambuco, 1969.

Park, Katherine. "Nature in Person: Medieval and Renaissance Allegories and
Emblems." In *The Moral Authority of Nature*, edited by Lorraine Daston and
Fernando Vidal, 50–73. Chicago: University of Chicago Press, 2004.

Pecci, Alessandra. "Images from the Codex." In *The World of the Aztecs in
the Florentine Codex*, edited by Monica Fintoni, Andrea Paoletti, and Paola
Vannucchi, 16–58. Florence: Mandragora, 2007.

Pereira, Kênia Maria de Almeida. *A poética da resistência em Bento Teixeira e
Antônio José da Silva, o Judeu*. São Paulo: Annablume, 1998.

Perelmuter-Pérez, Rosa. "El paisaje idealizado en *La Araucana*." *Hispanic
Review* 54, no. 2 (1986): 129–46.

Pérez de Moya, Juan. *Philosofía secreta de la gentilidad*. Edited by Carlos
Clavería. Madrid: Cátedra, 1995.

Saínz, Enrique. *Silvestre de Balboa y la literatura cubana*. Havana: Editorial
Letras Cubanas, 1982.

Seznec, Jean. *The Survival of the Pagan Gods: The Mythological Tradition and Its
Place in Renaissance Humanism and Art*. Translated by Barbara F. Sessions.
New York: Pantheon Books, 1953.

Siqueira, Sônia Aparecida. "O cristão-novo Bento Teixeira: crypto-judaísmo no
Brasil Colônia." *Revista de História* 44, no. 90 (1972): 395–467.

Sousa, J. Galante de. *Em tôrno do poeta Bento Teixeira*. São Paulo: Instituto de
Estudos Brasileiros, 1972.

Strong, Roy. *Art and Power: Renaissance Festivals 1450–1650*. Woodbridge, UK:
Boydell Press, 1984.

Tayler, Edward William. *Nature and Art in Renaissance Literature*. New York:
Columbia University Press, 1964.

Teixeira, Bento. *Prosopopéia*. Edited by Celso Cunha and Carlos Duval. Rio de
Janeiro: Instituto Nacional do Livro, 1972.

Teskey, Gordon. *Allegory and Violence*. Ithaca, NY: Cornell University Press,
1996.

Tilg, Stefan. "On the Origins of the Modern Term 'Epyllion': Some Revisions to a Chapter in the History of Classical Scholarship." In *Brill's Companion to Greek and Latin Epyllion and Its Reception*, edited by Manuel Baumbach et al., 29–54. Leiden: Brill, 2012.

Van Duzer, Chet. *Sea Monsters on Medieval and Renaissance Maps*. London: British Library, 2013.

Vitier, Cintio, ed. *Espejo de paciencia*. Havana: Publicación de la Comisión Nacional Cubana de la UNESCO, 1962.

– *Lo cubano en la poesía*. 2nd ed. Havana: Instituto del Libro, 1970.

Wakefield, Steve. "Three Lives of a Cuban Epic: Balboa, Echevarría, Carpentier and the *Espejo de paciencia*." Bulletin of Spanish Studies 83, no. 3 (2007): 387–414.

Warsh, Molly A. *American Baroque: Pearls and the Nature of Empire, 1492–1700*. Chapel Hill: University of North Carolina Press, 2018.

White, Landeg, trans. *The Lusiads*. Oxford: Oxford University Press, 1997.

Woods, M.J. *The Poet and the Natural World in the Age of Góngora*. Oxford: Oxford University Press, 1978.

3 Lyric as Temptation in Alonso de Ercilla and Torquato Tasso[1]

MERCEDES BLANCO

Tasso's *Gerusalemme liberata* and Ercilla's *La Araucana* are among the few Renaissance epics that enjoyed an early and lasting fame.[2] These long poems in ottava rima (twenty and thirty-seven cantos, respectively) deal with a military and historical subject: the capture of Jerusalem by the First Crusade under the command of Godfrey of Bouillon (1099); and the revolt of the Araucanians of Chile (1553) followed by the campaign to subdue them (1556–8) commanded by an extremely young Spanish nobleman, Don García Hurtado de Mendoza. Both works had a long and arduous gestation, and occupied, so to speak, the entire lives of their authors. Tasso was fifteen when he wrote in 1559 the first sketch of the *Gerusalemme*, still limited then to 116 stanzas. He published what he considered to be the culmination of his arduous quest of an ideal poem, the *Gerusalemme conquistata*, in 1593. He would die two years later.[3] Ercilla's vocation as an epic poet was almost as precocious since the first idea of what would become *La Araucana* probably dates from 1556, when, in his early twenties, he joined the Spanish expedition to Chile. His poem, printed in three separate parts over twenty years, was completed in 1589–90, four years before his death (1594).[4]

As far as we know, the two poems have never been systematically compared. In the first study to relate them, Imogen Choi has recently shown "the concealed presence of the *Gerusalemme* in the third part of *La Araucana*."[5] Tasso did not seem to have taken any notice of Ercilla, and the Spanish poet could not know Tasso's great poem before its first publication in the early 1580s. By that time, the first and second parts (the longest) of *La Araucana* had already enjoyed considerable success. Our comparison is therefore not based on the hypothesis of any sort of mutual influence. Besides, Choi claims that when, prior to composing the third and last part of his work, Ercilla became acquainted with the Italian poet, he was far from being seduced, and that an acute criticism transpires in his covert allusions, charged by an ironic or even sarcastic bias. In short, we are comparing two very different men, contemporary and sharing the same culture (humanist and Catholic), but in different languages and as members of two completely different political bodies, the small Italian princedoms and the powerful and plural Hispanic Monarchy. My essay has a heuristic purpose: showing how, in spite of these differences, both undertook a similar project of producing a new epic with the hope of surpassing Ariosto. The project was ambitious because it had the purpose of reconciling apparently incompatible poetic requirements. I claim that both men, in seeking the proper heroic tone, were ultimately doomed to give a prominent place in their works to the mood and ethos of lyric poetry, through intertextual connections with the foremost lyric poets in their respective traditions: Petrarch and Garcilaso de la Vega. It is as if modern poetry could not reach its audience without building on the best models, which were actually lyrical; or as if the aim of poetic delight, in the sixteenth century, was unattainable if the poet did not somehow adopt the moving, enthralling, and ennobling attitude of the Petrarchan lover.

A Long and Failed Struggle for Integration of Multiplicity

For Tasso as for Ercilla, the work that was meant to be one became finally multiple. Unity is strongly claimed by both authors in the initial stanza, where they give a distinct idea of what they want "to sing":

> Canto l'arme pietose e 'l capitano
> che 'l gran sepolcro liberò di Cristo. (*Gerusalemme*, I.1.1–2)

> Canto … el valor los hechos, las proezas,
> de aquellos españoles esforzados
> que a la cerviz de Arauco no domada
> pusieron duro yugo por la espada. (*La Araucana*, I.1.2–8)

The purpose seems simple, the road firmly set towards a satisfactory ending: in Tasso's poem, a glorious victory rewarding hard struggle for a high prize, the liberation of Jerusalem and of Christ's tomb; in Ercilla's *La Araucana*, the achievement of Spanish colonial order in the most remote part of America against a staunch Indigenous resistance. And yet, the more the poets go forward, the more they become entangled with complications.

At the end of Ercilla's tale, in spite of the Spanish victories, Arauco remains restive and the suppressed Araucanian uprising is ready to break out again. The rebellion is like the hydra: for one severed head, ten more grow back, and for one cruelly executed Indigenous leader, ten are already conspiring to start a new war. *La Araucana* nevertheless does have a kind of resolution: the tragic denouement for the Araucanian chief Caupolicán; the melancholic ending for the poet. More than an epic closure, the last stanza resembles those prologue-sonnets of collections of *rime* in which a meditative soul, as if awakening from a dream, casts a repentant glance at its own sad love story, seeing on the road left behind only wasted time, withered flowers, and illusory hopes:

> Y yo, que tan sin rienda al mundo he dado
> el tiempo de mi vida más florido,
> y siempre por camino despeñado
> mis vanas esperanzas he seguido,
> visto ya el poco fruto que he sacado,
> y lo mucho que a Dios tengo ofendido,
> conociendo mi error, de aquí adelante
> será razón que llore y que no cante. (XXXVII.76)

> (And I, who have so carelessly given the world / the most bountiful part of my life, / and always down cliff-strewn paths / have pursued my futile hopes, / seeing now the scant fruit I have been granted / and how greatly I have offended God, / realizing my error, from now on / it will be proper that I weep and no longer sing.)

The last word of this epic is thus lyric in nature and presents an unmistakable family resemblance with the famous opening sonnet of Petrarch's *Canzoniere*:

> Ma ben veggio or sì come al popol tutto
> favola fui gran tempo, onde sovente
> di me medesmo meco mi vergogno;
> e del mio vaneggiar vergogna è 'l frutto,
> e 'l pentersi, e 'l conoscer chiaramente
> che quanto piace al mondo è breve sogno.[6]

> (But now I see clearly how I was for quite a while / a fable among all people, so that I feel / often secretly ashamed of myself / and shame is the fruit of my vanities / and repentance, and to know / that whatever the world praises is a brief dream.)

This sad finale of *La Araucana*, modelled on a traditional Petrarchan lyrical opening, reverses the characteristic epic ending: the attainment of a grand design that gives sense to the hardships of history, as conceived by David Quint.[7] The *Aeneid* remains paradigmatic of such an epic of empire. The ultimate telos of Aeneas's wanderings and sufferings, conveniently remote from the poem's action, is less the announced foundation of Rome (*Tanta moles erat Romanam condere gentem*)[8] than the new Golden Age, with Augustus reigning in an everlasting pacified world dominated by the Eternal City. It is true that this imperial and triumphalist epic is more an idea than a reality; most epic poems, and certainly the best (including Virgil's), have a bitter aftertaste in spite of their glorious telos. As Ion acknowledges in Plato's dialogue, "tears are the best criteria of a rhapsode's success," since "the sharing of grief was perceived in the fourth century as the characteristic response to the most privileged poetry."[9]

But whereas the *Aeneid* tempers celebration with a sense of tragic grief, *La Araucana* is placed by Quint at the antipode of the idea of the victor's epic, which celebrates conquest and empire.[10] Such placement is understandable enough since the poem's modest aim, limited to the periphery of a vast empire, is attained in an almost ludicrous form. When we finally reach the real end of the long text, the achievement initially announced by the poet as the object of his celebratory singing – that is, the taming of Arauco by the sword of brave Spaniards – is barely reached. Indeed, Spanish success is threatened by a rebellion on the verge of erupting with renewed force. More than that, what is this Arauco so boldly trumpeted by Ercilla? A thin strip of land in long and narrow Chile, inhabited by a few thousand Araucanians, who are admittedly indomitable but also doomed to the defence of a ruined and wretched country. Between the vibrant epic *propositio* of the first canto and the repentant farewell of the last, written after a lapse of twenty years, many things intervened. Across these years, many battles, or rather bloody ambushes and skirmishes, discouraged the Spaniards in Chile. The poem itself also underwent many changes that its author could not have predicted. One of them, as we shall see, was the poet's unpremeditated yielding to the sirens of the lyric.

The long, unnamed poetic narrative that Torquato Tasso, then in his thirties, designated to his friends as the "poema di Goffredo," following the name of his elected hero, was preceded several years earlier by the very articulate program of the *Discorsi dell'arte poetica*.[11] Tasso's confessed ambition was to compose a perfect poem in which many characters and stories, in their beautiful variety, would all be subsumed under the Aristotelian unity of action. In 1575, Tasso could announce to his lord, Alfonso II d'Este, Duke of Ferrara, that he had reached his goal. Alas, what he had intended as a short, easy revision of the completed work became instead a tense struggle against both external censorship from a group of men of letters (based primarily in Rome) and internal self-reproach.[12] The so-called Roman revision, prolonged for more than a year, was in fact less achieved than interrupted. After a confused period spent in anguished attempts of fleeing Ferrara and its duke, Tasso was plunged into an annihilating crisis of paranoia, followed by a long confinement at Sant'Anna from March 1579 to August 1586. In the meantime, more than ten unauthorized editions of Tasso's epic, baptized by the pirate editors as *Gerusalemme liberata* (*Jerusalem Delivered*), appeared in Venice, Genoa, Parma, Mantua, Ferrara, and Casalmaggiore, achieving an outstanding success.

During the last half of his captivity and in his final years of wandering, Tasso undertook not only a revision of his poem but a "reform," a word fraught with religious meaning. The reformed poem, renamed *Gerusalemme conquistata* (Rome, 1593), was expanded to twenty-four books (following the *Iliad*), although it preserved almost word for word the vast majority of the stanzas in the *Liberata*. Claudio Gigante has shown that Tasso prepared this new poem by inserting additions into several of the pirated printings of the previous work.[13] And yet, as Matteo Residori has brilliantly demonstrated,[14] the *Conquistata* is based on another project and another aesthetic in much closer connection with Homer's *Iliad* and with Trissino's *Italia liberata dai Goti*.[15] For ideological, but also poetic, reasons, the reformed poem blurred the Aristotelian *favola* that characterized the *Liberata*, held together by the dynamics of action.[16] In the name of historical accuracy and religious decorum, Tasso mitigated or distorted his own earlier rule of verisimilitude, in view of which history is but one means among others. He likewise abandoned his desire to please a public of nobles and courtiers (*cavalieri*), and other moderately cultivated men. Finally, he suppressed (or at least tried to suppress) the moral ambiguities of the first poem, which for many readers and probably the majority, even in these times of religious passions, provide the work with its unique flavour and exquisite quality.

The *Conquistata* did not succeed in replacing the *Liberata*, its illegitimate elder sister, a poem snatched from its author that had to remain dearest to its readers. Tasso's passionate search for unity did not prevent his work from remaining open and becoming double, yielding to the demons of the shapeless. Since the *Liberata*, forever favoured by printers and readers, had no authorized edition (either by Tasso or by his manuscript editor, the scrupulous, learned, and generous Scipione Gonzaga), the task of fixing its text was doomed to try the resourcefulness, methodicalness, and patience of the Italian virtuosi of philology, becoming a textbook case of the field and an interminable endeavour. Luigi Poma, in several contributions collected in a recent volume,[17] though also synthesized earlier by Scotti,[18] has shown that none of the printed versions adequately represents the last stage of the process of correction in the years 1575–7, prior to the interruption of Tasso's work on the poem. A satisfying account of what the poet, before his madness and captivity, meant to be the final version of his *Poema di Goffredo* is better approached from the manuscript tradition, by now well established and explored, and which must therefore provide a basis for a true critical edition. And yet, after more than a century of efforts by some of the best Italian scholars, such an edition does not exist.

In short, the *Gerusalemme*, which aimed to become an indivisible monument set in inalterable marble, is no less multiple than the confessedly multiple *La Araucana*. Beyond its three parts, two prologues, and three suspended and inconclusive endings, the Spanish poem's *Tercera parte* also offers three long digressions: the life and death of the Carthaginian queen Dido, the exploration of several regions of southern Chile, and the annexation of Portugal by the king of Spain. Last but not least, corrections made by the author during the process of printing are so many that, as discovered by Juan Alberto Méndez Herrera,[19] there are no two identical copies of the first edition of the third part of the poem. As noted above, *La Araucana* enjoyed a resounding success, although limited to Spain and its territories. Ercilla oversaw several reissues of the two first parts, always providing a thorough revision of the text before and during the printing process.[20] While the manuscript tradition may be entirely absent, the number of variants offered by the printings is considerable.[21] As far as I am aware, no one has carried out an edition designed to shed light on this process of constant revision.[22] Nor does there exist an edition that takes care to provide, for each part, a text that reflects the poet's last revision.

Such coincidences between *La Araucana* and *La Gerusalemme* are all the more striking because it is difficult to find two more opposite profiles of men and of writers. If Torquato Tasso was a professional man of letters, a poet who cultivated all genres, and an intellectual who wrote in prose on almost all the fashionable subjects of his time, Alonso de Ercilla was the author of a single work.[23] Professionally he was a soldier, later a diplomat, and finally a businessman; that is, never purely, or even mainly, a man of letters. The Italian writer, who had admirers beginning in his early youth, lived on full display and left innumerable testimonies of his life and thought.[24] His great poem enjoyed an early and enduring glory, fostered by many editions and early translations into Spanish, English, and French, among other languages.[25] By contrast, the Basque captain seems to have been a reserved man, even secretive, and his fame was and remains, unjustly perhaps, narrower in scope.[26] Tasso was the son of a celebrated and erudite poet, and as a boy he was trained first by his father and then in the most learned circles of Naples, Rome, Paris, Padua, and Bologna. The education of Ercilla, an orphan raised in the travelling court of Prince Philip, was remarkably good too, but partly left to chance encounters and readings. If the first wanted to accomplish everything according to art, developing also a carefully considered poetics as a prerequisite to his poem, the second strove for artistic dissimulation, a know-how acquired through the example of poets and through experience, perhaps according to the ideal of sprezzatura. While Tasso does not hide his ambition to write a poem equal to Virgil's *Aeneid*, Ercilla apologizes for his awkwardness, poor wit, and crude style.

Furthermore, the two men seem unaware of each other's existence, at least until Ercilla read one of the editions of the *Gerusalemme* printed between 1581 and 1584. Ercilla's encounter with the work is highly probable, given its immediate impact, the acute interest in Spain for news of the Italian Republic of Letters, the ease of access to such news, and Ercilla's commitment to the epic as a form. Several pieces of evidence prove that the Italian poem was influential in Spain during the 1580s. For instance, the play attributed to Cervantes by Stefano Arata, *La conquista de Jerusalén por Godofre de Bouillon*,[27] contains a plot and characters borrowed from the *Gerusalemme*, and it could not be composed later than 1585. Moreover, Ercilla's interest would have been even greater due to his own deep involvement with Ariosto, a poet pulled into the orbit of Tasso's reception by the controversy that broke out in 1584 concerning the respective merits of the *Gerusalemme* and the *Orlando furioso*. Lastly, according to Imogen Choi, Ercilla's acquaintance with Tasso's poem is indisputable.[28] Yet, by 1580, when the first two parts of *La Araucana* were already famous, Ercilla's habits were too firmly established for the Italian to shape his own poem in a significant manner. The Spaniard also had a strong personality and, as Choi suggests, he virtually represents Tasso's opposite in terms of temperament, taste, and ideology. He was a good reader of Machiavelli,[29] mainly interested in legal discussions and casuistic literature, capable of humour, sceptical and ironic, and inflexible only in matters of justice and humanity. Ercilla was certainly ready to embellish history in order to render it enjoyable and intelligible, though not to erase whatever did not fit into some preconceived idea of holy war and God's cause, such as the one Tasso made the foundation of his epic. For all of these reasons, Ercilla adopts a critical attitude towards Tasso's work, observable in the handful of allusions to the *Gerusalemme* found in his poem.[30]

Coincidences between both poets could be explained by their common experience at court, and moreover by the pressure to undertake an ambitious epic project in the mid-sixteenth century.[31] The quest for epic poetry undertaken in these years by many young and talented writers in Italy,[32] Portugal,[33] and Spain[34] was rooted in deep social and cultural needs and was fuelled by the appeal and enormous success of Ariosto's *Orlando furioso* (1532). This colossal masterpiece was beyond doubt the starting point for both Ercilla and Tasso, and it captivated them as an admirable model. Their poems owe much to imitating Ariosto, a task achieved by Ercilla in a naive way and by Tasso with more sophistication.[35] In each case, however, the poet did not attempt to conceal his intent of emulation. Both wished to endow their creations with the powerful attraction of marvellous adventures and of astonishing martial prowess, elements to which Ariosto had yielded without guilt and even with a playful and cheerful mood. But Tasso and Ercilla were drawn even more to the lyrical charm in which Ariosto had indulged frequently. And yet, they hoped to exploit such lyricism without losing sight of their epic goals, which aimed at establishing prestige through the qualities of austerity and majesty. For Tasso, who methodically reflected on the art of the heroic poem, Ariosto was guilty not only of breaches of unity and verisimilitude, but also of a style that sometimes sinks to the comic and does not refrain from lyrical *concetti* unworthy of the epic's magnificence.[36] In Tasso's seminal investigations into poetics, "lyrical" means joyful, lascivious, turned towards pleasure (*fiorito, ridente, lascivo, ameno, dilettevole*). Even if Petrarch was for Tasso the first of lyrical poets, his idea of lyrical style and mood was very much in debt with the happy and pleasant atmosphere of Ariosto's world.[37] When he was conceiving his poem, Tasso did not connect them to spiritual lyric tradition, to *rime spirituali* or *rime sacre* as were Victoria Colonna's or as those he wrote himself in his last years. What we call lyrical temptation was connected with longing for pleasurable freedom and for sensuous delight. Ercilla, for his part, seems convinced that lyric charm depends quite simply on love. Without love, he admits with vexation before the end of the *Primera parte* (1569), nothing can go well, nobody can be playful, subtle, free, or amiable. He is forced to infer from these maxims, strange in the context of a sober narrative of war, that his initial commitment to the truth and his exclusive dedication to his dry and dark subject matter has doomed him to failure:

¿Qué cosa puede haber sin amor buena?
¿Qué verso sin amor dará contento?
¿Dónde jamás se ha visto rica vena
que no tenga de amor el nacimiento?
No se puede llamar materia llena

la que de amor no tiene el fundamento;
Los contentos, los gustos, los cuidados,
son, si no son de amor, como pintados.

Amor de un juicio rústico y grosero
rompe la dura y áspera corteza,
produce ingenio y gusto verdadero
y pone cualquier cosa en más fineza.
Dante, Ariosto, Petrarca y el Ibero,
Amor los trujo a tanta delgadeza,
que la lengua más rica y más copiosa,
si no trata de amor, es desgustosa. (XV:1–2)

(What good thing can exist without love? / What verse without love can bring joy? / Where has one ever found a rich vein / that does not have love as its source? / No subject can be considered whole / without having love as its foundation; / Joys, pleasures, courtesies, / if they are not for love, are daubed pretensions.

Love breaks the hard and rugged shell / of a crude and coarse mind, / breeds wit and true pleasure / and lends refinement to all things. / Dante, Ariosto, Petrarch and the Iberian [Garcilaso de la Vega], / Love led them to such subtlety, / since the richest and most copious language, / if not expressing love, is unpleasant.)

Their own declarations imply, therefore, that for Tasso as well as Ercilla, the lyric poet, even when unhappy, plaintive, and heart-rending, remains an enchanter. Although they do not admit it in such terms, lyric poetry – at that time overwhelmingly love poetry – seemed immensely pleasurable because it transported the reader into a land where desire takes precedence over the so-called reasons of the great collective causes to which the epic is devoted. Confronted with such ideas and feelings, both poets inevitably had to yield to lyrical temptation, which privileges fragmentation and deviation, subjectivity and passionate obstinacy. Consequently, their poems did not succeed in conforming to what they had dreamed them to be: a fully coherent work, pursued without concessions. Both poets struggled to finish their work, and ultimately they turned away from their task with a repentant attitude. Of course, it is partly thanks to their lapses and apparent inconsistencies that their poems became famous and still deserve to be read. This essay will explore the extent to which both poets' apparent antagonism towards the lyric is incoherent and unconvincing by engaging in a short examination of each text. *La Araucana* and *La Gerusalemme* are such stuff as lyric poetry is made of: a fabric of fancies of perfect love, voluptuous sorrow, and poetic glory. Even the war narrative, with its well-arranged plot, its historical, moral, and political lessons, and its pious and edifying exempla, is indebted to the trove of formulae and motives furnished by Petrarch and by a constellation of texts, ancient and modern, among which the Trecento poet was the brightest star. For Tasso, the paradoxical cooperation between lyric elements and epic construction, long recognized by commentators and critics of the *Gerusalemme*, was recently analysed by Ayesha Ramachandran[38] and, in a much more comprehensive manner, by Valeria di Iasio.[39] Prior to these studies, Claudio Scarpati[40] had shown that, in spite of the dense system of classical echoes and references in the final stage of the composition if the *Liberata*, his poem started from questions addressed by the vernacular literary tradition and mainly from Petrarch: from the poet of *Africa* and *Trionfi*, but also of the *Canzoniere*. As for the lyrical voices that reverberate in Ercilla's *La Araucana*, though rarely investigated by the poorer scholarly criticism on Ercilla, they have nevertheless been considered by Moore and thoroughly explored by Felipe Valencia.[41] Our comparison between the two cases will enrich these remarkable contributions.

Tasso: The Pyrrhic Victory of Order

In the juvenile *Discorsi dell'arte poetica* and later in the *Lettere poetiche*, Tasso affirms his desire to conquer the favour of the vast public who adored Ariosto's "stories of love and chivalry, adventures and enchantments."[42] The poet's stroke of genius was to give a major role to these alien components in the Aristotelian economy of the *múthos*. *Amori* and *incanti* are introduced as temptations of the most valiant champions of the Crusader army. These hindrances to the virtuous Goffredo's plan have, in the logic of the fable, the same function as the anger of Achilles, which forestalls the victory of the Greeks in Homer's *Iliad*. They constitute both the condition of a dramatic plot, and an element of philosophical, political, and moral significance.

During the "Roman" revision (evidenced mainly by the so-called *Lettere poetiche*) between March 1575 and July 1576,[43] love stories and magic spells were closely associated in Tasso's mind, and his first concern was to defend them from criticism. Indeed, Armida's story, which runs throughout the whole poem from the fourth to the last canto, shows in a prominent fashion the proximity of love and magical wonder. Armida's erotic appeal, employed as a mortal weapon against the Christian troops, is modelled on Laura's magic appeal to her lover:[44]

> Grazie ch'a pochi il Ciel largo destina,
> rara vertù non già d'umana gente,
> *sotto biondi capei canuta mente*
> e 'n umil donna alta beltà divina [...]
> coi *sospiri soavemente rotti;*
> da questi magi trasformato fui.[45]

(Graces that heaven bestows to the happiest few, / rare virtue, beyond human power / a wise mind under a blonde head of hair / high divine beauty in a simple girl [...] / with long sighs sweetly broken / by these magic spells I got transformed.)

When the lord of Damascus, the Muslim magus Idraote, sends Armida to the Christian camp to sow disorder and disruption, he gives to his dazzlingly beautiful and gifted niece instructions that are unequivocally allusive to this Petrarchan sonnet. Tasso borrowed from it the motifs of mature sense under blonde hair and of the broken sighs, both of which convey the magical power of erotic enslavement:

> Dice: O diletta mia, che *sotto biondi*
> *capelli* e fra sì tenere sembianze
> *canuto senno* e cor virile ascondi,
> e già ne l'arti mie me stesso avanze [...]
> Vanne al campo nemico: ivi s'impieghi
> ogn'arte feminil ch'amore alletti.
> Bagna di pianto e fa' melati i preghi,
> *tronca e confondi co' sospiri i detti* [...] (IV:24–5)

(O loved one, cried he, who underneath these locks of gold / and these looks of tender child / hide a mature sense and a manly spirit /and in your first youth could teach me my art / [...] Go to the Christians' host / and there employ all womanly tricks that awake love / plead with tears and implore with sweetness, / break and blur your words with sighs.)

Such a kinship between erotic appeal and magic emerges in the stories of Clorinda, Erminia, and even the holy martyr Sofronia, though in these cases the magic appears in more innocent and less self-conscious forms. These episodes underwent the most serious alterations in the reformed poem, the *Conquistata*, including the sacrifice of the character of Sofronia and the substitution of the passionate Erminia with the colourless and passive Nicea.

What acts as a temptation for the champions of Christ is also felt as a temptation by the readers: an attraction for a sensuous poetic delight sometimes tinged with morbidity, as when Clorinda's death is described ambiguously as a defloration. Hence the suspicion that the whole enterprise of the crusade might serve only as a pretext and a pious excuse for such immoral gratifications. What for the heroes is the lure of pleasure is for the poet the lyric temptation: by listening to the lyric sirens, he can ease the poetic reins, giving way to the playful refinements of *concetti* in the manner of Petrarch and Ariosto. They embellish what in the narrative appears as the attraction of sin, a sin veiled by chivalrous feelings.

The passionate bond of Tancredi with the dead Clorinda is unequivocally conceived according to Petrarch, whose love survives Laura's death. If Tancredi decides not to kill himself after unintentionally killing his beloved, it is because he listens to the Christian admonitions of Peter the Hermit, but moreover because he is consoled in a dream by an apparition of the warrior lady in angelic attire:

> Ed ecco in sogno di stellata veste
> cinta gli appar la sospirata amica:
> bella assai più, ma lo splendor celeste
> orna e non toglie la notizia antica;
> e con dolce atto di pietà *le meste*
> *luci par che gli asciughi,* e così dica:
> "Mira come son bella e come lieta,
> *fedel mio caro, e in me tuo duolo* acqueta." (XII.91)

(And suddenly in a dream, clad in starry veil / appeared the maid for whose sake he mourned, / much fairer than ever, but the heavenly beam / adorned without hiding the dear well-known face; / and wiping with a sweet compassion / the tears from his sad eyes, she seemed to say: / "See how fair I am and how radiant of joy, / dear faithful one: and calm your grief in me.")

The stanza resonates with the consoling apparitions of the dead Laura in sonnets 341 and 342 of the *Canzoniere*: "*Fedel mio caro,* assai *di te mi dole,*" she says: "Con quella man che tanto desiai, / *m'asciuga li occhi* …"[46]

These sublime appeasements given by the *donna angelicata* do not dispel the evil. Tancredi's adventure in the enchanted forest is commonly acknowledged as one of the best moments of the poem. The axe falls from his hands when he sees the blood gushing from the bark of a cypress that he has just split, and he hears the plaintive voice of Clorinda reproaching him for having wounded her for the second time. The consolations of lyric poetry prove to be illusions, and the poet's voice has already the anguished and ghastly tone that will dominate the Romantic era. The guilt is still there, together with the frightening belief in a carnal presence of the dead woman in the form of a phantom inhabiting a baleful tree. The cypress as symbolic tree of temptation was apparently chosen by Tasso because of the funereal meaning it possesses since classical antiquity and also for its pyramidal shape, also connected with funereal associations:

> Al fine un largo spazio in forma scorge
> d'anfiteatro, e non è pianta in esso,
> salvo che nel suo mezzo altero sorge,
> quasi eccelsa piramide, un cipresso.
> Colà si drizza, e nel mirar s'accorge
> ch'era di vari segni un tronco impresso,
> simili a quei che in vece usò di scritto
> l'antico già misterioso Egitto. (XIII.38)

(At last he glimpses a large circular space / like an amphitheatre bare of any plant /save that in the centre stands up with pride / like some tall pyramid, a black cypress. / There he goes and as he looks discerns / strange characters printed on the bark / like those which were used for writing / in the old and mysterious Egypt.)

This cypress bears magic inscriptions and evokes the mysteries of Egypt's sacred lore. The association between cypress and pyramid, well established already at the end of the Quattrocento in Colonna's *Hypnerotomachia Poliphili* and Sannazaro's *Arcadia*, had in these texts hermetic and melancholic connotations. Tasso was also fascinated by hieroglyphs and dedicated much of his dialogue *Il Conte overo de l'imprese* to reflecting on the magical power of ancient writing. In the *Gerusalemme* it seems further burdened with the vague terrors that torment a haunted mind, like Tasso's was at many moments during his life. The episode was impressively selected by Freud to illustrate the *Wiederholungzwang*, the compulsion of repetition, a fatal affliction by which humans invariably repeat actions that lead to what causes them pain:

Tasso gives a singularly affecting poetical portrayal of such a trend of fate in the romantic epic: "Gerusalemme liberata." The hero, Tancred, has unwittingly slain Clorinda, the maiden he loved, who fought with him disguised in the armor of an enemy knight. After her burial he penetrates into the mysterious enchanted wood, the bane of the army of the crusaders. Here he hews down a tall tree with his sword, but from the gash in the trunk blood streams forth and the voice of Clorinda whose soul is imprisoned in the tree cries out to him in reproach that he has once more wrought a baleful deed on his beloved.[47]

Such a bold interpretation, in metapsychological terms, is certainly distant from Petrarchan conventions, but not from the sense of fatal imprisonment that emerges from the *Canzoniere*'s images of love.

Further on, for Rinaldo, the tree in which temptation is concealed is a myrtle, from which sprang the still beguiling and sorrowful figure of the abandoned Armida. Tasso remembered certainly the myrtle into which Ariosto's Astolfo is transformed on Alcina's island, since Armida is similar by function and literary pedigree to Alcina, even if the two appealing magicians are almost as different as the poems in which they appear. Other elements of the story of the ghastly forest come from Dante's Inferno, and from the episode of the Wood of Suicide (canto XIII), where the damned Self-Murderers appear converted into trees. However, even for this detail we must not forget the lyrical background. In Petrarch's *Canzoniere*, the myrtle, Venus's tree, is mentioned only twice, and in both cases, it appears to make a pair with the laurel. Both are "*vaghi*," beautiful, both are evergreen, and together they symbolize the indissoluble bond of eroticism and poetry:

Qual vaghezza di lauro e qual di mirto?
Povera et nuda vai, filosofia[48]

(What appeal do you find in laurel and in myrtle? / Poor and naked goes philosophy …)

Né de l'ardente spirto
de la sua vista dolcemente acerba,
la qual dí et notte più che lauro o mirto
tenea in me verde l'amorosa voglia …[49]

(Not from the ardent spirit / of her sweet bitter gaze / that kept my loving desire green / day and night, more than laurel or myrtle …)

The tree of Aphrodite, which appears to conceal Armida's ghost, is therefore akin to the laurel, which in the *Canzoniere* shaded the country of love and poetic glory:

Quel, che d'odore e di color vincea
l'odorifero et lucido oriënte [...]
dolce mio lauro, ove habitar solea
ogni bellezza, ogni vertute ardente,
vedeva a la sua ombra honestamente
il mio signor sedersi e la mia dea.[50]

(That which in scent and colour overcame / the fragrant and the shining Orient [...] / my sweet laurel, where used to dwell / every beauty, every ardent virtue / saw honorably seating in its shade / my great lord and my fair goddess.)

Rinaldo, protected by magic weapons and divine favour, overcomes temptation. After a confused fight against what appeared first to be the sweet and mourning Armida, before becoming a terrifying crowd of giants and monsters, he strikes the enchanted tree with bold resolution. What under the spell of Ismeno's magic seemed an enormous myrtle reveals itself as a walnut (*noce*), a baleful and devilish tree (on account of the false etymology that connects the Latin word *nux* to *nocivus* or *nuxivus* – "harmful" – and the Italian word for walnut, *noce* with the verb *nocere*, "to harm). Thanks to his display of relentless cold-bloodedness, Rinaldo, elected by God as his champion, puts an end to the enchantments of the forest. Crusaders can now find the wood needed to build the assault towers that will lead to the conquest of Jerusalem. The tree of the cross triumphs over the tree of temptation. Nevertheless, scarcely has Rinaldo crushed the main forces of the Egyptian army when he puts aside his sacred mission. Acting like Antonius with Cleopatra, he follows his former lover and now mortal enemy Armida, who, like the legendary queen of Egypt, has fled the field of battle seeking escape from captivity by suicide (XX.117–18). Her faithful lover Tisaphernes, already doomed to fall in battle, would have been a more expedient embodiment of Antonius and was in fact meditating to imitate his lady in her flight. In the end, however, the role of the most illustrious among vanquished generals of Roman tradition, Antonius, is taken by Tisaphernes's victorious killer, the pious and invincible Rinaldo, who pursues his fair mistress, tenderly moved by her desperate situation. This unexpected return of a sinful passion, converted into holy feelings of compassion, or covered by them, allows the transformation of warrior into lover and of relentless victor into defender, knight, and servant. Such a metamorphosis is powerfully erotic, but it is also wondrous, and in it are connected the two major roots of poetic delight, love and marvel (*meraviglia*).

Just before the religious and surprisingly brief denouement, consisting in the consecration of Christ's sepulchre by Godfrey and his host in a Jerusalem purified by a river of blood, we see the woman who embodies temptation and the Christian conqueror in a loving embrace. The arm of the Crusader offers a "column" of support for her beautiful hip, as she faints of dread and pain:

> Ella cadea, quasi *fior* mezzo inciso,
> piegando il lento collo; ei la sostenne,
> *le fe' d'un braccio al bel fianco colonna*
> e 'ntanto al *sen* le rallentò la *gonna*. (XX.128.5–8)

(She was falling as a flower half sheared / with drooping neck, and he held her up, /her fair flank leaning on his arm as on a column; / he loosed meanwhile the dress about the breast ...)

The first readers could not miss the quotation from the famous canzone 126 of Petrarch, the same one that for Tasso in his *Discorsi* illustrated the blameworthy amenity of lyric *concetti*:[51]

> Chiare, fresche e dolci acque,
> ove le belle membra
> pose colei che sola a me par donna;
> gentil ramo ove piacque
> (con sospir' mi rimembra)
> *a lei di fare al bel fianco colonna*;
> herba e *fior'* che la *gonna*
> leggiadra ricoverse
> co l'angelico *seno* ...[52]

(Clear, fresh and sweet water / where rested her beautiful limbs / the only one who was to me a woman; / gentle branch wher it pleased her / (I remember it with longing) / to make a column for her lovely flank / grass and flowers which her dress / lightly covered / as it did the angelic breast ...)

This scene disappeared entirely from the reformed poem, the *Conquistata* (and actually, as Poma has shown, it was already suppressed in the manuscripts that represent the last stage of the "Roman revision";[53] it should therefore be absent in a philologically accurate critical edition of the *Gerusalemme*). Certainly, as Di Santo argues, it was incompatible with the important episode added by Tasso in the *Conquistata* regarding Rinaldo, whose name became Riccardo in the *Conquistata*. Through this new story, the affective weight of Armida's love is diminished by the passionate bond of Riccardo to Ruperto, modelled on Achilles's love for Patroclus. Even without the ideological shift that made necessary the suppression of the final victory of Armida's profane Eros, the reconciliation scene was to be erased in the reformed poem for structural and emotional reasons.[54] And yet, this suppression confirms what was obvious from the start for the most severe censors – that it is impossible not to see in this denouement a dangerous concession to the primacy of desire in the equilibrium of the entire composition. Tasso's first intention, his spontaneous movement, was to finish his tale with this scene, and without the intervention of his censors, it seems probable that he would have kept it.

When he was shaping the core of the *Gerusalemme liberata*, Tasso thought that he could yield to lyric temptation by submitting it to the rational order of the *verosimile*, going so far as to make of his Christian hero the perfect lover of the most desirable but certainly not the most virtuous woman. Heroes and heroines, in his opinion, were not subject to the norms of ordinary morality, and heroic virtues required overwhelming and uncompromising desires,[55] such as those sung by Petrarchan poets. The *Canzoniere*, the unsurpassed lyric expression of Eros understood as supreme delight and mortal alienation, furnished such capital elements to the ethos of the two strongest defenders of the Cross, Tancredi and Rinaldo, giving them feelings and attitudes that could be appreciated by a noble Italian (or European) audience of the sixteenth century. Moreover, as suggested by Ramachandran,[56] the *Canzoniere* provided the plot (the Aristotelian μῦθος or *favola*) with a subjective and introspective bedrock. The epic goal, the conquest of Jerusalem, must overcome obviously the obstacle represented by Ariosto and by the *romanzo*: that is, the centrifugal tendencies of the Christian warriors, fostered by diabolical and magical influences. Godfroy's companions must embark on the solitary and competitive adventures proper to errant knights, and be brought back to their duty by the authority of this perfect Christian chief. But these companions, and conspicuously the two best knights Tancredi and Rinaldo, live, each on his own, a story modelled on the Petrarchan plot of the *Canzoniere*: the juvenile error (*giuvenile errore*) that consists in a desperate love fused with a search for glory, leading finally to a repentance that in Tasso, like in Petrarch, remains ambiguous, since it is never fully assumed and expressed in the frame of the book. This poetically elegant solution, though ultimately unsatisfying to Tasso, did satisfy the vast majority of readers, who focused precisely on these moments of ambiguity, when we are far from Jerusalem and away from war, in a dreamy world, where no moral discipline can prevail over desire. There resound the voices of those who delight in their sickness and refuse to cure it, as do by rule Petrarch and his lyric followers: the voices of Tancredi, Erminia, Armida, and even Rinaldo.

Ercilla: Chivalric Heroes in a Disenchanted World

Ercilla's point of departure is again the example of *Orlando furioso*. While a page to the future Philip II, this gentleman spent his early youth in an itinerant court that contributed to spreading Ariosto's glory across Europe. In London, hearing of the Indigenous revolt in Chile, he asked permission from the prince to travel to America and fight against these bold Mapuche warriors to whom he would give the lasting name of Araucans or Araucanians. After spending less than two years in the wars of Chile, Ercilla left this country and soon America. If he had written, on the basis of this short experience, a history in prose, his narrative, maybe soon completed, would also, perhaps, have been soon forgotten. But he decided to write a poem, and he became, as a result, the founder of the colonial epic and one of the best early modern epic narrators.

Whereas Torquato Tasso wished to reconcile the popularity of Ariosto with Aristotle's rational rules, Ercilla aimed at an equally paradoxical goal: to emulate Ariosto while remaining a faithful historian of events that had not yet become the object of official or even unofficial chronicles. At least as far as public and printed accounts were concerned, Chile's history was still to be written, and Ercilla wanted to be its first historian, something between Homer and Herodotus. In the first stanza of his poem, he echoes the *propositio* of the Italian poem with the intention of overturning it. In Ariosto's text, one finds: "Le donne, i cavallier, l'arme, gli amori / le cortesie, l'audaci imprese io canto ..."[57] Ercilla writes:

> No las damas, amor, no gentilezas
> de caballeros canto enamorados,
> ni las muestras, regalos y ternezas
> de amorosos afectos y cuidados,
> mas el valor, los hechos, las proezas
> de aquellos españoles esforzados ... (I.1–6)

(Not of ladies, love, or the kindness / of enamored knights do I sing, / nor the gestures, signs, or tender words / of amorous affections and cares, / but the bravery, deeds, exploits / of those daring Spaniards ...)

For Ercilla's first readers, well acquainted with the *Orlando furioso*, the meaning of these lines was clear. From the very beginning, the poet sets forward his claims: I too sing and aspire to the glory that awaits the heroes and the poets. Like Ariosto, I undertake to compose a beautiful story in fine verse, a narrative that will delight you. On the other hand, my story is true in every particular and I do not sing of ladies and courtesy; I refuse the flattering pleasures of softness and lasciviousness. I will refrain from seducing you by tender feelings that would destroy my credit as a historian. My matter, austere and manly, is confined to war and victory.

Ercilla never flaunted his erudition, but it is possible to demonstrate by a careful reading of his text that he was nevertheless a cultivated man, familiar with ancient epic poetry: beyond doubt a reader of Virgil, Lucan, and Statius, and probably of the Latin translations of the *Iliad*. Since he wanted to write a poem and not a chronicle, he had to provide the enemies of Spaniards with heroic stature and assure them the reader's sympathy, as Homer did with the Trojans. This strategy is his great vindication and his lasting success: the invention of the Araucans, a remarkable people whose actions are worthy of memory: "Cosas diré también harto notables / de gente que a ningún rey obedecen / temerarias empresas memorables" (I.2.1–2) (I will say things that should be known / about people who do not obey to any king / feats of gallantry deserving memory). It is noticeable that the term *empresas* used by Ariosto, *audaci imprese*, is found in the second stanza of Ercilla's poem, *temerarias empresas memorables* (feats of gallantry deserving memory), but it is said about the Araucans and not about the Spaniards. Among the Indigenous warriors, there are heroes like Tucapel and Rengo, resembling those of Ariosto by their colossal strength, bravery, and pride. In order to keep his promise, Ercilla refrains from having them embark on amorous adventures. And yet we have seen that he was prone to the lyric temptation – and he finally succumbs to it with his main hero in the first part, Lautaro. In the third canto, Ercilla introduces this Lautaro as the favourite page of the conquistador Valdivia: a beautiful and strong Araucanian boy, very young and very wise, thirsty for freedom and for glory, not so different from Tasso's Rinaldo. Before any description, Ercilla artfully shows him in the process of becoming an admirable traitor. Betraying his masters, he takes the side of his people and gives them an unexpected and decisive victory. Much later in the poem, in the thirteenth canto, Lautaro, in the meantime promoted to main chief of the Indigenous rebellion after Caupolicán, is surprised in his fort by a Spanish detachment under the command of Villagrán. There, for the first time, ladies and love emerge in the poem. We discover the Araucanian leader, whom we knew only as a formidable warrior, an artful strategist, and an austere patriot, sleeping in the arms of a beautiful woman, whom he loves with ardent passion and who shares his fire:

> Aquella noche el bárbaro dormía
> con la bella Guacolda enamorada
> a quien él de encendido amor amaba
> y ella por él no menos se abrasaba. (XIII.43.5–8)

> (On that night the barbarian slept / in the arms of the beautiful and enamored Guacolda / whom he loved with burning passion / and she, feeling no less for him, was inflamed.)

Lautaro awakens from a nightmare of helplessness and death. Guacolda shares his dread and begs him to arm himself; the two exchange fervently amorous words. In the midst of this passionate scene, the Spanish attack. After so many fights and so much glory, an arrow, directed by death and fatality, ends the champion's short life.

Modern commentators have seen in this episode a moral lesson. Lautaro's loving weakness, his neglect and imprudence would be responsible for his downfall. In my opinion, it was not in these petty moralistic terms that Ercilla considered this scene, to which he dedicated his first verses of love, breaking the law he had given himself:

> Pero ya la turbada pluma mía
> que en las cosas de amor nueva se halla
> confusa, tarda y con temor se mueve
> y a pasar adelante no se atreve. (XIII.57.5–8)

> (But now my distraught pen / new to matters of love finds itself / confused, hesitant, and moving fearfully / not daring go further.)

In fact, Ercilla has not a single word of blame for the carelessness of Lautaro, but instead extols the virtue of women, proved by the pure love of a barbarous girl. He does not tell what happens to Guacolda after the death of her lover. He does not confirm that she committed suicide or died of a broken heart as she had protested to Lautaro that she would. Her lyrical complaints were for him, and most readers, a sufficient proof. This man, who had been engaged in a sordid war and seen so many horrors, and who had perhaps committed some himself, could certainly weep when he read love poems. If they were beautiful and noble, he ingenuously accepted the truth of the feelings they expressed.

Lautaro, a character dear to his creator and endowed with the greatest dignity upon his entrance into the poem, dies covered with laurels. He was the victim of Fortune and perhaps of his *hybris*, as befits a tragic hero. He was not punished for some erotic neglect, which actually enhances his nobility.[58] Early modern readers believed that lyric poetry (and particularly elegiac and Petrarchan poetry) was attuned to the generous mind and to the delicate taste of noblemen and ladies. Garcilaso de la Vega, the most illustrious lyrical poet of the Spanish Renaissance and to whom Ercilla's self-fashioning owes his own essential features,[59] epitomized such ideas. In the poetry that established his glory, Garcilaso, far from congratulating himself on his military exploits, modulates subtle amorous complaints and professes to abhor warfare. Instead of repenting, like Petrarch, for his juvenile errors, he displays them with a melancholic pride:

> ¡Oh crudo, oh riguroso, oh fiero Marte
> de túnica cubierto de diamante
> y endurecido siempre en toda parte!
> ¿Qué tiene que hacer el tierno amante
> con tu dureza y áspero ejercicio
> llevado siempre del furor delante?
> Ejercitando por mi mal tu oficio
> soy reducido a términos que muerte
> será mi postrimero beneficio.[60]

(Oh merciless, oh stern, oh fierce Mars / in diamond tunic garmented / and hardened always everywhere! / What must the tender lover do / with your severity and harsh exercise / driven headlong always by rage? / Exercising to my detriment your vocation / I am so far reduced that death / will be my final blessing.)

A few months after writing these verses, Garcilaso died in war, heroically and stupidly like Lautaro. In Ercilla's poem, the Indigenous leader is struck by an arrow that comes from nowhere, as he emerges from his tent and out of Guacolda's arms, without even taking the time to put on his armour. In a not dissimilar fashion, Garcilaso died while he was climbing a tower under the eyes of the emperor. Without wasting time to put on his helmet, he had escaped from the arms of friends who wanted to hold him back, and his head was fractured by a large stone torn from the wall and dropped by an anonymous hand. That historical death, which has the beauty and symbolic value of fiction, happened around twenty years before the probable date of Lautaro's death (the character is essentially fictitious, but embedded in a historical setting with a precise chronological frame). Another epic poet, Luis Zapata, who was also inspired by Ariosto, relates Garcilaso's death in these terms:

> Teníanle sus amigos abrazado
> porque le vían qu'estaba desarmado.
>
> Soltóse y corrió allá y subió ligero
> por la escala que al muro se arrimaba,
> tomando una ruin gorra antes de acero
> de un soldado a caso que pasaba;
> llegaba casi al escalón postrero
> cuando una grande almena que bajaba
> con gran dolor del campo allí presente
> le envió mortal a tierra finalmente.[61]

(His friends held him back / as they saw he was unarmed. // He broke free and ran there and swiftly climbed / the stairs that lead up the wall, / grabbing a shabby cap instead of a steel helmet / from a soldier who happened nearby; / he approached the final step / when a large stone unleashing / to the great sorrow of the troops / sent him to the ground with mortal wounds.)

Zapata's poem *Carlo famoso*, to which these awkward and moving lines belong, was published in 1566, three years before the first part of *La Araucana* (1569), and it is almost a certainty that Ercilla knew it. It is therefore not impossible that his treatment of Lautaro's death included a reminiscence of Garcilaso's absurd prowess:

> Revuelto el manto al brazo, en el instante
> con un desnudo estoque y él desnudo
> corre a la puerta [...]
>
> del toldo el hijo de Pillán salía
> y una flecha a buscarle que venía
> por el siniestro lado, ¡oh dura suerte!
> rompe la cruda punta y tan derecho
> que pasa el corazón más bravo y fuerte
> que jamás se encerró en humano pecho ... (XIV.15.1–3; 16.7–8 and 17.1–4)

(His mantle draped over his arm, in an instant / clasping his naked sword and himself naked / he runs to the door [...] / Pillán's offspring emerged from the tent / and an arrow that sought him / from the left side, oh cruel luck! / the harsh tip enters so precisely / that it pierces the boldest and strongest heart / that ever a human chest contained ...)

Like Garcilaso, Lautaro's end is caused by a lack of caution, but mainly by bad luck. It does not call into question the warrior's force and dexterity in fighting since it comes from afar, from a faceless enemy who threw a big stone, or from an arrow drawn by Fortune and Death. The man who dies has never been so dearly loved. Zapata mentions the grief of the whole camp attending Garcilaso's death; through the lamentations of Guacolda, Ercilla elicits similar compassion from his readers:

> ... y forzoso he de ver un mal tan fuerte,
> un mal como es de vos verme partida,
> dejadme llorar antes de mi muerte
> esto poco que queda de mi vida [...]
>
> Tras esto tantas lágrimas vertía
> que mueve a compasión el contemplarla
> y así el tierno Lautaro no podía
> dejar en tal sazón de acompañarla. (XIII.56.2–6 and 57.1–4)

(... and I am doomed to bear such grave calamity, / a blow as to see you parted from me, / let me weep before my death / this brief time that remains of my life [...] / Then so many tears she shed / that her sight stirs compassion / and so the tender-hearted Lautaro could not / but weep himself with her.)

The "tierno Lautaro," who cannot help but accompany the tears of his fair mistress, is the same figure who, some lines later, will be "el corazón más duro y fuerte que jamás se encerró en humano pecho" (the boldest and strongest heart / that ever a human chest contained). Similarly, the tender lover (el tierno amante) who complains in Garcilaso's second elegy and renounces his god, the fierce Mars, became an avatar of the same man who would run to death, bareheaded, climbing the Tour de Muy in Provence. Garcilaso's reality and legend shows the survival of a chivalric ideal in a renewed form, that of the Renaissance courtier. The courtier, a scholar of humanistic culture, also had to be a poet, a perfect lover when he loved, and a rash soldier in war at a time when gunpowder was rendering obsolete the sword and the spear.

Through the tale of Lautaro's death, Ercilla pledged allegiance to an ideal at the very core of Petrarchan practice of poetry in the Italian, and soon also in the European courts of the sixteenth century. His favourite hero must be fierce in war, but also tender in love, in spite of the demands of historical accuracy and pragmatism.

It is significant that Lautaro has to die immediately before the arrival of the soldier Ercilla on the stage of the Chilean war. From this moment, this new character splits into a poet and a soldier, a hero and a witness. As a narrator and also as a hero, he is the confidant and defender of the ladies, the one who protects, honours, consoles, and glorifies the widow Tegualda, the one thanks to whom Glaura recovers her beloved Araucan husband, the one who heals the wounded and grief-stricken Lauca, and the one who defends Dido's royal virtue against the slanderer Virgil.[62] Neither "Ercilla" nor Lautaro are simply quixotic fools: they are, to some extent with Caupolicán, the only complex characters of the poem, and their indulgence in lyrical impropriety is not a failure that must be judged in moralistic terms. For a public that has admitted once and for all that passionate love was an aristocratic attribute, such impropriety instead becomes the token of great minds.

The idealism and optimism that Ercilla maintains against the pressure of a reality whose violence and iniquity he does not dissimulate were shared by the young Tasso. A similar confidence fuels the Italian poet's hope of reconciling the imperatives of Aristotle and of the Christian *militia]* with the freedom of Ariosto and the pleasures of magic and love. In spite of being scarcely plausible, the program of both poets was accomplished. In *La Araucana*, as in the *Gerusalemme liberata*, readers would be able to enjoy the lively account of terrifying and courageous battles; they would find a defence and illustration of political virtues, and a censorship of their opposites. But they would also find poetry in accordance with their sensitivity: a lyric way of exalting human passions beyond or even against political and religious reasons.

However, in either case, the hard-won balance, the miraculous equilibrium of the masterwork, proved to be fragile. In Tasso's case, the loss of this balance was partly the result of a deep alteration of personality, which also expresses a sensitivity to the new requirements of the Catholic faith. After the Tridentine Reform, many Catholic leaders tried to surpass the Reformed churches in moral stringency and social discipline. Prominent participants of this renewal of uncompromising purity of faith and morals rejected openly the aristocratic values of honour and love as worldly temptations, diabolical or pagan illusions of delight and glory. Among them were some of the first censors of Tasso's poetry, to whom the poet chose to submit his work during the "Roman revision." The most rigorous member of this group, the future cardinal Silvio Antoniano, was a cultivated and refined man, who became at some point an intransigent defender of austere piety and uncompromising Christian behaviour. Such a position was not destined to prevail for long in Rome, but it had, in Tasso's time, an intimidating power that must not be underestimated.

In Spain, despite the confessional alignment of the monarchy with the Catholic Church, such feelings of pure and severe Christianity were never imposed on the majority of the clergy and, even less, on the class of noble laymen to which Ercilla belonged. Therefore the balance between lyricism and the historic narrative of war was not threatened by religious or moralistic considerations. Lyricism was nevertheless weakened or distorted since it became supported by the "barbarian" voices of Araucan women, mourning the loss of their beloved husbands or fiancés. Just as the epic was destabilized by the increasing consciousness of armed conflict that could not achieve enduring peace and by protests against the atrocities committed against the Araucanians, the Petrarchan lyric likewise yielded progressively to the tragic lamentation of the victims. The Araucanian women are, in the third part of the poem, equated with a Dido figure, Virgilian in her ardent and excruciating love, but also, as Justin's heroine, an example of queens and widows: a Dido who never met Aeneas, and who preferred suicide to a new marriage with an African king who would make her unfaithful to her dead husband.

Most readers of both poets retained only one side of the mixture of epic grandeur, lyric charm, and tragic pathos offered by these works. Some of Ercilla's readers, such as his Dutch translator, scoured his work for geographic and historical data with pragmatic aims. However, most preferred heroines and love stories.[63] Similarly, a majority of the many admirers of the *Gerusalemme liberata* retained the amorous laments of Armida, Tancredi, or Erminia, which would be extensively developed in the elegiac and operatic posterity of the poem. Faced with such a universal misunderstanding, Tasso would renounce his own masterpiece and construct a kind of *palinodia*, the *Conquistata*. Likewise, Ercilla imbued his account with a sinister ending, suspending his poem on a dissonant note of repentant melancholy.

NOTES

1 Several distinguished scholars and generous friends, Clizia Carminati, Imogen Choi, Christopher Geekie, Antonio Ricci, and Felipe Valencia, have read this paper. Their suggestions and corrections have immensely improved it, and I wish to thank them for their invaluable help.

2 For this essay, I have used the 1991 edition of Tasso's *Gerusalemme liberata* edited by Lanfranco Caretti and the 1993 edition of Ercilla's *La Araucana* edited by Isaías Lerner. Embedded page references in the article are to these two source texts. All translations are mine unless otherwise noted.

3 The best biography of Tasso is still Solerti's *Vita di Torquato Tasso*, issued in three volumes between 1895 and 1899. Baldassarri's "Torquato Tasso" of 1999 gives an excellent synthesis of Tasso's life and works; and Gigante's *Tasso* of 2007 is a likewise reliable account, one that also offers extended discussion of Tasso's later years, a period which has recently become a point of scholarly interest.

4 I use in this paper elementary data about Ercilla's life that have been well known since José Toribio Medina published his edition of *La Araucana* for the centenary of Chile's independence (1910–18). The third volume of this magnum opus was a well-documented biography of the poet, one that can be read in a more manageable format in its 1948 Mexican reprint *Vida de Ercilla*. Since then available information about Ercilla's life has made scarce progress, and the same is true regarding the philological knowledge of the text, which still lacks a critical edition. New and interesting elements on these two fronts can be found in Plagnard's *Une épopée ibérique* of 2019.

5 Choi, "La presencia oculta de Torquato Tasso en la *Tercera parte de la Araucana* de Alonso **de** Ercilla (1589–90)."

6 Petrarca, *Canzoniere*, I, 9–14.

7 Quint, *Epic and Empire*.

8 Virgil, *Aeneid* 1, 33.

9 Greene, "The Natural Tears of Epic," 190.

10 As Quint explains: "Ercilla finishes his poem three times, at the ends of each of its instalments, but in each case he provides images of aimless confusion, interruption and suspension, cyclical repetition. He does so knowingly, imitating and overturning epic models of closure, particularly Virgilian models that equate narrative completion with definitive military victory and political settlement." Quint, *Epic and Empire*, 168. It must be said, however, that for Quint and for the best critics, Virgil is not simply triumphalist, and he has been read in a different, even opposing, way.

11 Tasso dedicated a significant amount of time and energy to developing a coherent theory of poetry, in particular of epic genre (*poema eroico*). His main ideas are found in his youthful treatise *Discorsi dell'arte poetica*, composed in the early 1560s, though an authorized edition of this text first appeared in 1587. He later rewrote this work in a heavily expanded version, *Discorsi del poema eroico*, the printing of which he oversaw in 1594. Both texts were excellently edited by Luigi Poma.

12 Tasso, *Lettere poetiche*; Bocca, *Le "Lettere poetiche" e la revisione romana della "Gerusalemme liberata"*; and Russo, "*A ritmo di corrieri*."

13 Gigante, "L'elaborazione della *Gerusalemme conquistata.*"

14 Residori, *L'idea del poema.*

15 Di Santo, *Il poema epico rinascimentale e l'"Iliade" da Trissino a Tasso.*

16 Ferretti, *Narratore notturno.*

17 Poma, *Studi sul testo della "Gerusalemme liberata."*

18 Scotti, "Il problema testuale della *Gerusalemme liberata.*"

19 Méndez Herrera, "Estudio de las ediciones de *La Araucana* con una edición crítica de la tercera parte."

20 Méndez Herrera, "Estudio de las ediciones de *La Araucana* con una edición crítica de la tercera parte"; Martínez, "Writing on the Edge"; Plagnard, *Une épopée ibérique*; and now Gómez Canseco, "El retrato de Alonso de Ercilla en *La Araucana*: variantes y función."

21 The best philological investigation of Ercilla's text (the only one following modern scientific criteria), has been for a long time the PhD dissertation of Juan Alberto Méndez Herrera about the third part of the Araucana (Harvard, 1976). Unfortunately, it remained unpublished and was unknown or undervalued by scholars regarded as authorities in the field of Renaissance Hispanic Epic (a very narrow and marginal field): Frank Pierce, José Durand, and even Isaías Lerner, who was the curator of the only two editions that remain today easily accessible and possess a reputation for reliability (Madrid: Castalia 1983, and Madrid: Cátedra 1993). The two are identical (except for the introduction of the first by Morínigo), and the many reprints of the second do not introduce significant changes. The only apparent exception to this deplorable neglect was a rarely read paper of Álvarez Vilela, "La expedición a Ancud en *La Araucana* o la recuperación del mérito." As a consequence, for almost half a century, our views on the poem were distorted by the ignorance of what was really the third part, and of Ercilla's writing habits. As for me, having read Álvarez Vilela, I was acquainted with the main elements of Méndez Herrera's conclusions since I started to be interested in Ercilla; and my students Sarah Dichy-Malherme and Aude Plagnard took account of his work since 2008. We ordered a copy of the dissertation for the library of the École Normale Supérieure de Paris, perhaps the only one in Europe. Nevertheless, it is only recently that criticism has started to take advantage of Méndez Herrera's work. (For example, Martínez's "Writing on the Edge" offers an interesting approach based in material culture.) The section dedicated to "Édition et critique génétique: le cas de la *Araucana*" in Plagnard's book, *Une épopée ibérique,* is currently the only published investigation mapping the textual process of Ercilla's poem and it will soon be completed by the publication of the edition prepared by Gómez Canseco.

22 Luis Gómez Canseco has completed an edition of *La Araucana*, with the desirable amount of scientific accuracy, for the prestigious collection of classics published by the Real Academia Española. In recent articles, he has clarified many issues related with the history of the text and of his printings. I knew this edition, thanks to the generosity of its author, more than a year prior to its public issue, in the spring of 2022, when the present book was in the process of preparation.

23 That is, with the exception of a small number of lyrics and short proses, most written for the preliminaries of books of other authors. Due to the large success of *La Araucana* among Spanish readers, Ercilla became, in his last twenty years, a respected man of letters. Before 1580 he was appointed as one of the usual censors of books employed by the Royal Council, and his services were required for epic poetry and poetic matters in general. See "Aprobaciones de Ercilla" in José Toribio Medina, *Vida de Ercilla*, 199–215.

24 It was thought for a long time that the biographical material furnished by the impressive number of Tasso's letters, his dialogues, his lyrical poems, and his friend's eulogies was so abundant that it ought to suffice to build a complete and truthful narrative of Tasso's life. Solerti demonstrated the falsity of this assumption in his biography, based on a vast amount of documents emanated from other sources. See Solerti, *Vita di Torquato Tasso*, ch. X–XI.

25 Carpané, "La fortuna editoriale tassiana dal '500 ai giorni nostri."

26 See "Traductores de *La Araucana*" in José Toribio Medina, 1918. A Dutch translation by Isaac Ianz Byl (that is rather a kind of compendium) was published in 1619 in Rotterdam, for political more than aesthetic reasons, since the translator declares that he wanted to give useful information about a region that the Dutch judged interesting for their own imperial aims. The first literary translations into the French, English, and German languages had to wait for the pre-Romantic and Romantic times. It exists also as an early English translation in prose, made interesting by the implicit parallels between the Chili Conflict and the English colonial campaigns in Ireland. See Palmer, *The Severed Head and the Grafted Tongue*.

27 Arata, "La conquista de Jerusalén, Cervantes y la generación teatral de 1580."

28 Choi, "La presencia oculta de Torquato Tasso en la *Tercera parte de la Araucana* de Alonso de Ercilla (1589–90)."

29 Sutton, "'De gente que a ningún rey obedecen.'"

30 Choi, "La presencia oculta de Torquato Tasso en la *Tercera parte de la Araucana* de Alonso de Ercilla (1589–90)."

31 Zatti, *L'ombra del Tasso*; Sberlati, *Il genere e la disputa*; Jossa, *La fondazione di un genere*; and Sacchi, *Fra Ariosto e Tasso*.

32 Zatti, *The Quest for Epic*.

33 Alves, *Camões, Corte-Real e o sistema da epopeia quinhentista*.

34 Chevalier, *L'Arioste et l'Espagne (1530–1650)*.

35 One important example of this sophisticated and sometimes hidden imitation of Ariosto by Tasso was recently discovered by Carminati, "Una insospettata tessera ariostesca nella *Gerusalemme liberata* IV, 17."

36 Tasso, *Discorsi dell'Arte poetica. Discorsi del poema eroico*, 406, 501.

37 Moretti, "Tre maestri della tecnica epica tassiana," 39–43.

38 Ramachandran, "Tasso's Petrarch."

39 Di Iasio, "*Già grande vola, et già trionfa armato*."

40 Scarpati, "Geometrie Petrarchesche nella *Gerusalemme liberata*."

41 Moore, *Love, War and the Classical Tradition in the Early Modern Transatlantic World*; and Valencia, "Las muchas (aunque bárbaras) voces líricas de *La Araucana* y la índole poética de una historia verdadera."

42 Tasso, *Discorsi dell'arte poética e del poema eroico*; and Tasso, *Lettere poetiche*.

43 Tasso, *Lettere poetiche*.

44 Ramachandran, "Tasso's Petrarch," 189.

45 Petrarca, *Canzoniere*, 213, 1–4 and 13–14.

46 Petrarca, *Canzoniere*. My emphasis.

47 Freud, *Beyond the Pleasure Principle*, 16.

48 Petrarca, *Canzoniere*, 7, 9–10.

49 Petrarca, *Canzoniere*, 270, 63–6.

50 Petrarca, *Canzoniere*, 337, 1–8

51 Tasso, *Discorsi dell'arte poetica e del poema eroico*, 41.

52 Petrarca, *Canzoniere*, 126, 1–9.

53 Poma, *Studi sul testo della "Gerusalemme liberata."*

54 Di Santo, *Il poema epico rinascimentale e l'"Iliade" da Trissino a Tasso*, 233. "Se dunque nella *Liberata* la diversione dal compimento del telos epico della quale Rinaldo è protagonista e paradigma, si incentra sull'unico nucleo narrativo romanzesco della vicenda di Armida, nella *Conquistata* a questo primo nucleo diversivo se ne aggiunge un secondo, marcatamente epico, dovuto al radicalizzarsi della contesa con Goffredo e risolto nella tragica vicenda di Ruperto. É evidente, allora, che il taglio della riconciliazione finale tra Armida e il campione cristiano va imputato essenzialmente proprio a questo nuovo grande nucleo omerizzante che la critica preferisce ignorare: se già all'epoca della 'revisione romana' l'opportunità dell'episodio appariva dubbia per ragioni strutturali, proprio l'interposizione del nuovo nucleo emozionale della 'Patrocleia' di Ruperto risolve senz'altro la questione, rendendo impraticabile la ripresa del filo di Armida a tale distanza non solo testuale (che comunque nella *Conquistata* risulta notevolmente accresciuta : non più quattro canti ma ben undici), ma soprattutto narrativa ed emozionale."

55 Ferretti, "Pudicizia e *virtù donnesca* nella *Gerusalemme liberata*."

56 Ramachandran, "Tasso's Petrarch."
57 Ariosto, *Orlando furioso*, I, 1–2.
58 Blanco, "Fábulas de amores en la épica de guerra."
59 Valencia, "Las muchas (aunque bárbaras) voces líricas de *La Araucana* y la índole poética de una historia verdadera."
60 Garcilaso de la Vega, *Elegía II*, 94–102.
61 Zapata, *Carlo famoso*, 1566, fol. 220r.
62 Valencia, "Las muchas (aunque bárbaras) voces líricas de *La Araucana* y la índole poética de una historia verdadera."
63 Blanco, "Fábulas de amores en la épica de guerra."

WORKS CITED

Printed Sources

Álvarez Vilela, Ángel. "La expedición a Ancud en *La Araucana* o la recuperación del mérito." *Anales de Literatura Hispanoamericana* 24 (1995): 77–89.

Alves, Hélio J.S. *Camões, Corte-Real e o sistema da epopeia quinhentista*. Coimbra: Centro Interuniversitário de Estudos Camonianos, 2001.

Arata, Stefano. "La conquista de Jerusalén, Cervantes y la generación teatral de 1580." *Criticón* 54 (1992): 9–112.

Ariosto, Ludovico. *Orlando furioso*. Edited by Cesare Segre. Milan: Mondadori, 1982.

Baldassarri, Guido. "Torquato Tasso." In *Storia generale della letteratura italiana*, vol. 5, edited by N. Borsellino and W. Pedullà, 281–446. Milan: Federico Motta, 1999.

Blanco, Mercedes. "Fábulas de amores en la épica de guerra. De la *Araucana* al *Arauco domado*." *Bulletin hispanique* 121, no. 1 (2019): 17–54.

Bocca, Lorenzo. *Le "Lettere poetiche" e la revisione romana della "Gerusalemme liberata."* Alessandria, Italy: Edizione dell'Orso, 2014.

Carminati, Clizia. "Una insospettata tessera ariostesca nella *Gerusalemme liberata* IV, 17." *Schede umanistiche. Rivista annuale* 23 (2009): 151–9.

Carpané, Lorenzo. "La fortuna editoriale tassiana dal '500 ai giorni nostri." *Italianistica. Rivista di letteratura italiana* 24, nos. 1–2 (1995): 541–57.

Chevalier, Maxime. *L'Arioste et l'Espagne (1530–1650). Recherches sur l'influence du "Roland furieux."* Bordeaux: Université de Bordeaux, 1966.

Choi, Imogen (née Sutton). "La presencia oculta de Torquato Tasso en la *Tercera parte de la Araucana* de Alonso de Ercilla (1589–90)." *Bulletin hispanique* 121, no. 1 (2019): 73–21.

Colonna, Francesco. *Hypnerotomachia Poliphil*. Edited by Marco Ariani and Mino Gabriele. 2 vols. Milan: Adelphi, 1998.

Di Iasio, Valeria. *"Già grande vola, et già trionfa armato."*: *Aspetti della poesía tassiana tra epos e lirica*. PhD thesis. Tutor: Franco Tommasi. Padua, Università degli Studi, 2015.

Di Maldé, Vania. "Fortuna elegiaca della *Liberata*." In *Sul Tasso. Studi di letteratura e filología italiana offerti a Luigi Poma*, edited by Franco Gavazzeni, 161–94. Rome-Padua: Antenore, 2003.

Di Santo, Federico. *Il poema epico rinascimentale e l' "Iliade" da Trissino a Tasso*. Florence: Società Editrice Fiorentina, 2018.

Ercilla, Alonso de. *La Araucana*. Edited by Isaías Lerner. Madrid: Cátedra, 1993.

Ferretti, Francesco. *Narratore notturno. Aspetti del racconto nella "Gerusalemme liberata."* Pisa: Pacini, 2010.

– "Pudicizia e *virtù donnesca* nella *Gerusalemme liberata*." *Griseldaonline* 13 (2013): 1–43.

Freud, Sigmund. *Beyond the Pleasure Principle*. London: International Psycho-Analytical Press, 1922.

Gigante, Claudio. "L'elaborazione della *Gerusalemme conquistata*." In *Esperienze di filologia cinquecentesca (Salviati, Mazzoni, Trissino, Costo, il Bargeo, Tasso)*, 156–201. Rome: Salerno Editrice, 2003.

– *Tasso*. Rome: Salerno Editrice. 2007.

Gómez Canseco, Luis. "El retrato de Alonso de Ercilla en *La Araucana*: variantes y función." *Lemir* 23 (2019): 255–62.

Greene, Thomas M. "The Natural Tears of Epic." In *Epic Traditions in the Contemporary World*, edited by Margaret Beissinger, Jane Tylus, and Susanne Wofford, 190–201. Berkeley: University of California Press, 1999.

Jossa, Stefano. *La fondazione di un genere. Il poema eroico tra Ariosto e Tasso*. Rome: Carocci, 2002.

Martínez, Miguel. *Front Lines: Soldier's Writing in the Early Modern Hispanic World*. Philadelphia: University of Pennsylvania Press, 2016.

– "Writing on the Edge: The Poet, the Printer, and the Colonial Frontier in Ercilla's *La Araucana* (1569–90)." *Colonial Latin American Review* 26, no. 2 (2017): 132–53.

Medina, José Toribio. *La Araucana. Ilustraciones II*. Santiago de Chile: Imprenta Elzeviriana, 1909–18.

– *Vida de Ercilla*. Mexico City: Fondo de Cultura Económica, 1948.

Méndez Herrera, Juan Alberto. "Estudio de las ediciones de *La Araucana* con una edición crítica de la tercera parte." PhD diss., Harvard University, 1976.

Moore, Cyrus. *Love, War and the Classical Tradition in the Early Modern Transatlantic World: Alonso de Ercilla and Edmund Spenser*. Tempe: Arizona Centre for Mediaeval and Renaissance Studies, 2014.

Moretti, Walter. "Tre maestri della tecnica epica tassiana." *Annali della Scuola Normale Superiore di Pisa. Lettere, Storia e Filosofia, Serie II* 30, nos. 1–2 (1961): 1–59.

Palmer, Patricia. *The Severed Head and the Grafted Tongue: Literature, Translation and Violence in Early Modern Ireland*. Cambridge, MA: Cambridge University Press, 2013.

Petrarca, Francesco. *Canzoniere*. Edited by Marco Santagata. Milan: Mondador "I Meridiani," 1996.

Plagnard, Aude. *Une épopée ibérique. Alonso de Ercilla et Jerónimo Corte-Real (1569–1589)*. Madrid: Casa de Velázquez, 2019.

Poma, Luigi. *Studi sul testo della "Gerusalemme liberata."* Bologna: Clueb, 2005.

Quint, David. *Epic and Empire: Politics and Generic from Virgil to Milton*. Princeton, NJ: Princeton University Press, 1993.

Ramachandran, Ayesha. "Tasso's Petrarch: The Lyric Means to Epic Ends." *Modern Language Notes* 122 (2007): 186–208.

Residori, Matteo. *L'idea del poema. Studio sulla "Gerusalemme conquistata" di Torquato Tasso*. Pisa: Scuola Normale Superiore, 2004.

Russo, Emilio. *"A ritmo di corrieri*: Sulla revisione della *Liberata*." In *Festina lente: Il tempo della scrittura nella letteratura del Cinquecento*, edited by C. Cassiani and M.C. Figorilli, 183–203. Rome: Edizioni di Storia e Letteratura, 2014.

Sacchi, Guido. *Fra Ariosto e Tasso: Vicende del poema narrativo*. Pisa: Edizioni della Normale, 2006.

Sannazaro, Jacopo. *Arcadia L'Arcadie*. Text prepared by Francesco Erspamer. Paris: Les Belles Lettres, 2004.

Sberlati, Francesco. *Il genere e la disputa. La poetica fra Ariosto e Tasso*. Rome: Bulzoni, 2001.

Scarpati, Claudio. "Geometrie Petrarchesche nella *Gerusalemme liberata*." *Aevum* 67, no. 3 (1993): 533–70.

Scotti, Emmanuele. "Il problema testuale della *Gerusalemme liberata*." *Rivista di letteratura italiana* 24, nos. 2–3 (1995): 483–500.

Solerti, Angelo. *Vita di Torquato Tasso*. 3 vols. Turin: Loescher, 1895–9.

Sutton, Imogen [later Choi, Imogen]. "'De gente que a ningún rey obedecen': Republicanism and Empire in Alonso de Ercilla's *La Araucana*." *Bulletin of Hispanic Studies* 91, no. 4 (2014): 417–35.

Tasso, Torquato. *Discorsi dell'arte poética. Discorsi del poema eroico*. Edited by Luigi Poma. Bari, Italy: Laterza, 1964.

– *Gerusalemme liberata*. Edited by Lanfranco Caretti. Commentary and introduction by Giorgio Cerboni Baiardi. Ferrara: Franco Cosimo Panini, 1991.

– *Lettere poetiche*. Edited by Carla Molinari. Parma: Fondazione Pietro Bembo/ Ugo Guanda Editore, 1995.

Valencia, Felipe. "Las muchas (aunque bárbaras) voces líricas de *La Araucana* y la índole poética de una historia verdadera." *Revista de Estudios Hispánicos* 49 (2015): 147–71.

Vega, Garcilaso de la. *Obra poética y textos en prosa*. Edited by B. Morros. Barcelona, Crítica, 2001.

Virgil, *Aeneid*. Translated by F. Ahl. Edited by E. Fantham. Oxford: Oxford World's Classics, 2008.

Zapata, Luis. *Carlo famoso*. Valencia, en casa de Ioan Mey, 1566.

Zatti, Sergio. *L'ombra del Tasso. Epica e romanzo nel Cinquecento*. Milan: Mondadori, 1996.

– *The Quest for Epic. From Ariosto to Tasso*. Toronto: University of Toronto Press, 2006.

PART TWO

The Poet as Hero

4 The Many Voices of the Poet: Narrative Polyphony in *Os Lusíadas*[1]

MATTHEW DA MOTA

Não há também Virgílios nem Homeros;
Nem haverá, se este costume dura,
Pios Eneias nem Aquiles feros.[2]

(Have no Virgil nor Homer among us [the Portuguese]; / Nor will there be, if this continues, / Any pious Aeneas or fierce Achilles.)

The extensive critical literature about *Os Lusíadas* (1572) has drawn on themes that have become inextricably linked to how we think of the poem and its author. These include themes of maritime exploration, myth, cartography, and Portuguese imperial expansion in India. However, crucial elements of *Os Lusíadas* that are often overlooked include the way in which the text explores the idea of poetry, the value of poetry to history and culture, and the experience of writing poetry during Luís Vaz de Camões's epoch. An important line of enquiry into the role of the poet and the function of narrative voices in *Os Lusíadas* emerged in the mid-1990s in two essays by Marina Brownlee and Thomas Earle. Both articles were written seemingly without knowledge of the other essay but exploring very similar narrative elements of *Os Lusíadas* that both scholars recognize and theorize. In her essay, Brownlee identifies a tripartite structure of the narrative perspectives in *Os Lusíadas*: 1) the epic bard, deriving authority from poetic tradition and an anonymous voice; 2) the *histor*, who investigates the past and parses history from myth; and 3) the eyewitness, whose authority is derived from experience.[3] For his part, Earle analyses how Camões uses multiple narrators – an omniscient narrator and "restricted" or "limited" narrators, like the main character, Vasco da Gama – to construct an argument about the value of poetry.[4] Accordingly, Earle demonstrates how different narrative voices are used as didactic tools to forward specific arguments throughout the poem. In conjuction, the contributions by Brownlee and Earle map out a complex outlook on the narrative structure of Camões's epic, identifying disperate "voices" in the text and illustrating how the narrative voices in *Os Lusíadas* are both tropic and didactic.

In this essay I revise and expand the exploration of narrative voice in *Os Lusíadas*, which has since received little further attention. I would contend that the multiplicity of voices in the text and the seeming tension between voices is as important as the individual characteristics of each voice. In *Os Lusíadas*, Camões constructs a running dialogue of viewpoints on history, poetry, and empire that not only convey their perspectives to the reader but engage in an active argument with each other, each presenting differing perceptions on the central questions of the poem. These voices not only denote different standpoints but they each perform a type of poetic and narrative role in the text, working together to build a dialogue on the nature of poetry and its role in communicating history. Each voice presents part of a running dialogue throughout the text that ultimately arrives at a moment of covergence of all of the voices into one, at the end of the poem, in an instant of unity and revelation.

In the following pages, I will explore four types of narrative voice and their roles in the poem. The first voice is an omniscient narrator performing the detached voice of the epic narrators in Virgilian-Homeric epic. The voice of the omniscient narrator resurfaces throughout the ten cantos and structures the broad strokes of the poem. The second consists of the character-narrators (Vasco da Gama and Fernão Veloso), who embody the *histor* and the bard of Brownlee. However, I contend that each of these character-narrators presents an incomplete example of poetic narrative, one leaning too far on the historical and the other too steeped in the Romantic tradition of the bard, working together to show two essential sides of epic poetry. The third voice, a self-concious poet-narrator that matches the eyewitness of Brownlee to an extent but is far more personal. In my view, the poet-narrator speaks from a position of weaknes, struggling to tell a story that others will read while also trying to remain truthful and to survive in a world that has become hostile for a poet. Finally, at the end of the poem, all of the disparate and fragmented voices converge in a single unified voice to deliver an exhortation on the future of Portugal, the potential pitfalls of empire, the need for a great king to lead Portugal to correct the course of an ailing kingdom, and the hope that the poem itself, *Os Lusíadas*, has done enough to tell this essential story and to positively help to influence the future of Portugal.

An Anonymous Narrator Establishes the Authority to Speak

Os Lusíadas begins, "Of arms and great men" (As armas e os Barões as-sinalados) (I.1),[5] almost a direct quote of the opening of Virgil's *Aeneid*, "Of arms and a man I sing" (Arma virumque cano) (I.1).[6] Both lines explicitly signal the themes of each poem: arms, the men who wield them, and their deeds. However, implicit in the initial line of *Os Lusíadas* is the choice by Camões to emulate Virgil so closely, which, although reflecting a thematic affinity between the texts, also invokes questions of poetic genealogy and emulation. Camões's bold reference to Virgil makes it impossible for an informed reader to approach his text without establishing a link between the *Aeneid* and *Os Lusíadas*. More than invoking the theme of arms, this first line directs the reader towards a consideration of poetic history by associating a relatively unknown (at the time) Portuguese poet with Virgil, revered as the prince of epic poets, who reached the pinnacle of artistic excellence and imperial sponsorship. The first lines of *Os Lusíadas* signal a reflection on poetry and poetic influence by the poet while also displaying Camões's knowledge of classical epic. Having knowledge of epic influenced the form and style in Camões's writing, as we see in his direct reference to the *Aeneid* in the first line, but I would also argue that the narrator of *Os Lusíadas* emulates the narrators of both Homer and Virgil.

The early modern tradition of emulation of Virgil begins in the medieval era, with Petrarch as the figure who begins the humanist interpretation of Virgil. Hélio Alves argues that it was Petrarch's *Africa* that opened the space for modern epic, which took the spiritual allegory of medieval literature and used it to discuss worldly politics.[7] Petrarch's *Africa* employs Augustinian allegory in emulation of Virgil, which was a means of shedding the troubling multiplicity of romance in exchange for the "ideal unity of epic."[8] This would give way to a continued process of exegesis and emulation of the *Aeneid*, which transformed the epic into the foundational source for a new kind of poetry that could combine spirituality with moral philosophy, while also introducing subtle social and political critique in cultural, religious, and political context where such critique was difficult to get away with. The Latin origins of the *Aeneid* also positioned it as more accessible to Iberian poets of the sixteenth century, many of whom read Latin but were less likely to know Greek. The privileged position of Virgil's poem was amplified by the fact that the *Aeneid* was an essential element of Latin education.[9] Here it is worth recalling Juan Latino (ca. 1517–ca. 1594), a skilled Latinist and Europe's first known Renaissance poet of African descent, whose writings demonstrate a "profound engagement with Virgil."[10] For his part, Camões's proficiency in Latin is evident in his imitation of the culminating prophecy from Sannazaro's *De partu Virginis* (1526), an epic poem in Latin hexameters about the birth of Christ.[11] However, Homer can also be seen as an influence on Iberian poets both through Virgil's emulation and by way of a timely Spanish translation of the *Odyssey* by Gonzalo Pérez, personal secretary and advisor to Philip II. Perez's translation was completed in two stages in 1550 and 1556, and subsequently published in several different cities around Europe.[12] Hélio Alves suggests that although Camões may have read Greek, it was most likely through the 1550 partial translation by Pérez that Camões came to know the *Odyssey*.[13] While other Latin and Greek foundational texts contributed to the early modern humanist conception of epic, in this essay, references to classical epic refer specifically to Virgilian-Homeric epic, which I see as the most prominent classical sources for Camões.

The anonymous, epic narrator of *Os Lusíadas* presides over the majority of the text, remaining omniscient and rarely referring to himself. However, at the beginning of the poem the narrator makes references to an "eu," hinting at an individual poet, but remaining impersonal and performatively anonymous, like in Virgilian-Homeric epic. If the opening line of *Os Lusíadas* directly mimics and draws on the fame of the *Aeneid*, then in the third stanza the narrator speaks as a boastful poet, now challenging not only Virgil, but also Homer:

> Cessem do sábio Grego e do Troiano
> As Navegações grandes que fizeram;
> Cale-se de Alexandro e de Trajano
> A fama das vitórias que tiveram;
> Que eu canto o peito ilustre Lusitano. (I.3)

(No more about the long odyssey / Accomplished by the wise Greek and by the Trojan [Aeneas]; / Silence about Alexander and Trajan / and the famous victories they had; / I sing the illustrious Lusitanian courage.)

The explicit message of this stanza is to celebrate the success of the Portuguese for surpassing the achievements of the ancients. Then again, implicit in these lines is the theme of poetry and poetic lineage. The narrator compares the subject of his poem to earlier epics, particularly the conflict between Greeks and Trojans around which Homer's and Virgil's poems revolve. The narrator positions himself as both a descendant and a reformer of classical epic, bringing the scope of his poetic ambitions to his own time, in stanza eleven (I.11) by calling out

Boiardo and Ariosto directly, and completing the process of "throwing down his poetic gauntlet before the entire tradition of European epic."[14]

The use of "eu" in phrases like *eu canto* occurs several times in the opening stanzas of *Os Lusíadas*; it hints at an individual voice reciting the story, but it remains impersonal and performatively anonymous. Similarly, an "I" is implied when the narrator asks, "Give me now a loftier tone, / A style both grand and natural" (Dai-me agora um som alto e sublimado, / Um estilo grandíloco e corrente) (I.4). Both the "eu" and "-me" indicate a single origin of the text, an "epic bard" in the sense of Brownlee's definition, one who is singing the epic to listeners, or channelling it to the readers in written verse. The implied "I" here is similar to the "I" of Virgil's "Of arms and a man I Sing," and the "me" is that of Homer's "Tell me, Muse, of the man of many ways" (*Odyssey*, I.1). The "eu" introduced in the opening of *Os Lusíadas* is non-specific and not rooted to a particular body; it is a voice in a vacuum bringing the text to life out of a void but remaining detached from the author of the poem. This narrative voice is rootless so as to be able to move seamlessly through time, and speak to the Portuguese monarch, which Camões himself has little authority to do. This narrative voice is perfoming omniscience and detachment, emulating the voice of Virgilian or Homeric epic that is found at the beginnings of their epic poems, using "eu" but without any self attached to the first-person pronoun being used. There are other points in Virgil and Homer where the invocation of "I" is more personal,[15] but in this moment Camões is emulating the detached "I" of the authoritative narrative voice of an epic poem which can be found at the beginning of each text, far removed from the "I" of the individual poet which might introduce critique or lament the state of the world later in such poems and which is also found in the canto VII of *Os Lusíadas*.

In canto I, Camões dedicates his poem to King Sebastião I.[16] In his dedication, the narrator praises and venerates the young Portuguese king, and speaks as if preparing to sing the entire epic to Dom Sebastião in person. Camões was not alone in using apostrophe to invoke the presence of a monarch in an epic poem.[17] Alonso de Ercilla addresses King Philip II of Spain repeatedly at the beginning of *La Araucana*, with the caveat that Ercilla grew up in the Castilian court and travelled extensively in the entourage of the future king. As for Camões, he was not a member of the upper nobility, and most likely did not meet any monarch until later in his life. Only after publishing *Os Lusíadas* did Camões finally meet Dom Sebastião, who honoured the poet. Thus, there is a boldness to the direct address of the king at the beginning of *Os Lusíadas*, not in the content, but in the implied closeness and intimacy of the address.

The boldness of the narrator's address to Dom Sebastião is not mere poetic hubris; rather, it speaks to the great weight that the king's future held for the Portuguese as a figure of hope as well as a figure who sparked fear and pessimism for what might happen if he did not become a successful leader. Vitor Aguiar e Silva argues that the figure of Dom Sebastião in *Os Lusíadas* is not only the object of the dedication of the poem, "he is also the king, and the predestined hero, for whom the epic was written, with whom the poet speaks, whom he advises, whom he questions and appeals to, he is the heir and the culmination of the History of the Portuguese People."[18] Despite the fact that Dom Sebastião lived long after Vasco da Gama's journey and neither saw nor experienced the Portuguese navigation of the oceans, Aguiar e Silva argues that Camões constructs a "fantastic and symbolic authorial appropriation by the monarch which legitimizes an interpenetration or a fusion of the poetic plane of representation and the historical plane of the feats that have taken place."[19] This anachronistic, elusive combination of the king as both keeper of historical memory and embodiment of a heroic future for Portugal is only possible through Camões's delicate construction of this dedicatory and introductory section of the poem.[20] This introductory construct creates a "desired myth" around the figure of Dom Sebastião, one which transforms the king into a providential figure, destined to destroy the enemies of Portugal.

Complicating this intricate interweaving of history and future under the figure of Dom Sebastião, Brownlee argues that rather than simply building up the Portuguese and leading people to revel in glory, the poem "writes from the perspective of disillusion."[21] Although framed as incredibly important and a source of hope, the boy king Sebastião was also a source of pessimism for the Portuguese people, a pessimism which Camões addresses in the dedication and epilogue of *Os Lusíadas*, where he lists the problems facing Portugal, and tells the king what must be done about them.[22] However, Brownlee calls this appeal to Dom Sebastião "a failed speech act"[23] since the king's continued reckless behaviour led to his disappearance in the Battle of Alcazarquivir (1578), opening the door to Spanish dominion over Portugal for sixty years. Rather than being the saviour of the Portuguese Empire, Dom Sebastião would be the cause of its demise.

Unlike the narrators of the *Odyssey* and *Iliad*, for whom the muses are the primary objects of dedication of the poem and the main source of authority, in the case of early modern Iberian epic, narrators also address the king, in order to dedicate the poem to him and as a means of claiming poetic authority by way of the sovereign's authority. This patronage dynamic draws from the *Aeneid* wherein Octavian is the object of dedication and authority, but this dynamic becomes amplified in the Iberian context. The narrator's initial address of the Portuguese king does not actually name him directly, but instead uses different epithets: "And you, well-born guardian / Of Lusitania's ancient freedoms, [...] You, the new terror of the Moorish lancers" (E vós, ó bem nascida segurança / Da Lusitana antiga liberdade, [...] Vós, ó novo temor da Maura lança) (I.6); and "You, tender, young, budding branch / Of Christ's most precious tree" (Vós, tenro e novo ramo florescente / De uma árvore, de Cristo mais amada) (I.7). After two stanzas of addressing this unnamed "vós," just who is being addressed is finally revealed:

> Vós, poderoso Rei, [...]
> Vós, que esperamos jugo e vitupério
> Do torpe Ismaelita cavaleiro,
> Do Turco Oriental e do Gentio. (I.8)

> (You, mighty King, [...] / You, to whom we look to yoke and humble / Arabia's wild horsemen, / The eastern Turk and Gentile alike.)

The king is named directly and placed in literal opposition to Muslims and the Ottoman Empire, initiating an overarching theme of conflict between Christianity and Islam, West and East.

After expounding on the king's importance to Portugal and to Christians, the narrator addresses him with a tenderness uncharacteristic of a poet addressing a sovereign:

> Inclinai por um pouco a majestade
> Que nesse tenro gesto vos contemplo,
> Que já se mostra qual na inteira idade,
> Quando subindo ireis ao eterno templo;
> Os olhos da real benignidade. (I.9)

> (Descend a little from such majesty / For I see on your youthful countenance / Already inscribed that maturity / Which you will bear to eternity's temple; / Turn those royal and benign eyes.)

This address shows a lowly poet asking a godlike king to deign to give him a favourable look and a moment of attention. D. Sebastião is elevated to a divine level, which returns to Aguiar e Silva's discussion of the elevation of D. Sebastião. However, this moment also suggests a proximity of narrator and king, one in which the narrator is literally looking at the sovereign and asking him to turn his head a little so as to be better admired, like a painter directing his model. There is a physical closeness to this moment, with both men in the same room, as well as a social proximity suggested by the extended oration the poet is delivering to the king. Yet it is veiled in deference, and the poet's admiration is that of a loving subject seeking to elevate his beloved king. In this tender moment, the narrator also tells the king that the following verses of the epic will be for him and for Portugal: "[turn your eyes] Toward the ground, to see / This loving tribute of the most valiant deeds / Made into well-wrought verse" (Ponde no Chão: vereis um novo exemplo / De amor dos pátrios feitos valerosos, / Em versos divulgado numerosos) (I.9). The king becomes the source of inspiration for the epic, not only due to the sacred office he represents, but because his body and face embody the virtues and ideals he upholds. Unlike Homeric epic, the muses are not the sole focus of the poem's dedication:

> Ouvi, que não vereis com vãs façanhas,
> Fantásticas, fingidas, mentirosas,
> Louver os vossos, com nas estranhas
> Musas, de engrandecer-se desejosas. (I.11)

> (Behold, you will not hear your people acclaimed for counterfeit exploits, / Fantasies, frauds, lies, / Such as muses elsewhere have invented / eager to enhance themselves.)

The muses are reduced to peddlers of fantasy, whereas the epic that follows is characterized as truth, which exceeds the fantasies and myth of other epics.[24]

The relationship between poet and muse is a deferential yet erotic one, in which the female muses dole out the ability to sing, invoke fear in their capacity to revoke that ability, and inspire poetry through their beauty. The beauty of the muses is replaced at the beginning of *Os Lusíadas* by the promise and youthful beauty of Dom Sebastião, generating a kind of homoerotic or homosocial relation between the poet as inspired artist and the king as object of inspiration and desire. This is not to suggest an actual moment of physical proximity between Camões and D. Sebastião. Rather, this moment in which the worries and hopes of the Portuguese people are combined, where the king is being both instructed and warned, provokes an affective quality in the reader because it embodies such conflicting ideas and emotions. The narrator speaks to the king simultaneously in three modes: as a father to his son, lovingly yet sternly imparting wisdom; as a subject to his godlike king, praising his glory and anticipating greatness; and as a poet to an object of inspiration and desire, admiring and offering lavish praise, yet pained by the unrequited nature of his love. In summary, the omniscient narrator at the beginning of *Os Lusíadas* remains ambiguous and functionally anonymous. The narrator refers to a self, but this is a performance of selfhood to which there is no interior beyond the formulaic platitudes needed to begin the poem, and to establish the necessary authority to speak. This allows Camões to write in a way that encompasses complex emotional, practical, and historical concerns, both to praise and to criticize, in a manner that is both effective and affective, while adhering, at least in part, to the norms of epic poetry, but charting a different direction.

Vasco da Gama and Fernão Veloso Deliver Their Own Narratives

There are several character-narrators in *Os Lusíadas*, but two main Portuguese figures undertake the charge of telling a long story during their journey to India. The first, Vasco da Gama, tells the history of Portugal and of his own journey to his host, the Sultan of Melinde, over the course of cantos III to V. The second, Fernão Veloso, a distinguished soldier on one of the ships, recounts to his fellow sailors and soldiers a chivalric romance at the beginning of canto VI, which is cut short by a massive storm. These two character-narrators use different approaches to deliver their narratives, and the contrast between the two generates a dialogue on the nature of poetry and narrative. Earle argues that character-narrators are used by Camões to introduce his own opinion on certain subjects, and to demonstrate the importance of the poet in preserving the memory of heroes and their deeds, writing that "without the voice of the poet, the hero would be forgotten" (Sem a voz do poeta, o herói seria esquecido).[25] This position on the role of the character-narrators draws on Helder Macedo's similar conclusion that Camões uses his characters to deliver specific messages throughout the text, the characters being subservient to the mission and the will of the poet.[26] In this section, I will re-examine the narratives of da Gama and Veloso to show how these character-narrators not only voice their own arguments within the text but also lend their voices specifically to present fundamental elements of a broader argument on the nature and value of poetry that builds in the narrative.

I. Da Gama

Canto 3 describes the Portuguese arrival at the port of Melinde, where they are welcomed by the Sultan and his people. During their discussion, the Sultan asks da Gama to tell him about the Portuguese people. Inspired by the Sultan's request, da Gama tells him the history of

Portugal over the next two cantos. This historical narrative serves as a miniature epic within the broader poem, and it provides an opportunity for the omniscient narrator to comment on the use and value of poetry in the final stanzas of canto V. Da Gama's narrative history of Portugal follows the development of Portugal into a nation, focusing in particular on historical figures and their accomplishments. Da Gama's historical narrative can be seen as a minor epic within the broader text because it is preceded by an invocation of the muses: "Now, Caliope, teach me / What the Illustrious Gama told the king [of Melinde] (Agora tu, Calíope, me ensina / o que contou ao rei o ilustre Gama) (III.1). However, this invocation is not made by da Gama, who is ignorant of the norms of epic. Rather, it is the omniscient narrator's voice that delivers the invocation, preparing himself to retell da Gama's account of the history. Macedo suggests that this invocation serves to remind the reader that da Gama is a character in the text, and Camões is his author.[27] Thus, the character-narrator da Gama and all other character-narrators have been given the authority to speak only at Camões's discretion and are subservient to the will and plan of the epic's creator.

In this substantial section of the poem, da Gama is boastful and posturing. His source of pride is the Portuguese people and their history. He compares them and their deeds to the mythic heroes of antiquity, questioning whether poetry should capture the deeds of real men rather than the fictional deeds of mythic heroes; he offers a challenge to Homer and Virgil, using historical or non-fictional narrative to unsettle their fictional, mythic authority within the epic genre. Da Gama chastises the ancient poets for writing about such inadequate heroes:

> Cantem, louvem e escrevam sempre extremos
> Desses seus Semideuses e encareçam,
> Fingindo magas Circes, Polifemos, [...]
> Que, por muito e por muito que se afinem
> Nestas fábulas vãs, tão bem sonhadas,
> A verdade que eu conto, nua e pura,
> Vence toda grandíloca escritura! (V.88–9)

> (Let them sing on, piling praises
> On their more-than-human heroes,
> Inventing Circe and Polyphemus [...]
> However they polish and decorate
> With metaphor such vain fables,
> My own tale in its naked purity
> Outdoes all boasting and hyperbole.)

Ancient epic is criticized here as empty and deceptive, lacking historical grounding. Da Gama believes his narrative, *nua e pura*, is rooted in experience and fact rather than poetic artifice, and so it is superior to the Greek and Roman treatments of similar themes. Earle identifies these stanzas (88–9) as an admission by da Gama that his language is inelegant, but that the truth of his words matters more than the eloquence with which those words are delivered.[28] There is a particular regard for historical "truth" in da Gama's elision of epic poetry, which seems to contrast "truth" with "fiction," valuing the former over the latter. It would seem da Gama embodies the *histor* and not the epic bard in the sense of Brownlee's conception of narrative perspectives in *Os Lusíadas*,[29] while the epic narrator is a mix of both perspectives, respecting the importance of history while also defending the value of poetry. The epic narrator does not ever critique history as such, nor does he critique da Gama's arguments in favour of history. However, the epic narrator emerges from behind the mask of performed detachment to critique da Gama's ignorance of poetry. The two narrative voices of the character-narrator da Gama and the omniscient epic narrator work together to provoke an opportunity to argue the value of poetry. Earle demonstrates the instrumentality of da Gama's narration in facilitating this poetic argument, showing that da Gama is made to speak in unintended puns at several points throughout the end of the fifth canto, demonstrating that although he is unaware of his existence as a character in a text, claiming to detest poetry, he is being made to speak in a way that could only exist in a poem, one very carefully controlled and curated by the poet.[30] Further, Macedo writes that "Camões is the author of Vasco da Gama, as if by extension he, and the other historical characters of *The Lusiads*, had no other existence than the one that the poetic text confers on them."[31] Da Gama's purpose at the end of canto V is to provoke discussion of the role of poetry in Portuguese society. In contrast to da Gama's diatribe against poetry, the epic narrator begins to argue that it was Virgil who made Aeneas famous, and Homer who made Odysseus into a timeless hero (V.94), showing the debt characters and the historical figures owe to poets.[32]

Having established the importance of poets in preserving and elevating history, the epic narrator begins to speculate about why poetry is not valued by the Portuguese. Portugal, the narrator argues, gave birth to warriors, "But did not bestow such talents / The lack of which has made them hard and robust" (Mas não lhe dá contudo aqueles dões / Cuja falta os faz duros e robustos) (V.95). Those "talents" not bestowed on the Portuguese are the skills of poetic composition, the appreciation of reading, and also the ability to value poetry and writing as an essential element of a nation and a people. The narrator then explains that the Portuguese generally lack knowledge of poetry because they do not love the art form:

> Sem vergonha o não digo: que a razão
> De algum não ser por versos excelente
> É não se ver prezado o verso e rima,
> Porque quem não sabe arte, não na estima. (V.97)

> (I cannot admit without reproach / The reason we have so few poets / Is that poetry is not an art we love; / For who can cherish what he's ignorant of?)

This critique progresses from a generalized discussion of Portuguese anti-intellectualism to a specific critique of da Gama himself,

> ele, nem quem na estirpe seu se chama,
> Calíope não tem por tão amiga,
> Nem as filhas do Tejo, que deixassem
> As telas douro fino, e que o cantassem. (V.99)[33]

> (For in truth neither [da Gama] nor anyone in his lineage is named / For Calliope does not favour him, / Nor do the nymphs of the Tejo, enough to sing of him / Leaving aside their cloths of fine gold.)

Here da Gama is shown to be driven by patriotic passion, but lacking in the inspiration that comes only at the grace of the muses, the nymphs of the Tagus, and particularly Calliope, the muse of epic poetry. Thus, da Gama is not a poet and his epic cannot stand in as a suitable narrative of Portuguese history. Rather, this history must be told with the support and help of the muses in order to be successful. Da Gama has done a valiant job of trying to tell this story with limited resources and little outside help, but he lacks the proper inspiration. This lack of inspiration is the result of a hardening of the Portuguese people in the absence of great poetry, identified by the narrator.[34] Although Portuguese accomplishments might surpass those of mythic figures like Achilles and Aeneas, without a Portuguese Virgil or Homer to sing of their deeds, those deeds will not be remembered. The epic narrator claims the Portuguese "have no Virgil nor Homer among us; / Nor will there be, if this continues, Any pious Aeneas or fierce Achilles" (Não há também Virgílios nem Homeros; / Nem haverá, se este costume dura, / Pios Eneias nem Aquiles feros) (V.98). The hero and the poet are connected in an inextricable bond wherein the words of the poet preserve, enhance, and spread the story of the hero while the hero provides the material and inspiration out of which the poet writes.

Both Brownlee and Earle favour looking at da Gama's character as well as those of the other character-narrators in *Os Lusíadas*, in a way that focuses on their instrumentality in pushing forward specific arguments or ideas in the text. Rather than simply seeing references to classical epic and mythology in *Os Lusíadas* as examples of emulation, or of the poet paying homage to past poets, Earle suggests that we should understand the use of these sources as a thematic statement by the author about how to read the poem.[35] He argues that Camões is using references to show how wrong da Gama's perspective on poetry is, and to make a case for the importance of poetry in general.[36] These parallels should be considered by readers as instructional moments aimed towards specific didactic ends rather than moments of simple homage to great poets of the past. Brownlee takes up a similar perspective, exploring how negative myths are used to describe and evaluate da Gama throughout the epic and, "in so doing, Camões seeks to dramatize the fact that da Gama's success in pagan romance terms constitutes a failure in terms of Christian epic. The economy of *material values* and the economy of *spiritual values* are presented as being mutually defining negatively; one is the negation of the other."[37] Through this negative association we are shown that the hero da Gama is monstrous, or that his success can also be constituted as failure. Character-narrators, often historical figures, are used in *Os Lusíadas* as a means of drawing the reader to consider opposing sides of a conversation on the value and nature of poetry. I would contend that the character of da Gama is at once the hero of the epic and the means by which the anti-intellectual and anti-poetic sentiments of the Portuguese are exposed as well as a means of provoking a critique of the Portuguese aristocracy, of which da Gama is a representative. The back and forth between da Gama and the epic narrator runs throughout the text, constantly positioning and representing da Gama in ways that further the argument in favour of poetry.

II. Veloso

More than other character-narrators, Fernão Veloso works within the text to express, explicitly, not the value of poetry, but the principles on which good poetry should be based. On the journey from Melinde to India, da Gama's ships are caught in a storm. Shortly before this event, Veloso begins a poetic narrative, which will subsequently be cut short by the growing storm. First mentioned during da Gama's narrative, when he describes the ships' first landfall in Africa, Veloso is one of the men who goes ashore and is later chased back to the ships by enemies while da Gama is wounded in his efforts to help save Veloso and his other comrades (V.24–36). Earle draws parallels between Veloso's landfall and the episode of the Cicones in the *Odyssey* (9.39–61). The two works show the first disembarkations in both journeys, which lead to a skirmish with seemingly pacific strangers; both commanders (Odysseus and da Gama) being frustrated by delays in re-embarking their ships; and both commanders subsequently wounded in a battle by the shore.[38] The scene takes on an almost comical quality as the men laugh and joke about Veloso's near-death experience, which is in keeping with the swashbuckling, devil-may-care attitude of the historical figure Veloso.[39] This levity contrasts with the actual danger in which the men find themselves, something exemplified by da Gama's wound. From this early moment on, Veloso is established as a soldier and sailor who is deeply connected to the actual daily conflicts and struggles of enlisted men at sea; this positioning of the character comes to define how we read and understand Veloso's own poetic interlude in the text. Veloso relates a very different story than da Gama's history of Portugal. It is called the "Doze de Inglaterra," which offers an account of twelve Portuguese knights who go to England to fight in a tournament as the champions of twelve ladies. On the way to the tournament, rather than sailing with the others, Álvaro Gonçalves Coutinho, or O Magriço (the Skinny), decides to ride by himself to the tournament to explore and have an adventure, arriving just in time for the tournament. It is after the Portuguese knights win the tournament and are received by the Duke of Lancaster to celebrate and be honoured that the story is cut short by the storm.

The stanzas in which this episode is contained provide a vivid image of life at sea, with Veloso telling his companions a tale to which they listen attentively. Veloso's telling of the story is initiated by a fellow sailor, Leonardo, another distinct character in *Os Lusíadas*; he asks for a story about love to pass the time at sea with merriment, to which Veloso responds:

> Não é (disse Veloso) cousa justa
> Tratar branduras em tanta aspereza,
> Que o trabalho do mar, que tanto custa,
> Não sofre amores nem delicadeza;
> Antes de guerra, férvida e robusta
> A nossa história seja, pois dureza
> Nossa vida há-de ser, segundo entendo,
> Que o trabalho por vir mo está dizendo. (VI.41)

(It is not [said Veloso] right / To tell tender themes amid such harshness; / The work of the sea, which is so demanding, / Does not suffer love nor refinement; / Instead, war, fervid and rough / Must be the theme of our story / Grim days await us, as I understand, / The hardest work has yet to come.)

Veloso suggests that the harshness of the sea and of war justifies an emphasis on difficult topics in the story, rather than focussing on subjects that will distract from reality. The men agree with Veloso's argument, and so he begins,

Contarei (disse) sem que me reprendam
De contar cousa fabulosa ou nova;
E por que os que me ouvirem daqui aprendam
A fazer feitos grandes de alta prova,
Dos nacidos direi na nossa terra,
E estes sejam os Doze de Inglaterra. (VI.42)

(I will tell [my story] but let no one claim / I am telling fable or fiction / For those who listen to me will learn, / Of the great and honourable deeds / Of these men from our land [Portugal] / The Twelve of England.)

At the outset, Veloso warns against questioning the veracity of his account. The distinction between fact and fiction in his narrative is not to be questioned. Veloso then tells his story over the next thirty stanzas, when his narrative is cut off. As the crewmen urge Veloso to continue, they hear the bosun's whistle sounding the alarm for a coming storm, and the men are forced to join in to help save the ship. Again, Veloso is in the fray, participating in the daily tasks of life at sea, not spared from the responsibility of helping keep the ship afloat in a storm. Returning to Veloso's initial claim about the theme of his narrative, one of the harshest realities of the sea – a storm – comes to define this episode, cutting Veloso's story short. In similar manner to how da Gama's narrative is commented on by the epic narrator to expose irony or inconsistency in his position on poetry (being made to speak in puns or not realizing that he is a character in a poem), the action surrounding Veloso's narrative also intrudes upon his narration. However, in the case of Veloso, the intrusion on his narrative does not contradict his views, but reinforces his initial claim that poetry should reflect the harsh realities of life. Despite Veloso's appeal to poetic mimesis, the story of the Twelve Knights is a narrative that remains in the realm of romance in many ways, thus complicating our understanding of epic as an expansive genre. But, true to his claim that harsh reality be brought into conversation with fantasy and romance, his Chivalric romance is interrupted by a destructive storm and is never finished. Veloso is shown as a skilled poet, but the difficult realities of sailing and colonial expansion do not accommodate his type of narrative, a reality which he already acknowledges. Veloso is a man of another time, both in his poetic style and in his approach to military endeavours. He is a warrior poet, rooted in the codes of arms and letters, but he understands how this paradigm is outdated, and he seeks to embrace the realities of a new, shifting world. It is this internal contradiction in the character-narrator Veloso that is exposed by the interjection of the storm into his story. The epic narrator, performing anonymously now rather than directly commenting on Velosos's words, interjects into Veloso's romance to prove Veloso's earlier point that poetry should, in fact, reflect some elements of reality.

In *Os Lusíadas*, Veloso is the only character who is a poet. He is valued by his friends as a storyteller and begins to tell a story that is captivating and complex. We can contrast this with da Gama's narrative, which was more historical in nature: although it is an important story told by the hero of the epic, the reader learns that da Gama does not hold the favour of the muses. Da Gama's story lacks the poetic flare of Veloso's narrative, and though Veloso's lacks the rigorous historical basis of da Gama's narrative, he too acknowledges its importance. Veloso is interrupted by a storm, and we are not given the opportunity to hear the end of his story. We do, however, hear from him one last time as the ships arrive on the Isle of Love, where da Gama and his men receive the rewards for their journey.

In canto IX, as the sailors are exploring the Isle of Love, Veloso is amazed by the lush forests and the overall beauty of the island, saying,

> Mais descobrimos do que humano esprito
> Desejou nunca, e bem se manifesta
> Que são grandes as cousas e excelentes
> Que o mundo encobre aos homens imprudentes. (IX.69)

> (We have found more than the human spirit / Could ever desire: plainly, / Wonders exist, and marvels are apparent, / Though the world hides this from the ignorant.)

Here, near the end of the poem, Veloso suggests that it is only the wise – those who are neither reckless nor ignorant – who can see what is magical and truly spectacular in the world. In three short episodes, he shows the persistent potential for danger and violence in their journey to India (as well as the potential for comedy in otherwise terrifying moments); he argues for stories that reflect the harshness of life and, in turn, is interrupted by circumstances that illustrate the harshness of life; and, finally, at the end of the poem, he observes that there is great beauty and wonder in the world, but that it is not always apparent to those who do not have the wisdom to see it. For Veloso the world is revealed to him throughout the poem to be dangerous, harsh, beautiful, wondrous, and mysterious. Reality consists of all the good and the bad elements that Veloso identifies, but as he says in the ninth canto, the world hides beauty and wonder from those who are ignorant, from those who do not know how to see. The character in *Os Lusíadas* who we see continuously to be exposed as ignorant is da Gama, and in turn the Portuguese elite. If ignorance in the world of *Os Lusíadas* refers to ignorance of poetry, then Veloso can be understood to be advocating for poetry as a means of understanding the complex beauty and wonder of the world, something that is not easily revealed to those who do not have the knowledge that allows them to see it. Upon arrival at the Isle of Love, Veloso is struck by the physical beauty of the landscape, provoking a revelation about the nature of the world. It is no surprise that the only character that could be described in some sense as a poet is the one who arrives at this conclusion. It is Veloso's knowledge and appreciation of poetry that allows him to see what those who are ignorant of poetry do not.

Ultimately, whereas da Gama works to promote the importance of history, Veloso works to promote the value of the fictive elements of poetry. Veloso achieves that by experiencing a transformation from someone who argues that poetry should deal only in the harsh realities of life to someone who also appreciates the intangible beauty of the world, and the value of poetry in revealing that beauty. This is not a contradiction in Veloso's character. Rather, he first expresses the important idea that poetry should be mimetic, an idea which reforms da Gama's view of poetry, recognizing the importance of history that da Gama identifies, but combining it with the value of poetry in communicating and preserving that historical knowledge. As the narrator indirectly tells us, there will be no da Gama without a Camões. However, this view of poetry does not encompass Veloso's conception of poetry entirely as he goes on to tell a story that is thoroughly rooted in romance, telling his listeners not to question which parts of the story are fictive and which parts are real. Finally, upon arrival at the successful end of their pagan epic journey,[40] Veloso understands that his seemingly disparate positions on poetry are not in fact contradictory. Rather, Veloso arrives at a tentative but coherent theory of epic that combines the importance of history with the value of poetic artifice and the fabulous in order to create a more affective narrative.

The Poet-Narrator Reflects on His Life

At the end of canto VII, as da Gama rests and eats with his men on shore in Calicut, his brother Paulo da Gama invites Monçaide, the Muslim aide to the Samorin of Calicut, aboard their ship. Paulo da Gama conveys to Monçaide the history of Portugal by showing him oil paintings of various fictional and historical Portuguese figures. Paulo begins by showing Monçaide a painting of the mythic pre-Roman Portuguese figure, Lusus: "His costume was wholly Greek in manner; / In his right hand was a branch like a banner" (No trajo a Grega usança está perfeita; / Um ramo por insígnia na direita) (VII.77). In an instant, the register of the text shifts, becoming introspective. A new voice – neither that of Paulo da Gama nor the epic narrator that we have already encountered – interjects in the middle of the description of the painting,

> Um ramo na mão tinha … Mas, ó cego,
> Eu, que cometo, insano e temerário,
> Sem vós, Ninfas do Tejo e do Mondego,
> Por caminho tão árduo, longo e vário! (VII.78)

> (In his hand was a branch … But what / Blind folly is this that I embark, / On a voyage so hard, so long and varied / Without you, nymphs of the Tejo and Mondego?)

The sudden shift in conjugation from past tense to present is followed by an ellipsis, a figure not used anywhere else in the text, and which was printed in the original first edition of *Os Lusíadas*. This ellipsis reflects a thought pattern, a moment of hesitation and reflection, which gives way to an entirely new line of thinking,[41] one in which the narrative voice (whomever it might be that is narrating at this moment) begins to criticize himself about his own blindness, and to reflect on a need of the muses to continue his epic. This moment of hesitation constitutes a metatextual hesitation on the part of the narrator, which initiates a new poetic register in the narration. The narrator is no longer performing omniscience and detachment from the action in the text but is now the central subject of the action; the reader is temporarily transported out of the epic narrative of *Os Lusíadas* and into a completely different setting, a small space, perhaps a bedroom in which a poet reflects on a text he is writing. Self-reflective digressions such as this are rarely, if ever, encountered in epic, and it introduces an entirely new narrative perspective into *Os Lusíadas* which is only hinted at throughout the rest of the text – that of the poet himself commenting on the epic while he is composing it. The ellipsis disrupts the narrative time and initiates an introspective, subjective digression that completely departs from the narrative norms of Virgilian epic that have dominated the text until this point. This digression initiates more uses of the personal pronoun "eu," but not the performative "eu" from the beginning of the text: this new "eu" represents a historical and narrative "self" speaking within the text without the protection or comfort of the omniscient mask employed by the epic narrator throughout the text.

This new narrative voice, a poet-narrator, is a distinctly "real" figure interjecting into the text, wrestling with internal conflicts about his life and his writing. The poet-narrator has strayed from his intended path and now must ask for help from the muses:

> Vosso favor invoco, que navego
> Por alto mar, com vento tão contrário
> Que, se não me ajudais, hei grande medo
> Que o meu fraco batel se alague cedo. (VII.78)

> (I implore your help, for I am sailing / The high sea with such a contrary wind / That, if you do not help me, I fear / That my slight craft will soon flood.)

Sailing a rough sea is used as a metaphor for poetic composition, as if the narrator were navigating towards an unclear destination. Like Odysseus's appeal to the gods as his small craft is torn apart by a great storm on the way home from the Isle of Calypso, the narrator finds himself in troubled waters and in need of help, finally turning to the river nymphs and muses of Portugal to ask for aid in completing his fraught task.[42] There are several invocations of the muses in *Os Lusíadas*, but this one at the end of canto VII is unique in its pleading nature, and in the lack of confidence that it seems to betray in the poet. This is not an invocation by someone who is sure of the love the muses have for him, or who is confident that they will, in fact, answer his call.

The poet-narrator shows that writing poetry is unforgiving, and despite the purest intentions, does not ensure honours, wealth, or freedom. Poetry is characterized as a heroic pursuit that does not follow the classic model of glory and honour. Unlike the martial heroism of Aeneas, Achilles, Odysseus, and da Gama, poetry does not guarantee fame, and suffering is not a path to martyrdom but simply a reality to endure. Camões's life tells a similar story. He lived a hard life abroad, in exile for much of his adulthood, working as a low-level functionary, soldier, and sailor throughout the Portuguese Empire in Asia and Africa, writing poetry along the way but never working solely as a poet. He ultimately returned home to publish *Os Lusíadas*, which gave him some fame and success under the patronage of King Sebastião. However, until the publication of this text he did not live the life of a celebrated poet. When the poet-narrator says

Olhai que há tanto tempo que, cantando
O vosso Tejo e os vossos Lusitanos,
A Fortuna me traz peregrinando
Novos trabalhos vendo e novos danos (VII.79)

(Consider the years I have spent, singing / Of Your Tagus and your Lusitanians, / While fortune kept me drifting / From one task and trial to the next),

there is a resonance with the experiences of Camões's early life, that of being recognized as a skilled poet but also facing hardships.[43] *Os Lusíadas* was written abroad and, although this is not an explicit theme of the text, this self-reflective aside gestures at the material conditions in which the epic was written, and how those conditions might have shaped the narrative. At the end of the same stanza, the poet-narrator compares himself to Canace: "Like Canace who is condemned to death / In one hand always the sword and the other the pen" (Qual cânace que à morte se condena, / Nũa mão sempre a espada e noutra a pena) (VII.79). Brownlee describes Canace as the "putative author of Ovid's eleventh heroid" who writes a letter to her brother as she is preparing to commit suicide after unwittingly committing incest with the same brother.[44] Brownlee argues that this is a character who, by writing about incest, transgresses the laws of writing as well as natural laws by committing incest to begin with.[45] For Brownlee, Camões's decision to reference Canace is an acknowledgment of his own "double transgression for he is writing *of* transgression (that is, da Gama's transgression of enshrined epic values) while exposing the act of writing itself as a transgression against the institutionalized epic voice."[46] Camões's transgression of the "institutionalized epic voice" can be perceived in the text through the multiple narrative voices, the voices of the character-narrators, and the ways in which these voices play off each other to achieve specific goals throughout the text. The act of transgression in writing allows him to escape the wretched material circumstances in which he finds himself. Thomas Hart argues that Camões chooses to speak in his own voice, in spite of the powerful people who oppose his views, in order to enhance the dramatic implication of his text.[47] Although I disagree that it is Camões's own voice in the text, the implications of Hart's argument remain valid, as the poet-narrator speaks from a personal perspective, attempting to sway the opinion of a hardened and hostile Portuguese elite, creating an added sense of danger, drama, and urgency to the poet-narrator's plea.

The poet-narrator reflects on his wretched state of poverty, monotonous in its persistence and worsened by the inhospitable and foreign locale in which he finds himself. It is in this context of discomfort and exile that he chooses to write a poem celebrating his homeland, but the distance and precariousness of his situation wears on his ability to tell the story faithfully and with the level of focus needed. Having renewed hope for the future, the poet-narrator hints at new dangers that he faces, "Now on my back, life slipping away / That hung from a thin thread / Which by no less a miracle was saved" (Agora às costas escapando a vida, / Que dum fio pendia tão delgado / Que não menos milagre foi salvar-se) (VII.80). Pimpão argues that this moment of great bodily danger, when his life "hung by a thin thread" (dum fio pendia tão delgado), refers to the mythic shipwreck that Camões survived off the coast of China, which is thought to have been off the coast of modern-day Vietnam, near the Mekong Delta.[48] The shipwreck is presented in this moment of *Os Lusíadas* as an impediment to writing, a moment when individual experience injects into the world of the text, disrupting the structure and language in a way that makes the reader address the realities of the poet-narrator's life and its impact on the text. This is not a typical epic narrator who remains outside of time and tells the story as if it has been divinely inspired. Enduring hardship while writing further characterized the poet as a heroic figure who must overcome hardship in order to deliver his epic. The act of writing is placed on the same plane as the martial heroism of the other Portuguese heroes celebrated in the poem. The combination of the poet-narrator with elements of Camões's biography and the mythology surrounding the poet collapses the separate categories of author, narrator, and character, creating a complex intersection of perspectives, voices, and sources of authority.

Continuing his address to the nymphs and muses, the poet-narrator laments,

E ainda, Ninfas minhas, não bastava
Que tamanhas misérias me cercassem,

> Senão que aqueles que eu cantando andava
> Tal prémio de meus versos me tornassem. (VII.81)

> (And yet, my nymphs, it was not enough, / That such miseries surrounded
> me / But that the very men whose deeds I praised / Should reward my
> poetry as they did.)

He thought that singing about the heroes in the narrative would earn
the favour of the aristocratic class of which the heroes are members.
With this favour he hoped his suffering would end in praise and rewards for his work, but he only found more suffering. Although many
of the men mentioned in the poem are dead by the time Camões is
writing (1545–70), the class of "heroes" – the aristocratic ruling class –
remains intact, and perhaps even more in control of Portugal and its
empire than in the time of da Gama. It is this aristocratic class that
antagonized Camões through forced conscription, exile, arrest, imprisonment, and other indignities, a class which is, in turn, described
as antagonizing the poet-narrator in the text. The expectation that
such a celebratory, national poem should be greeted with praise is
disrupted by cruel, powerful men who disregard the value of poetry
and poets.

The poet-narrator asks for the favour of the muses so that he might
have the strength to continue writing despite the hardship in which he
finds himself:

> Pois logo, em tantos males, é forçado
> Que só vosso favor me não faleça,
> Principalmente aqui, que sou chegado
> Onde feitos diversos engrandeça. (VII.83)

> (So now, beset by such evils, your / Bounty must not fail me, especially /
> Now I approach a canto where / Further achievements must be praised.)

This vulnerable poet-narrator needs the muses in a way that the initial narrator of the epic did not. After he has established the stakes of
this bargain, the poet-narrator asks them to give favour only to him,
promising in return not to waste their imparted skill on the unworthy:

> Dai-mo vós sós, que eu tenho já jurado
> Que não no empregue em quem o não mereça,
> Nem por lisonja louve algum subido,
> Sob pena de não ser agradecido. (VII.83)

(Give but yourselves. I return my oath / I shall not waste it on the worthless, / Nor flattery of powerful men. / Since such ingratitude would be my just reward.)

Establishing a new covenant with the muses is followed by a list of negative qualities among the Portuguese "heroes" that should not be praised. He describes men who put self-interest, ambition, and vice above service (VII.84). He rails against others who misuse their authority to dominate, who are two-faced and deceitful "like proteus,"[49] and who pretend to please the king while robbing the poor (VII.85). Finally, he condemns those who are strict in their payments to workers while also taxing punitively, enriching themselves on the backs of the poor (VII.86). These are the kinds of false heroes the poet-narrator will no longer praise, resolving to focus only on the deserving. This promise to the muses marks a moment in which the poet-narrator takes control of the narrative and sets out a new trajectory, and what Aguiar e Silva calls a new "code of ethics of Camões' epic."[50] In the narrative world of *Os Lusíadas*, the poetic voice takes precedence over inherited titles or positions of power. This chastisement of the Portuguese elite in favour of the poor is a rare moment of political commentary that is not often seen in epic texts; it is a brief but jarring critique of the power structures in Portugal, and abroad in its colonies. Following his pledge to reorient and rededicate the poem, the poet-narrator makes one last statement at the end of the canto, before returning to the omniscient narrative voice:

> Apolo e as Musas, que me acompanharam
> Me dobrarão a fúria concedida,
> Enquanto eu tomo alento, descansado,
> Por tornar ao trabalho, mais folgado. (VII.87)

(Apollo and the Muses, who accompany me / Will double the fury they grant me / As I take a breath, well rested, / To return to my work with renewed energy.)

Now the pagan deities Apollo and the Muses assist him with his work moving forward, doubling his resolve to complete the task at hand. The final few lines of the seventh canto serve as a resolution of the interlude initiated by the ellipsis located ten stanzas earlier.

The Resolution of a Fractured Self

Following canto VII the text resumes its main narrative, detailing the betrayal of the Portuguese by the Samorin of Calicut and the unexpected assistance given by the Muslim Monçaide to aid the Portuguese escape. The story then follows da Gama and his men to the Isle of Love, where they finally rest and engage in orgiastic eating, drinking, and implied sexual intercourse with Thetis and the nymphs living on the island. It is strange that a text modelled on Virgilian and to a lesser extent Homeric epic should have a "homecoming," which is actually an arrival at a mythic place, far from home. Odysseus arrives at the island of Calypso, but eventually he must leave to achieve his homecoming in Ithaca. Aeneas also has his interlude of love with Dido, but this too must end so he can arrive in Italy and found Rome. For da Gama and his men not to have a proper homecoming is a rare diversion that is unique to *Os Lusíadas*. The men do in fact "arrive" at home just before the end of the epic, but the entire journey, from leaving the Isle of Love to arriving in Lisbon, is summarized in one stanza:

> Assi foram cortando o mar sereno,
> Com vento sempre manso e nunca irado,
> Até que houveram vista do terreno
> Em que naceram, sempre desejado.
> Entraram pela foz do Tejo ameno,
> E à sua pátria e Rei temido e amado
> O prémio e glória dão por que mandou,
> E com títulos novos se ilustrou. (X.144)

(So behold them ploughing the calm seas, / With friendly winds, not a hint of a storm, / Until their homeland, the country long / Yearned for, rose before their sight. / They entered the pleasant Tagus, and gave / Their country and their honoured king / The prize for which they sailed at his command, / Placing still greater titles in his hand.)

This is a brief mention of a long and arduous journey, one which skips over what traditionally spans much of the final third of any epic. Moreover, the moment of homecoming, of reuniting with family and friends, and of reporting successes and tragedies to the king and others, are all elements that are missed in the rush to finish the poem. However, though the narrative is rushed at the end, there are eleven stanzas after the brief homecoming where a new voice emerges to comment on Portugal and to give advice to the young king as he begins his ill-fated reign.

The new narrator speaks with the authority of the omniscient, classical narrative voice while also maintaining the self-conscious, embodied subjectivity of the poet-narrator of canto VII. The didactic monologue of the final stanzas begins by addressing the muses and referring to the body of the narrator:

Nô mais, Musa, nô mais, que a Lira tenho
Destemperada e a voz enrouquecida,
E não do canto, mas de ver que venho
Cantar a gente surda e endurecida. (X.145)

(No more, Muse, no more, my lyre / Is out of tune and my throat hoarse /
Not from singing but from wasting song / On a deaf and coarsened people.)

The lyre is out of tune, and the narrator's voice is hoarse from singing an epic for a deaf and fierce people. Aguiar e Silva calls this moment a "rupture of the epic song" that introduces the "narrator's pained voice which confesses his discouragement, his tiredness and his bitterness."[51] The narrative is inexhaustible, as it has divine origins, but the vessel through which it flows is mortal, prone to tiring and wearing out, a very embodied, human moment for the narrator. This plea is followed by the refrain that the Portuguese, for whom *Os Lusíadas* is being written, are unappreciative and undeserving of such a story:

O favor com que mais se acende o engenho
Não no dá a pátria, não, que está metida
No gosto da cobiça e na rudeza
Dũa austera, apagada e vil tristeza. (X.145)

(Those rewards which encourage genius / My country ignores, being given
over / To avarice and philistinism, / Heartlessness and degrading misery.)

The same complaints of the fifth and seventh cantos re-emerge, but now the narrator has the ability to end the story, having successfully completed his memorialization of the Portuguese people and of da Gama. Although the hoarse voice, the disappointment with his audience, and the address to the muse are in the voice of the poet-narrator, there is an assurance and firmness to the tone that does not ask permission to end the story, but tells the muse, "no more." The poet-narrator has taken full control of his own poem, no longer depending on others to give him fame or respect, or on the muses to give him the strength to tell his story. Rather, he decides now is the point at which to end. Once again, he speaks to the king directly with a familiarity that is uncharacteristic of a humble poet, as the disembodied "eu" did in the beginning of the text, but now the mask of anonymity has been removed, exposing the poet himself. The vulnerable, embodied poet-narrator finally overlaps with the confident, omniscient, epic narrator. This embodied narrative voice speaks as the architect of the text, commenting on his finished work, speaking as Camões the poet, whether this is an idea, or the voice of the poet himself matters very little. What is important, however, is the effect on the reader of arriving at an ending of the poem and then seeing a new narrative voice emerge to deliver a coda: "who am I that speaks, humble, low and rough, / Unknown, even undreamed of by you?" (Mas eu que falo, humilde, baxo e rudo, / De vós não conhecido nem sonhado?) (X.154). These words seem almost to tease the reader, asking "who am I?" before Camões the narrator reveals himself, claiming to have both martial and poetic prowess:

> Pera servir-vos, braço às armas feito,
> Pera cantar-vos, mente às Musas dada;
> Só me falece ser a vós aceito,
> De quem virtude deve ser prezada. (X.155)

> (In your service, an arm inured to battle; / In your praise, a mind given to the Muses; / All I lack is due approval where / merit should meet with esteem.)

Thus framing himself as the ideal Iberian epic poet. Martial experience was not an essential quality for the classical poet; however, in the world of Iberian epic, this discourse of experience became essential to the poet's persona.

This final narrative voice boasts of his abilities as an epic poet and argues for the need of a great epic poet and a great epic for the Portuguese people. Having argued throughout *Os Lusíadas* for the value of poetry and its invaluable role in preserving and amplifying history through the ages, the narrator makes a final case for why he should be the poet of the Portuguese and why this poem that the reader has just finished is the ideal epic poem for Portugal. He concludes,

> A minha já estimada e leda Musa
> Fico que em todo o mundo de vós cante,
> De sorte que Alexandro em vós se veja,
> Sem à dita de Aquiles ter enveja. (X.156)

> (My esteemed, beloved Muse / I sing of your exploits throughout the world; / So that Alexander in you is seen / No longer coveting Achilles's praise.)

This assertion appears at first as a final nod to the pagan muses of Olympus and the nymphs of the Tagus. The narrator is claiming that only through such an epic as Camões has written can Dom Sebastião achieve the fame and respect that Achilles enjoys, and heroes like da Gama can come to be known in the same register as their mythic counterparts. The mention of Alexander the Great refers to his supposed envy that Achilles had Homer to immortalize his deeds while he had no such poet to do the same for him. Here, Camões argues that D. Sebastião need not hold such envious sentiments towards the Greek hero now that he has his own Homer, Camões himself. The end of the poem advocates for a respect and veneration of poetry, not only in service of fame and glory but as a means of survival, a language and form through which history can be preserved, a vessel that contains identity and memory. The final lines of the text seek to justify and exalt the entire poem not only to the level of a national epic but to a universal status. The *Iliad*, the *Odyssey*, and the *Aeneid* are seen as more than mere poems; rather, they are vessels of imperial and historical authority.

NOTES

1 I owe a great debt of gratitude to several scholars who read earlier versions of this essay and provided valuable feedback: Hélio J.S. Alves, Mercedes Blanco, Thomas Earle, Jill Ross, and Emiro Martínez-Osorio.

2 *Os Lusíadas*, V.98.

3 Brownlee, "The Dark Side of Myth in Camões' 'Frail Bark,'" 177–8. Brownlee adapts her argument on narrative perspective in *Os Lusíadas* from Robert Scholes and Robert Kellogg, *The Nature of Narrative*, 242–3.

4 Earle, "Voz narrativa, ironia e a defesa de poesia n'*Os Lusíadas*," 294. Earle's text was first published in English in 1995. The version of his essay used for this chapter is a 2013 Portuguese translation and update to the original.

5 All translations are based on the Landeg White translation of *Os Lusíadas* with my own adjustments designed to preserve meaning rather than rhyme and metre, as White so artfully does. Citation places the number of the canto first, followed by verse number (i.e., "I.1").

6 Carlos Ascenso André points out that although both epics describe multiple armies and battles, the key distinction between the *Aeneid* and *Os Lusíadas*, as exemplified in the opening lines to each poem, is the object of their narratives. Where the *Aeneid* is about Aeneas, *Os Lusíadas* celebrates a collective hero, "o peito ilustre lusitano" (Camões I.3) *Eneida* e *Os Lusíadas* in *Diccionario de Luís de Camões* 337. However, in his extensive commentary

on the poem, Manuel de Faria e Sousa argues that "o peito ilustre" could refer to no figure other than Vasco da Gama, using extensive analysis of language use throughout the poem to show that the word "ilustre" is always used to refer to da Gama while other characters are referred to differently, thus complicating the meaning of the epithet. Camões, ed. Faria e Sousa I, column 148–53.

7 Alves, *Camões, Corte-Real e o Sistema da Epopeia Quinhentista*, 25.

8 Warner, *The Augustinian Epic*, 77.

9 See Warner, *The Augustinian Epic*, and Andrew Wallace's chapter "Forgetting Epic" in *Virgil's Schoolboys: The Poetics of Pedagogy in Renaissance England* for more on the impact of Virgil on early modern readers, particularly in the context of the use of the *Aeneid* as a tool of Latin language education. Warner's work details the most influential medieval editions of Virgil's works, including the *Aenied*, as well as the vernacular translations of the sixteenth century, which helped to shape humanist perspectives on epic poetry. Wallace explores the uses of Virgil's works in early modern education both in its influences in the classroom and in the anxieties and complexities provoked in schoolmasters by the *Aeneid*, which Wallace argues were a source of inspiration for English epic to "forget" epic and in turn to escape the trapping of epic poetry in pursuit of more productive modes of writing (226–7).

10 Wright, *The Epic of Juan Latino*, 29.

11 See Nicolopulos, *The Poetics of Empire in the Indies*, 189.

12 See Muñoz Sanchez's "'El mejor de los poetas' para 'el mejor de los príncipes'" which explores Gonzalo Perez's translation of the *Odyssey* and its implications both in the context of the early modern reception of Homer and the impact the translation had on Philip II. A complete edition of *La Ulixea de Homero* was published in 1562, having undergone significant changes. Muñoz Sanchez argues that Pérez's translation project constituted a politico-allegorical appropriation of Homer's poem to the end of making the future king "un auténtico principe del renacimiento" (148).

13 See Alves, "Presença da *Odisseia* em Camões." Alves gives the example of the divine council in *Os Lusíadas* (I.40), which shares more similarities with the *Odyssey* (I.80–6) than with similar episodes from the *Aeneid*, as evidence that Camões had at least some familiarity with Homer's epic. However, Alves also shows how some of the "Homeric" moments of *Os Lusíadas*, such as the episode with the giant Adamastor (V.39), are in fact more Virgilian than Homeric, emulating the Homeric moments of the *Aeneid* rather than directly emulating the *Odyssey*. Alves, "Presença da *Odisseia* em Camões," 41–3.

14 Nicolopulos, *The Poetics of Empire in the Indies*, 185. The intertextuality of Ariosto's and Camões's texts is explored extensively in Almeida, "Poesia,

furor e melancolia." For more on Boiardo, Ariosto, and Camões, see Ferro, "Boiardo," 94–9, and Marnoto, "Ariosto," 38–42.

15 For an example of the more personal "I," see the *Aeneid*, "Fortunati ambo! Siquid mea carmina possunt, / nulla dies umquam memori vos eximet aevo, / dum domus Aeneae Capitoli immobile saxum / accolet imperiumque pater Romanus habebit" (Virgil, *Aeneid*, 446–9).

16 It is likely that Camões began composing *Os Lusíadas* before D. Sebastião was born and certainly before he was king, making it difficult to know when the dedication was written. For a comprehensive discussion of the timeline of composition of *Os Lusíadas*, and specifically of the dedication, see Aguiar e Silva, "Camões e D. Sebastião," 129–31, and Houwens, "A Cronologia da Composição de Os Lusíadas," 301. Aguiar e Silva seems to agree with Houwens that it is likely that Camões returned to Lisbon before developing some of the more complex critiques and ideas surrounding D. Sebastião, as he would not have had the same access to information about the court and the king while abroad or at sea. Aguiar e Silva, "Camões e D. Sebastião," 131.

17 Oliveira e Silva explores the multiple addresses to the king in *Os Lusíadas* as a running process of rhetorical persuasion. See Oliveira e Silva, "Moving the Monarch."

18 Aguiar e Silva, "Camões e D. Sebastião," 129. Translations are my own.

19 Aguiar e Silva, "Camões e D. Sebastião," 129.

20 Aguiar e Silva, "Camões e D. Sebastião," 129.

21 Brownlee, "The Dark Side of Myth in Camoes' 'Frail Bark,'" 178.

22 Brownlee, "The Dark Side of Myth in Camoes' 'Frail Bark,'" 178.

23 Brownlee, "The Dark Side of Myth in Camoes' 'Frail Bark,'" 178–9.

24 The Tagides of the Tagus, Caliope, and other nymphs and muses do, also, play a major role in *Os Lusíadas*. See Pena's "As Musas," in *Diccionario de Luís de Camões*, 628–9.

25 Earle, "Voz narrativa, ironia e a defesa de poesia n'*Os Lusíadas*," 288. Translation is my own.

26 Macedo, "O braço e a mente," 61. Referenced by Earle in "Voz narrativa, ironia e a defesa de poesia n'*Os Lusíadas*," 289.

27 Macedo, "O braço e a mente," 61.

28 Earle, "Voz narrativa, ironia e a defesa de poesia n'*Os Lusíadas*," 293

29 Brownlee, "The Dark Side of Myth in Camoes' 'Frail Bark,'" 177–8.

30 Earle, "Voz narrativa, ironia e a defesa de poesia n'*Os Lusíadas*," 293.

31 Macedo, "The Poetics of Truth," 18. For more on the poetic text conferring meaning on characters in *Os Lusíadas*, see Figueiredo, *A Autocomplacência da Mimese*, chs. 3–4.

32 Earle, "Voz narrativa, ironia e a defesa de poesia n'*Os Lusíadas*," 288–9.

33 These lines are an allusion to Garcilaso de la Vega's third *Eclogue*: "Their woof was of the gold which Tagus brings / From the proud mountains in

his flow divine, / Well sifted from the sands wherewith it springs, / Of all admixture purified and fine" (Las telas eran hechas y tejidas / del oro que el felice Tajo envía, / apurado después de bien cernidas / las menudas arenas do se cría) (Écloga III, stanza 14). Translation from Wiffen's translation of Garcilaso's works.

34 Earle contends that this attack on da Gama at the end of canto V is an attack on anti-intellectualism in general, which was prevalent in sixteenth-century Portuguese society, even among elites (Voz narrativa, ironia e a defesa de poesia n'*Os Lusíadas*," 291). Earle writes that "Humanism arrived late to Portugal, and the aristocrats whom D. Manuel sent to command the forces in the East, were particularly against everything related to literature, even the act of writing itself." He goes on to quote the first viceroy to India, D. Francisco de Almeida, expressing his contempt for the expectation that he be a good writer in order to discharge his duty properly. Cited from Correia, *Lendas da Índia*, 1.910.2. Further, Earle highlights how Almeida's successor Afonso de Albuquerque could write well, but still hated and insulted writers, referencing Albequerque as quoted in *Cartas de Affonso de Albuquerque seguidas de documentos que as elucidam*, 1.157.

35 Earle, "Voz narrativa, ironia e a defesa de poesia n'*Os Lusíadas*," 294. Earle cites Faria e Sousa's discussion of the poem as an example of the misreading, or simplistic reading, of classical references in *Os Lusíadas*.

36 See Earle, "Voz narrativa, ironia e a defesa de poesia n'*Os Lusíadas*," 294–5. Earle suggests that evidence of didactic references to classical epic can be found in the parallels between the island of Circe in the *Odyssey* and Thetis on the Isle of Love in *Os Lusíadas* (cantos IX and X); the cyclops Polyphemus in the *Odyssey* (book 10) and the giant of the Cape of Good Hope, Adamastor, in *Os Lusíadas* (V.37–60); the Sirens in the *Odyssey* (10.39) and the nymphs of the Isle of Love (cantos IX–X).

37 Quote from Brownlee, "The Dark Side of Myth in Camoẽs' 'Frail Bark,'" 179. Brownlee provides several examples of this "negative mythology": da Gama's prolonged conflict with Bacchus, supposedly the first to discover India, as a transgression against a father-like figure like Lusus, the mythic progenitor of the Portuguese, who is either the son or close friend of Bacchus (180); at the end of canto V, when the narrator praises Alexander the great for his deeds (V.93), but denigrates da Gama (V.94–8) for his inability to appreciate the "exemplary figures from the past" (183); and the comparison of da Gama to Adamastor both for his defiance of the gods and for his coerced seduction of Thetis the sea nymph (canto IX), much like Adamastor forcing himself on a different Thetis, the wife of Neptune (184). Brownlee concludes that "If we are inclined to read this series of parallel features shared by the giant and the explorer as a mark of the latter's

prowess, we are called upon at the same time to view da Gama's behaviour as monstrous" (184). Emphasis mine.

38 Earle, "Voz narrativa, ironia e a defesa de poesia n'*Os Lusíadas*," 295–6.

39 Veloso is mentioned in Barros's and Castanheda's histories as a real figure on da Gama's voyage who achieved some fame through his exploits at sea and abroad. See Barros, *Da Ásia*, vols. 1, 3, & 4; and Castanheda, *História do descobrimento & conquista da Índia pelos portugueses*, vols. 1 & 2.

40 The term "pagan epic" comes from Brownlee's conception of distinct pagan and Christian epic journeys that take place in *Os Lusíadas*. See Brownlee, "The Dark Side of Myth in Camoẽs' 'Frail Bark,'" 179.

41 Delaney attributes a similar function to the use of a dash in a short story by Thomas M. Disch: "A voice begins, telling us an entire story in a single clause, then breaks off because the vision has suddenly cleared. The consciousness behind the voice has suddenly become aware, signed by the dash, that the story is more complicated than this opening clause states. The statement of the first clause has allowed the images all to move steps ahead in the many layered fields of mental resolution. Certainly, the voice intended to say more, but, in that dash, we may have a sign of how surprised the writer (not the speaker) was at the sudden awareness of how much more there was to say." Delany, *The American Shore*, 40–1.

42 This may also be a reference to Ariosto's "Hor, se mi mostra la mia carta il vero" in *Orlando furioso*, canto XLVI, ottave 1–2, in which he uses the analogy of a ship at sea to describe the composition of his poetry.

43 Although details of his life are difficult to confirm, it is generally accepted that Camões was forced to go to war in North Africa, where he lost his eye, and then was exiled to the Portuguese overseas territories shortly after his return to Lisbon, not returning to Europe for almost seventeen years. For more information on the life of Camões, see Matos, "Biografia de Luís de Camões," 80–94; the introductory pages to Faria e Souza's translation of *Os Lusíadas* (1639); and Storck, *Vida e Obras de Luis de Camões*.

44 Brownlee, "The Dark Side of Myth in Camoẽs' 'Frail Bark,'" 189.

45 Brownlee, "The Dark Side of Myth in Camoẽs' 'Frail Bark,'" 189.

46 Brownlee, "The Dark Side of Myth in Camoẽs' 'Frail Bark,'" 189.

47 Hart, "The Author's Voice in *The Lusiads*," 54–5.

48 Camões, *Os Lusíadas* [Pimpão edition], 421. This shipwreck is the setting for the, perhaps apocryphal, story of Camões swimming to shore with the manuscript of the unfinished *Os Lusíadas* in one hand, holding it above the water to save it from the sea.

49 Refers to Odysseus, the protean "Man of many ways" or "Man of twists and turns."

50 Aguiar e Silva, "Camões e D. Sebastião," 130.

51 Aguiar e Silva, "Camões e D. Sebastião," 133.

WORKS CITED

Aguiar e Silva, Vítor. "Camões e D. Sebastião." In *Diccionário de Luís de Camões*, edited by Vítor Aguiar e Silva, 228–34. Lisbon: Leya, 2011.

Albequerque, Affonso. *Cartas de Affonso de Albuquerque seguidas de documentos que as elucidam*. Edited by Raymundo Antonio de Bulhão Pato. 7 vols. Lisbon: Academia Real das Sciencias, 1884–1935.

Almeida, Isabel. "Poesia, furor e melancolia: notas sobre Ariosto e Camões." In *Magnum Miracolo est Homo: José Vitorino de Pina Martins e o Humanismo*, edited by Maria das Graças Moreira de Sá et al., 93–108. Lisbon: Universidade de Lisboa, 2008.

Alves, Hélio. *Camões, Corte-Real e o Sistema da Epopeia Quinhentista*. Coimbra: Por Ordem da Universidade de Coimbra, 2001.

– "Presença da *Odisseia* em Camões." *Revista Camoniana*, 3rd series, vol. 12. São Paulo, 2005.

Ariosto, Ludovico. *Orlando furioso*. 2 vols. Venice: Gabriel Giolito de Ferrari e fratelli, 1555–6.

Ascenso André, Carlos. "*Eneida* e *Os Lusíada*." In *Diccionário de Luís de Camões*, edited by Vítor Aguiar e Silva, 337–41. São Paulo: Leya, 2011.

Barros, João de. *Da Ásia*. 3 vols. Lisbon: Germão Galherde, 1552–63.

Brownlee, Marina. "The Dark Side of Myth in Camoẽs' 'Frail Bark.'" *Comparative Literature Studies* 32, no. 2 (1995): 176–90.

Camões, Luis vaz de. *Lusíadas*. Edited by Manuel de Faria e Souza. Madrid: Ivan Sanchez, 1639.

– *The Lusíads*. Edited by Landeg White. Oxford: Oxford University Press, 2001.

– *Os Lusíadas*. Edited by Álvaro Júlio da Costa Pimpão. Lisbon: Ministério dos Negócios Estrangeiros, 1972.

– *Os Lusíadas de Luis de Camões*. Lisbon: Antonio Gõçalves, 1572.

Castanheda, Fernão Lopes de. *História do Descobrimento & Conquista da Índia Pelos Portugueses*. Coimbra: Imprensa da Universidade, 1924–33.

Correia, Gaspar. *Lendas da Índia*. 4 vols. Coimbra, Imprensa da Universidade, 1922.

Delany, Samuel R. *The American Shore: Meditations on a Tale of Science Fiction by Thomas M. Disch – "Angouleme."* Middletown, CT: Wesleyan University Press, 2014.

Delasanta, Rodney. *The Epic Voice*. The Hague: Mouton, 1967.

Earle, Thomas F. "Voz narrativa, ironia e a defesa de poesia n'*Os Lusíadas*." In *Estudos sobre cultura e literatura portuguesa do Renascimento*. Coimbra: Imprensa da Universidade de Coimbra, 2013.

Ferro, Manuel. "Boiardo." In *Diccionário de Luís de Camões*, edited by Vítor Aguiar e Silva, 94–9. Lisbon: Leya, 2011.

Figueiredo, João R. *A Autocomplacência da Mimese*. Coimbra: Angelus Novus, 2003.

Garcilaso de la Vega. *Obras Completas con Comentario*. Edited by Elías L. Rivers. Madrid: Castalia, 2001.

– *The Works of Garcilaso de la Vega*. Translated by J.H. Wiffen. London: Printed by James Moyes, Greville Street, 1823.

Greene, Thomas. *The Descent from Heaven: A Study in Epic Continuity*. New Haven, CT: Yale University Press, 1963.

Hart, Thomas R. "The Author's Voice in *The Lusiads*." *Hispanic Review* 44 (1976): 45–55.

Houwens, H. Post. "A Cronologia da Composição de *Os Lusíadas*." *Occidente* 83 (1972): 293–316.

Homer. *Iliad*. Translated bvy Robert Fagles. New York: Penguin Classics, 2009.

– *Odyssey*. Translated by Emily Wilson. New York: W.W. Norton & Company, 2017.

Livy, Titus. *The History of Rome*. Cambridge, MA: Harvard University Press, 1997–2004.

Macedo, Helder. "O braço e a mente. O poeta como herói n'*Os Lusíadas*." *Arquivo do Centro Cultural Português* 16 (1981): 61–72.

– "The Poetics of Truth." In *The Traveling Eye: Retrospection, Vision, and Prophecy in the Portuguese Renaissance*, edited by Fernando Gil and Helder Macedo, 15–32. Dartmouth: University of Massachusetts Press, 2009.

Marnoto, Rita. "Ariosto." In *Diccionário de Luís de Camões*, edited by Vítor Aguiar e Silva, 38–42. Lisbon: Leya, 2011.

Matos, Maria Vitalina Leal de. "Biografia de Luís de Camões." In *Diccionário de Luís de Camões*, edited by Vítor Aguiar e Silva, 80–94. Lisbon: Leya, 2011.

Muñoz Sánchez, Juan Ramón. "'El mejor de los poetas' para 'el mejor de los príncipes': *La Ulixea de Homero, traducida de griego en lengua castellana por el secretario Gonzalo Pérez*, un tratado cortesano de educación principesca." *Calíope: Journal of the Society for Renaissance and Baroque Hispanic Poetry* 22, no. 1 (2017): 141–63.

Nicolopulos, James. *The Poetics of Empire in the Indies. Prophecy and Imitation in "La Araucana" and 'Os Lusíadas."* University Park: Pennsylvania State University Press, 2000.

Oliveira e Silva, John De. "Moving the Monarch: The Rhetoric of Persuasion in Camões's Lusíadas." *Renaissance Quarterly* 53 (2000): 735–68.

Pena, Abel N. "Musas (Mito das)." In *Diccionário de Luís de Camões*, edited by Vítor Aguiar e Silva, 628–9. Lisbon: Leya, 2011.

Quint, David. "The Boat of Romance and Renaissance Epic." In *Romance: Generic Transformation from Chrétien de Troyes to Cervantes*, edited by Kevin Brownlee and Marina Scordilis Brownlee. Hanover: University Press of New England, 1985.

Storck, Wilhelm. *Vida e Obras de Luis de Camões: Primeira Parte*. Translated by Carolina M. Vasconcellos. Lisboa: Academia Real das Sciencias, 1898. (Second volume planned but never completed.)

Scholes, Robert, and Robert Kellogg. *The Nature of Narrative*. Oxford: Oxford University Press, 1966.

Virgil. *Aeneid*. Translated by Robert Fagles. New York: Penguin Classics, 2009.

Wallace, Andrew. *Virgil's Schoolboys: The Poetics of Pedagogy in Renaissance England*. Oxford: Oxford University Press, 2010.

Warner, J.C. *The Augustinian Epic, Petrarch to Milton*. Ann Arbor: University of Michigan Press, 2005

Wright, Elizabeth R. *The Epic of Juan Latino: Dilemmas of Race and Religion in Renaissance Spain*. Toronto: University of Toronto Press, 2016.

5 Eyewitness, Hero, and Poet: Alonso de Ercilla in the Three Parts of *La Araucana*[1]

AUDE PLAGNARD

Dad orejas, señor, a lo que digo,
que soy de parte de ello buen testigo.[2]

(Lend ears, my Lord, to what I say, / For to a portion of it I am a faithful witness.)

With these introductory verses Ercilla transformed the epic genre's characteristic pact with the reader in an entirely original way. Unlike Virgil, who sang beseeching the muse's favour, Ercilla, imitating Ariosto, found inspiration in the attentive ear of his dedicatee: "Vi faro udir, se voi mi date orecchio" (I will relate to you, if you give me your ear).[3] However, whereas Ariosto's song captivated the listener's attention by the novelty and wonder of the tale – "cosa non detta in prosa mai né in rima" (Things yet unspoken in prose or rhyme)[4] – Ercilla put forth a more convincing argument for requiring an attentive ear: "I am a faithful witness."[5] By emphasizing Ercilla's status as a "faithful witness," the fifth stanza of *La Araucana* introduced an original strategy of self-representation in the modern epic, whereby the poet ascended all at once to the role of hero and of guarantor of his own epic fiction. Seen in this light, we could even conceive Ercilla's poem as "autobiographical epic" literature, one of the aspects of the text that has attracted the attention of scholars.[6]

Emerging from a rather marginal position of writing (literarily speaking) – that of soldier and poet in the military campaigns at the far reaches of the Hispanic monarchy – Ercilla effectively introduced into the high poetic register of his epic a mechanism of self-representation distinctive to the soldier's condition, undoubtedly contributing to the enormous success of *La Araucana*. Yet translating the perspective of a soldier and an eyewitness into poetic language could not be achieved immediately and required several experimental phases. This essay proposes a reconsideration of the structuring of Ercilla's testimonial poetics between 1557, the year of his earliest documented presence in America, and 1590, the year in which the first complete version of the poem in three parts was published, four years before his death. My hypothesis is that Ercilla's role as a "faithful witness," far from being immediately bestowed on him upon his return from the New World, entailed a long process of invention and a profound transformation of his image as an author.

Text and Author *in fieri*

The three parts of *La Araucana* retain traces of this slow maturation process. In the words of Mercedes Blanco, it is not a Greek temple but rather a "cathedral"; that is, as with many medieval cathedrals, it is an architectural assemblage made up of successive styles whose construction spanned several decades, if not centuries.[7] In contrast, the events narrated in the poem concern a relatively concise chronological period (1553–8), and the assembled thirty-seven cantos are remarkable for their coherence.

The first memorable event recounted in the poem dates back to the final days of 1553: the death of Pedro de Valdivia on 25 December narrated in the third canto. Around this time, or soon afterwards, while he was in England, Ercilla had the opportunity to speak with Valdivia's emissary to the throne, Jerónimo de Aldrete.[8] With Aldrete, who had been appointed governor of Chile, Ercilla travelled to America at the end of 1555, and later joined the army of Aldrete's successor, García Hurtado de Mendoza, who set sail from Lima for Chile in February 1557. Until Ercilla was exiled from that land, probably in December 1558, he had a little less than two years to formulate his project for an epic narration of the battles, learn how to compose verses on such subject matter, and, perhaps, draft a series of poetic sketches that would represent the initial tesserae for the future epic. The third part of the poem concludes on one hand with Ercilla's departure from Chile and his return to Europe, and on the other, in the thirty-seventh canto, with Philip II's annexation of Portugal, much more recent from the point of view of the author and his readers at the end of the 1580s. Ercilla joined the campaign in Portugal and, although he does not recount the battles in which he participated, he could also defend his position as an eyewitness to this event.

When *La Araucana* first appeared in 1569 – or rather what would eventually be its first part with fifteen cantos – Ercilla had just taken his place in the royal court and was still single; his poetic career was only just beginning, from zero, or almost. Although the fifteenth canto (García Hurtado de Mendoza's armada engulfed by a storm on their way from Peru to Chile) ends with the promise to continue the story and to appear as the witness Ercilla had announced, in truth nothing assured the reader that he would fulfil his manifest desire to continue the poem or that he knew how many parts he would add to conclude his story. Indeed, the title of the volume published in 1569 does not mention that this was a "first part," in contrast with other epic poems published in several instalments, and whose first part was identified as such from its initial publication, including those by Jerónimo Sempere, Juan de Castellanos, and Bernarda Ferreira de Lacerda.

In 1574, when Ercilla requested permission to reprint the first part, whose initial run had sold out, he again gave no sign that he was planning a continuation of the story, despite the fact that he was likely to have already been considering it at that point. He did not reveal his intentions between the publications of the second (1578) and the third (1589) instalments either, though once again he aroused a strong expectation for the story to continue when he suspended the action at the end of canto XXIX, freezing Tucapel's sword in mid-air for more than eleven years before it could finally plunge down upon Rengo. In other words, the exceptional coherence of the three parts of *La Araucana*'s final version – prepared in that manner for the 1589–90 edition while Ercilla was still alive – was devised a posteriori and for many years the poem remained a text *in fieri*.

At the same time, Ercilla's personal circumstances evolved significantly between 1569 and 1590. He went from being a young man to entering old age. From being a soldier whose service to the throne was poorly compensated, to a prosperous businessman and official representative of the Crown in diplomatic missions. From an unknown, in the eyes of contemporary poets and scholars, to an influential appraiser of works of poetry and protégé of the Council of Castile. In each of these stages, the representation of the author and his relationship with the characters in his own poem was modified considerably. Indeed, in 1569 *La Araucana* was the epic poem that, more than any other, ancient or modern, dealt with the most recent subject matter, as well as the most distant in geographic terms.[9] As a result, many of the poem's characters were still living at the time and were also included among the poem's first readers – and its author identified himself as the hero. For example, García Hurtado de Mendoza, who penned a beautiful laudatory poem included in the second part; or "those hoary heads once youthful" (jóvenes ya canos) who fought with Ercilla in Chile and reappear in the prophetic narration of the Battle of Lepanto (XXIII.84.8). This contemporariness also played an essential role in the development of his authorial perspective: the alterations between the Ercillan ethos and his intratextual figure in 1569, 1578, and 1589 show less the evolution of Ercilla as a protagonist of the wars of conquest than that of Ercilla, author and courtier in Madrid. The "faithful witness" defended in the fifth stanza was consequently modified.

Soldier and Eyewitness

The basis for the poem's *inventio* is Ercilla's presence as soldier and eyewitness to the wars in Chile. The prologue to part 1 dates the composition of the poem back to precarious circumstances of the military campaigns:

> este libro, [...] porque fuese más cierto y verdadero, se hizo en la misma guerra y en los mismos pasos y sitios, escribiendo muchas veces en cuero por falta de papel, y en pedazos de cartas, algunos tan pequeños que apenas cabían seis versos, que no me costó después poco trabajo juntarlos.

> (this book, [...] for greater veracity and authenticity, was composed at height of war, and in the very junctures and sites where I wrote many times on leather for lack of paper, and on scraps of letters, some so small that they barely contained six verses, joined together later at the cost of no little effort.)

Scholars disagree with respect to the credibility of these assertions. For Mercedes Blanco, only a naive reader would give a literal value to Ercilla's claims, contradicted by the long decade separating his testimonial experience and the publication of the first part of the poem, the majority of which Ercilla did not witness first-hand.[10] In contrast, Miguel Martínez documents the existence of a form of poetry (epic), beyond just the case of Ercilla, that was exercised in spaces of war, lending substance, weight, and historical authenticity to the fiction conceived by the poet.[11] Both critical positions are easily reconciled if we interpret Ercilla's words in terms of a self-fashioning: when he began composing *La Araucana*, he gave his text the appearance of a historical account and devised his position as author around the activity of the poet-soldier.

In effect, Ercilla made every possible effort to narrow the identification between the auctorial position – which defends the work's authorship in the legal paratexts, on the frontispiece of the volume, in the prologue to the reader, and the dedication to the king – and the first-person narrator. In the dedication to the king, which precedes the prologue, he adopts a biographical perspective and locates his epic tale within a long series of services offered to the Crown: by his father, Fortún García de Ercilla, deceased while he was still a member of the Royal Council; by his mother, Leonor de Zúñiga, head governess of Empress María's ladies-in-waiting; and by himself as a page to Prince Philip and later as a soldier who voluntarily enlisted to fight against Hernando Pizarro's rebellion and against the Mapuche. The dedication to the king is therefore inscribed in a continuum of a life of service and rooted directly in Ercilla's presence "amidst those very arms":

> paresciéndome que aún no cumplía con lo que deseaba, quise también el pobre talento que Dios me dio gastarle en algo que pudiese servir a vuestra majestad, porque no me quedase cosa por ofrecerle. Y así, entre las mismas armas, en el poco tiempo que dieron lugar a ello, escrebí este libro ... (1569, f. 4v)

> (feeling that I had yet to fulfil my purpose, I determined to spend the meager talent that God gave me on something that would serve Your Majesty, so as to not have anything else left to offer. And so, amidst those very arms, during the scant time afforded me, I wrote this book ...)

In other words, the value of Ercilla's offering to the king is based on the correlation between the conditions under which the poem was written and the historical content it narrates. This correlation is further reinforced by the five laudatory poems that, as the poem takes the shape of a book, precede (f. 8r–v) and follow (f. Ccr–Cc2r) the fifteen cantos: each one praises Ercilla for his dual talents wielding a sword and a pen, and one of the authors explicitly identifies himself as a soldier and veteran of the wars of conquest using the name "Cristóbal Maldonado el Indiano" (f. Ccr). To legitimize this first part of the poem, Ercilla did not surround himself with famous poets or other persons of note among the Republic of Letters at the time he gave a voice to those who could vouch for his experience as a soldier.[12] The portrait of the armour-clad poet, included at the end of the 1569 volume, contributed to the construction of this image (see fig. 5.1).[13] This is a fundamental aspect of the Ercillan ethos, one that was destined to endure. In 1589, some thirty years after having left America, and the same year as the publication of the final part of *La Araucana*, Ercilla once again underscored his American experience and his alleged role as eyewitness to authorize the publication of the second volume of Juan de Castellanos's *Elegías de varones ilustres de Indias*, in which he recognized "faithfully written many of the things and particularities that [he] saw and learned in that land during the time [he] spent there."[14] Also included in this third part was the "Lawyer Cristóbal Mosquera de Figueroa's Tribute [...] to Don Alonso de Ercilla" (Elogio del Licenciado Cristóbal Mosquera de Figueroa [...] a don Alonso de Ercilla). It opens with a splendid portrait of Ercilla "knight of vigorous determination and unacquainted with fear" (caballero de animosa determinación y ajeno de todo temor) during the wars in the Arauco region, which leads the author to celebrate the ideal of the union of arms and letters: "his glory comes as much from being a famous poet as from being a famous soldier" (se le debe tanta gloria por famoso poeta como por famoso soldado).[15] And there are several other examples of the same kind of praise that could be cited here.

This construction of Ercilla's role as a soldier and witness in order to legitimize his standing as a poet keeps with the actions that he undertook during that early period of his life to bring recognition to his services to the Crown. Thanks to José Toribio Medina, we have access to the transcripts of a considerable number of archival records related to Ercilla's life.[16] When examined along with his aforementioned *Vida de Ercilla*, these documents confirm that the poet's actions as a soldier during the military campaigns in the Arauco region are not recorded anywhere outside of his own testimony. In fact, in chapters IV and V dedicated to Ercilla's time in Chile, there are ample formulas that refer us back to *La Araucana* as the only source, a circular reasoning that bases the poet's life on his own poetic testimony.[17] There are, however, a total of five documents that mention Ercilla's services to the Crown in Chile between 15 September 1559 and 23 December 1560 and the compensation that he received in exchange. The first and most decisive of them, titled "Declaration by Don Alonso de Ercilla in the certified statement of achievements and services of Don Francisco de Irarrázabal (September 15, 1559)" (Declaración prestada por don Alonso de Ercilla en probanza de los méritos y servicios de don Francisco de Irarrázabal [15 de septiembre de 1559]),[18] contains fourteen statements given in Lima[19] by Irarrázabal, a soldier of Basque origin like Ercilla's family, and corroborated by the latter as his witness. Throughout declarations 1 to 14, we follow the parallel lives of the two men: both were pages to prince Philip in their youth (1) and travelled to America with Jerónimo de Aldrete in order to serve the Crown's interests in the Viceroyalty of Peru (2); both resided at the home of Viceroy Andrés Hurtado de Mendoza prior to enlisting in the army that was sent to Chile under the command of the Viceroy's son García Hurtado de Mendoza, appointed as the new governor of the region (3); they fought together in the same encounters (4–10), and together took part in the expedition to Ancud led by the governor (11) and the founding of the city of Osorno

Figure 5.1. Portrait of Alonso de Ercilla included in the first edition of *La Araucana* (1569). Courtesy of the Bibliothèque Nationale de France.

(12); and lastly, they left Chile at the same time with the intention of requesting compensation for the expenses they had incurred in service to the Crown (13–14).[20] Throughout this declaration, however, as the result of a procedural rhetoric characteristic of juridical documentation, we hear Ercilla mention time and time again how he bore witness to his compatriot's every action and experience. Not only does the word "witness" appear in each of Ercilla's answers (except for the fourth and sixth), but also his speech is full of verbs and expressions testifying to his presence at the site of the events, e.g., "he found himself," or with the senses on which his testimony is based, e.g., "he saw," "he heard."[21] Consequently, for Ercilla, his role as a witness in America was a legal reality long before it was expressed in his poetry. Capturing the attention of the king was the fundamental goal of this process.

Nevertheless, the similarities between Ercilla's status as a soldier-witness during the war efforts and as a poet-witness to the events that he narrates are confirmed by the manner in which he addresses the king. Among the extant documents written by Ercilla in America is a letter he wrote to Philip II on 31 October 1559 in which he asks for assistance, if not urgent help, in dealing with the expenses that he had incurred while taking part in the campaigns of conquest. While the letter from 1559 mentions financial motives and very clearly requests a *repartimiento* (a royal tribute grant of Indigenous people) as compensation for the expenses he incurred as a soldier, the poem's dedication to the king, published in part 1, expands the services offered to the Crown to include those from earlier in the poet's life as well as those of his family, requesting in exchange the king's support of the text. Furthermore, his *probanza de méritos* spans the whole of the poem and is epitomized in a fragment from the poem's third part, in which Ercilla repeats and summarizes the biographical list of services he rendered to the Crown (XXXVI.32–41).[22]

Another detail from his 1559 letter to the king also deserves our attention. In it Ercilla mentions an earlier letter sent from Chile in which, prior to his request for financial assistance, he had recounted all the events he had witnessed: "From Chile I wrote to Your Majesty making you aware of the events of that land as truthfully as I could at that moment" (Desde Chile escribí a V. M. haciéndole saber el suceso de aquella tierra lo más verdaderamente que supe hasta aquel punto).[23] If we trust the poet's statement, this first letter was in fact written amidst those very arms and certainly possessed the degree of authenticity that Ercilla later attempted to reconstruct, artificially, in his poem. The poem therefore could have been the extension of an earlier account, of which Ercilla hoped to take greater advantage. Indeed, the soldier received an answer to his petition in the form of a "Royal dispatch" (Real cédula) sent to the governor of Chile and signed on 23 December 1560 in Toledo, for which he received a *repartimiento de indios*.[24] This dispatch mentions the services that Ercilla had rendered to the Crown during his time as a soldier, but never any services as a witness or narrator of events. Upon his return to Spain, it is evident that Ercilla intended to make a name for himself in this second category, which would in turn set him apart from his military comrades.

Eyewitness, Historian, and Poet

Becoming the poet of a *historia verdadera* was not, however, an easy task. A possible approach, and one which Ercilla adopted at the outset of his poetic career, consisted in imitating the ethos and the style of a type of narrative that was very much in fashion at the time: that of the chroniclers, witnesses to the empire's distant wars.[25] In fact, the style of the first part of *La Araucana* imitates some of the characteristics of historical and testimonial prose. This is also the part that resorts least to amorous fiction, the one that excludes almost all marvellous elements, and the one that delivers the longest chronological and military sequence of the war in the Arauco region. These stylistic features are calculated so as to endow the poem with a resemblance to historiographical texts.[26] The soldier-witness is promoted to the rank of historian, via the imitation of an ethos convenient to the author of a chronicle or a written account.[27]

However, from this point of view, Ercilla's position is founded on a paradox: while he does in fact develop a series of rhetorical manoeuvres in the first part to establish his credibility as an eyewitness, he also admits that he only witnessed "part" of the events. In truth, the part that he was witness to was small, if not negligible, given that he only arrived in Peru and later Chile during the early months of 1557, that is, when the story of *La Araucana*'s first part concludes. Ercilla never set foot on Mapuche land *sensu stricto* during the span of time related in the poem's first fifteen cantos since the story stops during the storm that delayed the arrival of García Hurtado de Mendoza's armada in Chile. Therefore, the construction of his role as eyewitness requires a veritable act of funambulism on Ercilla's part. Excepting the prologue and the initial verses, which assume the testimonial aspect to be clearly established, the matter of Ercilla's presence is never considered until much later in the story and during an episode unrelated to the wars in Chile: the arrival of Viceroy Andrés Hurtado de Mendoza to Lima. This narrative, geographical, and military digression realized by the poet is justified by a poetic reflection on the story's degree of "authority" and the "credit" that the poet requires (XII.70.4 and XII.74.3). Both of these questions rely on various factors prior to and after the moment that Ercilla identifies as his arrival: "For the things I have thus far narrated / I, my Lord, was not present" (Hasta aquí lo que en suma he referido / yo no estuve, Señor, presente a ello) (XII.69.1–2).

Prior to introducing himself in the plot, Ercilla bases his story on a rigorous survey of "[im]partial interpreters" ([im]parciales intérpretes) and witnesses belonging to "both sides equally" (ambas las mismas partes) (XII.69.4–5); that is, he utilized the methods of a historian and compiler of sources. Afterwards, in contrast, his own testimony seems to be sufficient to assure the accuracy of the entire story: "I was present for the entire journey" (fui presente a toda la jornada) (XII.70.6). At the same time, the material body of the poet becomes the measure of the events – "There is no footprint in this region / which my feet have left unmeasured" (Pisada en esta tierra no han pisado / que no haya por mis pies sido medida) (XII.71.1–2) – asserting a shared authenticity with the chronicler-soldiers of the earlier phase of exploration and conquest and anticipating the second part of the poem.[28] Stanzas XII.70 to XII.74, therefore, play a key role in the evolution of Ercilla's testimonial poetics: whereas up to canto XIII Ercilla narrates events that he, as a war historian, reconstructs a posteriori, once he begins the second part, he follows the wandering trajectory of his presence in Mapuche lands. This last factor is decisive in the construction of the poem's *fabula*.

The Historical Fabula of *La Araucana*

There is a clear historical consistency among the episodes that Ercilla chooses to constitute the plot of his poem, particularly those in the first part, for which he was not present. The Araucanian warriors serve to strengthen the coherence of the military narrative. Cantos II and III introduce two warriors, key figures in the launching of the Indigenous rebellion: first, the appointment of Caupolicán as "captain" (capitán) (II.63.3), following his success during the trial of the tree trunk, and second, the appointment of Lautaro as "[his] lieutenant" ([su] teniente) (III.84.8). The deaths of these two characters – Lautaro in canto XIV (17– 18) and Caupolicán in canto XXXIV (27–32) – represent two decisive inflection points in the historiographical tale, which correspond with two watershed events in the conflict. The first, the death of Lautaro, highlighted in cantos XIV and XV by the defeat and massacre of part of the Araucanian troops, coincides with the arrival in a "Chile without governor"[29] of the representative of the authority of the monarch: Don García Hurtado de Mendoza, son of Andrés Hurtado de Mendoza, Viceroy of Peru and emblematic of Spanish dominion. Thus, the first part is measured in terms of Lautaro's military action, which coincides with the absence of Spanish leadership in Chile during the interim between the death of Pedro de Valdivia and the arrival of García Hurtado de Mendoza. The poem's three parts as a whole, in turn, correspond to the rebellion led by Caupolicán, which persists until the first months of Hurtado de Mendoza's government. However, Caupolicán's death does not provide a lasting solution to the conflict, and, on the contrary, results in an "ongoing war"[30] within the confines of this region.[31]

With respect to this framework, the final three cantos offer episodes that represent geographical as well as historical and military deviations in the story: the expedition to Ancud, Ercilla's exile from Araucanian territory, and the annexation of Portugal. The lexical field of detours and direction changes ultimately invades the text in these three fragments,[32] just as it does with Ercilla's conception of the direction and journey of the poem, that is, of its *fabula*. The notion of trajectory had already been fundamental prior to this moment and was largely a function of Ercilla's own footsteps.

The Testimonial Fabula of *La Araucana* (Parts 2 and 3)

The unity throughout the poem's second and third parts originates from Ercilla's presence in Chile and relies on the principle of testimony. Indeed, if we revisit Francisco de Irarrázabal's certified statement of services (*probanza de méritos*), we find that the military episodes in which Ercilla claims to have participated alongside his Basque comrade coincide almost entirely with those appearing in the poem. The primary military campaigns mentioned in Irarrázabal's written testimony possess an undeniable correlation with the historical subject matter of the second and third part of the poem.

Let us take a closer look at Irarrázabal's first-person account. The fourth question documents the arrival of the "aforementioned Governor [Don García Hurtado de Mendoza] in the city of La Serena." Ercilla involves himself in this event from the last canto of part 1, following the landing at La Serena where the Spanish troops "rested a month among much leisure" (un mes en mucho vicio reposaron) (XV.63.7). The fifth question recounts how after La Serena, they proceeded to rebuild the city of La Concepción:

> [...] después salí con el dicho vuestro Gobernador de la dicha ciudad de la Serena para ir a poblar y reedificar la ciudad de la Concepción y llegamos a una isla que llaman de Talcaguano, dos leguas de la dicha ciudad, con gran tormenta e riesgo de las vidas [...] y estuvimos en la dicha isla más de dos meses, pasando grandes trabajos y hambre y siempre en arma y centinela mandó el dicho Gobernador que saltásemos en tierra firme a hacer un fuerte, donde había sido poblada antes la dicha ciudad de la Concepción.[33]

> ([...] afterwards I departed with the aforesaid Governor from the city of La Serena to inhabit and rebuild the city of La Concepción and we came upon an island they call Talcaguano, two leagues from the city, through great storms and risk of life [...] and we were on that island for more than two months, suffering great toil and hunger and always armed and on alert; the aforesaid Governor ordered us to gain *tierra firme* and construct a stronghold, where the city of La Concepción had previously been inhabited.)

This episode serves as the underlying blueprint for cantos XVI and XVII, spanning the troop's arrival on the island of "Talca," (XVI.17.4) where they remained for "two months" (dos meses) (XVII.18.2), until erecting a fort in honour of Philip II and planting the royal standard: "In the sight of Arauco / fluttered the flag of Philip II, King of Spain" (siendo a vista de Arauco levantada / bandera por Felipe Rey de España) (XVII.26.5–6).

In the content of the declaration's ensuing episode (corresponding to the sixth question), Ercilla would insert the poem's first marvellous episode, which involved his dream about Bellona and Reason: while still in La Concepción, "having just finished building the fort, within eight days the entire band of natives from the region came to fight against those of us who were inside said fort" (acabado de hacer el dicho fuerte, dentro de ocho días vinieron a pelear toda la junta de los naturales de las comarcas con los que en el dicho fuerte estábamos).[34] In *La Araucana*, these skirmishes are spread over various episodes and are interspersed with his visionary and prophetic dream.[35] The seventh question details the beginning of the campaign inside the province of Arauco and to the south of the Biobío River:

> [...] después de llegado el socorro y los caballos de la ciudad de Santiago, salí con el dicho vuestro Gobernador al allanamiento y castigo de las provincias de Arauco y Tucapel, después de haberme hallado en la población e reedificación de la ciudad de la Concepción, y me hallé presente en otra junta y guasábara que todos los naturales de las comarcas nos dieron a la otra parte del río de Biobío.[36]

> ([...] after the reinforcements and horses had arrived from the city of Santiago, I departed with the foresaid Governor to raid and punish the Arauco and Tucapel Provinces, after having been present for the settling and rebuilding of the city of La Concepción, and I found myself involved in another uprising of the region's natives on the other side of the Biobío river.)

In Ercilla's poem we can recognize these same stages of advancing into Araucanian territory laid out by Irarrázabal: the arrival of reinforcements – "we also received news / that our warriors had left Mapochó" (también tuvimos nueva que partidos / eran de Mapochó nuestros guerreros) (XXI.14.1–2); and the arrival in Araucanian territory – "To the Araucanian valley we descended" (Al araucano valle, pues, bajamos) (XXIII.21.1). The skirmish (*guasáraba*) to which the testimony alludes coincides in the poem with the Battle of Penco, which ends in the exemplary punishment levied upon the Araucanian warrior Galvarino. This battle on land is then complemented, thanks the visionary arts of the Wizard Fitón, with the story of the naval battle at Lepanto in canto XXIV. The conclusion of this canto sets the stage for new conflicts with the Indigenous people:

> [...] nos partimos
> desmintiendo los pasos peligrosos,
> en su demanda, entrando por la tierra
> con gana y fin de rematar la guerra. (XXIV.99.5–8)

> ([...] we departed, / avoiding the perilous mountain passes / chasing the enemy, through the land / with the goal and desire to conclude the warfare.)

The eighth question recounts another military episode: the assault on Fort Millapoal: "[...] me hallé en otra junta e guasábara que todos los naturales de las comarcas nos dieron en el valle de Millapoal, que fue gran suma de enemigos, y en todos los demás rencuentros que nos dieron hasta llegar al valle de Tucapel" ([...] I was present for another clash and uprising of the region's natives in the Millapoal Valley, which involved an enormous sum of enemies, and for all the other encounters we had with them until arriving in the Tucapel Valley). In the poem, Ercilla gives the location of Millapoal another name, "Millarapué," where an extremely violent battle was fought, recounted from canto XXV.15 to canto XXVI.21. The subsequent cantos are rich in events that Irarrázabal's testimony does not identify with any precision. At the beginning of canto XXVI, Ercilla locates the story at the place where Pedro de Valdivia "built his stronghold, / and later received an infamous death" (fundó la casa fuerte / y le dieron después infame muerte): Tucapel (XXVI.38.7–8).

Here Ercilla recounts several battles, in the middle of which he grafts the marvellous vision of the world map inside Fitón's magical sphere, until they construct the fort at Tucapel – "It was decided / to hold up the fort" (fue acordado / sustentar el lugar fortificado) (XXVII.56.7–8) – and their return to La Imperial (XXVII.58.4). In canto XXVIII, he details the Araucanian attack in the ravine at Purén, an episode in which Ercilla fulfils an important role. Lastly, the ninth question documents Irarrázabal's presence during the construction of Cañete de la Frontera and its fort,[37] just as Ercilla also narrates in canto XXX: "first was planned and traced a city" (quedó primero la ciudad trazada) (XXX.29.5). This testimony marks the end of the historical material for the second part of *La Araucana*.

The four subsequent questions correspond to the material in part 3. Irarrázabal confirms at length how

> estando en la ciudad Imperial, hubo nueva que se habían tornado a rebelar las provincias de Tucapel y todas las comarcanas y se había juntado toda la tierra para dar en los españoles que habían quedado poblados en la ciudad de Cañete; y con esta nueva envió el dicho Gobernador desde la ciudad Imperial a socorrer la dicha ciudad de Cañete a treinta españoles de los que en su compañía tenía, entre los cuales fui uno de los dichos treinta que fueron al socorro de la dicha ciudad, a la cual fuimos a gran riesgo de las vidas, por hallar todos los naturales rebelados, como los hallamos, y haber de pasar por sus tierras y casas, y al fin entramos en la dicha ciudad donde los españoles estaban, y luego el día siguiente vino toda la junta de los naturales de las comarcas sobre nosotros a darnos guasábara y pelear, donde hubimos la vitoria y les hicimos retirar, y fui de los primeros que fueron a romper los escuadrones de los indios, como en todas las demás batallas, que fueron de gran peligro, por la mucha gente que hubo siempre.

> (arriving in the city of Imperial, news arrived that the provinces of Tucapel and every region had again risen up in rebellion and that all had joined forces to face the Spaniards who had stayed behind inhabiting the city of Cañete; and at this news, to aid the city of Cañete the aforesaid Governor sent thirty Spaniards from his company from the city of Imperial, amongst whom I was one of those thirty who went to the aid of that city, at great danger to our lives, since we found all the natives in revolt, as we did discover them, and being compelled to traverse their lands and homes, and finally entering that city where the Spaniards were, and then the following day the entire band of natives from the region descended upon us to battle and fight, where we achieved victory and forced them to retreat, and I was amongst the first who advanced to crush the Indian squadrons, just as in every other battle, which held great danger, because of the was always a vast number of warriors.)

This is the military episode at the beginning of cart 3, even if Irarrázabal does not mention the ploy of Andresillo, a local Indigenous man allied to the Spaniards, against the Araucanians that led to the tragic massacre of the Indigenous people at the Fort of Cañete.[38] Ercilla took part in this battle given that he was a member of the group of thirty Spanish cavalry soldiers who arrived as reinforcements and contributed to the success of the Spanish retribution. In *La Araucana* the episode is narrated from the Fort of Cañete's viewpoint: canto XXX relates how just when "to Imperial in safety we arrived" (a la Imperial llegamos salvamente) (XXX.30.7), the land rose up in rebellion – "the truce and contract broken" (rota la tregua y el contrato hecho) (XXX.32.5). Joining the thirty soldiers, he crossed through "Tiru's dense vegetation" (la espesura de Tirú) to the "Spanish fort" (presidio español) (XXX.33.3–8) where they were informed of the Araucanian attack and Pran's scheme, outwitted by the clever and traitorous Andresillo.

At this point of the action, Ercilla is only a spectator to this story told to the newly arrived soldiers by the group of Spaniards living in the fort. Nevertheless, he soon takes over the story on his own, addressing his ideal dedicatee, an intratextual reference to Philip II, and the reader:

> donde ya nuestra gente había tenido
> nueva del trato y tierra rebelada,
> que, por estraño caso acontecido,
> de la junta y designio fue avisada,
> y habiendo alegremente agradecido
> el socorro y ayuda no pensada,
> nos dio del caso relación entera,
> el cual pasa, señor, desta manera. (XXX.34.1–8)

(Here our friends had information / Of the rebel land's behaviour, / And by some strange hap admonished / Knew about their plot and union. / Happily they thanked us soldiers / For our aid so unexpected, / And a full report they gave us, / Which to this effect was worded.)

This allows Ercilla to go from being an indirect witness to a firsthand witness, thus justifying the hypotyposis in the description of the massacre.

After the imprisonment and torture of Caupolicán (XXXIII.56–XXXIV.33), the result of the previous episode, Ercilla recounts García Hurtado de Mendoza's expedition to previously unexplored lands in the south of Chile, in an episode that was interpolated in the 1589–90 edition and then integrated in all the editions after 1597. Two questions, eleven and twelve, are dedicated to this matter in Irarrázabal's testimony. The eleventh tells of the purpose for this expedition and its realization in two stages: "volví donde estaba vuestro Gobernador en la ciudad de Valdivia, de donde partí con él para el nuevo descubrimiento de las provincias e islas de Ancud"[39] (I returned to where your Governor was in the city of Valdivia, from where I departed with him on the new discovery of the provinces and the islands of Ancud). Ercilla also documents the return of García Hurtado de Mendoza from Cañete to

Ancud, specifying how he was among the troops who accompanied the governor: "where I also arrived / [since] his footsteps without delay I am following" (donde también llegué, que sus pisadas / sin descansar un punto voy siguiendo) (XXXIV.47.1–2). The troops finally arrive in Ancud by the end of canto XXXV (40.5–6).

The twelfth question recalls the expedition's return journey, when the foundation of the city of Osorno took place: "pasado el desaguadero del gran Lago de Valdivia, me hallé en el valle de Chaura en la nueva población de una ciudad que allí se pobló y fundó, nombrada la ciudad de Osorno del Lago" (having passed the watershed of the great Valdivia Lake, I found myself in the Chaura Valley for the new settling of a city that was populated and founded there, named the city of Osorno del Lago). This episode does not appear at all in Ercilla's poem despite the fact that the poet indicates that he had witnessed it. Finally, Irarrázabal used the thirteenth question to recount how he had left Araucanian territory and abandoned its wars:

> después de la dicha población y todo pacificado, me vine con el dicho Gobernador de V. A. a la ciudad Imperial, donde estuve algunos meses, sin haber más en qué servir, y desde allí, visto que en aquel reino ya no había más en qué servir a V. A. y que toda la tierra quedaba muy llana, quieta e pacífica, pedí licencia al dicho vuestro Gobernador para venir a servir a V. A. a estos reinos del Perú, para que en ellos vuestro visorrey me gratificase mis servicios y gastos y en nombre de V. A. me hiciese merced.

> (after the mentioned settling and everything at peace, I returned with Your Highness's Governor to the city of Imperial, where I remained for several months, there being no more need for my service, and from there, seeing as how in that kingdom there was no longer any way for me to serve Your Highness and the entire land was very calm, still and peaceful, I requested permission from your Governor to come and serve Your Highness in these kingdoms of Peru, so that here your Viceroy would reward my services and expenses and would in the name of Your Highness grant me favour.)[40]

Likewise, although under more conflictive causes,[41] Ercilla recounts how after arriving in Imperial (XXXVI.32.1), he left for "Lima's renowned Callao" (Callao de Lima celebrado) (XXXVI.37.8). In the final analysis, every military episode mentioned in the certified statement of services, and in which Irarrázabal and Ercilla declare to have participated alongside Governor García Hurtado de Mendoza, is reflected in the poem that otherwise limits itself to these events in the majority of the cantos. Certainly, there does exist an almost identical correlation between the military episodes involving the Irarrázabal-Ercilla pair and those that serve as the basis for Ercilla's narration, despite the obvious enhancement of the episodes featuring the Araucanians. Even so, we can identify two significant discrepancies between the legal and poetic testimonies. For one, Ercilla omits an important period in Irarrázabal's declaration regarding the account of García Hurtado de Mendoza's expedition to the island of Ancud: the founding of the city of Osorno during their return journey north, an episode not strictly military compared to the others.[42] Secondly, the abundance of details that Ercilla presents when recounting the battles between the Spanish and the Araucanians south of the Biobío is absent from the legal declaration. The historical material from cantos XXV to XXVIII corresponds to an elaboration of question eight, which is only a brief summary in Ercilla's legal testimony. Notably, the extent of his participation becomes greater on the battlefield precisely in these final cantos of part 2, as we shall see.

Ercilla's presence as a witness is therefore the criterion that largely determines the construction of the *fabula* in the poem's second and third parts – rather than the *relaciones* and chronicles handled by the poet, mainly those of Jerónimo del Villar and Alonso de Góngora Marmolejo.[43] Far from participating solely as a soldier and as a poet-witness, Ercilla explores throughout the historical narration, other modes of conduct, other positions, which evolve and transform his function as a poet. In what follows, I propose a more detailed analysis of the close relationship established between Ercilla's extratextual presence as a witness and his intratextual presence as a protagonist in the story. Essentially, it will involve an investigation of the relationship between the "progression of the actions and that of the words" (discurrir de las acciones y el de las palabras)[44] in the configuration of Ercilla's poetic ethos.

Soldier and Hero

The episodes where his substantial presence is made clear by the explicit use of the first person – oftentimes accentuated by the anaphoric subject pronoun "I" (yo) at the beginning of the stanza – are at the heart of this construction. Thematically and narratively, they can be classified into four sequences that keep neatly distinct, although they frequently overlap and are interwoven with one another:

- military episodes featuring Ercilla: Philip II's flag (XVI.83), Juan Remón's challenge (XXVI.2–20), the attack at the ravine of Purén (XXVIII.63–70), the surprise attack on Fort Penco (XXXI.33), and the testimonial stanza on the expedition to Ancud (XXXVI.19–29).

- marvellous episodes to which Ercilla alone has access: the dream about Bellona and Reason (XVI.34–XVIII.74), the vision of Lepanto in Fitón's cave: Lepanto (XXIII.21–XXIV.98) and the world map in Fitón's cave (XXVI.40–XVII.54).
- interventions on behalf of Indigenous warriors, to pardon their lives or alleviate their punishments: Galvarino (XXVI.22–30), Cariolano (XXVIII.45–52), and Caupolicán (XXXIV.31).
- interventions by Ercilla with Indigenous women, to prevent them from taking their own lives and to guarantee their safety and recovery: Tegualda (XX.21–XXI.12), Glaura (XXVII.57–XXVIII.44), Lauca (XXXII.32–42), and the story of Queen Dido (XXXII.42–XXXIII.54).

Military Hero and Defender of Indigenous Warriors

Let us return to the stanza in canto XIII where Ercilla pinpoints the start of his presence on American soil as a part of García Hurtado de Mendoza's army: "I with them also" (Yo con ellos también) (XIII.29). Here the poet stands apart from the group through the use of the first-person singular in opposition to a third-person plural. The formula "I saw" (Yo vi) (XV.16) (as well as various other uses of the verb "to see") validates this new modality in which Ercilla deploys his memories to complete the events he narrates and to give them presence and credibility. Following this modest introduction, several episodes in parts 2 and 3 of *La Araucana* attempt to give him a more substantial role, making Ercilla one of the heroes of the military campaigns in Chile. While the testimonial aspect is entirely absent in the prologue to the second part, at this point Ercilla begins to develop an essential element of his initial pact with the reader, well beyond his status as a witness.

In part 2, there are three strictly military episodes in which Ercilla intervenes: the landing on the island of Talcaguano (XVI), the defence of the Fort of Millarapué (XXVI), and the attack suffered by the Spanish at the ravine of Purén (XXVIII). His role grows increasingly until it becomes decisive in the last episode. Canto XVI narrates the arrival of García Hurtado de Mendoza and his fleet on the "small island" (isleta) near the port of Concepción. There, the point of view alternates between the plural third person – "the Spaniards" (los españoles) (XVI.24.2) – and the plural first person when he discretely includes himself in the story. In the canto's final stanza, Ercilla's presence is made explicit, marked by the narratorial voice's sudden interruption of Millalauco's speech:

Llegado al pabellón de don García,
hallándome con otros *yo presente,*

con una moderada cortesía
nos saludó a su modo, alegremente
levantando la voz … *Pero la mía*,
que fatigada de cantar se siente,
no puede ya llevar un tono tanto
y así es fuerza dar fin en este canto. (XVI.83.1–8 Italics mine).[45]

(At García's front pavilion / With becoming courteous posing, / He saluted us with blitheness; / *I myself stood there with others.* / Voice he raised, but *mine* more softly / Now will dwindle, hoarse from singing. / As my voice is less sonorous, / I shall close this sixteenth canto.)

As he had previously done in part 1 in canto XIII, Ercilla again casually indicates his presence among Don García's troops when demonstrating his Ariostan mastery of the narrative voice, enabling him to conclude the canto and resume it afterwards. It is not until canto XXVI that we see Ercilla become the protagonist of a military operation. In canto XXV, the Araucanians attack the Fort of Millarapué. The canto closes with the Araucanians' presumptuous triumph, since they claim victory too early, blind to Fate's warnings, whose unexpected twists constitute the theme of the prologue to the following canto. Indeed, the Araucanians had not counted on a Spanish squadron of reinforcements arriving at the last minute and reversing the fortunes of the respective armies on the battlefield. It is precisely in this squadron that we find Ercilla. We can note how the poet reasserts his position as a witness, "the last squadron, in whose ranks I marched as a witness" (el escuadrón postrero / adonde por testigo yo venía), while also actively engaging in the conflict (XXVI.3.1–2).

Upon the arrival of reinforcements, the intensity of the combat increases, so much so that Ercilla – now not the soldier, rather the poetic narrator – feigns his refusal to describe any more by way of a sort of preterition:

Así el entendimiento y pluma mía,
aunque usada al destrozo de la guerra,
huye del grande estrago que este día
hubo en los defensores de su tierra. (XXVI.8.1–4)

(Hence my quill and understanding, / Though inured to war's destruction, / Flees this day's momentous slaughter / Wrought on warders of their homeland.)

The poetic self's withdrawal, overcome by such violence, foreshadows that of the Araucanian warrior Rengo, who seeing that all is lost takes cover in the forest (XXVI.10–11) and joins the other warriors who had deserted the combat. In turn, this retreat coincides with Ercilla's debut, now not as a witness, but as an actor in the battle:

Yo, que de aquella parte discurriendo
a vueltas del rumor también andaba,
la grita y nuevo estrépito sintiendo
que en el vecino bosque resonaba,
apresuré los pasos, acudiendo
hacia donde el rumor me encaminaba,
viendo al entrar del bosque detenidos
algunos españoles conocidos. (XXVI.13)

(I, who rode in that direction, / Trailing every noise that rustled, / Heard the shouts and new-born uproar / In the nearby glade resounding. / Horse's hooves I shod with lightning, / Travelling where this growling guided, / And athwart the woodland's entrance / Spied some peers of my acquaintance.)

This remarkable stanza, using polysemy and semantic juxtaposition, weaves together action and narration (ride" [discurrir]), movement and perception (trailing noises, hearing resonances, "Travelling where this growling guided me" [el rumor me encaminaba]), giving new substance to the poetic testimony of *La Araucana*.

Three times Ercilla finds himself implicated in the story's development, and three times he underscores the fact anaphorically with the first-person subject pronoun or a self-mention at the outset of the stanza:

Estaba a un lado Juan Remón gritando:
"Caballeros, entrad, no temáis nada,"
mas ellos, el peligro ponderando,
dificultaban la dudosa entrada.
Yo, pues, a la sazón a pie arribando
donde estaba la gente recatada,
Juan Remón, que me vio luego de frente,
quiso obligarme allí públicamente,

diciendo: "*¡Oh don Alonso!* [...]"
Oyendo, pues, *mi nombre* conocido
y que todos volvieron a mirarme,
del honor y vergüenza compelido,
no pudiendo del trance ya escusarme,
por lo espeso del bosque y más temido

comencé de romper y aventurarme,
siguiéndome Arias Pardo Maldonado,
Manrique, don Simón y Coronado. (XXVI.14–16, italics mine)

(On one side Remón was shouting: / "Enter, gentlemen! Be cowed by nothing!" / But they pondered on the danger, / Deeming difficult the entrance. /
Then, from off my steed dismounting, / *I approached the hesitators.* / Juan
Remón, who saw me present / There, appealed to me in public: // saying:
"Don Alonso, […] // Hearing then *my name* made public, / and seeing all
turn round to look at me, / Chafed by itch of shame and honour, / And
unable to eschew the ordeal, / Through the dread of matted forest / I began
to break and venture, / followed by Arias Pardo Maldonado, / Manrique,
Don Simón and Coronado.)

This episode is less notable for our poet's military achievement than
for the objectification that his character attains. Whereas previously he
only had emerged as a part of his own testimony and use of the first
person (as a subject), Juan Remón's apostrophe endowed him with the
recognition of a third party, inscribing the name "don Alonso" into the
fabric of the narration, which links the poetic self with the author who
signs the work under the name Alonso de Ercilla. Thusly called, Don
Alonso is not only pointed out and identified, but he also heads up
the small troop that, despite the danger, accepts the risk of pursuing
the Araucanians into the forest. Five stanzas are enough to portray the
"cruel battle" (cruda batalla) in which the Araucanian warriors fall to
the Spanish swords rather than surrender (XXVI.17–21).

This hyperbole suggesting a massacre of the Indigenous soldiers is
accompanied by "a large number of prisoners" (un número copioso
de prisiones): twelve *caciques* are condemned to die by hanging from
a nearby tree. Among them is the warrior Galvarino, who had already
been made an example of and brutally punished in canto XXII – they
cut off both his hands as Ercilla looked on (XXII.46) – and who had since
become the voice and inspiration for the Indigenous armed resistance.
Twice Ercilla intervenes in an attempt to stay the cruel sentence, and
twice his efforts are frustrated, by his fellow Spaniards as well as the
Araucanian himself, who holds fast in his desire to die to avoid yielding to the Spanish enemy. In both cases, the anaphoric use of the subject
pronoun stresses Ercilla's intervention: "I, arriving at that moment" (yo
a la sazón al señalar llegando) (XXVI.23.1); "I, who fronted him, considering" (Yo, que estaba a par dél, considerando) (XXVI.29.1). We might
say that, at this crucial point in the story, the poetic and testimonial self
acquires a name, a character, and agency (albeit still ambiguous) in the

battles and in his relationship with the Indigenous people, although he is still unable to save the life of an Araucanian warrior.

Ercilla's final intervention in part 2 of *La Araucana*, in canto XXVIII, combines once again, though in inverse order, his prominence on the battlefield and his one-on-one relationship with the Araucanian soldiers. The second part of canto XXVIII tells of Ercilla's encounter with Cariolano, an admirable Araucanian warrior who, in spite of his great valour, agreed to be Ercilla's *yanakuna* (servant). Employing a strategy that we will see in later episodes involving Ercilla, this peaceful interaction with the adversaries is made possible by his moving out of the space controlled by Spaniards:

> Sabed, sacro señor, que yo venía
> con algunos amigos y soldados,
> después de haber andado todo el día
> en busca de enemigos desmandados;
> mas ya que a nuestro asiento me volvía
> con diez prisiones bárbaros atados,
> a la entrada de un monte y fin de un llano
> descubrimos muy cerca a Cariolano. (XXVIII.46)

> (August lord, know I was coming / With some comrades and some soldiers / After having marched the day through / Hunting enemies disbanded; / But as to our camp I turned me, / With barbaric prisoners fettered, / At the plain's edge and the mount marge / We discovered Cariolano.)

After seeing the incredible resilience of Cariolano in combat, Ercilla expresses his admiration for the brave Araucanian to the Spaniards who accompany him and, by sparing Cariolano's life, he creates a debt that compels the noble warrior to show his gratitude, loyalty, and friendship.

After this remarkable moment of mutual recognition of valour between enemies, Ercilla makes his final appearance in the story in a few, but very important, stanzas in canto XXVIII (stanzas 63–70). Under attack in a ravine and with no hope of escaping, the Spaniards survive thanks only to Ercilla's involvement. Accompanied by a small troop of soldiers, he climbs to the top of the mountain (XXVIII.64.3), from where he is able to surprise and disperse his attackers. Ercilla assigns himself the role of strategist in this final battle, insisting on the urgency of the moment – "sudden" (súbito), "immediately" (al momento), "without delay" (sin dilación) – and the decisive effect of the surprise realized by the sudden charge of eleven soldiers under his command. Together, they comprise a group of heroes, akin to the "doce de la Fama" (Twelve of Fame) referenced in part 1 (IV.23.8. Quite distinct from the heroic Cariolano, here Ercilla faces, conveniently, a different type of Indigenous warrior, morally corrupt and characterized by their greed and their incompetence in battle. The "exemplary punishment" (ejemplar castigo) (XXVIII.71.8) levied against his own men by the Araucanian leader does not provoke the poet's disapproval. With this heroic action, Ercilla's participation as a military hero in the story reaches its climax.

In part 3 his distinction as a soldier becomes intentionally more discrete. We have already seen how his presence among the reinforcements who contributed to the tragic victory at Fort Penco and participated in the massacre of a considerable number of Araucanian troops (cantos XXX–XXXII) did not lead to a prominent role for Ercilla. What is emphasized is not his military action, rather the contrary, his consternation as an eyewitness who must recount the massacre. Even more striking is the episode, in many ways conclusive, that relates the execution of Caupolicán, who is submitted to the horrible torture of being simultaneously impaled and killed with arrows. Although Ercilla devoted careful attention to this distressing scene and was set on making it particularly emotional for his readers, he also explicitly renounced his status as a witness, emphasizing in the often-commented verse: "I was not present" (no estuve yo presente) (XXXIV.31.4). This deliberate distancing from the bellicose actions of the Spanish can be explained by his disapproval of the merciless retaliation that had been carried against the Mapuches. However, his own point of view is made clear not only by his absence or distancing from the actions carried out by the Spanish but also by his exploration of new ways of being present and giving testimony throughout the second part of the poem.

The Fictional Hero

Ercilla's authority as eyewitness extends beyond the warlike content to another, more conciliatory, type of encounter with the Indigenous people. In these, he blends war with other themes: magic and fantasy in his encounters with the wizard Fitón; love and sorrow when he confronts Indigenous widows. These episodes explore new ways of being a poet and reconfigure the Ercillan ethos.

The "web of epic prophecy"[46] in part 2 links cantos XVI and XVII (his dream about the Battle of Saint Quentin), XXIII and XXIV (prophesy of the Battle of Lepanto), and XXVII (ekphrasis of Fitón's world map) into a single storyline that parallels the Araucanian war, both narrative threads alternating by way of an Ariostan *entrelacement*. We can read these episodes as Ercilla's attempts to show himself able to create poetry on the battlefield.

However, these efforts do not follow the testimonial logic announced in the prologue, which entailed observing and providing a written account amidst the war and on scraps of parchment or paper – a method that is rescinded almost immediately on Ercilla's arrival in Chile. The stanzas in which the poet recounts how he fainted and suffered an attack when he sought, for the first time in the poem, "of some of the recent events, / by the pen to alleviate my memory" (de agunas cosas desta historia / descargar con la pluma la memoria) (XVII.34.7–8) are well known and have received considerable attention. Rendering a testimony impossible, this accident and the subsequent dream propel Ercilla into a very different poetic role: that of the inspired dream, modelled after Cicero's *Dream of Scipio* and, more broadly, after the tradition of the prophetic dream.[47] Employing this device, Ercilla regains his testimonial capabilities, albeit supernaturally and for imaginative events. Fundamental to this experience is the act of travelling the world in order to bear witness to these original events outside of the territories controlled by the Spanish. Ercilla tells of how Bellona transports him through pleasant landscapes to "its highest summit" (la más alta cumbre) (XVII.49.7) from where, like a falcon, he was able to "review the scenes she had promised" (ver lo prometido) (XVII.52.3). As Bellona encourages the poet to look – "you will be able to see," "you will see," "you from here may look, attentive" (podrás ver, verás, podrás mirar atento) – a new form of wartime writing begins, characterized by the same impartiality that Ercilla endorsed regarding the Araucanian war:

Tú desde aquí podrás mirar atento
las diferentes armas y naciones
y escribir de una y otra la fortuna,
dando su justa parte a cada una. (XVII.59.5–8)

(You from here may look, attentive, / on the different arms and nations, / writing down their respective fortunes, / giving each his just appraisal.)

The strategy employed here balances the following elements: writing, mobility (we could refer to Ercilla's "footsteps" [pisada] or "journey" [recorrido]), and vision. These elements evolve in inverse proportions over the following fictional episodes featuring Ercilla. In the two encounters with Fitón, all allusions to Ercilla's activity as a writer disappear. On the contrary, he enhances the staging of an initiatory journey that allows the poet and soldier to reach distant places, granting his testimony originality and value: first, Ercilla loses his way while successively pursuing "a weary Indian" (un indio laso) (XXIII.24.5), "a meek roebuck" (una mansa corcilla) (XXIII.27.7), and lastly, "an old man" (un hombre anciano) (XXIII.32.8) who leads him to Fitón's cave; later, he is guided by the magician himself along a different course to the "room / of the miraculous globe" (pieza / del milagroso globo) (XXVI.50.7–8). In both cases, Ercilla accomplishes the incredible detour by straying from the Spanish faction not only in dreams, but also physically. The encounters with Fitón even involve Ercilla wandering into a territory that is completely beyond his control:

> Perdí el rastro y cerróseme el camino,
> sobreviniendo un aire turbulento,
> y así de acá y de allá, fuera de tino,
> de una espesura en otra andaba a tiento.
> Vista pues mi torpeza y desatino,
> arrepentido del primer intento,
> sin pasar adelante me volviera,
> si alguna senda o rastro yo supiera. (XXIII.31)

> (Trail I lost; the road closed on me; / Murky airs about me hovered. / Here and there I groped, dazed, nonplussed, / From one coppice to the other. / Fretting now for stupid blundering, / Sorry for my first intention, / I would fain turn back, not passing, / If I could but find an exit.)

On his return to camp, he intentionally underscores how his men "had judged [him] lost" ([le] juzgaban por perdido) (XXIV.98.4) or "were frantically searching (for him)" ([le] andaba[n] a buscar confusamente) (XXVII.54.8). Throughout this surprising scheme, Ercilla applies the same principles to the realm of marvellous fiction that guaranteed the accuracy of his earlier accounts as a soldier, making his "footstep" (pisada) the measure of its authenticity. This evolving ability to reach places that offer a new form of revelation closely follows a progression from night "amidst the silence and dark night" (en medio del silencio y noche escura) (XXIII.23.2) to day, from darkness to clarity (XXVI.40.1–2). Leaving the camp allows his senses and perceptions to be heightened, maximizing his abilities as a witness. His vision of Bellona explicitly illustrates this. The "accident" (accidente) leads to the retreat of the "sense / in the body's noblest part" (sentido / en la más noble parte recogido) (XVII.37.7–8) and, in turn, the mobilization of his other senses, namely hearing and sight, which are summoned upon Bellona's deafening appearance:

> No bien al dulce sueño y al reposo
> dejado el quebrantado cuerpo había,
> cuando oyendo un estruendo sonoroso
> que estremecer la tierra parecía,
> con gesto altivo y término furioso
> delante una mujer se me ponía,
> que luego vi en su talle y gran persona
> ser la robusta y áspera Belona. (XVII.38)

(Hardly had my shaken body / Found repose and dulcet slumber / When I heard a crash sonorous / Rumbling from terrestrial bowels. / Fierce of speech, with surly gestures, / In my presence stood a woman, / Whom I recognize by stature / As the stout and fierce Bellona.)

In the account of the Battle of Lepanto, replicated in miniature inside Fitón's magic sphere, sight stands as the fundamental modality: the formula "I saw" (vi) is repeated on multiple occasions, and it twice begins the first verse, as if sight itself is taking the place of the lyrical voice. Ercilla uses this opportunity to invent a new type of sight in motion that depends on Fiton's magic and on Ercilla's role as a witness, both of which breathe life into the ekphrasis. The result is the quintessence of a *living description*, where the portrayed actions come to life inside the written discourse:

> No acabó de decir bien esto, cuando
> las aguas en el mar se alborotaron
> y, el seco Lesnordeste respirando,
> las cuerdas y anchas velas se estiraron;
> y aquellas gentes, súbito anhelando,
> poco a poco moverse comenzaron,
> haciendo de aquel modo en los objetos
> todas las demás causas sus efectos. (XXIII.83).[48]

(Hardly had he finished speaking, / When the ocean's flood grew fervid, / And the east-northwest wind, puffing, / Tautened billowing sails and tackle. / Suddenly those panting sea-wolves / Moved in gradual navigation, / and in the same way all the other causes / made their effects in the objects.)

In canto XXVII's ekphrasis of the world, the visual component acquires critical importance, amplifying the usual sight-related verbs – "Look" (mira) / "You see" (ves) – repeated anaphorically over forty-eight stanzas to call the spectator's attention. Ercilla's own mobility within Mapuche territory enables him to develop his visual and testimonial potentialities via his privileged interactions with several Indigenous figures who are not part of the warring factions.

A similar conclusion can be reached from the elegiac episodes in which Ercilla explores his abilities as a lyric poet[49] when presenting the three Indigenous widows Tegualda, Glaura, and Lauca, modelled after the great heroines of the Roman epic and tragedy, who search for the bodies of their husbands in order to give them a proper burial.[50] In fact, the two series of episodes, prophetic and elegiac, are in many ways similar.

First of all, in both cases we see Ercilla relinquish his role as author-witness in favour of a new experience of oneiric and fantastical nature, but that eventually regains the accessibility of daytime. The first encounter, with Tegualda, occurs under very similar circumstances to those that gave rise to his dream about the Battle of Saint Quentin.[51] At the day's end, weary from fighting, Ercilla pauses to consider the painful conditions of soldierly life, which he describes in detail in canto XX (stanzas 22–4). He concludes his reflection returning not to document a failed attempt at writing, but to remember his condition as a soldier-poet and, imitating Garcilaso de la Vega, to describe himself with "pen now in my hand, now the spear" (la pluma ora en la mano, ora la lanza) (XX.24.8). As in the Saint Quentin and Lepanto episodes, the encounters with Tegualda and Glaura take place respectively at night, "obscure and murky" (lóbrega y escura) (XX.27.1), or "at the break of dawn" (al romper del alba) (XXVII.60.5). Night is a space that promotes Ercilla's solitude and closeness with the characters who cross his path, advancing throughout the episodes from dead of night to sunrise. Following the same dynamic, the final elegiac encounter, with the widow Lauca, occurs during the day (XXXII.31) as does the final encounter with Fitón (XXVII).

Another point of contact between the two series of episodes is that they originate from a topographical distancing, when Ercilla leaves the Spanish camp to explore his surroundings: "from one side to another scouting" (de un canto al otro canto paseando) Ercilla comes upon the young Tegualda (XX.25.4). At the end of canto XXVII, it is his disposition to explore that again leads him to his encounter with the fugitive Glaura:

Iba yo en la avanguardia descubriendo
por medio de una espesa y gran quebrada,
cuando vi de través salir corriendo
una mujer, al parecer turbada. (XXVII.61.1–4)

(I scouted in the vanguard's fore, / through a deep ravine and coppice, / when I glimpsed a woman / running away, patently distressed.)

The encounter with Lauca comes about during another of the poet's excursions – "One day, as I scouted / through untraversed trails and footpaths" (saliendo yo a correr la tierra un día / por caminos y pasos desusados) – which takes him to a "hidden Indian settlement" (oculta ranchería) (XXXII.31.1–5). In the prophetic episodes as well as during his encounters with the Indigenous widows, Ercilla goes out of collective spaces and, guided by the Araucanians or his own senses, reaches spaces of authentic revelation. Indeed, the way in which the three women appear to Ercilla is increasingly clear for the character. The appearance of Tegualda is undoubtedly the most laborious and the one that requires the keen senses of the poet, on this occasion turned hunter of a female prey.[52] Eye and ear are both mobilized, first, his sense of hearing:

[…] yo, que estaba
con ojo alerto y con atento oído,
sentí de rato en rato que sonaba
hacia los cuerpos un ruido,
que siempre al acabar se remataba
con un triste sospiro sostenido
y tornaba a sentirse, pareciendo
que iba de cuerpo en cuerpo discurriendo. (XX.26)

([…] I was with / Eye alert and ear attentive, / Heard an intermittent murmur / Sounding faintly by the cadavers, / Long sustained and ever dwindling / Into saddened suspirations. / Yet again weird moans unmanned me, / As it seemed to move from body to body.)

And then the sense of night vision:

[…] vi entre los muertos ir oculto
andando a cuatro pies un negro bulto.
Yo, de aquella visión mal satisfecho,
con un temor, que agora aun no lo niego,
la espada en mano y la rodela al pecho,
llamando a Dios, sobre él aguijé luego. (XX.27.7–8 and XX.28.1–4)

([…] I saw a blackish object / Crawling, hidden 'midst the corpses. // I, distraught by the eerie vision, / With a fear e'en now admitted, / Sword in hand, my buckler girded, / Swooped, invoking God, upon it.)

Ercilla's hesitance when identifying this blurry mass leads him to overcome his fear as well as his defensive and offensive soldierly reflexes. Recognition occurs much more easily in the case of Glaura – "I glimpsed a woman / running" (vi de través salir corriendo / una mujer) (XXVII.61.3–4) – and later, in the case of Lauca, there is never a doubt, as if Ercilla's ability to enter into that privileged contact with the Araucanian heroines had also improved. This contact, both in the case of Fitón and the widows, gives way to the emergence of other voices, creating a true polyphony in the poem.

In the case of the Araucanian widows, Ercilla offers a first-person narrative of his inconsolable interlocutors: "I beseeched her ... to relate to me" (yo le rogué ... me contase) (XX.35.5–8); "I craved to know why she had come" (Yo, queriendo saber a qué venía) (XXVIII.5.1); "I inquired what had brought her" (pregunté qué ocasión la había traído) (XXXII.33.1). Galvarino, Cariolano, and Fitón are three other figures characterized by their extensive first-person discourse. The first develops a political argumentation, which results in the elaboration of a collective first person, an Araucanian "we" (nosotros). The cases of Cariolano and Fitón are distinct in that, originally speaking about themselves, they later initiate a dialogue with Ercilla, a demonstration of trust and friendship.

Along with Elizabeth Harvey and Felipe Valencia, I read it as an act of ventriloquism through which the poet appropriates the vanquished voices of the Araucanian warriors and widows. I would argue that in *La Araucana* the proximity to the narrator-protagonist's "I" favours diegetic imitation over mimesis and that the poetic self spotlights these characters surrounding him on the fictional stage of the war, just as we would in theatre.

Soldier and Poet: Audience, Orality, and the Materiality of Writing

Ercilla's development as a character in his own poem is set apart by a growing autonomy, visionary ability, and the capacity to act and be persuasive in the presence of his contemporaries. Indeed, while the marvellous encounters with the wizard Fitón occur in solitude and his military interventions are carried out as a part of the action of the group, the poet's other quests are made public when the character triumphs. With Glaura and Cariolano, Ercilla "was coming / with some friends and soldiers" (venía / con algunos amigos y soldados) (XXVIII.46.1–2) and a large part of his accomplishment consists of convincing his comrades that Cariolano deserves admiration and respect. In that same canto, during the attack at the ravine of Purén, Ercilla successfully unites and coordinates the actions of eleven other soldiers to victory. Finally, in part 3, he encounters Lauca while scouting the land accompanied by "a group of experienced soldiers" (una escuadra de pláticos soldados) (XXXII.31.4). This handful of soldiers plays the unprecedented role of being Ercilla's first audience as a character: the first intradiegetic audience, which replaces the fictional "Lord" (Señor) to whom this episode, and the entire poem, is dedicated. At their insistence, and to correct the offensive and inaccurate Virgilian image of Queen Dido, Ercilla commences his long tale, modelled after Justinus's historical version. This retelling takes place "as we walked back to the fortress […] I was chatting with the soldiers" (la vuelta del presidio caminando ... iba con los soldados platicando) (XXXII.43.1–3).[53]

Dido's digression accomplishes Ercilla's objective of diversifying the story's military content, embedding this poetic imperative within the conditions of the life of a soldier and justifying the evolution of his poetics based on his own experience as a participant in the war.[54] This clarification is minimal, and yet it forces us to reinterpret the stylistic and poetic change that Ercilla sought to implement in his poem in the final prologue of the first part (canto XV), when he complained of "remaining so close to the truth" (ir a la verdad tan arrimado) (XV.4.3); and when in the prologue to the second part, in which he bemoans the "matters so harsh and so little varied" (materia tan áspera y de poca variedad) in his poem, he decided to introduce episodes of war featuring his king and dedicatee. The amorous episode between Lautaro and Guacolda (canto XIV) and the array of possibilities presented by the introduction of this material and the love lyric into the epic tale (XV.2) are clearly powerful justifications for this change.[55] From part 3's canto XXXII on, however, Ercilla invites us to reread this inflection as a practical necessity, for the soldiers, to distract from the war. In other words, he tailors his own character as a soldier, witness, and poet to his poetic choices. Thus, Ercilla abandons the epic singing for the benefit of a story he "tells," and that emerges "in the unexpected circumstances / presented by this rare example and occasion" (en esta no pensada coyuntura / por raro ejemplo y ocasión traída) (XXXII.48.1, 3–4); that is, it is determined by the needs and possibilities of the practical life of the soldier. This story addresses not only the fictional dedicatee, in second person, but also its listeners within the fiction, whose journey back to the fortress determines the length of the tale. Two stanzas explicitly superpose the characteristics of the diegetic journey and the poem's stylistic trajectory:

> Que el áspero sujeto desabrido,
> tan seco, tan estéril y desierto,

y el estrecho camino que he seguido,
a puros brazos del trabajo abierto,
a término me tiene reducido
que busco anchura y campo descubierto
donde con libertad, sin fatigarme,
os pueda recrear y recrearme.
Viendo que os tiene sordo y atronado
el rumor de las armas inquïeto,
siempre en un mismo ser continuado,
sin mudar son ni variar sujeto,
por espaciar el ánimo cansado
y ser el tiempo cómodo y quïeto,
hago esta digresión, que a caso vino
cortada a la medida del camino. (XXXII.50–1)

(This insipid theme I follow, / Dry and sterile, long and tiresome, / And this narrow road I open / At the cost of swink and sweating, / Hold me bound by such restrictions / That I seek broad panoramas, / Which will freshen and beguile us / With free leisure's recreation. // You are stupefied and deafened / By war's loud reverberations, / In its character consistent, / Never changing sound or subject; / So, to expand your straitened spirits / On this opportune occasion / I shall here digress, and wander / On a trail perchance well-patterned.)

The timeliness on the part of the storyteller ("que a caso vino") is not enough to conceal the incredible coincidence between the poetics developed by the author and the path traversed. That is, in these final cantos of the poem, Ercilla is no longer concerned solely with remaking the poetics of his story, as he had done so masterfully between the first and second parts, but also with adjusting his own character to it and giving substance and life to his relevant abilities as a narrator.

Thusly executed, Ercilla's first successful attempt at narrating manifests itself through oral, not written, expression and is applied to an ancient story, not to the wartime matters of his present. Ercilla gains his authority here not as eyewitness, since the chronological separation prevents any correspondence between him and the subject of his story, but from the knowledge of historical culture that he acquired while at the court and his contact with other men of letters. And yet his success as a storyteller is perfectly suited to the practical needs and rhythm of the soldiers resting between battles. It is noteworthy that Ercilla, in taking this decisive step in his representation as poet, storyteller, and author, appeals to the story of Dido, a prolific and highly political subject in the poetry of the 1500s, an episode that embodies the evident tensions between the military logic of empire building and the profoundly divided and contradictory mindset of the lyric poet.[56]

The epic proposition introduced by Dido's digressive episode was inserted a posteriori in various copies of the 1589 and 1589–90 editions so as to better emphasize its poetic importance. It is an indication of the attention that Ercilla gave to this episode. However, the other interpolated fragment, that of the expedition to Ancud (cantos XXXIV–XXXVI), is, as far as he is concerned, decisive in the evolution of Ercilla's authorial figure: for the first time, we find him capable of successfully executing the type of writing he longed for since the outset of the poem, as we will see.

The account of the expedition to Ancud, led by Governor García Hurtado de Mendoza, represents one of his attempts to deviate from the dead end that was the Araucanian war. In particular, it affords Ercilla an excuse for not having witnessed the execution of Caupolicán, from which he distances himself entirely. In this new episode, Ercilla underscores his presence and role as eyewitness on more than one occasion: "Here alike, I arrived, / following closely every one of his steps, without respite" (donde también llegué, que sus pisadas / sin descansar un punto voy siguiendo) (XXXIV.47.1–2); "I was present, and attentive to his instructions" (presente yo, y atento a las señales) (XXXV.4.7). This episode sets the stage for Ercilla's most renowned feat and the one that won him the most fame as a writer: an expedition within an expedition in which he ventured beyond the farthest point previously known to the Spanish, "accompanied by some young men" (de alguna gente moza acompañado) (XXXVI.19.5). Arriving at the "end and far reaches" (remate y fin postrero) (XXXVI.22.4) of the lake that they had been exploring, Ercilla set off, along with ten companions, on this "uncertain… enterprise" (empresa… dudosa) (XXXVI.27.5) that he would carry out, alone, though not without witnesses and perhaps even admirers:

> Pero yo por cumplir el apetito,
> que era poner el pie más adelante,
> fingiendo que marcaba aquel distrito,
> cosa al descubridor siempre importante,
> corrí una media milla, do un escrito
> quise dejar para señal bastante,
> y en el tronco que vi de más grandeza
> escribí con cuchillo en la corteza:

> "Aquí llegó, donde otro no ha llegado,
> don Alonso de Ercilla, que el primero

en un pequeño barco deslastrado,
con solos diez pasó el desaguadero
el año de cincuenta y ocho entrado
sobre mil y quinientos, por hebrero,
a las dos de la tarde, el postrer día,
volviendo a la dejada compañía." (XXXVI.28–9)

(I, to slake the thirst that seared me, / And to be the first to trample / Soil, with foot of exploration, / Quenchless dream of all seafarers, / Ran a half mile farther southward, / And I notched with my sharp knife-blade / In the bark of one huge tree-trunk / This inscription as a record: // "Here, where others have not trodden, / I, Don Alonso de Ercilla, / In a bark without ballast / Came with ten, and crossed the channel. / Fifteen fifty-eight the year is; / Final day of February, / Two o'clock, and after noon-tide; / Ere returning to our comrades.")

This fragment is significant for several reasons. The signature of his full name confirms the shared identity of the character (heretofore referred to either in the first person, or as "don Alonso" in the episode with Juan Remón) and the author. Furthermore, this signature is not recorded on leather or scraps of letters mentioned in the opening prologue, impermanent materials and writing instruments for times of war, but rather on the land itself, explored and reached by Alonso de Ercilla. The first testimony of Ercilla's poetic ability emerges from these particular circumstances as the result of the gradual maturation of his project of self-representation. Evidently, the inscription on the tree trunk is a response to the practical and strategic need to mark the territory and establish a date. The date and time are included to create an *effet de réel*,[57] all the more significant given Ercilla's sparing use of precise dates in the poem.[58] But the elaboration of the message, chiselled into stanza form, adjusted to fit the poem's metre, is intended to illustrate the soldier's ability in verse. This stanza links Ercilla's American experience to his subsequent poetic adventure: the first of the poem's stanzas to be composed, if we place our trust in fiction, also appears among the work's last and could only have been penned after Ercilla had already dedicated thirty-five cantos to sculpting his own character as eyewitness, hero, and poet.

A comprehensive reading of *La Araucana* that takes into account the poem's textual history and the unique chronological dimensions of its composition invites us to reconsider the often-remarked absence of a hero in *La Araucana*. In effect, just as poets like Luis de Camões and Jerónimo Corte-Real were doing at that same time, the poem's proposition identifies a collective hero: "those daring Spaniards" (aquellos españoles esforzados) (I.1.6), whose great numbers are discovered throughout the battles and who inspire, in particular, the many stanzas constructed using onomastic parataxis.[59] The figure of the governor, absent from the first part, following the death of Pedro de Valdivia, and substituted by García Hurtado de Mendoza in the second and third parts, does not fill this void, although the latter's actions and decisions are closely documented throughout at least half of the poem. This absence is what affords the text the necessary freedom to give its full attention to another device through which the author becomes the witness to the action and the hero of his own verses, as Dante had done several centuries earlier. Ercilla made use of a privileged situation that allowed him to guarantee the veracity of his story, an essential requirement for an epic poem whose pact with the reader rests on the accuracy of the historical material and runs counter to the fantastic and magical subject matter of the Ariostan model. Although Ercilla always had this objective in mind, a careful study of the three parts reveals that in each one he had a different way of approaching it and of giving consistency to his character: his status as eyewitness enables him to also be the historiographer, the hero, and finally, the poet of his own poem. His ability to tell true stories (Dido) and write verses (the stanza carved beyond Ancud), anticipated since *La Araucana*'s initial publication in 1569, is not accomplished until the end, in part 3 in 1589. Thus, a *rétrolecture* presents itself as one of the fundamental tools for according the complex textual construction of *La Araucana* its full meaning and significance.

NOTES

1   Translated from the Spanish by Sean Manning and Emiro Martínez-Osorio.

2   *La Araucana*, I.5.7–8. All quotations from *La Araucana* follow Luis Gómez Canseco's edition and appear in the text.

3   Ariosto, I.4.6, p. 88.

4   Ariosto, I.2.2, p. 86.

5   Translations of *La Araucana* were made in consultation with those of Charles Maxwell Lancaster and Paul Thomas Manchester (*The Araucaniad*, Vanderbilt UP, 1945) and appear in the text. Modifications have been made to give a more literal translation.

6   See the chapter titled "Una epístola autobiográfica" in Gómez Canseco's critical edition of *La Araucana*.

7   Blanco, *Tópica de la metaficción*, 117.

8 For this biographical reconstruction, I rely primarily on Medina's *Vida de Ercilla*.

9 Regarding this, one can compare the earlier poems from Baltasar de Hierro, studied by Miguel Martínez (*Front Lines*, 90–100), and the "Caroléidas" (Vilà, *Épica e imperio*, 475–82), although the latter follow a much more Ariostan poetical structure and centre on the life of a deceased emperor, not a military event.

10 Blanco, *Sur les frontières mouvantes*, 247.

11 Martínez, *Front Lines*; "Writing on the Edge."

12 Plagnard, *Une épopee ibérique*, 62.

13 Gómez Canseco, "El retrato de Ercilla."

14 Ercilla's approval remained unpublished until the publication of the *Elegías* as part of the *Biblioteca de Autores Españoles* in 1874 (180). See also Medina, *Vida de Ercilla*, 240.

15 Ercilla, 1589–90, f. §§5r–§§§8v. See Valencia, *The Melancholy Void*.

16 See Medina, *Documentos*.

17 "Es Ercilla quien, asimismo, lo cuenta …" (It is Ercilla who, himself, tells it …) (29), "Escogido […] el lugar, que fue, como refiere Ercilla …" (Chosen […] the place, which was, as Ercilla recounts…) (39), "pues él mismo refiere que…" (well he himself recounts that …" (53), "Cuenta, pues, él …" (He tells us then …) (56), "Refiere Ercilla que …" (Ercilla recounts that …" (61), "Ercilla nos informa que …" (Ercilla informs us that …) (63), etc. The abundance of quotations from *La Araucana* in this part of his biography is striking. The same biographical circularity is documented in the case of Luis de Camões (Plagnard, "Une poétique des confins," 2020).

18 Medina, *Documentos*, 28–32.

19 This information regarding the location does not appear in the document as it was transcribed by Medina, but it can be deduced from the prosopography that he proposes in the second part of his *Ilustraciones* (33).

20 "[…] pidió licencia el dicho don Francisco para venir a este reino del Perú para que el Visorrey le gratificase lo que había servido e gastado; e sabe este testigo que está empeñado en no en cuánto, mas de que ha menester que Su Majestad le haga merced para poderse desempeñar" ([…] the aforesaid Don Francisco requested permission to come to this kingdom of Peru so that the Viceroy might reward him for what he had served and spent; and this witness knows him to owe monies though not how much, but that it is necessary that Your Majesty grant him royal favor so he can pay his debtors) (13).

21 The same can be observed, albeit to a lesser degree, in the "Declaración de don Alonso de Ercilla en la probanza de los servicios de don Miguel de Avendaño y Velasco hecha en la ciudad de Los Reyes. 1.º de marzo de 1560" (Declaration by Don Alonso de Ercilla Attesting to the Services of Don

Miguel de Avendaño y Velasco Made in the City of Los Reyes. March 1st, 1560), in which Governor García Hurtado de Mendoza's military actions in the vicinity of Villarica and Concepción are also documented (Archivo de Indias, Patronato, 1–4-14/19, ramo 13; Medina, *Documentos*, 37–40).

22 See also Davis, *Myth and Identity in the Epic of Imperial Spain*, 26–9.

23 Medina, *Documentos*, 32.

24 Archivo de Indias, 128–4-6; Medina, *Documentos*, 40.

25 Albarracín-Sarmiento, "Pronombres de primera persona y tipos de narrador en *La Araucana*."

26 Plagnard, *Une épopée ibérique*, 67–109.

27 This subject has been extensively documented. See Albarracín-Sarmiento, "Pronombres de primera persona y tipos de narrador en *La Araucana*," and Blanco, "Sur les frontières mouvantes."

28 Plagnard, "Une poétique des confins."

29 See Errázuriz, *Historia de Chile sin gobernador*.

30 Quint, *Epic and Empire*, 160.

31 Plagnard, "Une poétique des confins."

32 See the following verses: "querría / [...] alcanzar, si pudiese, a don García / aunque es diversa y larga la carrera" (I wanted / [...] to reach, if possible, Don García / though the road is long and winding) (XXXIV.45.1–4); "fue forzosa ocasión de mi destierro" (was the imposed reason of my exile) (XXXVI.34.2); "aceleré mi súbita partida" (I hastened my sudden departure) (XXXVI.36.6); "tomar otro camino largo quiero / y volver el designio a nuestro polo" (I'll wend another long path / and turn my attention to our sphere) (XXXIV.44.3–4); "Veo toda la España alborotada" (I see all of Spain in upheaval) (XXXVI.45.1).

33 Medina, *Documentos*, 29.

34 Medina, *Documentos*, 29.

35 *La Araucana*, XVII.29–33; XVIII.74–XX.18. Francisco de Irarrázabal appears as Francisco de Andía in canto XIX (48.2), among the soldiers that formed García Hurtado de Mendoza's army in Chile (see Luis Gómez Canseco's notes to this stanza).

36 Medina, *Documentos*, 29.

37 "[...] me hallé en el dicho valle de Tucapel en la población y edificación de la ciudad de Cañete de la Frontera, en la sustentación de la cual y en la conquista e defensa que se les hizo a los naturales me hallé y en hacer otro fuerte que allí se hizo" ([...] I was present in that Tucapel Valley for the settling and construction of the city of Cañete de la Frontera, for its securing, and for its conquest and defense realized against the natives I was present and for building another fort that was made there).

38 Blanco, "Un episodio trágico."

39 Medina, *Documentos*, 29.
40 The fourteenth question further develops this last part, expanding
    on the expenses undertaken by the soldier and requesting greater
    reimbursement.
41 Medina, *Vida*, 92.
42 For Dichy-Malherbe (122–33), this omission is explained by the emphasis
    Ercilla places on the centrifugal movement of Spanish expansion.
43 See Cordero and Plagnard, *Une épopée ibérique*.
44 Blanco, "Tópico de la metaficción," 134.
45 *La Araucana*, XVI.83.f. 17r, italics mine.
46 Nicolopulos, *The Poetics of Empire in the Indies*.
47 In the sixth book of Cicero's *De Republica*, Scipio Emilian sees his ancestors
    Scipio the African and Paul Emilian in a dream. They reveal to him the
    structure of the cosmos and explain the Platonic doctrine of the immortal-
    ity of the soul. It was particularly through Macrobius's commentary that
    this text circulated and became known during the Renaissance.
48 *La Araucana*, XXIII.83.
49 Valencia, *The Melancholy Void*, 57–85.
50 Schwartz Lerner, "Tradición literaria y heroínas indias en *La Araucana*,"
    615–25.
51 The beginning of the reign of Philip II of Spain was marked by the war
    against the France of Henry II. In August 1557, fighting brought the Span-
    ish troops before the French town of Saint Quentin, whose prolonged
    resistance (17 days) led to the siege of the same name. On 10 August, Saint
    Lawrence's Day, the Spaniards won a bloody victory over the French,
    which was a milestone in the history of Philip II's reign: he was sometimes
    mistakenly considered to be present at the battle and it was in commemo-
    ration of this inaugural victory – which had no great strategic or military
    consequences – that the monarch had the Royal monastery of San Lorenzo
    de El Escorial built.
52 Valencia, *The Melancholy Void*, 83.
53 The story of Queen Dido comprises a total of 102 stanzas
    (XXXII.43–XXXIII.54).
54 In their representations of soldiers and sailors, respectively, there are
    clearly many points of contact between this episode of *La Araucana* and
    the heroic tale of the Twelve of England that Fernão Veloso narrates to the
    weary sailors in canto six from *Os Lusíadas* (VI.41–69). I am thankful to
    Mercedes Blanco, who led me to explore this similarity.
55 For Valencia, this reorientation also coincides with the painful abandon-
    ment of a poetic trajectory that could have been but was never realized.
    See *The Melancholy Void*, 57–85.

56 Helgerson, 14–21. For a political reading of the story of Dido in *La Araucana*, see Galperín, "The Dido Episode in Ercilla's *La Araucana*" and Plagnard, *Une épopée ibérique*, 328–35.

57 For structuralist theory, the presence in a text of descriptive elements referring to the real world without making sense for the action produces an
effect of reality, i.e., it summons the concrete real world as a framework
for fictional action. For Jacques Rancière, these elements do not testify to a
realist logic that would be measured by the yardstick of a real world as an
absolute reference, but rather to the emergence of a new mode of experience and perception. It is in this sense that Ercilla's American experience,
as translated in *La Araucana*, could be an effect of reality.

58 Only once previously to lend veracity to the appearance of the Virgin, Protector of the city of Concepción on "April 23rd 1554" (IX.18). The date here,
suspect and mistaken, matters less than its feigned precision modelled
after the dates that characterize historiographical discourse.

59 This is a characteristic of Ercilla's poetics rooted in one of the missions
of the historiographical poet: "nomear todos os fidalgos e soldados que
deste cerco se acharam" (to name all the noblemen and soldiers who participated in this siege), to use the words of Jerónimo Corte-Real from his
prologue to *O Segundo cerco de Diu* (Corte-Real, 3; quoted in Plagnard, *Une
épopée ibérique*, 49n.38). Medina dedicates hundreds of pages to identifying
these soldiers from the wars in Chile whom Ercilla rescues from anonymity (Ilustración XVII," *La Araucana: Ilustraciones II*, 5–342).

WORKS CITED

Albarracín-Sarmiento, Carlos. "Pronombres de primera persona y tipos de
narrador en *La Araucana*." *Boletín de la Real Academia Española* 46.178 (1966):
297–320.

Ariosto, Ludovico. *Orlando furioso*. Edited by Cesare Segre et María de las
Nieves Muñiz. Madrid: Cátedra, 2002.

Blanco, Mercedes. "Sur les frontières mouvantes de l'historiographie et de
l'épopée: l'*Araucana* d'Alonso de Ercilla (1569–1589)." In *La Renaissance des
genres. Pratiques et théories des genres littéraires entre Italie et Espagne (XVe–
XVIIe siècles)*, 241–65. Dijon: Presses de l'Université de Dijon, 2012.

– "Tópico de la metaficción en *La Araucana* de Alonso de Ercilla." *Metaficció:
Reinaixement & Barroc*. Lleida, Spain: Punctum, 2018.

– "Un episodio trágico en *La Araucana*: la traición de Andresillo (cantos 30–32)."
In La Araucana (1569–2019), a special issue of *Revista Canadiense de Estudios
Hispánicos* vol. 45, no. 1 (2020): 33–62.

Castellanos, Juan de. *Primera parte, de las elegías de varones illustres de Indias*.
Madrid: en casa de la viuda de Alonso Gomez ..., 1589.

Cordero, María de Jesús. *The Transformations of Araucania from Valdivia's Letters to Vivar's Chronicle*. New York: P. Lang, 2001.

Davis, Elizabeth B. *Myth and Identity in the Epic of Imperial Spain*. Columbia: University of Missouri Press, 2000.

Dichy-Malherbe, Sarah. "Le Chili d'Ercilla: poésie géographique ou cartographie impériale ?" Paris: Sorbonne, 2011.

Ercilla y Zúñiga, Alonso de. *The Araucaniad*. Translated by Charles Maxwell Lancaster and Paul Thomas Manchester. Nashville: Vanderbilt University Press, 1945.

– *La Araucana*. Madrid: Pierres Cossin, 1569.

– *La Araucana*. Salamanca: Domingo de Portonariis, 1574.

– *La Araucana*. Edited by Luis Gómez Canseco. Madrid: Real Academia Española, 2021.

– *Primera, segunda, y tercera partes de la Araucana de don Alonso de Ercilla y Zúñiga*. Madrid: Pedro Madrigal, 1590.

– *Primera y segunda parte de La Araucana*. Madrid: Pierres Cossin, 1578.

–*Tercera parte de la Araucana*. Madrid: Pedro Madrigal, 1589.

Errázuriz, Crescente. *Historia de Chile sin gobernador: 1554–1557*. [s.l.]: [s.n.], 1912.

Galperín, Karina. "The Dido Episode in Ercilla's *La Araucana* and the Critique of Empire." *Hispanic Review* 77, no. 1 (2009): 31–67.

Gómez Canseco, Luis. "El retrato de Alonso de Ercilla en *La Araucana*: variantes y función." *Lemir Revista de Literatura Española Medieval y del Renacimiento* 23 (2019): 255–62.

Góngora Marmolejo, Alonso de. *Historia de todas las cosas que han acaecido en el Reino de Chile y de los que lo han gobernado*. Edited by Miguel Donoso Rodríguez. Madrid/Frankfurt: Iberoamericana/Vervuert, 2010.

Harvey, Elizabeth D. *Ventriloquized Voices: Feminist Theory and English Renaissance Texts*. London: Routledge, 1992.

Helgerson, Richard. *A Sonnet from Carthage: Garcilaso de La Vega and the New Poetry of Sixteenth-Century Europe*. Philadelphia: University of Pennsylvania Press, 2007.

Lacerda, Bernarda Ferreira de. *Hespaña libertada: parte primera*. En Lisboa: en la Officina de Pedro Crasbeeck, 1618. catalogo.bne.es Library Catalog. Web.

Martínez, Miguel. *Front Lines: Soldiers' Writing in the Early Modern Hispanic World*. Philadelphia: University of Pennsylvania Press, 2016.

– "Writing on the Edge: The Poet, the Printer, and the Colonial Frontier in Ercilla's *La Araucana* (1569–1590)." *Colonial Latin American Review* 26, no. 2 (2017): 132–53.

Medina, José Toribio. *La Araucana. Documentos*. Santiago de Chile: Imprenta Elzaviriana, 1918.

- *La Araucana. Ilustraciones* II. Santiago de Chile: Imprenta Elzaviriana, 1918.
- *La Araucana: Vida de Ercilla.* Santiago de Chile: Imprenta Elzaviriana, 1916.
Nicolopulos, *James. The Poetics of Empire in the Indies: Prophecy and Imitation in "La Araucana" and "Os lusíadas."* University Park: Pennsylvania State University Press, 2000.
Plagnard, Aude. *Une épopée ibérique: Alonso de Ercilla et Jerónimo Corte-Real (1569–1589).* Madrid: Casa de Velázquez, 2019.
- "Une poétique des confins: *La Araucana* (Chili, second XVIe siècle)." *Crisol* (2020): n.p. Web. https://crisol.parisnanterre.fr/index.php/crisol/article/view/257/322.
Quint, David. *Epic and Empire: Politics and Generic Form from Vigil to Milton.* Princeton, NJ: Princeton University Press, 1993.
Schwartz Lerner, Lía. "Tradición Literaria y Heroínas indias en *La Araucana.*" *Revista Iberoamericana* 38, no. 81 (1972): 615–25.
Sempere, Jerónimo. *Primera [Segunda] parte de la Carolea: trata las victorias del Emperador Carlos V Rey de España* ... Valence: Joan de Arcos, 1560.
Valencia, Felipe. *The Melancholy Void: Lyric and Masculinity in the Age of Góngora.* Lincoln: University of Nebraska Press, 2021.
Vilà, Lara. *Épica e imperio. Imitación virgiliana y propaganda política en la épica española del siglo XVI.* Barcelona: Universitat Autònoma de Barcelona. Serveix de Publicacions, 2001.
Vivar, Jerónimo de. *Crónica de los reinos de Chile.* Edited by Ángel Barral Gómez. Madrid: Dastin, 2001.

PART THREE

Gendered Epics

6 The Voice and the Veil: Pearls, *Villancicos*, and Dissent in Juan de Castellanos's "Elegy 14"[1]

EMIRO MARTÍNEZ-OSORIO

"In prose and in art, pearls opened the door to reflections on the nature of empire."[2]

Juan de Castellanos's rendering of Pedro de Ursúa's expedition in search of the Kingdom of Omagua and El Dorado along with Lope de Aguirre's subsequent rebellion stands out for at least two reasons. First, because there are places in "Elegy 14" that make no attempt to offer a realistic account of what unfolded during the journey.[3] Instead, Castellanos adds scenes that do not appear in the testimonies of eyewitnesses, idealizes the landscape, and narrates events using a poetic discourse that is filled with intertextual references and allusions to the poetic conventions championed in Spain by courtier-poets like Juan Boscán and Garcilaso de la Vega. The poetic liberties taken by Castellanos are so pronounced that it has prompted one critic to suggest that, at times, he "writes more like a pastoral poet than a rhyming chronicler."[4] On the other hand, Castellanos's narration of the events that unfolded deep in the Amazon jungle around 1561 also stands out because he combines the description of Ursua's expedition (cantos III through VII) with his account of the apogee and demise of the pearl fisheries on the island of Margarita (canto I). As we know, the island of Margarita had little or nothing to do with the initial objectives of Ursúa's expedition but was raided by Lope de Aguirre and his followers prior to Lope de Aguirre's defeat and execution in Barquisimeto, Venezuela. In my view, by joining these two seemingly mismatched topics, Castellanos offers readers a poem that speaks about the maritime-centred focus of the early phase of expansion as well as the land-centred priorities of exploration that followed. But more importantly, by producing a poem that bridges different stages and modalities in the expansionist enterprise, Castellanos is able to place the theme of political and poetic dissent at the forefront of his writings. Certainly, even though other expeditions had led to mutiny or failed calamitously, seldom had one expedition so radically severed the bonds of solidarity among Spanish explorers or unleashed such a degree of self-destructive violence. In a social context marked by conflict, in very few cases the discontent of those soldiers who felt that they had not been properly rewarded for their services went so far as to express itself with such overt disregard for the authority of the king or his representatives. On the other hand, by the time the first volume of the *Elegías* is published in 1589, the pearl fisheries in the Caribbean had come "to be understood as an egregious example of mismanagement of human and natural wealth, an embarrassing product of ineffective royal policy."[5]

In her study of the historiographic and literary tradition that emerged from accounts of Lope de Aguirre's rebellion, Ingrid Galster acknowledges that Petrarchism is one of the main elements of some sections of Castellanos's "Elegy 14," but she sidesteps its significance by casting it as an ornamental aspect of the text, or by downplaying Castellanos's abilities as a writer. For example, when referring to the section of canto III that narrates the tragic end of the love affair between Pedro de Ursúa and Inés de Atienza, Galster limits her remarks to suggesting that "readers familiar with Petrarchist motifs might find the narration of the episode pleasurable" (los lectores familiarizados con el conjunto de motivos de la literatura petrarquistas hallarán placer en ella). In relation to Castellanos's rendition of nature's expression of sorrow after the death of Inés de Atienza, Galster proposes that similar depictions of nature can be found "with greater poetic perfection in Garcilaso."[6] And yet, Petrarchism is a very common feature of many texts that accompanied Iberian expansion and, far from an ancillary aspect of these texts, operates as "an original imperialist discourse in the Americas."[7]

In this essay, I approach "Elegy 14" as Castellanos's most productive engagement with some of the tenets of Petrarchism. In this poem, the author endeavours to situate the New World on comparable footing to prestigious imperial locations such as the city of Granada, as referenced by Juan Boscán in his famous letter to the Duchess of Soma, or the cities of Toledo and Naples in the poetry of Garcilaso de la Vega. From this perspective, Castellanos's recalibration of Petrarchist conventions in canto III of "Elegy 14," and the celebration of traditional expressions of Castilian poetry elsewhere in the poem, serve as the fulcrum for the negotiation of symbolic capital and the promotion of a divergent vision of imperial expansion and masculinity in contrast to the one embraced by courtier-poets at the service of the Hapsburgs. Indeed, "Elegy 14" affords Castellanos not only with an outlet to distance the *encomendero*[8] class of New Granada from the violence and excesses associated with Lope de Aguirre's rebellion but also with a large canvas on which to sketch the profile of a male subject who lacks the ideological fissures scholars have identified in the poetry of Garcilaso de la Vega, or in poets who used Garcilaso as a model, chiefly Alonso de Ercilla.[9] From this perspective, one of the main unifying threads that binds the divergent material included in the seven cantos of "Elegy 14" is the fashioning of a complex poetic self (*yo*) who emerges as eyewitness, long-term resident on the island of Margarita, historian, friend, moral authority, and, not surprisingly, poet and lover. In my analysis, I assign special attention to pearls as one of the most sought after goods associated with the early phase of transatlantic exploration and to the style of women covering their faces in public, which became a characteristic marker of social transgression in the Iberian Atlantic circuit by the end of the sixteenth century.[10] Pearls and the controversial fashion of veiled ladies (*tapadas*) converge in the poem's depiction of the mestiza Inés de Atienza, who embodies the *encomenderos*'s aspirations of social mobility, wealth, and prestige, all of which were diminished by the promulgation of the New Laws (1542) and the administrative apparatus at the service of the Hapsburgs. Rather than rejecting the generic indeterminacy of Castellanos's *Elegías*, this reading welcomes it, and offers a more multifaceted image of Castellanos as a writer than the two-dimensional portrait of a clergyman that adorns the first volume of his writings.

From Heroism to Patriotism, from Biography to Chorography

"Elegy 14" is quite different from other poems in the first volume of the *Elegías* for several reasons. First, as critics have observed, up until "Elegy 12" Castellanos arranges his material in chronological order and focuses loosely on the figure of an explorer.[11] "Elegy 1" and "Elegy 4" are devoted to Christopher Columbus; "Elegy 2" to Rodrigo de Arana; "Elegy 3" to Francisco de Bobadilla; "Elegy 5" to Diego Colón, and so on. In contrast, the last two poems of the first volume focus on concrete geographic locations. "Elegy 13" memorializes the rise and fall of the pearl fisheries on the island of Cubagua, and "Elegy 14," as noted earlier, recounts the apex and demise of the neighbouring island of Margarita. The full title of "Elegy 14" is "Elogio de la isla Margarita donde se da relación de la vivienda de la gente que allí reside y de los infortunios que ha padecido, con otras muchas particularidades dignas de memoria" (A tribute to Margarita Island with an account of the lives of its inhabitants and the misfortunes they have suffered, along with many other details worthy of remembrance).

The shift from honouring the illustrious gentlemen (*varones ilustres*) heralded in the title of his volume of poems to celebrating New World locations could have been the result of Castellanos's awareness of the increasing popularity of chorography, "a genre whose authors served the particular historical interest of individual cities and whose outlook of the past was distinctly local."[12] As Richard Kagan has shown, the interest in chorography "served as the inspiration for many of the geo-historical projects launched by Philip II, including the *Relaciones geográficas*; [Ambrosio de] Morales' compendium of Spanish antiquities; and the ... views of Spanish cities that Philip II commissioned from the Flemish painter, Anton van den Wyngaerde."[13] In turn, the popularity of chorography and the impact of the questionnaire of the *Relaciones geográficas* in the Spanish American colonies, in particular, must have played a role in the production of the maps that accompanied the manuscripts of the *Elegías*, one of which depicted the Gulf of Venezuela, as noted by Luis Fernando Restrepo.[14]

By combining the showcasing of a New World setting in canto I with the narration of Lope de Aguirre's rebellion in cantos III through VII, Castellanos establishes a tension between loyalty to one's *patria* (the island of Margarita and the New Kingdom of Granada) and loyalty to the monarch, which were the key elements of chorography vs. royal history demonstrated by Kagan. After all, it is by celebrating the memory of a bygone era on the island of Margarita that Castellanos finds the pretext to write at length about Lope de Aguirre. If indeed Castellanos aimed to produce a more local view on historical events, capitalizing on the popularity of chorography offers a more effective solution than arranging the material around the figure of a single explorer, in this case Captain Pedro de Ursúa. In "Elegy 9" Castellanos declares himself indebted to Ursúa and announces his intention to write at length about Ursúa's deeds as explorer and soldier.[15] Yet the expectations of a martial narrative centred on Ursúa never materializes since "Elegy 14" offers a rather anticlimactic ending for the first volume of the *Elegías* by pivoting on the themes of failure, treason, and deception. More precisely, in the second stanza of canto I, Castellanos explicitly narrows the scope of his approach to Ursúa's accomplishments by announcing he will provide only a "brief summary" of Ursúa's ordeals.[16] In addition, the portrayal of Pedro de Ursúa in cantos II to IV, far from sketching the profile of a heroic military leader, casts Ursúa as a tragic figure at best, or a blinded lover at worst. Certainly, the flaws in Ursúa's character become patently evident in his failure to pay heed to successive warnings that foretell his imminent doom, and his sheer inability to lead the expedition or recognize the danger around him. The first warning is offered by an experienced soldier named Pero Alonso, who counsels

Ursúa to pay less attention to his lover and to be more cautious (630). The second is given by Inés de Atienza, when she shares with her lover the premonitions she has in a series of dreams (632–3).[17] The final warning is provided by a black slave named Joan Criollo, who overhears a group of men plotting to kill Ursúa (634). In this context, rather than highlighting his noble equanimity as hidalgo, Ursúa's final words to his murderers enhance his ineptness at addressing the task at hand: "and realizing he was seriously wounded / [Ursúa] exclaims 'what is the reason for this, gentlemen?'" (Él viéndose herir de golpes fieros / les dice: ¿por qué es esto caballeros?) (635).

In "Elegy 14" the remembrance and narration of a particular place is intimately tied to the fashioning of the self of the poet who remembers it. Certainly, "Elegy 14" differs from other poems in the first volume of the *Elegías* because in this poem Castellanos moves from offering passing references to himself to occupying a more prominent role in his own writing. Castellanos situates himself at the centre of his narrative by stating in the opening stanza: "Let us deal with the island of Margarita / about whose description I have much to say" (Tratemos de la Isla Margarita, / En cuya descripción tengo yo voto) (591). Rather than a gratuitous autobiographical gaffe, the interplay between the New World locale and the poet expresses poignantly the tug of war between imperial priorities and royal administration, on the one hand, and individual initiative and local custom, on the other, during the heyday of the pearl fisheries on the island of Margarita.[18] Moreover, Castellanos's assertion of his individuality and experience at the start of the poem makes clear that neither the loyal but weak Pedro de Ursúa nor the rebellious and violent Lope de Aguirre can match his overarching presence throughout the poem.[19] And what better way to boost his own authority early in canto I than by providing a portrait of himself as a young man while employing a central motif of European literature, the *locus amoenus*, to depict one of the earliest experiments in wealth accumulation across the Atlantic, the pearl fisheries on the "violently cosmopolitan" island of Margarita?[20]

The Voice: A New Lyric for a New (Albeit Fleeting) World

Another reason why "Elegy 14" differs from other poems in the first volume of the *Elegías* has more to do with literary than historiographic conventions. In "Elegy 1" Castellanos states that his work is devoid of poetic embellishment and suggests to readers that the sole criterion to judge its merits should be by his ability to tell the truth.[21] At the beginning of "Elegy 14," however, the poetic voice appears quite aware of poetic conventions and invokes assistance from the heavens to put forth his best writing style:

> Provea de favor el alto Cielo
> enriquezca mi vena y el estilo
> porque proceda yo mejor que suelo
> en la prolija trama de este hilo. (592)

> (Grant me your favour, Heaven above, / Grace me with inspiration and style, / So that I may proceed better than usual / In the intricate weaving of this thread.)

For readers who ignore the significance of this shift, Castellanos circles back a few stanzas later and likens his poem to a literary and musical salad. The use of this culinary metaphor brings to mind the musical salads by Mateo Flecha Sr. and introduces into the poetic discourse not only the possibility of reconciling different themes and sources, as Marrero-Fente points out,[22] but also the elements of music, performance, and theatricality. Thus relying on classical, biblical, and contemporary sources, Castellanos transforms the pearl settlement into an elaborate *locus amoenus*. The island – whose economy thrived owing to the rapacious extraction of pearls destined for consumers elsewhere – is depicted as a safe, bountiful, and beautiful dwelling place where explorers and soldiers leave behind the affairs of war and enjoy a life of leisure that includes singing *canciones* and *villancicos* under the auspices of Polymnia and Erato, the Greek muses of religious and lyric poetry. Hence, the principal sounds evoked in the first half of the first canto of "Elegy 14" are not those of martial trumpets or drums that call to battle, but "of voices tuned to perfection" (voces concertadas en su punto) and musical instruments that accompany lyric poetry:[23]

> Allí se cuelgan las pendientes camas
> adonde templan aires los calores,
> entre las espesuras de las ramas
> hay cantos de suaves ruiseñores;
> con cuyo son las damas y galanes
> encienden más sus pechos y amores:
> allí mirar, allí la dulce seña,
> que el ardiente deseo les enseña.

> Allí también dulcísimo contento
> de voces concertadas en su punto,
> cuyos conceptos lleva manso viento
> a los prontos oídos por trasunto:
> corre mano veloz el instrumento
> con un ingenioso contrapunto,

enterneciéndose los corazones,
con nuevos *villancicos* y *canciones.*

Porque también Polimia y Erato,[24]
con la conversación del duro Marte
de número sonoro y verso grato,
tenían deste tiempo buena parte:
rara facilidad, suave trato,
y en la composición ingenio y arte,
de los cuales discípulos y alumnos
podríamos aquí decir algunos.

Y aun tú, que sus herencias hoy posees
no menos preciarás saber quién era
Bartolomé Fernández de Virués
y el bien quisto Jorge de Herrera:[25]
hombres de más valor de lo que crees,
y con otros también de aquella era
Fernán Mateos, Diego de Miranda,
que las musas tenían de su banda. (597)

(There [in the Valley of San Juan] hang the hammocks / Where passion
warms the air, / Among the dense branches / Sweet nightingales sing
their songs; / With whose sound the ladies and sirs / Further inflame their
hearts with love: / Look there, there the sweet sign / That burning desire
reveals to them. // There also the sweetest pleasure / Of voices tuned to
perfection, / Whose lyrics are carried by the gentle wind / Echoing towards eager ears: / The nimble hand strums the instrument / With clever
counterpoint, / Endearing hearts, / With new *villancicos* and *canciones.* //
Because Polymnia and Erato, / Together with the resilient Mars and his
dialogues' / Resounding rhythm and pleasant verse, / Were also very important during this time: / Uncommon ability, pleasant style, / And in
composition, inventiveness and art, / Whose disciples and students / We
could name here quite a few. // And even you, who today enjoys their
legacy / Would not refuse learning of / Bartolomé Fernández de Virués, /
And the renowned Jorge de Herrera: / Men of greater courage than you
think, / As well as many others also from that time, / Fernán Mateos,
Diego de Miranda, / Whom the muses had smiled upon.)

Assuming that the commoners singing poetry are also some of the
same men to whom the poetic voice refers as "courageous soldiers"
(valerosísimos soldados), the last line of the last stanza (que las musas
tenían de su banda) is significant. It would recall a somewhat similar

line from book 9 of the *Aeneid* in which Virgil recounts how one of the
men killed in battle by Turnus was not only a soldier but also a poet:

> Cretheus, friend of the Muses, the Muses' comrade,
> Cretheus always dear to his heart the song and lyre,
> turning a verse to the tout strings; always singing
> of cavalry, weapons, wars and the men who fight them. (bk. 9, 873–6)

In that section of the *Aeneid*, Virgil could be imitating a passage from
Homer's *Iliad* in which Achilles appears "playing his lyre and singing of 'men's deeds of renown' to his dear comrade Patroclus."[26] As
pointed out by Timothy Power, another important model for Virgil
could have been Homer's Demodocus, whom the "muse loved exceed-
ingly," or Apollonius's Orpheous, "who contributes to the Argonautic
mission not with a weapon, but his lyre."[27] In any event, while the
gathering of poets on the island of Margarita does not take place prior
to or after a battle like in Virgil's or Homer's works, the description of
the setting as a place of safety, harmony, and peace is constructed upon
the premise that those individuals deserve to be there. That is, this
island is a sort of reward for the risks they have taken, the hardships
they have endured, and the daring deeds they have accomplished. In
this regard, it is worth noting again that the poets on the island of Margarita sing under the auspices of Erato, the muse who also "presides
over those who sing the great accomplishments of heroes and unde-
feated men" ([p]reside a los que cantan las hazañas de los héroes e
invictos varones).[28]

If Castellanos is one of the poet-musicians who participated in these
gatherings, then the implications are dual: first, he was more prolific
than previously thought; and, second, it would appear that he had an
interest in traditional expressions of Castilian poetry long before starting to write his narrative heroic poems in *octavas reales*. Castellanos's
keen evocation of these *canciones* and *villancicos* is probably one of the
few traces of them that remain since they have been lost and we do not
know what melodies accompanied their singing. In hindsight, we can
speculate that Castellanos could be referring to them, or to similar compositions, when in his last will he entrusts Gabriel de Rivera not only
with the manuscripts of his *Elegías*, but also with "all the other papers
and notebooks related to poetry that might be found in the desks at my
houses" (los demás papeles y cartapacios tocantes a poesía que en mis
casas y sus escritorios se hallaren).[29] While that could be a possibility,
it is worth stressing that, in the stanzas cited above, Castellanos associates himself with a poetic tradition distinct from the practice of lettered

noblemen emphasizing their excellence with the sword and the pen. Indeed, rather than a sword and a pen in the manner that Garcilaso de la Vega and Alonso de Ercilla portray themselves in their poems, these men appear to be wielding their musical instruments (likely *vihuelas*) and their voices.[30] Accordingly, the *canciones* Castellanos refers to are not the type of *canciones* produced by Garcilaso de la Vega or Fernando de Herrera, but the poetic forms included in the *Cancionero general*, the same collection of poetry Boscán associates with plebeians in his letter to the Duchess of Soma.[31]

The scene described in the stanzas cited above is remarkable for several reasons. First, the description of this group of commoners engaged in playing music and singing is the focal point of the first half of canto I. The poem starts by offering a panoramic view of the entire island, next proceeds to narrow the frame to a group of valleys, and finally to one valley in particular, the Valley of San Juan, and then focuses on a single colossal ceiba tree whose vast shade provides the lovely setting where the gathering occurs. Visually, therefore, the jamboree of poets and musicians enjoying *otium* constitutes the central point of the landscape that the poem is trying to reconstruct. If we accept that Castellanos is in the group, he would be placing himself in his role as a poet in the foreground of the vast landscape and the enormous poem he writes about it. On the other hand, the stanzas stand out in the context of the entire poem. The poem includes no descriptions of any physical structures built by residents on the island such as houses, churches, or piers, yet it offers an unobstructed view of the gathering, and dedicates four stanzas to evoke the sounds of *canciones* and *villancicos* and to celebrate the memory of those men who sang them. The poem therefore elevates the ability to create, perform, and enjoy poetry and music as one of the cornerstones of the emerging society on the island and of the project of expansion the inhabitants on the island had envisioned. To be clear, far from a veritable arcadia fully cut off from worldly concerns, what the first canto of the poem depicts is a community that combines the privileges afforded to men of arms within Spanish society with the rewards of new extractive economies, made possible through the enslavement and forced labour of Indigenous peoples and Africans.[32] In fact, halfway through the first canto Castellanos clarifies that the seemingly idyllic world he describes only started to decline after the depletion of the pearl fisheries and the promulgation of the New Laws limiting the enslavement of Indigenous peoples:

Porque como las perlas se acabaron
en aquella sazón ya repetida

> y luego los esclavos se quitaron
> a causa de la ley establecida. (599)

Moreover, the simile that conveys the eventual decline of the colony on the island reveals the financial incentives that led to its founding in the first place, and the intersection between exploration, trade, and the ephemeral character of the boom town:

> Bien como cuando veis a gran mercado
> ocurrir de gentío peregrino
> tal número que tienen ocupado
> la plaza, la calzada y el camino,
> y aquel contrato hecho y acabado,
> se vuelve cada cual por donde vino
> dejando vacos los lugares llenos,
> y los que en ellos quedan son los menos. (600)

> (Like when you see a great market / Spring up among migrant peoples / So great in number that they pack / The square, the sidewalk, and the road, / And once the business has been carried out, / Each one of them returns from whence they came / Leaving vacant those filled places, / And those who remain are very few.)

The explicit mention of the types of compositions these commoners are performing (*canciones* and *villancicos*) is noteworthy because they were typically associated with traditional Castilian poetry as opposed to the new Italian-style poetry embraced by courtiers like Juan Boscán, Garcilaso de la Vega, and others.[33] It is as such that *canciones* and *villancicos* are grouped together with *coplas españolas* and *romances* in Cristóbal de Castillejo's well-known "Reproof against those Spanish poets who write in Italian metres" (Reprensión contra los poetas españoles que escriben en verso italiano):[34]

> Mas ellos [Garcilaso de la Vega and Juan Boscán], caso que estaban
> sin favor y tan a solas,
> contra todos se mostraban
> y claramente burlaban
> de las coplas españolas,
> *canciones y villancicos*
> romances y cosa tal
> arte mayor y real
> y pies quebrados y chicos
> y todo nuestro caudal.[35]

It is vital to acknowledge the reference to *canciones* and *villancicos* in "Elegy 14" in light of the controversy regarding the appropriation of Italian verse forms in Spain because the debate hinges on the intersection of taste, masculinity, and authority, which are also central themes in Castellanos's writings. From the very title of his collection of poems, which translates to *Elegies of Illustrious Men of the Indies*, Castellanos works to align explorers and soldiers in the New World, not so much with contemporary generations of noblemen who could use the sonnet "as court coin, a stamp of a certain degree of erudition and an affiliation with the institutions of power,"[36] but with the older Castilian tradition of military excellence that preceded the Hapsburgs. Therefore, in the context of the evolving identity of Spain and the implications of poetry for models of masculinity, authority, and taste, there is an intriguing tension at play in the stanzas that use *octavas reales* not to chastise but to celebrate traditional Castilian poetry like *canciones* and *villancicos*. This tension is compounded if we consider that the use of the noun wit (*ingenio*) and the adjective witty (*ingenioso*) in relation to the ability to compose and perform *canciones* and *villancicos* negates Boscán's pejorative assessment of traditional poetic expressions that preceded the rise of Italianizing poetry in Spain. It is worth recalling that in his letter on poetry, Boscán informs the Duchess of Soma that a central topic of his memorable conversation with the Italian ambassador Andrea Navagero in Granada had been "matters of wit and letters" (cosas de ingenio y letras).[37]

It is equally significant that Castellanos states that the poems and songs they are performing are new. I do not think he is referring to *canciones* or *villancicos* brought to the New World from Spain but of new poems composed by the residents of Margarita after their arrival on the island. Certainly, *nuevos* is a loaded term in a context in which poetic experimentation favoured imitation, parody, contrafactum, and plain hybridity, of which Castellanos's writings offer multiple examples. The use of the adjective *nuevos* draws attention to the New World, not only as a new geography, but also in relation to creative processes that had remained hidden or unknown and that emerged in association with the enterprise of expansion. In this sense, Castellanos would be using the word in a manner similar to the way in which Christopher Columbus uses it in a letter he wrote after his third journey. Columbus refers to the lands he had encountered as "the new heaven and world that had until then remained hidden" (Al nuevo cielo y mundo que fasta entonces estaba oculto).[38] Had they survived, these *canciones* and *villancicos* might be crucial to understanding the role of traditional Castilian poetry in mediating the encounter between the Old World and the New. As far as Castellanos's poem is concerned, the stanzas dedicated to the gathering of poets offer testimony of a poetic renewal that takes place in a distinctly American setting, under the shade of the enormous ceiba tree at the centre of the *locus amoenus*:

Y a sombra de la ceiba deleitosa
admirable de grande y hermosa.

Con cierta cantidad no señalamos,
por increíble cosa, tronco y cepa,
pues toma tal espacio con sus ramos
que dudo que mayor otro se sepa:
tan bella, tan compuesta la pintamos,
que hoja de otra hoja no discrepa;
allí con el frescor del manso viento
daba cien mil contentos un contento.

En torno de la cual los verdes prados
de naturales y traspuestas flores
estaban todos tiempos estampados
de pinturas diversas en colores;
y a vista grande copia de ganados
que rodeaban rústicos pastores,
y debajo de ramas tan amenas
asientos puestos y las mesas llenas. (596)

(And in the shade of the enchanting ceiba tree / Admirable in its size and beauty. // We cannot count them with precision, / Because it is an impressive sight, its trunks and roots, / For it occupies such great space with its branches / That I doubt another greater is known: / So beautiful, so dense do we describe it, / That one leaf is indistinguishable from the next; / There in the coolness of the gentle wind / One delight led to one hundred thousand more. / Around it the green meadows / And their native and transplanted flowers / Were perpetually decorated / With the hues of assorted colours; / And large herds of livestock in view / Surrounding pastoral shepherds, / And beneath its pleasant branches / Chairs were placed and the tables filled.)

Finally, the description of the Valley of San Juan on the island of Margarita shares some of the elements of the description, in canto IX of Camões's *Os Lusíadas*, of the *vale ameno* on the island of love (*ilha namorada*) conjured by Venus, and the site where a nymph sings "Orphic song" accompanied by musical instruments.[39] Yet the similarities can only go thus far. In Castellanos's poem the island is not inhabited by playful nymphs ready to reward explorers who are on their journey back to Europe, but by virtuous wives whose home is in fact the New World. Incidentally, far from serving as a vantage point to exalt a monarch, as Camões does for the young Portuguese king in the closing cantos of *Os Lusíadas*, "Elegy 14" partially puts the responsibility for the demise of the pearl fisheries on the detrimental effects of royal policy. In this regard, it merits further scrutiny to determine if the poetic voice is addressing Philip II directly when he uses apostrophe to declare "and even you who now possess their inheritances" (y aun tú que sus herencias hoy posees). This is not the type of veneration demonstrated by poets like Ercilla in his frequent use of apostrophe to link his poem to the monarch. Rather, it is more in line with the type of dissent encoded by rebel Lope de Aguirre in his letter to Philip II.

The Island of Margarita is Not a Place for Unrequited Love

After making his presence known in the opening lines of the poem, Castellanos goes on to sketch a self-portrait, not merely as a long-time resident of the island and eyewitness to some of the events he narrates, but also as a knowledgeable historian who can debunk the myth of the presence of the amazons in the New World (615), and as a loyal subject who at one point merges the act of writing his poem with the act of pursuing the rebel Lope de Aguirre (662). Accordingly, on two occasions in the final canto, Castellanos boasts his loyalty to the king by declaring that the punishments imposed on Lope de Aguirre and his supporters should have been harsher. Moreover, in the context of the dominant discourses that accompanied transatlantic expansion studied by Greene and others, Castellanos also depicts himself as a lover. At the end of canto III, the poetic voice links himself again to the island of Margarita by revealing that his fondness for that place comes from it being the site where he had found love as a young man:

> Hágales Dios el bien que yo deseo,
> que cierto quiero bien aquella tierra,
> pues por allí gasté mi primavera
> y allí tengo también quien bien me quiera. (662)

> (God grant them the good fortune I request, / I do indeed love that land, / For it was there I spent my youth / And there I also have someone who loves me deeply.)

Since these lines appear in a section of the poem that narrates Lope de Aguirre's takeover of the island of Margarita and the letter the rebel leader addressed to Philip II,[40] it is imperative to probe the function of such a clear affirmation of requited love beyond the merely autobiographical. What is the poetic voice signalling by encoding such a clear sense of completeness, confidence, and reciprocity in the declaration of his lover's requital and enduring loyalty? Or, more concisely, is there a connection between the poet's expression of romantic love and the administrative and political conflicts his poem is addressing? We can begin to approximate an answer to these questions by examining the relationship between imperial geography and poetic self in the poetry of another agent of empire, Garcilaso de la Vega. When reading "Elegy 14," it is crucial to recall Garcilaso's ability to sketch a map that links lyric voices to imperial endeavours in the Mediterranean, whether it be Carthage, Naples, Sicily, Barcelona, or, above all, Toledo. Here we can recall that moment from Garcilaso's "Elegy 2," in which the poetic persona who has presented himself as a soldier accompanying the emperor's troops at Sicily refers to Naples as a place of leisure and love, and as the place where he had left his beloved, and he ponders if she might have found another love:

D'aquí iremos a ver de la Serena
la patria, que bien muestra aver ya sido
de ocio y d'amor antiguamente llena.
Allí mi corazón tuvo su nido
un tiempo ya; mas no sé, triste, agora
o si estará ocupado o desparcido. (246)

(From here we will go to see from Serena / the homeland, which clearly had been / replete with leisure and love long ago. / There my heart had its nest / once; but now, sadly, I do not know / whether it is inhabited or abandoned.)

Without providing the name of the beloved, or describing any of her attributes, the lyric voice is able to anchor his poetic discourse in a specific imperial geography and a set of circumstances that would eventually put his personal interest at odds with his duties as a courtier and soldier. Garcilaso's ability to transform Naples, retrospectively, into a dear and intimate location must be taken into consideration when reading sections of "Elegy 14," chiefly the ending of canto III. Castellanos has no interest in emulating Garcilaso's painful examination of the burden of sexual jealousy and rather immodestly declares (presumably three decades after abandoning the island) that the lover he left behind on the island of Margarita still remains faithful, which could imply turning Garcilaso's use of the adverb *allí* on its head. Yet, the important thing to remember is that, in his "Elegy 2," Garcilaso uses the topic of jealousy to skilfully explore the difficulty in reconciling love and war while in the service of the emperor.[41] However, in these lines and throughout the entire poem, Castellanos and the group he represents appear to have no qualms about reconciling love with exploration and war, and thus they emerge as subjects devoid of the ideological fissures that scholars have identified in Garcilaso de la Vega and in epic poets like Alonso de Ercilla. Accordingly, rather than unrequited love, the bonds of marriage (*los ñudos conyugales*) are placed at the forefront of Castellanos's effort to convey the detrimental effects of what he sees as unjust royal measures. Notice that prior to turning to the topic of piracy in the second half of canto I, Castellanos closes the section about the demise of the pearl fishery at Margarita by celebrating the memory of the women who lived on the island and the loyalty they exhibited to their husbands. While death is a core theme of the *Elegías*, a palpable subtext of the stanzas cited below is the Petrarchan theme of the death of a beautiful and dearly beloved lady. Notice how the words *bella*, *belleza*, *hermosa*, or *hermosura* in relation to the physical attributes of the women appear eight times in the next seven stanzas. However, Castellanos refracts the Petrarchan topic by linking the weight of post-Tridentine religious reform of marriage to his criticism of what he considers the detrimental effects of royal mismanagement:

> Allí también señoras principales,
> en vida marital y mas segura,
> asidas con los ñudos conyugales
> frecuentaban también esta holgura,
> en aviso y belleza tan cabales
> que nadie tuvo mas de hermosura;
> pues con lo menos de su gracia dellas
> se pudieran decir algunas bellas.
>
> Catalina de Rojas, que señora
> fue de dicho valle y pertenencia,
> y de sus hijos debe ser ahora
> como de sucesores por herencia,
> tal fue que la mas bella se desdora
> ante su graciosísima presencia
> pues en donaire, gracia y en talante,
> allí no vimos cosa semejante.

La otra, de su nombre dicha Ana,
Ana de Rojas, digo, cuya cara
podía convencer la de Diana,
en gracia, resplandor y lumbre clara:
mas ¡ay dolor! Que contra la tirana
furia su pulcritud no la repara;
pues quien domaba tigres y leones,
no domó los humanos corazones.

Y Francisca Gutiérrez, que de Haro
estirpe clara tiene y generosa,
necesidad no tuvo de reparo
para ser con extremo muy hermosa,
suprema discreción, aviso raro,
conversación suave y amorosa,
cuyas gracias, facecias, cuyas sales,
no hallan semejantes ni aun iguales.

E Isabel de Reina, que no en calma
se queda, pues podía serlo dellas
en el cuerpo hermosa y en el alma,
santas costumbres, proporciones bellas,
claro triunfo, vitoriosa palma
de las graciosas dueñas y doncellas,
a la cual Dios en juventud florida
sacó de los peligros de la vida.

Y María de Lerma, cuya gracia
esmero parecía de natura,
si no fuera cubierto de falacia
el rostro de la humana hermosura:
pues ya sin esta fuerza y eficacia
lo come la terrena sepultura,
por ser al fin aqueste el paradero
de lo cabal y de lo más entero.

¿Qué podremos deciros de su hermana,
Joana de Ribas, que es también difunta,
sino que allí pintó natura humana
cuanto bueno se pinta y se trasunta?
virtud, bondad, honor, intención sana,
honestidad con hermosura junta,
cabal en todos dones de natura,
y no menos cabal en la ventura. (597–9)

(There also were gentlewomen, / Living a secure honourable life, / Bound by the bonds of marriage. / They also frequented in this place, / So exemplary were their prudence and beauty / That no one possessed greater allure; / For with just an ounce of their grace / Other women could be considered beautiful. // Catalina de Rojas, who was / the lady of this valley and tenure, / Which should belong to her children now / Being they the inheritors of her legacy, / So lovely was she that the greatest beauty tarnished / When in her charming presence, / For in finesse, grace and in demeanour, / We never saw there her equal. // The other was named Ana, / Ana de Rojas, I mean, whose face/ Could impress even Diana's, / In grace, radiance and glowing light: / Yet – what sorrow! – against cruel / Force, her beauty could not withstand; / For though it (her beauty) tamed tigers and lions, / it could not tame the human heart. // And Francisca Gutiérrez, who from Haro / Brought her pure and generous lineage, / Had no need of help / To be extremely beautiful, / The utmost discretion, rare prudence, / A gentle and affectionate voice, / Whose charm, wit, whose vigour, / Were incomparable and unequalled. // And Isabel de Reina, who does not sit / In sorrow, for she could be one of them [important women] / With her beautiful body and her soul, / Virtuous manners, lovely figure, / Evident victory, triumphant glory / Over the elegant madams and maidens, / Who was taken by God in her budding youth / Away from the perils of this life. / And María de Lerma, whose grace / Closely resembled that of nature, / If it were not for the deception that conceals / The face of human beauty: / Now without this strength and virtue / It is devoured by its earthly tomb, / For that is the final resting place / For the honest and for all. // What can we tell you about her sister, / Joana de Ribas, who is also deceased, / Except that in her existed such human nature / As good as any that ever was exuded? / Virtue, kindness, honour, pure intentions, / Honesty together with beauty, / Exemplary in every gift of nature, / And no less exemplary in happiness.)

In a manner similar to the male counterparts memorialized elsewhere in the *Elegías*, in these stanzas Castellanos gives the name and the physical and moral qualities of each individual. In the stanza dedicated to María de Lerma, this strategy acquires enhanced poignancy as the poet briefly evokes the site of her burial (*la terrena sepultura*). Thus, the broad scope that allowed readers to grasp the entirety of the island of Margarita is replaced by the narrow confines of María de Lerma's tomb. By devoting an entire stanza to each of the six women, "Elegy 14" momentarily yields the male-centred logic of its poetic discourse, and speaks of a type of heroism not necessarily tied to military dexterity. Castellanos acknowledges that these are not the only women from the island who are worthy of praise, and offers as a disclaimer that his memory fails him. He then goes on to suggest that he will write in similar detail about those women when he writes about the other locations. While that promise never materializes, the pivotal role assigned to women in the first half of canto I finds its counterpart in the attention devoted by the poet to Inés de Atienza elsewhere in "Elegy 14." As a result, when a reading of it takes into consideration the ideological implications of the depiction of its female characters, "Elegy 14" has far more thematic coherence than its broad geographic and chronological sequence might at first suggest.

The Veil: Cannibalizing the Poetry of Garcilaso de la Vega

To appreciate fully how Castellanos recalibrates some of the tenets of Petrarchism according to New World realities, in this section I will focus on the description of Inés de Atienza, the young widow who accompanied Pedro de Ursúa on his expedition. Inés de Atienza and Pedro de Ursúa died at the hands Lope de Aguirre's followers. Her presence on the expedition is confirmed by several sources, none of which come close to devoting as much attention to her as cantos III and IV of Castellanos's poem. Accordingly, no other source portrays Inés de Atienza as a veiled lady from Lima (*limeña tapada*) or describes a parade organized in her honour at any time during the journey. Furthermore, Castellanos devotes a considerable portion of canto III to setting up a love triangle among Pedro de Ursúa, Inés de Atienza, and an explorer named Lorenzo de Salduendo.

Inés's crucial role in "Elegy 14" is reinforced by the rich description of how the surrounding landscape displays sorrow after listening to her distressed plea when she is facing her imminent death. Unlike other sections of the poem, in the stanzas cited below, Castellanos introduces a poetic language similar to that found in Garcilaso de la Vega's bucolic poetry. In particular, the conventional terms used to personify nature and describe the sympathetic reaction of the landscape are either identical (*aves, árboles, fieras*), or come from the same semantic field as the elements employed by Garcilaso to describe how nature reacted after listening to Salicio lament the suffering caused by his unrequited love for Galatea in "Eclogue 1." An important difference when comparing the personification of nature in these two poems is that, while Salicio expresses his lament as he is figuratively dying of love for Galatea, in "Elegy 14" nature's reaction takes place immediately preceding Inés's violent and unjust death:

> Arroyos claros van por las mejillas
> y por hermosos pechos de la dama,
> que puestas por el suelo las rodillas,

piedad, piedad a voces clama.
El eco va haciendo maravillas,
con acento que al aire se derrama
endurecidos robles hacen blandos,
mas no los duros pechos y nefandos.
Las aves por los árboles gemían,
las fieras en el monte lamentaban
las aguas sus discursos detenían,
los peces en el centro murmuraban;
los vientos con los sones que hacían
tan execrado hecho detestaban:
salió de las cavernas un ruido
que perdieron de hombres el sentido. (647)

(Tears stream down the lady's cheeks / And over her beautiful breasts, / Her knees dropped to the ground, / Mercy, mercy she cries out: / The echo works its wonders, / Her voice spilling forth into the air / Makes the hardened oak trees bow with compassion / But not the hard-hearted and the vile. / The birds in the trees wailed, / The beasts of the forest mourned, / The waters ceased to flow, / The fish midstream moaned; / The winds with the sounds they made / Deplored such a loathsome act: / Out of the caves came a noise / That drove the men to lose their reason.)

Here I am reminded of Mary Barnard's analysis of Garcilaso's "Eclogue 1," and how she speaks of the authority bestowed upon Salicio and Garcilaso by using the mantle of Orpheus.[42] One of the key issues in Castellanos's "Elegy 14" is also poetic authority, particularly the authority to express views that carry an overt criticism of royal policies regarding the administration of the pearl fisheries, or the authority to narrate a rebellion that essentially rejected the social and political order represented by the king. While Castellanos goes to great lengths to distance himself from Lope de Aguirre, my contention is that the free adaptation and transformation of the conventions of the dominant form of amatory poetry is pivotal, not merely to make the New World experience intelligible to European readers, but also to create a privileged space of interpretation in which Castellanos can express political dissent and invite readers to consider alternative poetic and political arrangements.

Inés de Atienza's significance in "Elegy 14" is also confirmed by the inscription carved into the trunk of a tree, which marks the place where her body was buried. The transcription of the epitaph casts Inés de Atienza as an individual whose memory should be preserved, boosting

the authority of the poetic voice by retrieving and offering readers
something that would otherwise have been inaccessible or lost:

> Encubren estos laureles
> aquella que extremo fue
> de hermosas y fieles
> a quien sin qué ni por qué
> mataron manos crueles. (648)

> (Beneath these laurels lies / She who was supreme / Among the beautiful
> and devout, / Who without rhyme or reason / Was killed by cruel hands.)

The identity of the individual who wrote Inés's epitaph is not stated
as it is irrelevant. Nor does it matter who would be the audience that
will read the epitaph after the explorers continue their journey. What
matters is that the allusion to Petrarch is sufficient for readers to situate
and assess the characterization of Inés de Atienza within the poetic tradition metonymically expressed through the laurel tree. To be sure, all
along the first volume of the *Elegías* Castellanos has been transcribing
to the pages of his *Elegías* the epitaphs written to memorialize several
other explorers and conquistadors, including Joan Ponce de León (298),
Diego Velázquez de Cuellar (307), Francisco de Garay (334), Agustín
Delgado (489), Jerónimo de Ortal (499), Antonio de Sedeño (533), and
Pedro de Ursúa (640). But Inés's tomb stands out as it is the only one
adorned with leaves from a laurel tree. Accordingly, if in other instances
the transcription of the epitaphs serves to enhance Castellanos's authority as an eyewitness – "y yo vi que decían sus renglones / estas
mismas palabras y razones" (And I saw that its lines read / These very
words and reasons)[43] – Inés's epitaph is a highpoint in Castellanos's
strategy to write her name (and his own name) in relation to an established poetic tradition.

Taking into consideration the celebration of an American cornucopia,
and the prominence assigned to the ceiba tree in canto I, the allusion to
Petrarch's tree in a scene that takes place deep in the Amazon jungle
could seem out of place to some readers. However, the explicit reference to the laurel tree in Inés's tomb expresses poignantly not only the
intersection of poetry, exploration, and empire building, but also the
multiple ways in which poetry was embedded in the social fabric of
early Spanish-American society. On the other hand, although similar
gestures of carving messages on trees or rocks appear in multiple early
modern European texts, and go as far back as Ovid's writings,[44] Inés's
epitaph could also be interpreted as an allusion to Garcilaso's Elisa,

whose epitaph was carved into the bark of a tree in the climatic section of "Eclogue 3." In support of that reading, one can cite the fact that, after Inés de Atienza is buried, a group of nymphs (*driades*, *amandríades*, *nayades*) (648) come to mourn her passing. The anonymous nymphs who emerge from the river in "Elegy 14" bring to mind the four river nymphs weaving tapestries on the shores of the Tagus River in Garcilaso's poem: Filódoce, Dinámene, Climene, and Nise.

After it is established that there are repeated allusions to the poetry of Garcilaso de la Vega in key passages of "Elegy 14," we are better prepared to recognize the implications of Inés de Atienza's description as a veiled lady, and how the stanzas that describe her arrival at the campsite stage several commonplaces of Petrarchist love poetry. Prior to her arrival, Castellanos builds up anticipation for this scene by stressing Inés's physical beauty and referring to her as "the beautiful Inés" (la bella Inés). For competent readers, the epithet *bella* recalls the widely popular amorous episodes of Alonso de Ercilla's *La Araucana*, particularly the one involving Lautaro and Guacolda, as Ercilla introduces Lautaro's love interest as "the beautiful Guacolda" (la bella Guacolda).[45] In her contribution to this volume, Mercedes Blanco reveals the depth of Ercilla's debt to Garcilaso in that particular episode.[46] Interestingly enough, the two traits memorialized on Inés de Atienza's epitaph are two of the characteristics Ercilla assigns to the majority of the female Indigenous characters of *La Araucana*: physical beauty and fidelity.

If Petrarchist poets were fond of producing poetic portraits that assembled the female body through the description of a sequence of fetishized body parts (blonde braids, forehead, eyes, lips, neck, etc.), such a poetic portrait never materializes in "Elegy 14" because Inés arrives at the camp with her head and face partially covered. Readers gather that her physical features are there, but they cannot be visually apprehended. Certainly, Inés's body parts are depicted according to Petrarchan iconography of beauty (*aureo cabello*, *mejillas blancas*, and *blanco cuello*) but will only become fully visible to readers after Inés finds out about the death of her lover (636) or in the scene that describes the moment when she is struck with mortal wounds (648). For now, rather than dwelling on specific elements of her body, the poetic voice first describes Inés's attire and then moves upwards to describe the elaborate headdress she is wearing. In particular, in the first stanza the poetic voice details the elegant, colourful, and costly dress Inés is wearing, which combines prized commodities from Indigenous and European systems of exchange, such as feathers, pearls, and fine cloth. This description hence stresses Inés's socio-economic status, making her appear out of reach, impenetrable to those who behold her. Similarly, for

readers of the poem, the range of chromatic elements in the first stanza
(white, velvet, purple, blue, golden) signals an increased attention to
the sense of sight, a cornerstone of Petrarchan poetics:

En un cuartago blanco pequeñuelo
iba, pero muy bien aderezado,
basquiña de lustroso terciopelo,
un galdresillo de color morado,
las guarniciones de color de cielo,
con cristalinas perlas estampado,
capelete con plumas y medalla,
con el mas aderezo que se calla.

Rebozada hacía gran destrozo
de ánimas en esta compañía,
y mucho más después que cierto mozo
le dijo "por merced, señora mía,
os pido que quitéis ese rebozo,
veremos ya la luz del claro día,
que no sé cómo puede velo solo
cubrir rayos más claros que de Apolo."

Ella, de comedida cortesana,
el antifaz quitó luego a la hora.
Atónita quedó la gente vana
De ver rostro do tanta beldad mora:
Deshízose la lumbre de Diana
Sobrepujó lo claro de la aurora:
Dijeras en el alma más reclusa
Obrarse los efectos de Medusa.

En amoroso fuego van ardiendo
hasta los recatados y discretos,
y en el desventurado de Salduendo
hacen más impresión estos efectos;
pues en las muestras iba descubriendo
sus apasionadísimos concetos;
y aunque cesó la fiesta de aquel día,
nunca cesó su loca fantasía. (623–4)

(On a small white pony, / She rode, but well attired, / A lustrous velvet
skirt, / A cloak purple in colour, / Adornments the colour of the sky, / Decorated with sparkling pearls, / A headdress with feathers and gold / With

too much jewellery to describe. // With her veiled face she laid waste / To the spirits in this company / And even more so after a particular young man / Said to her: "out of kindness, my lady, / I beg you to remove your veil, / We then shall see the light of this bright day, / For I know not how but a single veil / Can contain rays brighter than those of Apollo." // She, a prudent woman, / Then removed her covering. / The vain crowd was left stunned / When they saw a face so full of beauty: / It eclipsed Diana's glow / Outshined the light of dawn: / One could say even the most impassive of souls / Was under the power of Medusa. // Love's flames had consumed / Even the most reserved and discrete, / And on the ill-fated Salduendo / The impression she made was much greater; / Throughout this exhibition he began to recognize / His passionate desires; / And though the celebration that day ended, / His wild fantasy never did.)

The brief mention of the pearls that adorn Inés's dress serves as a link between the account of Ursúa's expedition in canto IV, and the narration about the pearl fisheries at Margarita in canto I. But more crucially, if in canto I the poem says nothing about the callous labour regime that enabled the extraction of pearls, in canto IV the display of pearls as jewellery silences the intricate networks of exchange that allowed for the pearls to come into Inés's possession. This seems fitting for a poem in which the social groups who bore the burden for extracting pearls from the oyster reefs – enslaved Indigenous and African divers – are relegated to the background or are excluded altogether from the poem. In this sense, the pearls on display on Inés's dress are both an "emblem of maritime expansion"[47] and a symbol of the defiance of the increasingly bureaucratic structures of the Spanish Monarchy, even at the expense of naturalizing the violence inflicted against Indigenous peoples, Africans, and the natural environment.

The most important piece of clothing in Inés's attire is the veil (*rebozo, velo, antifaz*) that covers her face, which is mentioned in lines 1, 5, and 7 of the second stanza. In the second half of the sixteenth century, women on both sides of the Atlantic began to appear in public with their faces partially covered. This new style of clothing was referred to as veiled, or *tapado*, and women who dressed in this fashion were known as veiled ladies, or *tapadas*.[48] Since the veil prevented other people from recognizing the identity of the person wearing it, it is not difficult to imagine how this style of clothing could afford some women (or men, for that matter) a degree of agency, mystery, and power. This anonymity might be particularly useful if it allowed a woman to move easily in and out of public spaces without being recognized by her own relatives or peers. For the purpose of this study, it is worth noting that Inés is a veiled lady and appears confident, mysterious, and alluring, but only for the men who passively witness her arrival with expectation. In this sense, the manner in which Inés conducts herself in front of male spectators "porque su buen donaire y su meneo / ponía mil espuelas al deseo" (because her grace and movement / filled a thousand spurs [soldiers] with desire) and the fact that she is introduced in the poem as part of a love triangle also confirm her characterization as a *tapada* as a literary type. To borrow a phrase from Laura Bass and Amanda Wunder, Inés's characterization "evokes the flirtatiousness, freedom, and rivalries typically associated with the veiled woman."[49]

However, Inés is certainly not a veiled lady or *tapada* for the poet (or the readers of the poem). Prior to describing the moment of her arrival, Castellanos has already disclosed her full name, place of origin, social background, and the name of her father. By disclosing Inés's identity in this manner, any type of agency, disruptiveness, or empowerment associated with the social phenomenon of the *tapado* fashion is transferred to the poem itself, and particularly to the poetic voice. It is ultimately the poet who emerges as a more powerful agent because he is the one choosing to disclose information at his own will, and capable of discerning what lies beneath the surface. Notice that in this scene Inés is never given the opportunity to speak, and the episode quickly moves from the description of Inés's external appearance to Lorenzo de Salduendo's inner monologue. In addition, in the last line from the first stanza cited above, it is the poetic voice, not Inés, who asserts his own will to reveal or withhold information: "con el más aderezo que se calla" (with too much jewellery to describe).[50] For all of the reasons identified above, by introducing Inés in this manner, the poem's narrator emerges as the antithesis of a fragmented and subjugated Petrarchan speaker.

Although the detailed depiction of Inés as a veiled lady probably has something to do with the shifting expectations for the conduct of women in public places in early Spanish-American society, the scene has less to do with "the problem of social legibility,"[51] and more to do with the expectations for writing and reading poetry on opposite sides of the Atlantic. In this sense, Inés's veil is a powerful metaphor for both the blank page and the role assigned to ocular desire in the dominant expressions of amatory poetry. Notice that after Inés lifts her veil, the poem proceeds to unveil some of the worn-out conventions of the dominant form of love poetry. That is precisely what occurs when Lorenzo de Salduendo's infatuation quickly runs out and he begins to ponder whether Inés could even notice or understand his feelings or intentions, and particularly when Salduendo goes on to refute altogether the metaphor of love as illness:

> Al fin el regocijo ya desecho
> y todos los guerreros escuadrones,

el Salduendo tomó luego su lecho
sin esperar a mas conversaciones
su corazón bestial y falso pecho
distraído con mil vacilaciones
pero todas y todos sus cuidados
van a doña Inés encaminados.

Decía: "¡si su vista halagueña
acaso contempló mi buen talante
al tiempo que salí de la reseña
e hice las levadas de montante!
¡o si quiso notar aquella seña
que le hice pasando por delante!
parecióme cebar en mi los ojos …
pero creo que son vanos antojos.

Porque ¿qué ocasiones o qué prenda
hay para penetrar mis pensamientos?
o ¿qué le dije yo para que entienda
estos mis congojosos sentimientos?
¿O qué quiere decir tomar contienda
con quien es el señor de sus intentos?
¿Quién no dirá ser el intento mío
grandioso locura y desvarío?

O ¿cuál de las mujeres adivina
el mal y la congoja de sirviente
con una sola vista repentina
sin le decir jamás el mal que siente?
o ¿quién pudo dar cierta medicina
a los inocentes males del doliente?
¿en que buena razón o seso cabe
querer curar el mal que no se sabe?" (624)

(Once the festivities had concluded / And the soldiering squadrons dispersed, / Salduendo made his way to his bed / Without entertaining any other conversations: / His savage heart and dishonest soul, / Confused by a thousand doubts, / But all of them and all his attention / Were directed at Doña Inés. // He said: "And if her flattering eyes / By chance beheld my remarkable skill / When I rode forth from the line of troops, / And raised my steed upon his hind legs! / Or if she took notice of that gesture / I made as I passed before her! / It seemed that she fixed her eyes on me … / But I think these are all fruitless desires. // For what opportunity or what token / Could express my thoughts to her? / Or what might I have said for her to understand / These tormented feelings of mine? / Or what would it mean to clash / With he who is the master of her affection? / Who would not say that my affection / Is raving madness and absurd? // Or what woman would recognize / The pain and suffering of her admirer / With nothing but a hurried glance / Without him ever telling her the pain he is feeling? / Or who could administer the proper medicine, / For the unexpressed pains of the sufferer? / Whose sound reasoning or mind / Would lead them to cure an unknown pain?")

What we have, therefore, is a highly ironic scene that stages and re-works the poetic language of unrequited love, and draws the attention of readers to the acts of writing and reading texts per se. In this sense, it is remarkable that in only eight stanzas several conceits associated with that tradition are all put on display, frustrated, or questioned, including the poetic blazon; the depiction of love at first sight; the notion of love entering through the eyes; the metaphor of love as a flame; the comparison of love to an illness; the notion of referring to the beloved as cure; and even the feasibility of mute speech between two lovers.

Final Considerations: Between Clio, Calliope, and Erato

The first canto of "Elegy 14" offers one of the rosiest depictions of the early phase of exploration of the New World included in the first volume of Juan de Castellanos's *Elegías*. The depiction of the island of Margarita as an idyllic place is conveyed through references to pleasurable weather, the successful husbandry of crops and animals brought from the Iberian Peninsula, the safety and leisure enjoyed by Spanish colonists, the submissiveness of the native population, and the nostalgic remembrance of poetic jamborees. By characterizing it in this manner, Castellanos expresses a genuine concern with the fate of the Spanish residents in Margarita following the economic decline of the island. The effort he puts forth to memorialize their experience explains why so many Spanish residents are singled out with their proper names while Indigenous peoples remain anonymous or are referred to collectively, and their labour, knowledge, and expertise are stripped of any authority.[52] Accordingly, as he retells a time-tested story of arriving in paradise and subsequently being expelled from it, Castellanos appears impervious to the violence imposed on enslaved Indigenous and African peoples as well as to the toll on maritime ecosystems owing to the harvesting of millions of pearls from the ocean floor. In "Elegy 14" readers can find the antithesis of the depiction of the Pearl Coast (Costa de las Perlas) offered by Fray Bartolomé de Las Casas in his *Brevísima relación de la destrucción de las Indias* (1552). In one of the chapters of his impassioned pamphlet, Las Casas describes the harsh fate of the enslaved pearl divers who succumb to malnutrition, excessive labour, beatings, or are killed by sharks. Las Casas goes on to describe how the dehumanizing conditions under which the enslaved divers extract the pearls transform them into "monsters in human form or some other species" (monstruos en naturaleza de hombres o de otra especie).[53] The shared interest and incongruities between Castellanos's and Las Casas's accounts of what unfolded in that region confirm Rolena Adorno's argument that the texts produced in Colonial Spanish America are to a large extent the result of what she defines as "the polemics of possession"; that is, they are part of a web of "texts always centered on the rights of conquest and the treatment of Amerindians."[54]

As an organic product, pearls came in different shapes, sizes, colours, and intensity of lustre, and their variety made it difficult to establish and fix their monetary value. Despite their importance to the economy of the island of Margarita, in "Elegy 14" Castellanos does not describe pearls in any significant detail and only references them in passing. Accordingly, Castellanos's description of the island bypasses any concrete details related to pearl-fishing operations; when pearls are mentioned, it is either to celebrate their abundance: "and the sea in the distance / nurtures an abundance of clear pearls" (la mar en su distancia / cría de claras perlas abundancia) or to lament their scarcity, "because the pearls ran out" (porque como las perlas se acabaron).[55] However, elsewhere in the *Elegías*, Castellanos includes information that discloses his knowledge of the day-to-day function of the pearl fisheries, and of the terminology used to refer to the most coveted type of pearls: *caconas*.[56] For example, in "Elegy 3," Castellanos describes an Indigenous woman of high standing within her community as "heavily adorned and profusely attired / with what they call here *cacona*" (muy llena y adornada su persona / de lo que por acá llaman *cacona*).[57] Nonetheless, notions regarding value are central to "Elegy 14," not in relation to the price of pearls, but to the worth and contributions to empire building made by the men who appear singing *canciones* and *villancicos*.

In *Antología de poetas hispanoamericanos* (1894), Marcelino Menéndez y Pelayo proposes that if Castellanos had written his *Elegías* in prose (instead of verse) he would have produced one of the best and most prolific chronicles of the conquest of the New World.[58] In making this appraisal, Menéndez y Pelayo concurs with Agustín de Zárate's view that the author of the *Elegías* is first and foremost a historian. As censor of the first volume of the *Elegías*, Zárate was the first to suggest that Castellanos had originally written a historical chronicle in prose and then spent ten years translating it into verse (gastó más de diez años en reducir la prosa en verso).[59] But Zárate does not elucidate if Castellanos's history in prose (*historia en prosa*) would have been in line with the perspective offered by royal historians or chorographers. Certainly, as a historian who received a royal endorsement to publish a history of Peru, Zárate would have been sensitive to such issues. Although expressed more than three hundred years apart, Menéndez y Pelayo's and Zárate's assessments are informed to some degree by Aristotle's notion that it was possible to write history in verse, which was a matter of debate since it was introduced in Aristotle's *Poetics*. A closer examination of this issue exceeds the scope of this chapter. For now, suffice it to note that Zárate does not fully address what would have been the advantages of offering Philip II a history written in verse, "no de las redondillas que comunmente se han usado en nuestra nación, sino en estilo italiano, que llaman octava rima" (not in the *redondillas* that are commonly used in our country, but in the Italian style called ottava rima). As censor, Zárate simply suggests that given its length and difficulty it must have been an exercise for Castellanos "to display [through arduous labour] the eminence of his talent" "(por mostrar la eminencia de su ingenio). By establishing a difference between Spain and Italy in terms of poetic metres, Zárate's approval of the *Elegías* is revealing, not only about the link between poetic trends and empire building but also about the connection between state-sponsored censorship and the practice of literary criticism. In turn, offered at a time when empire building was no longer sustainable or desirable for Spain, Menéndez y Pelayo's appraisal would seem to strip Castellanos's work of its political thrust, regardless of whether it had been written in prose or verse, or transmitted orally as in the case of the *villancicos* and *canciones* referenced in this essay. To put it directly, if Castellanos had attempted to publish his *Elegías* in prose rather than verse, the contentious nature of the topics he examines would most likely had prevented his work from receiving approval for publishing or it would have drawn not praise but suppression, as occurred with the works of Francisco López de Gómara and Bartolomé de Las Casas after they appeared in print.

While there is little doubt that Castellanos's writings engage directly with evolving historiographic and cartographic practices, this essay has shown that his perspective about the enterprise of expansion acquires greater potency when placed in the context of the existing and emerging poetic traditions in the Iberian Peninsula. In "Elegy 14," in particular, Castellanos offers readers a privileged space of interpretation around the celebration of traditional expressions of Castilian poetry, and frequent allusions to the language and some of the conventions associated with the dominant expression of amatory poetry. Since there existed "a metonymic association between Petrarchist lyric and the Spanish empire,"[60] contemporary Iberian readers steeped in Petrarchist poetic practices (individuals like Pedro Sarmiento de Gamboa or Alonso de Ercilla, who served as censors for other portions of Castellanos's writings) would have been able to recognize not only the aesthetic but also the ideological import of Castellanos's poetic experiment, and the merits and shortcomings of his effort to place the New World on par with other poetic locations on the imperial map. In addition, readers familiar with Juan Boscán's translation of Baldassarre Castiglione's *Il libro del Cortegiano*, or versed in the ambitious poetic program offered in Garcilaso de la Vega's "Eclogue 3," would have had no difficulty in recognizing Castellanos's direct request for assistance to improve his own writing style as a mechanism to distance "Elegy 14" from the highly regarded principle of sprezzatura, which ultimately implied that poetry was not only "an aristocratic activity, but an exclusively aristocratic activity."[61] Finally, the connection Castellanos establishes among pearl fisheries, poetry, and political dissent eloquently encapsulates an early chapter of the expansionist project that deserves further attention. While Castellanos did not possess the temperament or the ethical concerns that allowed other writers to offer a more balanced assessment of the expansionist project, his unconventional poetic experiment still endures in his innovative approach to recount imperial setbacks and in his imaginative formulation of his expansive self, from fortune seeker on the islands of Cubagua and Margarita to defender of Inés de Atienza.

NOTES

1 I wrote the bulk of this chapter while I benefited from a non-stipendiary fellowship at the Centre for Renaissance and Reformation Studies at Victoria College in the University of Toronto. I am grateful to Ethan Matt Kavaler and to Natalie Oeltjen for their support and collegiality. I am grateful to Mercedes Blanco and Luis Fernando Restrepo for reading earlier drafts of this essay and offering valuable suggestions.
2 Warsh, *American Baroque*, 247.
3 My reference text for this chapter is Juan de Castellanos, *Elegías de varones ilustres de Indias*. In general, future page references from this work will be indicated parenthetically in the text of this chapter. Unless otherwise noted, all English translations from the *Elegias* are my own.
4 Markham, "Introduction," xxxvii.
5 Warsh, *American Baroque*, 6.
6 (con perfección poética mucho mayor, en Garcilaso.) Galster, *Aguirre o la posteridad arbitraria*, 118.

7 Greene, *Unrequited Conquests*, 6.

8 An *encomendero* received a royal tribute grant for his services to the Crown during the campaigns of conquest and was expected to protect and envangilize the natives entrusted to them.

9 For Garcilaso de la Vega, see Cruz, "Self-Fashioning in Spain," and two works by Middlebrook: "The Poetics of Modern Masculinity" and *Imperial Lyric*. See also Graf, "From Scipio to Nero to the Self." For Ercilla, see Davis, *Myth and Identity*, and the first chapter in Valencia, *The Melancholy Void*.

10 See Bass and Wunder, "The Veiled Ladies of the Early Modern Spanish World."

11 See Marrero-Fente, *Poesía épica colonial del siglo XVI*, and Kohut, "Las *Elegías de varones ilustres de Indias* de Juan de Castellanos y el problema de la épica Indiana de los siglos XVI y XVII."

12 Kagan, "Clío and the Crown," 84.

13 Kagan, "Clío and the Crown," 86.

14 According to Restrepo, both maps were suppressed by censors, and the map of Venezuela did not survive. See *Un nuevo reino imaginado*, 197–8. See also Restrepo, "Land and Sea in Juan de Castellanos."

15 "Y Ursúa, capitán tan excelente / cuanto pudieron ser los más cabales, / a quien los que vivimos de presente / debemos alabanzas inmortales, / y de quien trataré más largamente, / celebrando sus tristes funerales / por el orden que de presente llevo / pues si muchos le deben yo le debo." (Ursúa, an outstanding captain / whose excellence matches that of the best / and those of us alive today / owe him everlasting praise, / I will describe at length his unfortunate passing / in due time following this sequence, / because I am indebted to him like many more.) Castellanos, *Elegías*, 347.

16 "Pedro de Ursúa, capitán famoso, / de cuyos trances mi cansada pluma / querría dar alguna breve suma." (Pedro de Ursúa, famous captain / whose ordeals my weary pen / would provide a short summary.) Castellanos, *Elegías*, 592.

17 The epitaph in Ursúa's tomb highlights the pre-eminence of Inés's forewarning by declaring that Ursúa died "por no creer el aviso / de doña Inés su querida" (for ignoring the warning / of his beloved Inés). Castellanos, *Elegías*, 640.

18 See Warsh, *American Baroque*.

19 In relation to the protagonist of "Elegy 14," Avalle-Arce argues: (el lector debe caer en la cuenta de que el protagonista no es la isla de Margarita como parece anunciar el epígrafe y como lo fue la isla de Cubagua en la elegía anterior sino que el protagonista es el propio vesánico Lope de Aguirre.) See *La épica colonial*, 81–2. According to Marrero-Fente, in "Elegy 14," (hay diferentes protagonistas, pues reúne tres narraciones diferentes: la de

Jacques de Sores, la de Pedro de Ursúa y la de Lope de Aguirre.) See *Poesía épica colonial del siglo XVI*, 190.

20 I am borrowing the phrase "violently cosmopolitan" from Jorge Cañizares-Esguerra. See his book review of *American Baroque*, 1411.

21 For an analysis of the opening stanzas of "Elegy 1," see Martínez-Osorio *Authority, Piracy and Captivity*, 1–14.

22 Marrero-Fente, *Poesía épica colonial del siglo XVI*, 181.

23 The sounds evoked in the poem change significantly in the second half of the first canto as the blowing of trumpets and screams are linked to the attacks by French pirates.

24 In addition to Polymnia and Erato, in canto I the Roman goddess Ceres also appears as one favouring the harvests at the island of Margarita.

25 By including Jorge de Herrera, Castellanos establishes a connection between "Elegy 14" and "Elegy 13," the poem about the demise of the island of Cubagua. At the end of "Elegy 13," Castellanos transcribes a poem written by Herrera prior to abandoning the island of Cubagua. See Castellanos, *Elegías*, 591.

26 Martínez, *Front Lines*, 11. See also Homer, *Iliad*, 9.186–91.

27 Powers, "Vergil's Citharodes: Cretheus and Iopas Reconsidered," 97.

28 Covarrubias, *Tesoro de la lengua castellana o Española*, 800.

29 Rojas, *Juan de Castellanos*, 308.

30 Although Castellanos does not name the specific instruments employed in these performances, archival research confirms the importation of *vihuelas* to the Pearl Coast as early as 1530. See Domínguez-Torres, "Nel piu ricco paese del Mondo," 29, and Otte, *Las perlas del Caribe*, 390.

31 See Navarrete, *Orphans of Petrarch*.

32 The earliest licence issued by Charles V to bring enslaved Africans to the neighbouring island of Cubagua dates from 1526. See Domínguez-Torres, "Nel piu ricco paese del Mondo," 24. A royal decree from 1558 states that "only African slaves could be used for pearl fishing." See Domínguez-Torres, "Pearl Fishing in the Caribbean," 76.

33 In *Tesoro de la lengua castellana o española*, Sebastián de Covarrubias writes: "Las canciones que suelen cantar los villanos cuando están en solaz; pero los cortesanos, remedándolos, han compuesto a este modo y mensura cantarcillos alegres. Ese mismo origen tienen los villancicos tan celebrados en las fiestas de Navidad y Corpus Christi" (cited in León, 3, "MI-RE-MI-SOL-ESCONDIDO," 68). According to Baehr, "el villancico es una poesía estrófica de composición fija, pero variable forma métrica, de manera que autores, épocas y las colecciones de poesía prefieren una u otra. Los elementos de su composición (tal como ocurre con el estribote o la canción) son un estribillo inicial (llamado cabeza, villancico, letra de invención o tema) y la estrofa dividida en tres partes, dispuesta en dos mudanzas rigurosamente simétricas y una vuelta." See *Manual de*

versificación española, 320–6. For a recent study of the development of the genre of *villancicos* in the New Kingdom of Granada, see Sebastián León, "MI-RE-MI-SOL-ESCONDIDO."

34 The translation of the title is by Middlebrook, "The Poetics of Modern Masculinity in Sixteenth-Century Modern Spain," 155.

35 Rivers, *Antología de la poesía del siglo de Oro*, 53. Italics are mine.

36 Middlebrook, "The Poetics of Modern Masculinity in Sixteenth-Century Modern Spain," 163.

37 Boscán, *Obras*.

38 Wey Gómez, *Tropics of Empire*, 29.

39 Nicolopulos, *The Poetics of Empire in the Indies*, 188.

40 During his uprising, Lope de Aguirre wrote three letters: one to Pablo Collado, governor of Venezuela, one to Fray Francisco de Montesinos, and one to Philip II. See "Appendix" to Jos, *La expedición de Ursúa al Dorado*.

41 Cruz, "Self-Fashioning in Spain."

42 Barnard, *Garcilaso de la Vega and the Material Culture of Renaissance Europe*, 152–70.

43 Castellanos, *Elegías*, 489.

44 See Phaethon's epitaph in Book II of Ovid's *Metamorphoses*, and the reference to the inscription on a poplar tree in the letter from Oneone to Paris in Ovid's *Epistles*.

45 Ercilla, *La Araucana*, XIII.43.6.

46 See Blanco, "Lyric as Temptation in Ercilla and Tasso" in the present volume, *The War Trumpet*. See also Lerner, "Garcilaso en Ercilla," and Valencia, "Las 'muchas (aunque bárbaras) voces líricas de *La Araucana* y la índole poética de una 'historia verdadera.'" For the sharp differences between Ercilla and Castellanos, see Martínez-Osorio, *Authority, Piracy, and Captivity in Colonial Spanish American Writing*.

47 Warsh, *American Baroque*, 243.

48 In some cases, veiled ladies covered one eye to appear more seductive. Prior to the emergence of this controversial fashion, veiling had a long tradition in the Iberian Peninsula and was typically associated with feminine modesty or with an ideology that assigned a submissive role for women. See León Pinelo, *Velos antiguos y modernos*.

49 Bass and Wunder, "The Veiled Ladies of the Early Modern Spanish World," 101.

50 Although produced in a different context, it is worth recalling here Sor Juana's assertive unveiling of Sor Filotea at the end of her autobiographical letter "Respuesta de la poetisa a la muy ilustre Sor Filotea de la Cruz." See Cruz, *The Answer/La Respuesta*, 102.

51 Bass and Wunder, "The Veiled Ladies of the Early Modern Spanish World," 102.

52 Castellanos refers to Indigenous peoples as "indios naturales" (549), "sirvientes cautivos de tierras comarcanas" (597), and "esclavos" (599).
53 Casas, *Brevísima relación*, 144–5.
54 Adorno, *The Polemics of Possession*, 6.
55 Castellanos, *Elegías*, 594–9.
56 According to Jorge Cañizares-Esguerra, the word *cacona* derives from *caca* (shit) and is related to the fact that enslaved pearl divers swallowed the best pearls and then recovered them from their own faeces in order to buy their freedom. See Cañizares-Esguerra, "Review of *American Baroque*."
57 Castellanos, *Elegías*, 161.
58 "(hubiéramos tenido una de las mejores y más caudalosas crónicas de la conquista" (We would have had one of the best and most prolific chronicles of the conquest). Menendez y Pelayo, *Antología de poetas hispanoamericanos*, XII.
59 (escribió primero el discurso desta historia en prosa … [and late] gastó más de diez años en reducir la prosa en verso" (He first wrote the particulars of this history in prose … [and later] spent more than ten years in translating the prose into verse). Zárate, "Censura de Agustín de Zarate el Consejo Real," 50–1.
60 Navarrete, *Orphans of Petrarch*, 2.
61 Navarrete, *Orphans of Petrarch*, 48.

WORKS CITED

Adorno, Rolena. *The Polemics of Possession in Spanish American Narrative*. New Haven, CT: Yale University Press, 2007.

Aristotle. *Poetics*. Translated by Gerald F. Else. Ann Arbor: University of Michigan Press, 1970.

Avalle-Arce, Juan Bautista de. *La épica colonial*. Pamplona: Universidad de Navarra, 2000.

Baehr, Rudolf. *Manual de versificación española*. Madrid: Editorial Gredos, 1989.

Barnard, Mary E. *Garcilaso de la Vega and the Material Culture of Renaissance Europe*. Toronto: University of Toronto Press, 2014.

Bass, Laura R., and Amanda Wunder. "The Veiled Ladies of the Early Modern Spanish World: Seduction and Scandal in Seville, Madrid, and Lima." *Hispanic Review* 77, no. 1 (2009): 97–144.

Blanco, Mercedes. "Lyric as Temptation in Alonso de Ercilla and Torquato Tasso." In *The War Trumpet: Iberian Epic Poetry (1543–1639)*, edited by Emiro Martínez-Osorio and Mercedes Blanco, 96–128. Toronto: University of Toronto Press, 2023.

Boscán, Juan. *Las obras de Boscán y algunas de Garcilasso de la Vega, repartidas en quatro libros*. Barcelona: Carles Amorós, 1543.

Camões, Luís Vas de. *Los Lusíadas. Poesías, Prosas*. Edited by Elena Losada. Madrid: Biblioteca de Literatura Universal, 2007.

Cañizares-Esguerra, Jorge. "Review of *American Baroque. Pearls and the Nature of Empire, 1492–1700* by Molly A. Warsh." *Renaissance Quarterly* 73 no. 4 (2021): 1410–12.

Casas, Bartolomé de. *Brevísima relación de la destrucción de las Indias*. Madrid: Ediciones Cátedra, 1995.

Castellanos, Juan de. *Elegías de varones ilustres de Indias*. Vol. 1. Bogotá: Editorial A.B.C., 1955.

Castiglione, Baldassarre. *Il libro del Cortegiano*. Edited by Walter Barberis. Turin: Einaudi, 1998.

Covarrubias Horozco, Sebastián de. *Tesoro de la lengua castellana o española*. Madrid: Iberoamericana, 2006.

Cruz, Anne J. "Self-Fashioning in Spain: Garcilaso de la Vega." *Romanic Review* 83, no. 4 (1992): 517–38.

Cruz, Sor Juana Inés de la. *The Answer/La Respuesta, Including a Selection of Poems*. Edited by Electa Arenal and Amanda Powel. New York: The Feminist Press at the City University of New York, 1994.

Davis, Elizabeth B.. *Myth and Identity in the Epic of Imperial Spain*. Columbia: University of Missouri Press, 2000.

Domínguez-Torres, Mónica. "'Nel piu ricco paese del Mondo': Cubagua Island as an Epicenter of the Early Atlantic Trade." In *Circulación: Movement of Ideas, Art and People in Spanish America*, edited by Jorge Rivas, 14–39. Denver: Frederick & Jan Mayer Center, Denver Art Museum, 2018.

− "Pearl Fishing in the Caribbean: Early Images of Slavery and Forced Migration in the Americas." In *African Diaspora in the Cultures of Latin America, the Caribbean, and the United States*, edited by Persephone Braham, 73–82. Newark: University of Delaware Press, 2016.

Ercilla, Alonso de. *La Araucana* Edited by Isaías Lerner. Madrid: Cátedra, 2002.

Galster, Ingrid. *Aguirre o la posteridad arbitraria: la rebelión del conquistador vasco Lope de Aguirre en la historiografía y ficción histórica*. Bogotá: Universidad Javeriana/ Universidad del Rosario, 2011.

Graf, E.C. "From Scipio to Nero to the Self: The Exemplary Politics of Stoicism in Garcilaso de la Vega's Elegies." *PMLA* 116, no. 5 (2001): 1316–33. Greene, Roland. *Unrequited Conquests: Love and Empire in the Colonial Americas*. Chicago: University of Chicago Press, 1999.

Jos, Emiliano. *La expedición de Ursúa al Dorado y la rebelión de Lope de Aguirre según documentos y manuscritos inéditos*. Huesca, Spain: Talleres Gráficos Editorial V. Campo, 1927.

Kagan, Richard L. "Clio and the Crown: Writing History in Hapsburg Spain." In *Spain, Europe and the Atlantic World: Essays in Honour of John H.*

Elliot, edited by Richard L. Kagan and Geoffrey Parker, 73–99. Cambridge: Cambridge University Press, 1995.

Kohut, Karl. "Las *Elegías de varones ilustres de Indias* de Juan de castellanos y el problema de la épica indiana de los siglos XVI y XVII." In *Épica y Colonia. Ensayos sobre el género épico en Iberoamérica (siglos XVI y XVII)*, edited by Paul Firbas, 151–92. Lima: Universidad Nacional de San Marcos, 2008.

León, Sebastián. "MI-RE-MI-SOL-ESCONDIDO: Poesía cantada en la catedral de Bogotá." In *Esencias y pervivencias Barrocas en el Nuevo Reino de Granada*, edited by Adrián Contreras-Guerrero and Humberto Borja, 367–93. Seville: Universidad Pablo de Olavide, 2021.

León Pinelo, Antonio de. *Velos antiguos y modernos en los rostros de las mujeres.* 2 vols. Santiago de Chile: Centro de Investigaciones de Historia Americana, 1966.

Lerner, Isaías. "Garcilaso en Ercilla." *Lexis* 2, no. 2 (1978): 201–21.

Markham, Clements. "Introduction." In *The Expedition of Pedro de Ursúa and Lope de Aguirre*, edited by William Bollaert, i–liii. New York: Lenox Hill, 1971.

Marrero-Fente, Raúl. *Poesía épica colonial del siglo XVI. Historia, teoría y práctica.* Madrid: Editorial Iberoamericana, 2017.

Martínez, Miguel. *Front Lines. Soldiers' Writing in the Early Modern Hispanic World*. Philadelphia: Penn State University Press, 2016.

Martínez-Osorio, Emiro. *Authority, Piracy and Captivity in Colonial Spanish American Writing: Juan de Castellanos' Elegies of Illustrious Men of the Indies.* Lewisburg, PA: Bucknell University Press, 2016.

Menéndez Pelayo, Marcelino. *Antología de poetas hispanoamericanos. Volume III.* Madrid: Rivadeneira, 1894.

Middlebrook, Leah. *Imperial Lyric: New Poetry and New Subjects in Early Modern Spain*. University Park: Pennsylvania State University Press, 2009.

– "The Poetics of Masculinity in Sixteenth-Century Modern Spain." In *The Poetic of Masculinity in Early Modern Italy and Spain*, edited by Gerry Milligan and Jane Tylus, 143–67. Toronto: Centre for Reformation and Renaissance Studies, 2010.

Navarrete, Ignacio. *Orphans of Petrarch. Poetry and Theory in the Spanish Renaissance*. Berkeley: University of California Press, 1994.

Nicolopulos, James. *The Poetics of Empire in the Indies: Prophecy and Imitation in "La Araucana" and "Os Lusíadas."* University Park: Pennsylvania State University Press, 2000.

Otte, Enrique. *Las perlas del Caribe: Nueva Cádiz de Cubagua.* Caracas: Fundación John Boulton, 1977.

Ovid. *Metamorphoses.* Translated by Charles Martin. New York: W.W. Norton & Company, 2004.

Palacios, Mariantonia. *Noticias musicales en los cronistas de la Venezuela de los siglos XVI–XVIII*. Caracas: Fundación Vicente Emilio Sojo, 2000.

Powers, Timothy. "Vergil's Citharodes: Cretheus and Iopas Reconsidered." *Vergilius* 63 (2017): 93–123.

Restrepo, Luis Fernando. *Un Nuevo reino imaginado: Las Elegías de varones ilustres de Indias de Juan de Castellanos*. Bogotá: Instituto Colombiano de Cultura Hispánica, 1999.

Restrepo, Luis Fernando. "Land and Sea in Juan de Castellanos." In *The Rise of Spanish American Poetry 1500–1700: Literary and Cultural Transmission in the New World*, edited by Rodrigo Cacho Casal and Imogen Choi, 205–21. Oxford: Legenda, 2019.

Rivers, Elías, ed. *Poesía lírica del Siglo de Oro*. Madrid: Ediciones Cátedra, 1997.

Rojas, Ulises. *El Beneficiado Juan de Castellanos, cronista de Colombia y Venezuela. Estudio crítico-biográfico a la luz de documentos hallados por el autor en el Archivo General de Indias de Sevilla y en el histórico de la ciudad de Tunja*. Tunja, Colombia: Biblioteca de Autores Boyacenses, 1958.

Romero, Mario Germán. *Joan de Castellanos: un examen de su vida y de su obra*. Bogotá: Banco de la República, 1964.

Valencia, Felipe. *The Melancholy Void: Lyric and Masculinity in the Age of Góngora*. Lincoln: University of Nebraska Press, 2021.

Valencia, Felipe. "Las muchas (aunque bárbaras) voces líricas de *La Araucana* y la índole poética de una historia verdadera." *Revista de Estudios Hispánicos* XLIX, no. 1 (2015): 147–71.

Vega, Garcilaso de la. *Obras completas: con comentario*. Edited by Elías L. Rivers. Madrid: Editorial Castalia, 1981.

Virgil. *Aeneid*. Translated by Robert Fagles. New York: Penguin, 2006.

Warsh, Molly A. *American Baroque: Pearls and the Nature of Empire, 1492–1700*. Chapel Hill: University of North Carolina Press, 2018.

Wey Gómez, Nicolás. *Tropics of Empire: Why Columbus Sailed South to the Indies*. Cambridge, MA: MIT Press, 2008.

Zárate, Agustín de. "Censura de Agustín de Zarate el Consejo Real." In *Elegías de varones ilustres de Indias*, 49–51 Bogotá: Editorial A.B.C., 1955.

7 Domestic Bliss and Strife: Fresia and Caupolicán in Alonso de Ercilla's *La Araucana* and Pedro de Oña's *Arauco domado*[1]

NICOLE DELIA LEGNANI

This is my prayer; this last utterance I pour out
With my blood. Then do you, Tyrians, persecute with hate
His stock and all the race to come, and to my dust offer
This tribute! Let no love or treaty unite the nations! Arise
From my ashes, Unknown Avenger, to harass the Trojan
Settlers with fire and sword – today, hereafter, whenever
Strength be ours! May coast with coast conflict, I pray,
And sea with sea, arms with arms; war may they have,
Themselves and their children's children! (Virgil, *Aeneid* bk. 4, 621–9)

With this curse, Dido, queen of Carthage, seeks her vengeance on Aeneas and his descendants, the vanquished exiles from the Trojan War, who are also the future founders of Rome. For Virgil's readers in Augustan Rome, the unknown avenger (*aliquis … ultor*) would have been a clear reference to Hannibal (247 BCE–ca. 183 BCE), the oath to forever emerge from the queen's remains, phoenix-like, an allusion to the three Punic Wars (*Aeneid* bk. 4, 625).[2] Her passion for Aeneas metamorphoses into hate, prefiguring the hostilities not only between two cities but generations of ruling elites on opposing shores of the Mediterranean. Thus, Dido's curse of Aeneas serves figuratively and narratologically as an explanation for the recurrent apparition of Rome's enemy over generations. Inasmuch as Hannibal does play the historical role of "unknown avenger" in that he *did* cross the Pyrenees and the Alps with his fearsome Carthaginian soldiers and war elephants (218–204 BCE), he was ultimately vanquished for his armies were forced into a retreat from Italy (203–201 BCE). Two generations later, Carthage was razed to the ground during the Third Punic War (149–146 BCE) and left in ruins until a new Carthage was built near the original site as a Roman city under Augustus (r. 27 BCE–14 CE). In this epic chronotope set in the aftermath of the Trojan War before Rome's founding, the native woman's curse serves to foretell recent history and contemporary events in Augustan Rome. In so doing, it may have provided some measure of narrative closure to Virgil's contemporaries: finally, in recent memory, Carthage had been defeated, despite the enemy's best efforts to destroy Rome over centuries.

Within the *Aeneid*'s storyline, Dido's invocation of natural forces, such as storms, only serves to delay Aeneas and his son by Creusa, Ascanius, from reaching Italy's promised shore. Shortly after cursing her former lover, the desire for revenge turns on its source: Dido dies by suicide on Aeneas's sword and destroys the city she had worked so hard to build. Her death also puts to rest any possibility that a child born to Dido and Aeneas would challenge Ascanius (or Iulus) for rival ascendancy in North Africa. The risk that would have been posed to Ascanius by a pregnant Dido serves Virgil as a transparent allusion to the threat posed by Ptolemy Caesar (47 BCE–30 BCE) to Octavian (63 BCE–14 BCE). Claimed to be the son of Julius Caesar (100 BCE–44 BCE) by his mother, Cleopatra, queen of Egypt (69 BCE–30 BCE), Ptolemy Caesar was also known as Caesarion, or "little Caesar," a diminutive nickname formed from the (putative) father's name and given to the child by his mother. Caesarion's death was ordered by Octavian, the adopted son of Caesar, who would be known for posterity as Caesar Augustus and, also, Virgil's patron.[3]

The story of Dido and Aeneas explores different models of imperialism and their connection to endogamous and exogamous alliances and partnerships among natives and foreigners. It is, among other things, also a tale of matrimony and patrimony that calls into question the strength of a native woman's speech act. In Virgil's account, Dido is a queen foresworn; left a widow by the death of her first husband, Sychaeus, a Phoenician exile like herself, she swears fidelity to him beyond death. Her oath allows her to ward off the advances of Iarbas, a local chieftain, from whom she purchased the land on which to build her city, while constructing and protecting Carthage in her industrious widowhood. In Virgil's account, by succumbing to Aeneas's charms and engaging in a concubinage over months, the queen of Carthage breaks her oath to Sychaeus and risks retaliation from Iarbas. However, Aeneas breaks off his relationship with Dido, once he learns of his destiny to found a new dynastic line among the Latins on the Italian peninsula. Thus, he abandons the queen of Carthage out of a sense of duty to the fate of his son, Ascanius, and any descendants Aeneas may have with his future wife, Lavinia. It is not clear, however, whether

Aeneas broke his word to Dido. Were Dido and Aeneas married before consummating their love in a cave? The strength of the binds tying the Trojan exile to the Libyan queen are purposefully tenuous. On the one hand, the narrator asserts that lightning alone bears witness to their union (fulsere ignes et conscius Aether / conubiis) (*Aeneid* bk. 4, 167–8); on the other, the narrative voice states that it is nuptial Juno herself, along with primal Earth, who gives the sign for the storm to proceed (prima et Tellus et pronuba Iuno / dant signum) (bk. 4, 166–7). Yet the narrator also suggests that Dido "calls it marriage and with that name veils her sin" out of guilt (coniugium vocat; hoc praetexit nomine culpam" *Aeneid* bk. 4, 172); in her entreaties to Aeneas, she later refers to "the marriage that is ours, the nuptial rites begun" (conubia nostra, per inceptos hymenaeos) (*Aeneid* bk. 4, 316). Aeneas denies that a marriage ever took place or that he promised himself to her (*Aeneid* bk. 4, 338–9). Upon returning to the bedroom that she shared with Aeneas in Carthage, only to find the clothes and sword he left behind, Dido laments, "sweet relics, while the fates and gods did allow" (Dulces exuviae, dum fata deusque sinebat) (*Aeneid* bk. 4, 651). These belongings epitomise her losses, past and future: the marriage that was not, the child that could have been. Having cursed Aeneas, she nonetheless mourns his loss with tenderness, only to direct this frenzy of love and hatred against herself and her city. Beyond their contested versions of what took place in that cave, their private shelter from the storm, the concubinage and later enmity of Aeneas and Dido foreground the complexity of imperial relations – wrought through and against conquest, customs, and law – among different peoples.

Dido's marriages, her curse of Aeneas, and subsequent self-immolation tie together several thematic threads that are topical in poetry written within or against the epic tradition: the fraught relationships, both intimate and legal, between natives and foreigners, domestic partners and political opponents; the power of public and private speech acts, such as oaths, curses, and promises; and the characters' sense of duty to "future" generations, often the intended readers of the epic in question. As subsequent authors sought to inscribe their poems within the epic genre, which necessarily reflects on the political circumstances at the moment of each poem's composition, the spectre of Dido's curse has been summoned as a means to comment on the imbricated futures of both victors and vanquished.

The comparatist approach has divided post-Virgilian epic in two camps – epics of the vanquished, beginning with Lucan's *Pharsalia* or Ovid's *Metamorpohoses*, and epics of the victors, beginning with the *Aeneid* itself. Dido's curse – itself a Virgilian twist on Polyphemus's curse on Odysseus and his men in Homer's *Odyssey* (bk. 9, 528–36) – reappears as a topos of the native curse and its power (or not) to ultimately derail the hero from his destiny. For David Quint, the native curse reinforces imperial ideology because no matter how far it may force the hero to stray from the straight and narrow, ultimately, he and his followers are able to overcome the obstacles and fulfil their destiny.[4] This is not to say, however, that the affects raised by Virgil's poem, especially surrounding the queen of Carthage, are not so complex that even if one may recognize an ideological bent to the poem in question, it does not detract from the subtlety of appeals, political questions raised, or admiration and empathy shown by Virgil's poetic voice for Dido and her people.

Defining any given epic's ideology is a complex endeavour, and this is especially true of *La Araucana*.[5] If Quint's thesis rests on a correlation between literary form and ideology, taking Virgil's *Aeneid* and Lucan's *Pharsalia*, or Ovid's *Metamorphoses*, as opposite ends of the spectrum, an inclination for greater political liberty is articulated in the genre by a proliferation of voices, a meandering plot, an inconclusive ending, in short, a tendency towards romance that in the early modern period is exemplified by Ariosto's *Orlando furioso*, which receives its Virgilian response in *La Gerusalemme liberata* (1580–1) by Torquato Tasso. Thus, within Quint's taxonomy of epic, *La Araucana* falls within the "epic of the vanquished" tradition because of its sprawling narrative edifice and its lack of resolution in the South American theatre of war. By the end of the third part, Ercilla, as narrator, must abandon the Chilean setting and turn his sights on Europe because the Araucanian insurgency rages on. Evidence that Ercilla's poem was interpreted as pro-Araucanian by his contemporaries may be found in Pedro de Oña's *Arauco domado* (1596), which, per Ramona Lagos and Elide Pittarello,[6] by its very title betrays the criollo author's intention to put a final stop to the Araucanian insurgency, if only in the literary terrain.[7] This interpretation has been supported by the work of Pittarello and James Nicolopulos, who have both seized on the erotic encounter of Fresia and Caupolicán in Book 5 of *Arauco domado* as an intervention made by Oña to domesticate the native couple – as synecdoche for the Araucanian insurgency – where Ercilla, both as author and narrator, could not or would not.

Though I recognize the ideological ambivalence of Ercilla's *La Araucana*, in this essay I explore the potency of the curse levelled by Fresia against her husband, Caupolicán, and their infant child within epic tropes of indigeneity that engage with Virgilian Dido in all her facets: Phoenician settler, native queen of Carthage, faithful widow, oath-breaker, passionate lover, cursing native, would-be mother, self-destructive woman. I frame the implications of Fresia's public dissolution of her marriage to Caupolicán in the context of Tridentine reforms and their ramifications for marriage in Spanish America as well as Europe. I then show how Ercilla introduces similar questions about marriage and indigeneity in his account of Philip II's annexation of Portugal. Following this line of analysis, I examine the possibility of reading *La Araucana* in light of Pedro de Oña's *Arauco domado*, as David Quint, James Nicolopulos, Elide Pittarello, and Mercedes Blanco have done before me, but to other ends.[8] I contend that in canto 5 of *Arauco domado*, Oña (1570–1643) reasserts the union between Fresia and Caupolicán by restoring the gender binary between spouses. Set in a *locus amoenus*, their scene of marital bliss erases the horrors of the impalement of Caupolicán and the eradication of his lineage meted out, in part by Fresia, in canto XXXIII of Ercilla's poem. As a correction to Ercilla's cruelty shown towards the native couple and their descendants, Oña's treatment of their union reveals a criollo ambivalence on indigeneity in the Spanish Empire, one that exalts the virtues of the land of his birth while advocating for its cultivation and settlement by Hispanic mores and people.

Cursing Wives, Native Women

As Ricardo Padrón has argued, the third part of Ercilla's *La Araucana* emasculates the Mapuche warrior Caupolicán, first through his wife Fresia's curse, in which she claims that his "robust / body has been turned into the female sex" (membrudo / cuerpo en sexo de hembra se ha trocado) (XXXIII.81.5–6) and then in his execution by impalement, whose setting for the public execution the narrator Ercilla compares to a "wedding bed" (tálamo) (XXXIV.28.8).[9] In this way, Fresia's symbolic transformation of her husband from man to woman in her curse is then reinforced by the comparison between the method of execution (impalement), as suffered by the Indigenous warrior, to a wedding one canto later. Impalement should not be conflated with anal sex, nor anal sex with emasculation, but I contend that this epic poem makes these connections through its figurative language and the performative potency of Fresia's curse.

Impalement has been employed as a form of torture and execution across centuries and by various societies. Nevertheless, as Louise Vásvari observes in her essay on the *Libro de Buen Amor*, "the semiotics of phallic aggression and anal penetration refers to sex not as a hetero- or homosexual act but as a game of dominance and submission reinterpreted as insertive and receptive sex roles, where the male organ becomes a kind of weapon and where the passive position is equated with dishonor, weakness, feminization."[10] What is notable about the description of Caupolicán's execution is that he is impaled even after he has embraced Christianity and that his torture and death are met by comparisons to the traditional site for the consummation of marriage; that is, the figurative connection between impalement and sexual penetration is made by Ercilla the narrator, who goes into exhaustive detail of the execution even as he confesses that he did not bear witness to it. Moreover, Caupolicán's impassivity throughout the ordeal "neutralizes our empathy for the body in pain as it highlights the warrior's indomitable courage ... Ercilla also makes sure to let the reader know that he was not present ... One wonders what was the purpose of providing a detailed description of an execution that he did not witness, if it was not to verbally violate Caupolicán's body."[11] In Lucas Marchante-Aragón's reading of the simile of stake and scaffold to nuptial bed, he argues that the image "diverts momentarily the reader's attention from the act of torture in order to frame the narrative in the positive conception of the penetration as a sought-after union" within cultural production of the Hapsburg Empire that emphasized marriage as a means for incorporating the Other.[12] Marchante-Aragón maintains that Caupolicán's impalement is, indeed, a form of rape but one "over which the poet nor the monarch have had control ... Ercilla narrates the death of the chieftain in a way that personifies Arauco valor in the body of Caupolicán to then co-opt it for the empire as the act is represented as one which is at the same time rape and marriage" (168). To this reader of *La Araucana*, the scene's reminiscence of epithalamium poetry does not so much divert attention from the sexualized violence of the impalement but rather confirms the process of the Araucanian hero's emasculation, which begins with Fresia's curse.

As explored in this chapter, Caupolicán's torture and death by impalement fulfils the symbolic emasculation of Fresia's curse earlier in the poem, implicating female Indigenous agency in the unmanning and death of an Indigenous male leader whose impalement is amply documented in the historical record. Yet before I consider what Ercilla, the author, *does* to Caupolicán through Fresia's curse, it is important to reflect on what epics generally *do* with representations of warriors, and their wives and lovers; also, when it comes to cursing, it bears recalling who curses whom and if – conventionally speaking – these curses are successful. In other words, in order to situate Fresia's propriety or impropriety as a native woman who curses in a Spanish epic, I explore what Judith Butler has conceptualized as the performativity of gender and identity through the exterior "stylized repetition of acts,"[13] but within the genre; within the poem itself, the portrayals and speech acts of other women – Spanish and Indigenous alike – are equally important.

In *La Araucana*, there are no less than four speeches made by Indigenous women – all qualified as "barbarous" (bárbaras) – avowing their love and fidelity for their Indigenous beloved men, dead or alive.[14] As Lía Schwartz has demonstrated, their laments often recall verses from Garcilaso de la Vega's sonnets and songs.[15] However, beyond a rhetorical flourish (adorno retórico) that contributes to the thematic variety of the poem, as Schwartz discussed,[16] Felipe Valencia asserts that with these speeches Ercilla's "poetic persona repeatedly underscores the colonial thrust of his transvestite ventriloquism when he reminds readers of the unmistakable alterity in terms of language, religion, and political allegiance of the women whose voices he ventriloquizes. Guacolda is the 'bárbara moza'; Tegualda, the 'infelice bárbara hermosa'; Glaura, 'la bárbara'; and all of them together, including Lauca, 'bárbaras.'"[17] In the case of Fresia, her curse on husband and son ventriloquizes Garcilaso de la Vega's poetic persona, who, in sonnet 10, had emoted for a lost lover via Dido. As it opens with a counterfactual gaze back on her child with Caupolicán as a "wretched belonging," which he "should have looked at" (miraras a esta prenda desdichada), Fresia's speech thus converts Dido's lament for lost patrimony into a curse on native matrimony. It is an allusion to the opening verse of sonnet 10 by Garcilaso de la Vega (1503–6), "Sweet belongings, sadly found by me" (Oh, dulces prendas, por mi mal halladas),[18] itself a trope on Dido's lament, "sweet relics, while the fates and gods did allow" (Dulces exuviae, dum fata deusque sinebat) (*Aeneid* bk. 4, 651). Their citation by Fresia underscores the reversals in affect, from love to hatred and vice versa, which, in turn, index the inversions between subject and object of the native woman's speech act, from curse of the departing foreigner to destruction of herself and her people, mediated by melancholic lament. In recollecting Virgilian Dido's lament via Garcilaso de la Vega in the third part of *La Araucana*, Fresia summons the spectre of Virgilian Dido's pained survey of Aeneas's abandoned possessions even as the historical authenticity of Virgilian Dido is denied in canto XXXII. Fresia is given the last word among the Araucanian women, one that serves to reinforce imperial hegemony, but in a way that breaks the fragile bonds of heteronormativity in Spanish America under the new Counter-Reformation codes for marriage.

In canto XXXIII of *La Araucana*, Fresia revives the fatalism promised by the likes of Hector's tearful farewell to his son Astynax and wife Andromache in Homer's *Iliad*[19] while restoring the spectre of Dido's curse on Aeneas in *Aeneid* (bk. 4, 607–29), which seemingly had been put to rest earlier in the same canto, and in canto XXXII, through a defence of the historical Dido, who lived and died at least one hundred years *after* the events of the Trojan War and its aftermath. The "defence" of the historical Dido, who committed suicide so that she could safeguard her people and her honour by choosing loyalty to her dead husband Sychaeus over life with Iarbas, the local African king, already enjoyed a long tradition in the medieval and early modern Spanish Republic of Letters.[20] However, even as Ercilla denies the historicity of Virgilian Dido's tragic love for Aeneas, he invokes the pathos and the potency of her curse and lament. This puts Fresia in the position of cursing her lawful husband and her child, and unlike other curses cast by "the vanquished" in the epic tradition, her curse has the potential to wield lasting damage. As Quint has argued, the topos of the curse by the "vanquished," such as those performed by Polyphemus, Dido, Adamastor (and the Acomans in Villagrá's *Historia de la Nueva México*), fulfils an ideological function in that the curse reinforces the epic plot whose ending characteristically establishes and celebrates the triumph of the "vanquishers."[21] If it serves to define the impotence of the "vanquished" and, ultimately, to justify violence against the natives,[22] then the retelling of Dido's story – her *true* history in cantos XXXII and XXXIII – alludes to the ideological function of the curse by its omission, perhaps annulling it. However, Dido's spectre returns, affectively and effectively, via Fresia's curse in what is most certainly an inversion of the Virgilian model, precisely because native curses gain potency with Ercilla's revision, but only when natives wield the curse against one of their own.

Virgilian Dido's curse is undone in historical terms with the narration of the *true* history of Dido and her fidelity beyond death to Sychaeus in cantos XXXII and XXXIII of *La Araucana*, where Aeneas is made conspicuous by his absence. After his encounter with Lauca, Ercilla, the character "was chatting with soldiers / about the faithfulness of Indian women" (iba con los soldados platicando / de la fe de las indias y constancia) (XXXII.43.3–4). A young soldier attempts to correct him (XXXII.44.1), citing Dido's passion and frenzy in book 4 of the *Aeneid* as a counterexample to the chastity and loyalty of the "barbarous women" Ercilla had just exalted based on his own personal experience. The soldier's riposte to Ercilla's exaltation of Indigenous women underscores the fallacy of imperialist logic. After all, how can a North African queen's actions taken, or not, more than a thousand years before the Araucanian insurgency reflect on the character of Indigenous women in the Americas of the sixteenth century? Rather than contest the premise for his interlocutor's comparison, Ercilla, the character, recollects the Hispanic "defence" of the historical Dido, allowing him to "defend" Dido and Araucanian women both without questioning the soldier's logic, thus upholding the imperial paradigm afforded by the epic genre. In Ercilla's contestation of *Aeneid* bk. 4, there can be no curse of Aeneas because Aeneas and Dido had never been a couple, as Aeneas did not even exist during her time: "As we see by [reckoning with] time [that] / Aeneas [lived] one hundred years before Dido" (vemos por los tiempos haber sido / Eneas cien antes que fue Dido) (XXXII.46.7–8), hence there could be no broken promises made in a cave to inspire the Carthaginian queen's self-destructive wrath. Rather than the lustful woman who curses, to no avail, as it turns out, and destroys herself and her burgeoning empire in the process, Dido is presented as a virtuous widow, herself a wanderer, who founds a peaceful, vast, and just empire. Indeed, Dido in *La Araucana* offers an alternative to the Spanish modus operandi of conquest, described by the poetic voice earlier in that same canto:

> pues con modo inhumano han excedido
> de las leyes y términos de guerra,
> haciendo en las entradas y conquistas
> crueldades inormes nunca vistas. (XXXII.4.4–8)[23]

(for they have inhumanly exceeded / the laws and limits of war / by committing enormous, unprecedented acts of cruelty / in their raids and conquests.)

La Araucana thus reminds readers of the historical Dido, the faithful widow who kept her word to her husband and to her new settlement at Carthage.

According to this counter-Virgilian – or historically accurate – narrative, Dido "pacified" the natives, thereby offering a "different model" of how to colonize a land, as opposed to the brute force (*merum imperium*) of Spanish conquest.[24] But does Ercilla's Dido truly stand as a foil to the Spaniards, as Karina Galperín has contended?[25] In the historical version of Dido's pacification of the territory that will become Carthage, she famously purchases a bullhide's worth of land from a nomadic herder, only to lay down the law, the *nomos*, through a trick: by cutting the hide into strips, she is able to enclose more land for her future city. And yet, in this topical comparison, if Dido *did* found her city by fully compensating the natives for this enclosure destined to be Carthage, thus eschewing with the greed (*codicia*) and unbridled violence of raids (*entradas*), how is that any different from the reformist vision of the 1573 Ordinances of the Spanish Crown for the "discovery, settlement, and pacification" (descubrimiento, población y pacificación) of new lands and peoples, which regulated *conquista* to the point of erasing its mention?[26] Among other things, these ordinances compelled colonists (*pobladores*) to avoid enclosing Indigenous lands at all costs, and to keep their word in their negotiations with native populations; and yet, if native lands had to be enclosed, the law *also* compelled colonizers to provide proper compensation.[27] Moreover, "indios vacos" – that is, Indian nomads – would be enjoined by the colonizers, in an apropos amphibology, to "vacar" – that is, to herd cattle within an *encomienda* for two lives, or three lives if the settlements were for "our ports and main towns" (puertos y *caueçeras* para nos – for the Crown in a *repartimiento*).[28] Ordenanza 136 contemplates the possibility of Indigenous resistance and also asks settlers to "make friends with them and teach them to live in a civilized manner" (hazer Amistad con ellos y enseñarlos a bivir politicamente), but without taking "their lands and other property" (haziendas o lo que fuere particular de los indios) – unless the natives give their consent.[29] Settlers are asked to "requerir" several times, and if they are met with resistance still, then and only then may they settle "without hurting them beyond what may be needed for the defense of settlers so that the settlement is not impeded" (su poblaçion … sin hazerles más daño del que fuere menester para la defensa de los pobladores y para que la poblaçion no se estorue).[30] This economy of violence is mitigated by the law's optimistic program for settlement.[31] The contradictions and anxieties, even the ambivalence surrounding imperial enterprise, are found in the very discourse of the law set in place not only to domesticate the natives (*naturales* or *indios*, used interchangeably), but also to tame the native Spanish subjects who served as the Crown's and the Church's agents overseas.

Topically speaking, the 1573 Ordenanzas were openly anti-*conquista* and condemned the unbridled greed of conquistadors: the question was precisely how to bridle the violence and *cupiditas* to achieve a *pax hispanica*. The (in)famous Ordinance 29, for example, argued that the word *conquista* had impelled the Spanish Crown's subjects and agents to act in ways that contradicted the Crown's desired objectives, of both a material and religious order, for its new subjects in the empire. The rationale behind Ordinance 29 seemingly argues in favour of a correspondence between the name for violence (conquest, discovery, or pacification) and the actions performed under its aegis, "for [as this activity is] to be done with as much peace and charity as we so desire, we do not wish for the name to give occasion for the use of force or injury against the Indians" (pues hauiendose de hazer con tanta paz y caridad como deseamos no queremos que el nombre dé ocación ni color para que se pueda hazer fuerça ni agrauio a los Indios).[32] The passage offers a striking contrast in subject positions, between the active "royal we" (*deseamos, queremos*) and the impersonal construction for both prescribed and proscribed actions (*haviendose de hazer, se pueda hazer*). The erasure of *conquista* and *conquistador* attempts to annul the individualism of the *empresarios* within the larger imperial enterprise. There is little room for heroism and the naked lust and greed (*cupiditas*) condemned by the 1573 ordinances, but these had already been the target of Charles V as early as the 1526 Ordenanzas and the New Laws of 1542. In this way, one could argue that Ercilla in his diatribes against greed (*codicia*) and conquest (*conquista*) was, in fact, towing the party line of the Spanish Empire. Simply put, massacre is nonsensical when the end goal is conversion and new subjects who pay tribute, though that is not to say that violence in excess – that which was not sanctioned by the Laws of the Indies – did not take place. It is the very unruliness of the conquistadors and *encomenderos* that brings Ercilla to the New World, as he reminds Philip II in canto XXXVII: defence of the Spanish king's interests against the rebellion of *encomenderos* in 1553 (XXXVII.67–8), whose leader – Francisco Hernández Girón – protested the limits placed on native dispossession by the 1542 New Laws.

The Dido episode in *La Araucana* both plays out a reform of Spanish empire, as envisioned by the Crown and the Council of the Indies, and underscores the sanctity of marriage, as understood after the Council of Trent. The importance of four marriage-involved plots and their reversals in the third part of *La Araucana* are made even more salient in light of the binding and sacramental nature marriage takes on during the Tridentine reforms (1545–63). By the *Tametsi* decree, given during the twenty-fourth session, on 11 November 1563, the definitive ritual of marriage was set in place, requiring clergy to perform the celebration and witnesses to validate it. As Asunción Lavrín argues in her seminal *Sexuality and Marriage in Colonial Latin America*, post-Tridentine reforms emphasized the power of the public betrothal to initiate a marriage, in this way resolving, doctrinally speaking, the positions taken by Peter Lombard (1096–1160) and Gratian (d. ca. 1159) who held that promises to marry were binding even when they were made in private, on the one hand, and that of Pope Alexander III (r. 1159–81), who held that a verbal promise was revocable, as long as carnal consummation had not taken place.[33] This does not mean, however, that the medieval Iberian ritual of the promise to wed (*palabra de casamiento*) made in private fell into disuse, both on the Iberian Peninsula and in the Spanish American colonies following Trent. Regular and irregular relations between men and women continued to be initiated through such promises. As legislated in the *Siete partidas* of Alfonso X (r. 1252–84) and performed in Spanish plays ad nauseam in the seventeenth century, both consummated and unconsummated betrothals (*desposorios*) could be compelled to marriage (*matrimonio*) by the bishops to fulfil promises to marry if they were given by mutual consent, and even if they had been exchanged without witnesses present, although Trent emphasized publicity with the *Tametsi* decree. In *La Araucana*, the Indigenous noblewomen who populate its episodes of romance fall squarely within the *palabra de casamiento* tradition.

The treatment of Indigenous unions in the second and third parts of *La Araucana*, published in 1578 and 1589–90, respectively, displays a troubled awareness of the complexities of translating the already contradictory Counter-Reformation ideology overseas, which is absent in the first part of Ercilla's poem, published in 1569. In this respect, I follow a longer tradition of scholars who have observed and explained the marked contrast between part 1 and parts 2 and 3 of the poem in different ways. This contrast has been widely construed, especially per Quint, following Ramona Lagos,[34] as a pessimistic rendering of the Spanish imperial project, especially in its colonies, which Galperín, in her reading, translates back onto the European arena of war through the Dido episode in cantos XXXII and XXXIII.[35] Elizabeth Davis, for her part, has pointed to the widely observed reversal of the second and third parts from the first as an "increasingly panegyrical view of the entire Hapsburg imperial program," attested by the inclusion of San Quentin and Lepanto.[36] And yet, as Leah Middlebrook has argued based on the openings of the first and second parts of *La Araucana*,

> the different ways in which Ercilla framed the two parts of his poem for his cultured and courtly readership indicates the challenges faced by a poet attempting to accommodate epic to the ideologies and social organization of early Modern Spain … In part one, Ercilla portrays himself as invested with the responsibility of commemorating heroes and the actions they undertake in remote reaches of the globe. In part two, his task is different: now he must inscribe, using all the persuasive power of modern rhetoric, the subjection of the world and its inhabitants to God and the Sovereign.[37]

It is in the third part, however, that the "penetration of the political and religious reforms of the Counter-Reformation into late sixteenth-century poetic discourse" becomes more troubled and troubling,[38] particularly for those new subjects of Spain and neophytes of the Church in *ultramar*. This troubled and troubling gender violence becomes particularly salient in portrayals of Indigenous conjugal unions in the poem, *especially* in light of post-Tridentine reforms.

We might recall, for example, that, in a dream sequence that follows the prophecies of the Indigenous necromancer Fitón, Ercilla's poetic voice takes some respite from the action in canto XVIII of the second part of *La Araucana* to praise the beauty of Spanish women, including, notably, that of his betrothed, María de Bazán, a very public declaration of their *desposorio* (XVIII.68–73).[39] That the promise to marry is binding and, even, prophetic is reaffirmed by the fidelity of the Araucanian women to their men throughout all parts of the poem, except, notably, for Fresia. In terms of John L. Austin, whose own example for the force of what he called "illocutionary acts" used the social context of the marriage pronouncement, the assertions surrounding marriage in *La Araucana* are particularly forceful, or happy;[40] the repetitive avowals of fidelity before witnesses, such as Ercilla's character in the epic poem, reinforce the importance of a public rite or, at the very least, the presence of witnesses to give faith to betrothal. In the colonies, the force of the public *desposorio* was not only felt in the Inquisition's cases regarding Spanish and criollo unions, but also in the emphasis placed on the sacrament of marriage, and the extirpation of polygamy and other so-called deviant practices by the *doctrineros* (missionaries) among Indigenous converts to Catholicism. In *La Araucana*, as has been widely noted, the Araucanian women behave like exemplary Spanish betrothed wives, or widows, like the exemplary, historical Dido who, as I have noted before, does not curse.

The Indigenous curse, in the context of epics written by the victors, is notably impotent, the failed speech act par excellence.[41] Yet in another inversion of this epic trope in *La Araucana*, Fresia's speech acts in canto XXXIII – directed towards her husband – are immediately carried out.[42] The scene begins by recalling the tenderness of *Iliad* bk. 6, 466–81, when we first encounter Fresia and her child, captured by a Black slave while fleeing a native house (*toldo*). Though she and Caupolicán are not, in fact, together, we are given a spectral image of domestic bliss:

> llevaba un mal envuelto niño al pecho
> de edad de quince meses, el cual era
> prenda del preso padre desdichado,
> con grande estremo dél y della amado. (XXXIII.74)

> (She had a poorly swaddled child at her breast / who was fifteen months old [and] / belonged to the wretched, imprisoned father / [a child] immensely beloved by him and her.)

In an archetypal image of femininity and motherhood, Fresia carries the unnamed fifteen-month-old at her breast, who is defined as the darling property (*prenda*) of the absent father. The alliteration of the plosives in the stanza similarly underscores Caupolicán's status as the paterfamilias; though imprisoned (*preso*), he has a patrimony that is expressed, to his credit, in the form of a pledge (*prenda*). The *niño*, who is also his *prenda*, serves as the symbolic collateral, made flesh, of the couple's promises made to each other in marriage. Not yet patrimony, the Indigenous child nevertheless is the physical token that signifies his parents' matrimony at the moment of his capture. This invocation of the child as bond both reverses Garcilaso's allusion to Dido's lament and foreshadows Caupolicán's unmanning via Fresia's curse as she dissolves the pledge by disowning the child.

In this scene of mother and son's shared captivity, their captor fails to recognize her noble status, and Fresia is allowed to wander freely among her vanquished compatriots.[43] In this way, she happens upon Caupolicán, now her imprisoned husband (marido que preso iba adelante) (XXXIII.75.6), and the spectre of *Iliad* 6 is revived once more through its many reversals: rather than a tearful farewell made by the father to the son and wife in private *before* battle, the wife disowns her son and her husband in a public display of fury, emasculating the husband following his capture.

First, Fresia suggests that committing suicide would have been preferable to capture since Caupolicán should have died fighting. As her public shaming (*escarnio*) of her husband proceeds, Fresia cites her disappointment that Caupolicán's promises to conquer *las Españas* did not come to fruition (harking back to VIII.16). She suggests that, if his "effeminate right hand" (afeminada diestra" [XXXIII.76.6]) could not mete out a victory, he should have committed suicide, like Virgilian Dido, since he was not even capable of dying heroically, that is, like Hector (*Iliad* 22). The right hand is the sword hand, and Virgilian Dido in book 4 of the *Aeneid* stabs herself with the sword, one of the sweet possessions (dulces exuviae) left behind by Aeneas, her lover or husband. The reference to Dido's lament thus alludes to the ambiguous nature of Aeneas and Dido's union that had been topical in Augustan Rome and would have resonated with the diverse denizens of Spanish empire post-*Tametsi*. Via Fresia's curse, the allusion to the scorned queen's suicide in *La Araucana*, unmans Caupolicán while prefiguring the horrific torture and death that is to come.

In Fresia we can also hear echoes of the Castilian heroine Doña Mencia de Nidos. In canto VII, though feeble, ill, and bedridden (estando flaca y enferma en la cama), Mencia shows her true mettle as a "noble, intelligent, valiant, and bold" woman (noble, discreta, valerosa y osada), when she rises up and unsheathes a sword to call back her retreating countrymen to defend Concepción (con la espada desnuda los seguía), thus achieving "as much fame / as is denied to men at this time" (tanta fama / que en tiempo a los hombres es negada) (VII.20–2). The series of rhetorical questions, underscored by the use of anaphora, to berate the fleeing men, are similarly employed by Fresia against Caupolicán. They culminate with the disavowal of both the son and the father in a turn that projects Dido's lament onto the warrior, while she keeps the potency of the Carthaginian queen's curse, though this time it is directed against her native husband, a latter-day Sychaeus who is also figured, ironically, as Aeneas:

> Miraras a esta prenda desdichada,
> pues que de ti no queda ya otra cosa,
> …
> toma, toma, tu hijo, que era el ñudo
> con que el lícito amor me había ligado;
> que el sensible dolor y golpe agudo
> estos fértiles pechos han secado.
> cría, críale tú que ese membrudo
> cuerpo en sexo de hembra se ha trocado;
> que yo no quiero título de madre
> del hijo infame del infame padre. (XXXIII.80–1)

(You should have looked at this wretched belonging / for nothing of yours remains … / Take [him], take your son, who was the knot / that bound me in lawful love; / for the deeply felt pain and sharp blow / have dried up these fertile breasts. / Raise [him], you raise him for that robust / body [of yours] has been turned into the female sex; / because I don't want to receive the title of mother / to the infamous son of the infamous father.)

The repeated references in *La Araucana* to the son of Fresia and Caupolicán as a *prenda*, highlighted by the narrator through alliteration earlier on, and professed by Fresia just as she is disowning her child, not only recall Dido's lament via Garcilaso, but also allude to the tempest in Ovid's *Metamorphoses* and another ignominious death for a warrior-king, a watery grave.[44] In Ovid, Ceyx thinks of his wife and son, also described in similar terms to the *prenda*, or bonds, while he drowns with flotsam in his right hand rather than his kingly sceptre (11.544–6; 11.560–9).

Though counter to Counter-Reformation prescriptions on marriage, whose dissolution in Catholicism were notoriously difficult even prior to the Council of Trent, Fresia's invocation of lawful love (*lícito amor*) refers to Indigenous unions that were, paradoxically, notoriously difficult to legislate. Since Caupolicán only converts to Christianity immediately prior to his death, we may assume that in this speech Fresia is referring to a union that would have been recognized as legal within Spanish jurisprudence's recognition of *jus gentium* (local customs and traditions), but only to the extent that such a union was not construed as *contra natura* or contrary to nature. In this way, Fresia cuts the proverbial ties that bind in a kind of legal ruse, reminiscent of the wiles employed by Dido, to enclose more land for her future city with the purchase of the nomadic herdsman's hide. The child – referred to as being bound to her breast (*ñudo, prenda*) in the earlier stanza – is shunned as her milk dries up and she feminizes Caupolicán and curses her husband, her child, and herself. In this moment, she transforms both her husband and herself into one archetypal, unnatural mother (*madre desnaturalizada*), though one split into two opposing bodies as they are no longer made one flesh by marriage.[45] Her words are enough to undo their marriage vows, and deny their consummation and fruition in the form of a child. In one fell swoop, she informs both her former husband and the witnesses to his public shaming that she and Caupolicán are no longer man and wife, and she is no longer a mother.

The status of Fresia, now under the yoke of the Spanish *imperium*, recurs ironically to the strictures of Tridentine reforms in order to undo her marriage: the eighth canon on marriage of the General Council of Trent, for example, entertains the possibility that couples may be separated indefinitely, in terms of sharing a bed or cohabitation.[46] Such a separation would need validation by an ecclesiastical authority, however. Precisely how the eighth canon was to be applied to Indigenous neophytes in the colonies was just beginning to be regulated in the Viceroyalty of Peru with the Third Council of Lima of 1582–3. From Lavrín's work, we know that violence in a marriage was often invoked by women as a just cause for separation and accepted by ecclesiastic authorities in the seventeenth century.[47] In this sixteenth-century epic, Fresia alludes to a "deeply felt pain and sharp blow" (sensible dolor y golpe duro) (XXXIII.81.3–4) that have transformed her body violently, making it less maternal but not, I would argue, less feminine. As a result, by the end of her speech, what was once a heteronormative marriage between *naturales* (natives, but also of nature) becomes, in an uncanny poetic conceit, *contra natura*, between two feminine or quasi-feminine subjects. In any case, with Caupolicán's torture and execution, which occurs promptly after his conversion to Christianity, Fresia is truly unbound from the Christian rite of marriage, and Caupolicán is returned to his "proper" place in the epic. Denied the heroic death of Hector, he suffers, stoically, the sharp pain of the penetrating stick tearing apart his insides as his torture, and then the mutilation of his cadaver, become a spectacle. These acts are disciplinary, and therefore public, but the ironic conceit of the poem compares his composure during impalement to the privacy of marital consummation, as if Caupolicán were "being seated on his wedding bed" (que si asentado en tálamo estuviera) (XXXIII.28.8) like a bride.

But what of the nameless child? Ercilla, as author, shows him no small mercy. In historical accounts, such as that of Gerónimo de Vivar in his *Crónica y relación*, Fresia was said to have killed her own child by flinging his small body against a tree.[48] At the close of *La Araucana*'s scene in Chile, we have no Astynax, or Ascanius. For the purposes of the epic, Caupolicán is the principal native hero and Fresia was his noble wife, his *palla*. If the historical Quepolicán, according to Alonso de Góngora Marmolejo,[49] was but one leader among many, this matters little within the Arauco of the epic poem and its poetic fictions. There is no heir who could carry out Caupolicán's threat in the poem "that later there would be one thousand Caupolicáns more" (que luego habrá otros mil Caupolicanos) (XXXIV.10.3). Though the Araucanians assemble to choose a new general shortly thereafter (XXXIV.38–43), a role that an infant would be unable to perform in any case, we are left with scenes of tumult but no acclamation.

Writers on political theology, including but not limited to Carl Schmitt, Ernst Kantorowicz, and Georgio Agamben, have all observed that the death of any people's leader, especially that of a military commander, often results in a tumult that can lead to the investiture of a ruler, and with him (often *him*), a new political paradigm. Beyond the symbolic, the performative nature of literal investiture (*mutatio vestis*), in particular the donning of the purple and the fasces, is explored by Agamben as foundational to the formation of imperial power as the military might (*imperium*) exercised outside of Rome latches onto these civic insignia so that "the new imperial power will be defined precisely as the extension and fixing of the triumphal right in a new figure" via acclamation.[50] While recognizing, as does Kantorowicz, that the acclamation progressively becomes a litany when republican Rome's imperial might is transformed into imperial Rome and sedimented in imperial Christianity,[51] the role of the people in recognizing and clamouring for the new ruler, during the triumph which often coincided with funerary rites, is indeed imperative for the investiture to be realized, that is, personified in the emperor.[52] Much as Macchiavelli does in the *Discorsi* with his commentary on Livy, Agamben concerns himself with understanding the moments in history when civil strife, rebellion, in short, tumult is "crowned" by the personification of power into a governing lineage. As Imogen Choi (see Sutton) has demonstrated, Ercilla was a keen reader of Machiavelli and of his classical sources, and applied lessons from European history to his observations of Araucanian practices. Ercilla would have been familiar with the Florentine author's appraisals of tumults and transitions and his estimations of the conditions that both generate and are generated by them. I believe the descent into chaos after the death of Caupolicán is one such moment that, in the poem, remains inconclusive for the people of the Arauco but was, nevertheless, full of potential. In my estimation, Fresia's curses are instrumental to the impediment of one possible outcome from Caupolicán's conversion to Christianity and subsequent death: the acclamation of a new lineage for Indigenous rule even as such an investiture would have incorporated foreign mores.

The scenes of chaos in canto XXXIV provide a contrast with the scenes of collective decision-making in the second canto, when Caupolicán was chosen as the general of the coalition of Araucanian militias, from among sixteen leaders who, Ercilla notes in the first canto, were "born of barbarous mothers" (de bárbaras madres han nacido) (I.13.14). Choi has identified the election of Caupolicán in the second canto as a constitutive moment in primitive state formation, in line with Machiavelli's commentary in the *Discorsi* on the benefits and limits of republicanism.[53] If the Araucanians' republicanism serves as a foil for European monarchic models in the first part of *La Araucana*, as Choi has argued, the scenes of anarchy in canto XXXIV in the third part ensure that no other Araucanian military commander will be made emperor of the Arauco. As for the anonymous child, he is quickly given to another woman, also anonymous, to serve as his new mother. They both disappear into the larger group of prisoners who will bear witness to their general's grisly torture and execution in the next canto (XXXIII.83).

The entire scene, and the anonymous orphan, *do* trouble the epic form. Perhaps *La Araucana*'s open-endedness does lean, in this way, towards the counter-Virgilian position of Lucan's *Pharsalia*, but it also has a native mother perform an act of ideological violence against her own kith and kin. Regardless of how many classical and literary models one may find for Fresia's comportment, by disowning her child and shaming her husband in public, Fresia impedes their ability to lead honourable lives and deaths within Spanish American colonial society. If her implacable standards for Indigenous manhood lead Fresia to castigate them both, and, in so doing, offer a measure of resistance to Spanish mores, she nevertheless ensures their inability to flourish in a society where marriage and primogeniture were the standard social mechanisms for transmitting power and wealth among the ruling class. In this way, though

La Araucana does condemn some forms of colonial violence, it performs others, and even has the native Other perform it, reviving the spectre of the Virgilian Dido's self-immolation. Much like the contradictory discourse of the civilizing love of the Spanish laws of the Indies, such tensions are impossible to reconcile; but in an epic poem famous for its inconclusiveness, Ercilla does seem to put a final stop to the futurity promised by the lineages of Indigenous elites in the New World.

Crises of Succession, Juxtaposed

The final canto (XXXVII) of the third part of *La Araucana* justifies Spain's belligerence towards Portugal, which led to the Iberian Union (1581) following the Portuguese crisis of succession that was occasioned by the death of King Sebastião of Portugal (r.1557–78), who died without a direct heir at the time of his failed invasion of Alcazarquivir (Ksar el-Kebir, Morocco). Ercilla's epic therefore does not close with the lack of succession in the New World, but in the Old. By juxtaposing two succession crises – one in the Arauco, the other on the Iberian Peninsula – the poem promotes the rules of succession among European royalty in order to justify Spain's war against Portugal, while painting Araucanía as a place where none – including the Spanish conquistadors – are beholden to these rules. The canto opens with an overview of the just and unjust causes of war widely debated and elaborated by the Schools of Salamanca and Alcalá de Henares (XXXVII.1–13),[54] followed by a justification of Philip II's annexation of Portugal (XXXVII.14–64), and finally with a call to other poets to sing of Philip II's exploits now that Ercilla's own travails and song have ended (XXXVII.64–76).

The defence of Philip II's annexation of Portugal begins with a claim that the Spanish monarch's hand was forced. Law-abiding Philip II could not have acted out of greed or in a power grab "for his sceptre and reign extend / thence the sun sets its course" (pues se estiende su cetro y monarquía / hasta donde remata el sol su vía) (XXXVII.14.7–8). The Spanish king's military offensive will not be described in terms of invasion, but rather as a civil war.[55] What follows is an analysis of the king's use of violence or clemency to rule properly (i.e., not tyrannically). Through a series of phrases that echo the torture and execution of Caupolicán in canto XXXV, the reader is asked to engage in an economy of violence, to consider how punishment is meted out against rebels, and to what end on a universal scale.

Should it be public and spectacular (XXXVII.23)? When should the king show mercy (XXXVII.24)? The French armada led by Felipe Strozzi against the Portuguese-held Azores is described as powerful (pujante) but also, saliently, penetrating (*penetrante*) (XXXVII.17. 3). "Puesto en el palo" (XXXVII.23.7), the phrase used to invoke the power of a public hanging to elicit good behaviour in the king's subjects, refers to a hanging in the poem, but it also literally means impaled. What the poet presents as a digression plotted from "point to point" (*punto en punto*) (XXXVII.26.1) is an excursus in the adequate punishment for *rebels* that glosses over one of the major critiques levelled by Las Casas against the Spanish Crown's involvement in the Indies, namely, "nobody is nor can be called a rebel, unless he or she was first a subject" (ninguno es ni puede ser llamado rebelde si primero no es súbdito).[56] The last canto of *La Araucana* skirts around the lascasian defence of Indigenous insurgency in the New World even as it endeavours to bury it once and for all. In this way, the last canto explores all the facets of *imperium*, point by point, the full reach of the sovereign's decision from the fate of one individual to that of a nation with alliterations that echo the plosives from Fresia's curse and Caupolicán's impalement.

The ongoing comparison between the Araucanian couple and Portuguese insurgents is brought home in ottava 29, when resistance to the Iberian union is described in terms of self-immolation:

> ¿Qué ciega pretensión, qué embaucamiento,
> qué pasión pertinaz desatinada
> saca así la razón tan de su asiento,
> y tiene vuestra mente trastornada,
> que una unida nación por sacramento
> y con la cruz de Christo señalada,
> envuelta en crueles armas homicidas
> dé en sus propias entrañas las heridas,
>
> Y unas mismas divisas y banderas
> salgan de alojamientos diferentes,
> trayendo mil naciones estranjeras
> que derraman la sangre de inocentes
> y introducen errores y maneras
> de pegajosos vicios insolentes
> dejando con su peste derramada
> la católica España inficionada. (XXXVII.30–1)

(What blind arrogance, what hoax, / what obstinate and nonsensical passion / is able to remove reason from its seat / and has your mind unhinged, / for one nation united by sacrament / and marked by Christ's cross, / [is now] involved in cruel, homicidal arms / [and] wounds itself in the gut, //

so that the same sigils and banners / arise from different accommodations, / bringing a thousand foreign nations / that shed the blood of innocents / and introduce the errors and manners / of insolent, contagious vices / that leave behind a spreading plague / in Catholic, infected Spain.)

The alliterative plosives in ottava 30 reinforce the association between indigeneity and irrationality (obstinacy and passion) through the amphibology of *pertenencia* (belonging) and *pertinaz* (obstinate) that echoes the similarly alliterative plosives of "parientes pechos" (kindred chests) being torn apart by the lances brandished by the Castilian people (*pueblo castellano*) and the Portuguese kingdom (*reino lusitano*) against each other, the image of internecine strife on the Iberian Peninsula that opens the last canto of *La Araucana* (XXXVII.1). Both the alliteration and the themes in ottavas 1 and 30 of this final canto recall the blood relations produced by marital unions, such as the beloved pledge (prenda preciada), the child of Fresia and Caupolicán, who was so quickly discounted by his mother in earlier cantos.

The comparison between the Portuguese and the Araucanians is made explicit in the lines that follow, as the narrator reminds the Portuguese of their bonds to one another as a people united sacramentally in a *corpus mysticum* (que una unida nación por sacramento) through shared faith (y con la cruz de Christo señalada) signified by the sigil of the Five Wounds of Christ; and yet these bonds have come undone through Lusitanian self-immolation (dé en sus propias entrañas las heridas).[57] The Portuguese people's refusal to accept Philip II as their rightful king through lawful inheritance has led them to act irrationally, much like the Virgilian Dido, and in so doing, they have cursed themselves and opened the Iberian Peninsula to invaders. Much as the defence of the historical Dido informs the scenes of Fresia's curse and Caupolicán's torture and death, the return "home" of *La Araucana*'s plot and setting turns once more to a ruler dying with no succession.

In the octaves that follow the poet's condemnation of the Portuguese propensity for self-immolation, we are reminded of how the crisis of Iberian succession occurred in the first place: the impetuous Sebastião chose to invade Africa, despite his Uncle Philip's best efforts to dissuade him (XXXVII.33–8); Sebastião's frail and ailing great-uncle, a childless cardinal, inherits the throne and rules from 1578–80 (XXXVII.40–1); intuiting that Enrique would expire soon and that the time for him to advocate for his own succession to Portugal's throne was drawing near, Philip gathers a council of learned Christian men to evaluate the contenders, including Catherine of Medici (1519–89) and Don António (1531–95), Prior of Crato (XXXVII.43). The former's equal claim by proximity of blood (descendientes del tronco en igual grado) (XXXVII.46) is discredited by virtue of Philip II's seniority; the latter's claim, as the grandson of Luís, Duke of Beja, and Violante Gomes, is discredited as a consequence of his having been born out of wedlock: António is a natural-born son and, thus, illegitimate (XXXVII.43). Finally, a native son of Portugal, Cristóbal de Moura (1538–1613), who is also a subject of Spain, decides in favour of Philip II's claim "by law, reason, local law, and by nature" (por ley, razón, por fuero y por natura) (XXXVII.51.7–8). In these octaves the category of the *natural* (as native-born, as born outside of wedlock) does the work of legitimizing Philip II's claim, but as the poem approaches its close, it also comes undone as a category of discreet boundaries.[58] Unsettled though the boundaries of *natura* may be, and thus too the law, it is brute force (*merum imperium*) that has the final say in the matter of the Iberian Union: the Portuguese people raise arms against the foreign king, but their insurgency is pacified by force (XXXVII.60–1).

Closer to home on the Iberian Peninsula, however, Ercilla's poetics do not indulge in the same queering of the *natural*. Don António, Prior of Crato and natural-born grandson of Manoel I (1469–1521), does not suffer the same fate as the son of Caupolicán and Fresia. His ancestry is not subject to the violence of a curse similar to that of Fresia towards her own child. This responds, in part, to the Mapuches' own practices of inheritance and rulership, which did not hew to Iberian laws and mores. One could argue that the force behind the letter of the law on the Iberian Peninsula makes the violence of the Indigenous curse gratuitous. But as the last canto itself shows in its dénouement, the status of Don Antonio's claim to the Portuguese throne was not automatically discounted due to his illegitimate ancestry by his Portuguese followers. If the unmarked heir was male, born in wedlock, and native, the crisis of the Portuguese succession, as played out in the last canto of *La Araucana*, acknowledged a preference by the people for the native-born when all the default conditions of inheritance could not be met. In the poem, Moura, male and Portuguese, serves Spanish imperial ideology in much the same way as Fresia did, but rather than curse the native-born *natural* son, he gives his blessing to Philip II to invade Portugal. It would be gratuitous to curse the child, or the terrain of the Iberian Peninsula at the outset of the Iberian Union, made one nation through the sacrament of marriage.

Oña's *Arauco domado* Ties the Knot

Published less than a decade after the third part of *La Araucana*, the *Arauco domado* shows a similar sensibility towards recently constitutive and constituted authorities, including, notably, the figure of Viceroy García Hurtado de Mendoza (1535–1609), 5th Marquis of Cañete, whose portrayal in *La Araucana* was hardly favourable. At the same time, Oña takes care to restore the ties that bind between Caupolicán and Fresia, exalting the lineage of Mapuche elites at every opportunity. For example, one of Oña's favourite epithets with which to refer to Caupolicán is "son of Leocán" (hijo de Leocán) (IV.92.2; V.33.5; VI.72.8), while he exalts Fresia's royalty as *palla* and her fertility (V.8.6–V.11.8) as one that is shared by the native soil, making reference to the "rich and fertile field" (rico y fértil prado) (V.12.1) and "fertile slopes" (fértiles vertientes) (V.11.3). In the fifth canto, he creates an erotically charged bathing scene for Fresia and Caupolicán; it marks a classic *locus amoenus* in which the flora reproduces the embraces of the native husband and wife:

También se ve la yedra enamorada
que con su verde braço retorcido
ciñe lasciva el tronco mal pulido
de la derecha haya levantada;
y en conjugal amor se ve abraçada
la vid alegre al olmo envejescido,
por quien sus tiernos pámpanos prohija,
con que lo enlaza, encrespa y ensortija. (V.16.1–8)

(The ivy is also in love / [and] with its twisting green arm / it clings lasciviously to the poorly polished trunk / of the straight and tall beech; / in conjugal love embraced are / the cheery vine and the aging oak, / for whom it produces tender shoots / with which it ties, twines, and curls.)

In this scene, Oña's ivy favours this European vine's traditional association with marital love. As widely noted by readers of Oña, his celebration of the cornucopia of America's bounty largely avoids the representation of local flora and fauna in his epic,[59] even as it is populated with words from Quechua, Aymara, and Mapundungun.[60] This conceit – the use of European flora to symbolize Indigenous marriage – displays a criollo sensibility for the exaltation of the native soil in which all plants, especially the non-native, may take root, as metonymy for Spanish civilization and for the reproduction of American-born criollos. As the 1573 *Ordenanzas* made clear, one of the best examples of the benefits of Spanish civilization (*poliçía*) was the introduction of Spanish seeds such as grapevines, rice, wheat, and olives. In *Ordenanza* 149, commonplace figures for Indigenous monstrosity and savagery go hand in hand with a litany of objects that characterize the good life cultivated by exposure to Spanish products:

> y los tenemos en paz para que no se maten ny coman ni sacrifiquen como en algunas partes se hazia y puedan andar seguros por todos los caminos tratar y contratar y comerçiar aseles ensenado puliçia visten y calçan y tienen otros muchos bienes que antes les heran prohibidos aseles quitado las cargas y serbidumbres aseles dado vso de pan vino azeyte y otros muchos mantenimientos paño seda lienço cauallos ganados herramientas armas [...] y que de todos estos bienes goçaran los que vinieren a conoçimiento de nuestra santa fee catholica y a nuestra obediencia [...][61]

> (And we have pacified them so that they do not kill, or eat, or sacrifice one another as they did in the past. And they can travel, and trade, and do business on the roads safely; we have taught them to live in polite society. They dress and wear shoes, and have other goods that were previously prohibited to them. We have removed their burdens and servitude, and given them the custom of [eating and drinking] bread, wine, and oil, and other sustenance. Cloth, linen, horses, livestock, tools, and weapons [...] all these benefits they will enjoy, if they come to the knowledge of our holy Catholic faith and to obey us [...])

The barrenness in that gap between the *hijo natural* and *contra natura* explored by Ercilla in his descriptions of Chilean terrain, and in the denaturalization of the native mother, is returned to the promise of Spanish law and, especially, settler colonialism in Oña's epic as the descriptions boast of fertility in their depiction of Indigenous conjugal love. In order to achieve this, Oña must first revisit all signs of gender trouble surrounding the pair from the epic precedent established in *La Araucana*. The Creole author alludes to the fraught nature of his task in his prologue to *Arauco domado*, where, in a moment of *captatio benevolentae*, Oña acknowledges his temerity in following in the footsteps of the celebrated Ercilla, but he does so in the guise of a bloodhound, "following the trail of his [predecessor's] scent" (preciándome mucho de ir al olor de su rastro), if only "to recall what he [Ercilla] left behind to be forgotten" (traer a la memoria lo que él [Ercilla] dexó al olvido) (548). The criollo writer as indefatigable dog following the peninsular author's trail exemplifies what Juan Vitulli has called "criollo deixis" (deixis criolla), the singular positioning of the lettered criollo through an imitative gesture that seeks to participate in the symbolic and material networks of transatlantic power in the construction of his own figure as an alternate in command of cultural authority (21). Leading from behind, so to speak, Oña then frames his motivation to supplement *La Araucana* with the *Arauco domado* as a "desire to serve [his] native land, one born out of love" (el solo desseo de hazer algún servicio a la tierra donde nací–¡Tanto como esto puede el amor a la patria!) (549). As the native (*natural*)-born son, Oña positions himself to love Chile thoroughly in a way that Ercilla could not. He achieves this commitment, in part, by rebinding together Caupolicán and Fresia and, in so doing, metaphorically revives the Indigenous (*natural*) and natural (*natural*) fertility of their native land while staking a claim to it.

In Oña's epic, Fresia repairs the bonds undone by her alter ego in *La Araucana*, referring to Caupolicán as her "beloved owner" (dueño amado) and "dear spouse" (caro esposo) (V.29.1, V.30.1). Any comparisons made between Dido (historical or mythical) and Fresia are glossed over in favour of Daphne, the nymph whose cries at her violation are rendered mute as she is transformed into the laurel tree, whose leaves adorn the brow of the male victor in arms and in letters:

> Abrásase, mirándola, dudoso
> si fuese Dafne, en lauro convertida,
> de nuevo al ser humano reduzida
> según se siente de ella cudicioso. (V.36.1–4)

> ([Caupolicán] burned, [while] looking at her, doubtful / if she had been Daphne converted in the Laurel tree, / reduced once more to human form / as he lusted for her.)

As the scene unfolds, the binary in gender roles between Lover and Beloved, male and female, active and passive, speech and silence becomes even more marked, so that the epic may specify that their breasts cannot "penetrate each other," but rather that their embraces will result in reciprocated "knots" (*ñudos*):

> Los pechos, antes bellos que velludos,
> ya que se les prohíbe el penetrarse,
> procuran lo que pueden estrecharse
> con reciprocación de ciegos ñudos. (V.40.1–4)

> (Their chests, beautiful rather than hairy, / as they are forbidden to penetrate each other, / attempt to get closer / with the reciprocity of blind knots.)

The description of the pair reaches its climax with references to figures with whom they clearly do *not* identify, such as Hermaphroditus (*Troco, el zahareño*) and Salmacis, the nymph enamoured of the son of Hermes and Aphrodite.

According to Ovid in the *Metamorphoses*, Salmacis gave her name to a pool of water in Caria, which had the ability to combine two sexes into one, after her own efforts to remain forever embraced with Hermaphroditus are favoured by the gods (IV.373–533). Though the description of the native married couple's embraces resembles the metaphors of twining plants and vines used by Ovid to describe the union of Hermaphroditus and Salmacis, the narrator insists instead in the *Arauco domado*:

> No están allá los Géminis desnudos
> con tan fogosas ansias de juntarse,
> ni Sálmacis con Troco el zahareño,
> a quién por verse dueña amó por dueño. (V.40.5–8)

(The nude Gemini twins they are not, / so anxious in their desire to re-unite, / nor Salmacis with Hermaphroditus, the wild one, / whom she loved as a master so that she could be [his] mistress.)

In this way, the mythological figures offered as counter-examples in the *Arauco domado* respond to the gender-troubling of Fresia and Caupolicán in the third part of *La Araucana* by rejecting the imagery of same-sex union, though rather than two women, the counter-example is homosocial and fraternal, embodied by the Gemini twins Castor and Pollux – or emasculation, as promised by a dip in the pool of Salmacis. Like Daphne returned to human form earlier in the same canto, the pool in which Fresia and Caupolicán swim serves to reverse the troubling transformations of Ovidian epic, and through these allusions to Ovid's gender-bending, seeks to undo the damage both to their marriage and their bodies in *La Araucana*.[62] Rather than the Indigenous child, the only knot to unravel in the scene is that of Fresia's dress, which slips open just as she slips it off, feigning female modesty: "Once the knot comes undone / and she feigns elusiveness and slips away" (Alguna vez el ñudo se desata, / y ella se finge esquiva y se escabulle) (V.41.1–2). However, even as canto V in the *Arauco domado* responds to and erases every instance of gender-troubling endured by the couple in Ercilla's epic, the native child, the fruit of Caupolicán and Fresia's encounter, remains but a promise: conceived, perhaps, in this very scene, but as yet unborn.

Oña divorces the native human from the native soil, just as the laws of the Indies predicate the cultivation of civilizing seeds, products, and practices. It is easy to see how the metaphor of the union of native, fertile soil with foreign seeds would be intriguing to Oña as a native-born son of Spanish parentage. His celebration of Indigenous marriage aligns native unions with the fertility of the land, no longer barren as Ercilla had left it, even as the male seed of Caupolicán is not given the opportunity to bear fruit in the form of a native son. Figuratively, this clears the forest of the *locus amoenus* for the *nomos*, the furrows, and the law of settler colonialism by which wheat, olives, and grapes may flourish and grow.

NOTES

1 I am grateful for the comments and suggestions of Mercedes Blanco, Emiro Martínez-Osorio, Felipe Valencia, and the anonymous reviewer from their careful reading of earlier versions of this essay.
2 I have used the edition of Virgil's text edited by G.P. Goold. Subsequent references to the *Aeneid* draw on this edition and appear in the text.
3 Eidinow, "Dido, Aeneas, and Iulus," 264–7; Barrett, "Dido's Child: A Note on *Aeneid* 4.327–30," 51–3.
4 Quint, *Epic and Empire*, 111–18.
5 For this essay, I am using the 1993 edition of Alonso de Ercilla's *La Araucana*, edited by Lerner. References in my text refer to this edition and appear in the text.
6 Lagos, "El incumplimiento de la programación épica en *La Araucana*." Pittarello, "*Arauco domado* de Pedro de Oña o la vía erótica de la conquista."
7 I am referencing the 2014 edition of Pedro de Oña's *Arauco domado*. References in my text refer to this edition and appear in the text.
8 Quint, *Epic and Empire*; Nicolopulos, *The Poetics of Empire in the Indies*; and Blanco, "Fábulas de amores en la épica de guerra."
9 Padrón, "Love American Style."
10 Vásvari, "The Semiotics of Phallic Aggression and Anal Penetration," 130.
11 Rabasa, *Writing Violence on the Northern Frontier*, 151.
12 Marchante-Aragón, "Conquest, Rape, and Marriage," 171.
13 Butler, *Gender Trouble*, 191.
14 The speeches are made by Tegualda, Glaura, Lauca, and Guacolda. In the latter case, Guacolda predicts the death of Lautaro, another instance of a native woman's potent speech act in the epic poem. However, the characterization of Lautaro falls short of the transgressive reversals seen in the treatment of Caupolicán.
15 Schwartz, "Tradición literaria y heroínas indias en *La Araucana*," 619–25.
16 Schwartz, "Tradición literaria y heroínas indias en *La Araucana*," 625.

17 Valencia, *The Melancholy Void*, 81.

18 Vega, *Obra poética y textos en prosa*, 31.

19 Homer, *Iliad* bk. 6, 390–502. My references are to the Wyatt edition and Murray translation. Subsequent references to the *Iliad* draw on this edition and appear in the text.

20 See Rosa Lida de Malkiel's study *Dido en la literatura española: su retrato y defensa*.

21 Quint, *Epic and Empire*, 111–18.

22 Rabasa, *Writing Violence on the Northern Frontier*, 145.

23 Unless otherwise noted, all translations in this essay are my own.

24 Quint, *Epic and Empire*, 185–6.

25 Galperín, "The Dido Episode in Ercilla's *La Araucana* and the Critique of Empire," 33.

26 Edited and published by Morales Padrón in *Teoría y leyes de la Conquista*, 489–518.

27 *Ordenanzas*, Ordinance 139.

28 *Ordenanzas*, Ordinance 58.

29 *Ordenanzas*, Ordinance 136.

30 *Ordenanzas*, Ordinance 136.

31 For example, Ordinance 139 places its faith in commerce and trade for "the pacification" of the natives: "through commerce and trade make friends with them, showing them much love and caressing them and giving them some things so that they take a liking to them, and by not showing any greed for their things, make an alliance through friendship with the lords and leaders who seem to be in favour of their land's pacification" (por via de comercio y rescates traten amystad con ellos mostrandolos mucho amor y acariçiandolos y dandoles algunas cossas de rescates a quellos se afiçionaren y no mostrando codiçia de sus cossas assientese Amistad y aliança con los señores y prinçipales que paresçieren ser mas parte para la paçificacion de la tierra). *Ordenanzas*, Ordinance 139.

32 Morales Padrón, *Teoría y leyes de la Conquista*, 495.

33 Lavrín, "Introduction," 5–6.

34 Quint, *Epic and Empire*, 178 and 181–2; and Lagos, "El incumplimiento de la programación épica en *La Araucana*," 180–5.

35 Galperín, "The Dido Episode in Ercilla's *La Araucana* and the Critique of Empire," 57–62.

36 Davis, *Myth and Identity in the Epic of Imperial Spain*, 23.

37 Middlebrook, *Imperial Lyric*, ch. 4n.18.

38 Middlebrook, *Imperial Lyric*, ch. 4n.18.

39 Note that by the time of publication of the second part of *La Araucana* in 1578, Ercilla was already married to Bazán (the marriage took place in 1570). The events narrated in *La Araucana* are set in 1557–8.

40 Austin, *How to Do Things with Words*, 13–24.

41 Rabasa, *Writing Violence on the Northern Frontier*, 152.

42 Significantly, Sabat de Ribers has argued that Fresia's unmanning of Caupolicán influences the way readers are meant to evaluate the native hero, eventually condemning him with her and, ultimately, his Spanish captors. Sabat de Rivers, "*La Araucana* bajo el lente actual: el noble bárbaro humillado,"118–19.

43 Fresia's nobility is connoted in the poem by the use of the epithet *palla*, which had been used by the Inca elites to denote women of high status. It was registered by conquistadors early in the conquest of Peru.

44 Ovid, *Metamorposes*, 11.533–47. My references are to Goold's edition. references refer to this edition and appear in the text.

45 In canto X, the narrator attributes the Araucanians' victories, in part, to the native women who follow their husbands into battle (vienen acompañando a sus maridos), after trading in their spinning wheel (la rueca) for manly vigour (varonil esfuerzo) (X.7.1; X.3.3–4). In a paradoxical play on the polysemous word *natural* (native, but also of nature) the narrator comments that pregnant Indigenous women have the best stamina on the battlefield, running faster than the rest (antes corren mejor las más preñadas) (X.5.8), thereby suggesting that native (*natural*) motherhood is somehow contrary to nature.

46 Session XXIV, Canon 8, *General Council of Trent*.

47 Lavrín, "Introduction," 27.

48 Vivar, *Crónica y relación*, 207.

49 Góngora Marmolejo, "Historia de Chile," 135.

50 Agamben, *The Kingdom and the Glory*, 183.

51 Kantorowicz, *The King's Two Bodies*, 87–192.

52 Agamben, *The Kingdom and the Glory*, 190.

53 Choi (see Sutton), "'De gente que a ningún rey obedecen,'" 421–2.

54 For Ercilla's engagement with the debates on the just and unjust causes of war, as elaborated by Francisco de Vitoria, Juan Ginés de Sepúlveda, and Bartolomé de Las Casas in the first part of *La Araucana*, see Choi (Sutton), "'De gente que a ningún rey obedecen.'" For the debates surrounding the just causes of war in the Indies, see Anghie, "Francisco de Vitoria and the Colonial Origins of International Law"; and Hanke, *The Spanish Struggle for Justice in the Conquest of America*.

55 Plagnard, "Geografías épicas nas obras de Jerónimo Corte-Real, Alonso de Ercilla e Luís de Camões," 22–3. In her comparison of the poems by Ercilla, Camões, and Corte-Real, Plagnard shows that Iberian poets created a shared epic terrain in which they explored the similar challenges faced by the Iberian empires. As noted by Plagnard, through their epics, which dialogue with one another – *La Araucana* (1569, 1578, 1589–90), *Os Lusíadas*

(1572), and *Cerco de Diu* (1569), and *Vitoria de Lepanto* (1575) – the authors cast the Spanish and Portuguese empires as doing battle against a shared enemy, Indigenous pagans, and Muslim infidels alike, on various frontiers around the globe. By the time Ercilla writes the third part to *La Araucana*, the shared enterprise of the Iberian empires, at least in epic terrain, allows him to cast the Portuguese insurgency against the Spanish invasion as a rebellion.

56   Las Casas, *Brevíssima relación de la destruição de las Indias*, 112.
57   Beginning in the fourteenth century, though drawing on earlier traditions, the metaphor of marriage to signify the union of a people with their ruler – whether that be Christ or the king – was increasingly employed by jurists to signify the inalienability of fiscal property, and the indissolubility of the body politic by extension. Kantorowicz, *The King's Two Bodies*, 212–23.
58   As I have discussed elsewhere, *naturaleza* in sixteenth-century Spanish can refer both to a subject's community of belonging – synonymous with the *patria* – and to nature. Legnani, "Invasive Specie," 128–9.
59   See, for example, Medina, "El anotador al lector," viii; Chevalier, *L'Arioste en Espagne*, 145; Huidobro Salazar, "El territorio de Chile en la poesía épica del siglo XVI," 38.
60   Iglesias, *Pedro de Oña*, 410–68.
61   *Ordenanzas*, Ordinance 149.
62   In her reading of *Arauco domado*'s treatment of Caupolicán and Fresia, Blanco argues that Oña provides a celebration of conjugal love that reverses the emasculation of the Mapuche warrior. Similarly centred around canto 5, her interpretation focuses on Oña's treatment of Hermaphroditus (*Troco*) and Salmacis, though her reading depends on the influence of Vitruvius and this author's rejection of the emasculating properties of the Salmacis pool. Blanco, "Fábulas de amores en la épica de guerra," 51–3. Though there may be an intertextual dialogue with Vitruvius, I do not believe it is necessary to establish influence of Vitruvius on Oña as the criollo author clearly rejects the Ovidian exempla in canto 5, as discussed above, though his understanding of the myth of Salmacis and Hermaphroditus may have certainly been informed by such a counter-Ovidian reading.

WORKS CITED

Printed Sources

Agamben, Giorgio. *The Kingdom and the Glory: For a Theological Genealogy of Economy and Government*. Translated by Lorenzo Chiesa and Matteo Mandarini. Stanford, CA: Stanford University Press, 2011.

Alfonso X. *Las siete partidas*. Edited by Robert I. Burns. Translated by Samuel Parsons Scott. 5 vols. Philadelphia: University of Pennsylvania Press, 2001.

Anghie, Antony. "Francisco de Vitoria and the Colonial Origins of International Law." *Social and Legal Studies* 5, no. 4 (1996): 321–36.

Austin, John J. *How to Do Things with Words.* Oxford: Clarendon, 1975.

Barrett, A.A. "Dido's Child: A Note on *Aeneid* 4.327–30." *Maia* 25 (1973): 51–3.

Blanco, Mercedes. "Fábulas de amores en la épica de guerra. De la *Araucana* al *Arauco domado.*" *Bulletin Hispanique* 121, no. 1 (2019): 17–54.

Butler, Judith. *Gender Trouble: Feminism and the Subversion of Identity.* Abingdon, UK: Routledge, 2010.

Chevalier, Maxime. *L'Arioste en Espagne (1530–1650): Recherches sur l'influence du "Roland furieux."* Bordeaux: Institut d'études ibériques et ibéro-américaines de l'Université de Bordeaux, 1966.

Davis, Elizabeth. *Myth and Identity in the Epic of Imperial Spain.* Columbia: University of Missouri Press, 2000.

Eidinow, J.S.C. "Dido, Aeneas, and Iulus: Heirship and Obligation in *Aeneid* 4." *Classical Quarterly* 53, no. 1 (2003): 260–7.

Ercilla, Alonso de. *La Araucana.* Edited by Isaías Lerner. Madrid: Cátedra, 1993.

Galperin, Karina. "The Dido Episode in Ercilla's *La Araucana* and the Critique of Empire." *Hispanic Review* 77, no. 1 (2009): 31–67. doi:10.1353/hir.0.0046.

Góngora Marmolejo, Alonso de. "Historia de Chile." In *Crónicas del reino de Chile*, edited by Francisco Esteve Barba, 77–226. Vol. 131 of *Biblioteca de autores españoles.* Madrid: Ediciones Atlas, 1960.

Hanke, Lewis. *The Spanish Struggle for Justice in the Conquest of America.* Dallas: Southern Methodist University Press, 1949.

Homer. *The Iliad.* Edited by W.F. Wyatt. Translated by A.T. Murray. Cambridge, MA: Harvard University Press, 1924. doi:10.4159/DLCL. homer-iliad.1924.

– *The Odyssey.* Translated by Emily Wilson. New York: Norton, 2018.

Huidobro Salazar, María Gabriela. "El territorio de Chile en la poesía épica del siglo XVI: Un imaginario sobre los desafíos de la Conquista de Arauco." *Alpha* 47 (2018): 31–46.

Iglesias, Augusto. *Pedro de Oña: Ensayo de crítica e historia con un apéndice sobre los chilenismos y americanismos dispersos en el vocabulario de "Arauco domado."* Santiago de Chile: Editorial Andrés Bello, 1971.

Kantorowicz, Ernst. *The King's Two Bodies: A Study in Medieval Political Theology.* Princeton, NJ: Princeton University Press, 2016. https://doi. org/10.1515/9781400880782.

Lagos, Ramona. "El incumplimiento de la programación épica en *La Araucana.*" *Cuadernos Americanos* 40 (1981): 157–91.

Las Casas, Bartolomé de. *Brevísima relación de la destruición de las Indias.* Edited by André Saint-Lu. Madrid: Cátedra, 2005.

Lavrín, Asunción. "Introduction: The Scenario, the Actors, and the Issues." In *Sexuality and Marriage in Colonial Latin America*, edited by Asunción Lavrín, 1–43. Lincoln: University of Nebraska Press, 1989.

Legnani, Nicole D. "Invasive Specie: Rabbits, Conquistadors, and Capital in the *Historia de Las Indias* (1527–1561) by Bartolomé de Las Casas (1484–1566)." In *Latin American Culture and the Limits of the Human*, edited by Lucy Bollington and Merchant Paul, 127–49. Gainesville: University of Florida Press, 2020. https://doi.org/10.2307/j.ctvzgb67d.

Leonardo, Francesco, and Catholic Church, Province of Peru. Concilio Provincial (3rd: 1582–1583). *El Tercer Concilio Limense y la aculturación de los indígenas sudamericanos.* Salamanca, Spain: Universidad de Salamanca, 1990.

Lida de Malkiel, Rosa. *Dido en la literatura española: su retrato y defensa.* London: Tamesis, 1974.

Livy. *History of Rome, Volume X: Books 35–37*. Edited and translated by J.C. Yardley. Loeb Classical Library 301. Cambridge, MA: Harvard University Press, 2018.

Lucan. *The Civil War (Pharsalia)*. Translated by J.D. Duff. Loeb Classical Library 220. Cambridge, MA: Harvard University Press, 1928. DOI:10.4159/DLCL.lucan-civil_war.1928.

Marchante-Aragón, Lucas. "Conquest, Rape, and Marriage: Forced Miscegenation in the Hapsburg Empire." *eHumanista* 11 (2011): 161–84.

Medina, J.T. "El anotador al lector." In *Primera Parte de Arauco domado*, by Pedro de Oña, v–xiii. Madrid: Ediciones Cultura Hispánica, 1944.

Middlebrook, Leah. *Imperial Lyric: New Poetry and New Subjects in Early Modern Spain.* University Park: The Pennsylvania State University Presses, 2009.

Morales Padrón, Francisco. *Teoría y leyes de la Conquista.* Seville: Universidad de Sevilla, 2008.

Nicolopulos, James. *The Poetics of Empire in the Indies: Prophecy and Imitation in "La Araucana" and "Os Lusíadas."* University Park: Pennsylvania State University Press, 2000.

Oña, Pedro de. *Arauco domado.* Edited by Ornella Gianesin. Como-Pavia: Ibis, 2014.

Ovid. *Metamorphoses, Volume I: Books 1–8*. Translated by Frank Justus Miller. Revised by G.P. Goold. Loeb Classical Library 42. Cambridge, MA: Harvard University Press, 1916. DOI:10.4159/DLCL.ovid-metamorphoses.1916.

– *Metamorphoses, Volume II: Books 9–15*. Translated by Frank Justus Miller. Revised by G.P. Goold. Loeb Classical Library 43. Cambridge, MA: Harvard University Press, 1916. DOI:10.4159/DLCL.ovid-metamorphoses.1916

Padrón, Ricardo. "Love American Style: The Virgin Land and the Sodomitic Body in Ercilla's *Araucana*." *Revista de Estudios Hispánicos* 34, no. 3 (2000): 561–84.

Pittarello, Elide. "*Arauco domado* de Pedro de Oña o la vía erótica de la conquista." *Dispositio* 14 (1989): 247–70.

Plagnard, Aude. "Geografías épicas nas obras de Jerónimo Corte-Real, Alonso de Ercilla e Luís de Camões." *Veredas* 23 (2015): 9–25.

Quint, David. *Epic and Empire: Politics and Generic Form from Virgil to Milton.* Princeton, NJ: Princeton University Press, 1993.

Rabasa, José. *Writing Violence on the Northern Frontier: The Historiography of Sixteenth-Century New Mexico and Florida and the Legacy of Conquest.* Durham, NC: Duke University Press, 2000.

Sabat de Rivers, Georgina. "*La Araucana* bajo el lente actual: el noble bárbaro humillado." In *La cultura literaria en la América virreinal: concurrencias y diferencias,* edited by Pascual Buxó, 107–23. Mexico: UNAM, 1996.

Schmitt, Carl. *Political Theology II: The Myth of the Closure of Any Political Theology.* Translated by Michael Hoelzl. Cambridge: Polity, 2008.

Schwartz Lerner, Lía. "Tradición literaria y heroínas indias en *La Araucana.*" *Revista Iberoamericana* 38, no. 81 (1972): 615–25.

Sutton, Imogen. "'De gente que a ningún rey obedecen': Republicanism and Empire in Alonso de Ercilla's *La Araucana.*" *BHS* 91, no. 4 (2014): 417–35.

Valencia, Felipe. *The Melancholy Void: Lyric and Masculinity in the Age of Góngora.* Lincoln: University of Nebraska Press, 2020.

Vasvári, Louise. "The Semiotics of Phallic Aggression and Anal Penetration as Male Agonistic Ritual in the *Libro de buen amor.*" In *Queer Iberia. Sexualities, Cultures, and Crossings from the Middle Ages to the Renaissance,* edited by Josiah Blackmore and Gregory S. Hutcheson, 130–56. Durham, NC: Duke University Press, 1999.

Vega, Garcilaso de la. *Obra poética y textos en prosa.* Edited by Bienvenido Morros. Madrid: Crítica, 1995.

Villagrá, Gaspar de. *Historia de la Nueva México.* Albuquerque: University of New Mexico Press, 1992.

Virgil. *Eclogues. Georgics. Aeneid: Books 1–6.* Translated by H. Rushton Fairclough. Revised by G.P. Goold. Loeb Classical Library 63. Cambridge, MA: Harvard University Press, 1916.

Vitulli, Juan. *Instable puente: la construcción del letrado criollo en la obra de Juan de Espinosa Medrano.* Chapel Hill: University of North Carolina Press, 2013.

Vivar, Gerónimo de. *Crónica y relación copiosa y verdadera de los Reynos de Chile hecha por Gerónimo de Bibar natural de Burgos MDLVIII.* Edited by Irving Leonard. Santiago de Chile: Fondo Histórico y Bibliográfico José Toribio Medina, 1966.

Electronic Sources

General Council of Trent, 1545–63 AD. Church Councils. *Papal Encyclicals Online.* Online at https://www.papalencyclicals.net/councils/trent.htm.

PART FOUR

New Historiographic and Cartographic Boundaries

8 "Así el cielo lo quiso": Christopher Columbus and the Anonymous Pilot in *Carlo famoso* by Luis Zapata de Chaves

JASON McCLOSKEY

In *Los perros del paraíso*, Abel Posse's historical novel about Christopher Columbus, the Italian seafarer is said to have first learned about the sea in his youth as he contemplated it from the shore. The novelist relates that "It was at that point that the boy realized the sea was another universe. He learned that it was a cranky, angry, amoral god [...] To calm the infuriated deity – when his rage lasted more than three days – a deformed man was brought from some neighboring town and hurled off the cliff ringed with a necklace of dried figs and covered with chicken feathers to aid the sacrificed man in his flight to the limbo of idiots."[1] In this passage, Posse satirically alludes to the practice of scapegoating, and for all its mocking hyperbole, it raises questions about who benefits from the sacrifices of others, and how suffering can be rationalized by those who stand to gain from it. In Posse's novel, the victim is considered expendable because of his alleged deformity, and his death in the turbulent waters below is thought to restore the sea to conditions more propitious for fishing. The death of the innocent man is presented as a sacrifice required by a god angered for some unknown reason, but it is certainly not Columbus who is called upon to make the sacrifice. Rather, he watches, aloof, and presumably entertained by the spectacle that has become familiar in its ritualistic absurdity.

Some four centuries before Posse's novel, Luis Zapata de Chaves (1526–95) also featured a scapegoat in his account of Columbus in his epic, *Carlo famoso* (1566). And although Zapata's portrayal of the scapegoat is much more understated, it does force readers to reflect on the suffering and death inherent in transatlantic seafaring and the construction of early modern empires. In Zapata's poem, the scapegoating of an anonymous pilot subtly acknowledges, and yet symbolically releases, Columbus from any assignment of guilt for the ravages of conquest and colonization. Columbus is depicted as a pious Christian who perseveres in the face of hardships and fulfils his promise to the Catholic monarchs by bringing salvation to the Indies as part of God's providential plan. However, the narrative suggests that he was not adequately acknowledged for his accomplishments, and the underlying recognition of guilt and Zapata's own irreverent tone makes the narrative potentially unsettling for its dedicatee, Philip II. This essay focuses on the portrayal of Columbus in relation to early modern historiography and analyses what Zapata's account reveals about his attitude towards his monarchs and the controversies surrounding the Spanish conquest of the New World. It further argues that the scapegoating of the same legendary pilot who allegedly informed Columbus about the existence of the Indies evokes earlier criticisms levelled by Bartolomé de las Casas against the Spanish conquistadors.

Zapata's account of Columbus spans a mere thirty-seven stanzas (XI.16–52)[2] in an incredibly long poem of fifty cantos that is otherwise dedicated to the exploits of Charles V in Europe. Zapata's Columbus narrative draws extensively on historical, mythological, and religious discourses, and appears as a digressive interpolation in an account of Hernán Cortés's campaign to conquer Tenochtitlan. And although this portion of the epic has been excerpted, edited, and published on its own, it has generated relatively little critical interest.[3] Today *Carlo famoso* is probably best known for the asterisks that the publisher inserted in the margins of the text to warn readers of fictional passages, and also for being represented, in *Don Quixote*, as one text among others condemned to burn for purportedly promoting dangerous falsehoods.[4] Recent scholarship on *Carlo famoso* continues to reflect a similar interest in the distinctions and tensions between poetry and history in the conception of the poem. These studies examine the influence of poetic models and the ideals of chivalry on Zapata's panegyric to Charles V, and the depiction of events that took place during his reign.[5] Yet there may be more to Cervantes's apparent censure of *Carlo famoso* than meets the eye, and some scholars have emphasized Zapata's direct and indirect criticism of the eponymous hero of the poem and its dedicatee Philip II.[6] Indeed, something within the text of *Carlo famoso* appears to have severely upset Philip II because the king ordered Zapata to be imprisoned the same year the poem was published.[7]

Returning to an Undiscovered Land

Like many other sixteenth-century writers, Zapata maintains – against Columbus's emphatic insistence otherwise – that the Genoese sailor intended to sail to the New World. To explain how he had knowledge of a continent unknown to the rest of Europe, Zapata relies on a legend that, according to Las Casas, had long enjoyed widespread credence in the Indies.[8] The legend described an anonymous pilot, blown off course during a storm in the Atlantic, who saw this previously unknown land and, after a difficult return voyage during which much of the crew perished, communicated its existence to Columbus just before he himself died. Not surprisingly, this story was polemical because of its political, economic, and even symbolic implications. David A. Lupher calls this legend an "anti-Colón story,"[9] and it was, indeed, perceived that way by some, both in Spain and abroad. As Natalie Hester has shown, the Italians Giovanni Battista Ramusio and Girolamo Benzoni both expressed indignation over the story, believing it deprived Columbus of due recognition for his achievement.[10] However, it must not have been regarded as all that damaging to Columbus's reputation given that his son Fernando validated the basic premise of the myth in the biography he wrote about his father.[11] Other Spanish writers, such as Gonzalo Fernández de Oviedo, professed to be more circumspect about the myth, and for Las Casas, the effect of the legend on Columbus's claims to priority mattered much less than did its supposed revelation of the role of providence in Columbus's voyages.[12]

As José Toribio Medina and Manuel Terrón Albarrán have shown, Zapata's version of the anonymous pilot myth derives largely – sometimes almost verbatim – from Francisco López de Gómara's *Historia general de las Indias* (1552).[13] A passage from Gómara's history, in which he summarizes what he considers to be the undisputed facts of the story, gives a sense of the similarities between the two texts. Gómara writes: "All of them agree only that the pilot died in the house of Christopher Columbus, in whose possession remained the writings from the caravel and the account of the entire long voyage with the markings and height of the lands recently seen and found" (Solamente concuerdan todos en que falleció aquel piloto en casa de Cristóbal Colón, en cuyo poder quedaron las escrituras de la carabela y la relación de todo aquel luengo viaje, con la marca y altura de las tierras nuevamente vistas y halladas).[14] The essentials of this plot are reiterated in the following stanza from Zapata's poem:

Allí él del nuevo mundo a do aportado
así había, a Colón hizo que supiese,
para que en una carta que mostrado
le había, las nuevas tierras le pusiese:
mas en muy breve tiempo el desdichado
piloto, allí Dios quiso que muriese,

donde dejó a Colón las escrituras,
y de las nuevas tierras las alturas. (XI.24.1–8)[15]

(There, he informed Columbus about the New World, where he had landed, so that he [Columbus] could put the new lands on a map that he had shown him. Yet God willed the unfortunate pilot to die shortly later, where he left Columbus with the writings and the height of the new lands.)

Yet there are also subtle, meaningful differences between these two accounts. Gómara relates simply that the height, or latitude, of the newly found lands are left in Columbus's possession, but in the stanza above Zapata goes further, asserting that Columbus was responsible for charting that nautical information. This description is consistent with his portrayal of Columbus as a learned map maker – "a great master of maps and tables" (de mapas y tablas gran maestro) (XI.20.3) – and indeed, with his assertion that Columbus "was a great cosmographer" (cosmógrafo era grande) (XI.28.3). By contrast, however, Gómara maintains that "Christopher Columbus was not learned, but he was smart" ([n]o era docto Cristóbal Colón, mas era bien entendido,)[16] by which he appears to concede that Columbus was clever, but not educated or learned, and certainly not a cosmographer.[17] Zapata himself invites readers to compare his version of the events with his possible sources by calling attention to his professed consultation of written accounts.[18] The effect of this deviation from Gómara is to evoke the significant differences in education and social standing between pilots and cosmographers, two groups that were vying for control of seafaring when Zapata was engaged in composing his poem.[19] The poem implies that, without Columbus's expertise, a repeat of the accidental discovery would be difficult if not impossible. Thus, in *Carlo famoso*, it is Columbus's cosmographical learning that allows him to convert chance into divine purpose: he is the right person at the right time and place.[20]

In this respect, the poem is in line with Las Casas's portrayal of Columbus early in his *Historia de las Indias*.[21] After recounting many similar reports of islands sighted by sailors far west of the Azores and the Canary Islands, Las Casas writes of their effect on Columbus:

Cosas eran todas éstas ciertamente para él que tan solícito ya vivía desta negociación, se abrazase ya con ella, y señales con las cuales parece que Dios lo movía con empellones, porque la Providencia divinal, cuando determina hacer alguna cosa, sabe bien aparejar los tiempos, así como elige las personas, da las inclinaciones, acude con los adminículos, ofrece las ocasiones, quita eso mismo los impedimentos para que los efectos que pretende finalmente se hayan por sus causas segundas de producir.[22]

(Certainly, all of these things, for him, who lived so attentively by this enterprise, made him burn even more for it, and were signs with which it seems that God moved him by pushing, because divine Providence, when it determines to do something, knows well how to prepare the time and likewise it chooses the people, gives inclinations, provides the tools, presents occasions, and similarly removes obstacles so that the desired effects are at last produced by secondary causes.)

In Las Casas's interpretation, these kinds of stories brought back by lost sailors about mysterious islands were the secondary causes by which God could enact his providential plan for the discovery of the Indies. According to this vision, Columbus was divinely appointed to carry out his voyages in order to bring the Christian faith to the New World as the *Christum ferens*. However, as will be discussed later, Las Casas also thought Columbus fell short in fulfilling his calling. Zapata's poem is thus one of the first texts to present the Christum-ferens trope described by Jorge Cañizares-Esguerra: "'Christum-ferens,' an epic hero bringing the liberating message of Christ into a land long in the hands of Satan, became a staple of the Catholic Atlantic."[23] It puts into effect the epic portrayal of Columbus as Christum-ferens already modelled by Las Casas. As Cañizares-Esguerra writes, "[i]t was Las Casas's *Historia de las Indias* (1552–61), which circulated in manuscript, that first portrayed the life of Columbus in epic terms by elucidating all the obstacles the devil threw in the hero's path."[24]

Much more than Gómara, Zapata likewise emphasizes the active role that God took in initiating a providential enterprise. God's involvement in the course of events is highlighted three times in the anonymous pilot story. First, after the sailor takes refuge in Columbus's home, the narrator asserts laconically that "God willed him to die there" (allí Dios quiso que muriese) (XI.24.6). Then, in the following stanza, when the unknown identity of the pilot is emphasized, the narrator again insists that "Heaven willed it thus" (Así el cielo lo quiso) (XI.25.8). And finally, the narrator explains that, with the information provided by the anonymous pilot and his subsequent death, "God willed to put this memory in the head of Columbus alone" (Dios quiso en Colón solo / Poner, y en su cabeza esta memoria) (XI.27.1–2). In these three instances, the verb "quiso" is employed to express rather emphatically that the will of God, or heaven, is responsible for the pilot's death, for his anonymity, and for placing this memory in the head of Columbus. As in Las Casas's interpretations of previous voyages to the Indies, the seemingly random expedition of the anonymous pilot in *Carlo famoso* is given a greater purpose by God, but Zapata goes even further to assert that God willed the death of the sailor. However, unlike Las Casas, who gives many of the names of those sailors who preceded Columbus, Zapata – like Gómara – insists that the identity of the pilot who died in Columbus's home is unknown and lost to oblivion.

As will soon become clear, despite his vital contribution, the hapless pilot is made to bear only guilt for his discovery. All the credit is given instead to Columbus: "May all the world, from one pole to the other, give perpetual glory to Columbus alone" (A solo Colón de uno al otro polo, / Todo el mundo le dé perpetua gloria) (XI.27.3–4). This insistence on acknowledging only Columbus contradicts Gómara's version of two co-discoverers,[25] but it recalls similar comments made by Oviedo. This historian unequivocally rejects what he considers the myth of the anonymous pilot and makes abundantly clear who should receive credit for the discovery: "in truth, although something else may be concluded from contrary evidence or stories to lessen the praise of Christopher Columbus, they should not be believed. His is the glory, and to Columbus alone, after God, do the past Catholic, the present, and the future kings of Spain owe it to him" (en la verdad, aunque otra cosa se pudiese presumir de los contrarios indicios o fábulas, para estorbar el loor de don Cristóbal Colom, no deben ser creídos. Suya es esta gloria, y a solo Colom, después de Dios, la deben los reyes de España pasados e católicos, e los presentes y por venir).[26] Zapata likewise insists that "[Columbus alone] should receive the 'glory'" (solo Colón […] gloria) (XI.27.3–4) if Spain enjoys the benefits that his discovery has made possible: "If transitory life so greatly esteems silver and the bright gold of Apollo, if (it so greatly esteems) lording over other lands and peoples, which today Spain will owe to his descendants" (Si la plata, si el rubio oro de Apolo / Tanto estima esta vida transitoria, / Si tanto el señorear tierras y gentes, / Que España hoy deberá a sus descendientes) (XI.27.5–8). In fact, Zapata is so biased towards Columbus that he risks insulting the memory of the very person whose glories his poem *Carlo famoso* professes to sing. By asserting that Spain owes a debt to Columbus's descendants – "That today Spain owes to his descendants" (Que España hoy deberá a sus descendientes) (XI.27.8) – he appears to contradict the decision that Charles V ratified in 1536, which limited the privileges and benefits that the descendants of Columbus could rightfully claim.[27]

The rights, privileges and titles originally accorded to Columbus, should he make landfall, were spelled out in the *Capitulaciones de Santa*

Fe. They had been agreed upon in 1492 by Fernando and Isabel in Santa Fe, a military base from which the Spanish monarchs had been laying siege to Granada, the last Muslim city in Spain. The decision taken by Charles V in 1536 altered the terms of the *Capitulaciones*, but Zapata emphasizes the sanctity of the original contract by reflecting on the literal meaning of Santa Fe, or Holy Faith. He writes:

> En Santa fe (donde se funda y cría
> Cualquier cosa perpetua y duradera)
> Se tomó con Colón en todo asiento,
> Y se despachó, y fue alegre y contento. (XI.31.5–8)

> (In Santa Fe [where anything perpetual and lasting is founded and raised], everything was established in a contract with Columbus, and he was dispatched and went away happy and content.)

In the context of his preceding praise of Columbus, and the claim of what is owed to his descendants, Zapata's comments on the symbolism of Santa Fe appear admonitory. He suggests that – like the place from which it issued – the commission should be perpetual and lasting. That Zapata would assume this tone, and risk chastising the very namesake of his poem, appears to be in keeping with his contrary personality, but it likely stems also from his own familial connections to the historical circumstances. Zapata's grandfather served as an adviser to Ferdinand and Isabel, and perhaps not surprisingly, the narrator praises the monarchs' advisers, boasting of the sovereigns' "select council [...] worthy of praise" (escogido/ Consejo, [...] de loor digno [...]) (XI.30.5–6), and contends that, because of poor advisers, kings of other nations declined to support Columbus's enterprise (XI.29.1–8).

Having secured royal patronage, Columbus equips his ships and then departs for the Canary Islands and beyond. He is "inflamed with a great love that the Indies be discovered by him" ([...] inflamado de amor grande/ Que las Indias por él se descubriesen) (XI.28.1–2), and he sets his course by the path of the sun: "following the sun as it goes to its place, he sets sail on the surrounding high sea" ([...] tras el sol yendo a sus lugares,/ Se metió en alta mar por esos mares" [XI.33.7–8]). The literal light of the sun then gives way to a more metaphorical light:

> O cierto de morir en agua o en guerras,
> o de salir con lo que osado había:
> Atrás dejar Colón se veía las sierras,
> las que él como sus manos conocía,

> por ir en busca de las nuevas tierras,
> que todo el mundo aún de ellas no sabía,
> siguiendo una luz chica como a tiento,
> que le encendía de llama el pensamiento. (XI.34.1–8)

(Either certain to die in water or in wars, or to accomplish what he had dared to do: Columbus was seen leaving behind the mountains that he knew like the back of his hands to go in search of the new lands, of which the world did not know, following, as if by touch, a small light that ignited his thought in flame.)

The mountains of the Canary Islands, symbolic of the limits of all knowledge prior to Columbus, fade from view. And, as the sun sets in the west (XI.33.3–6), Columbus, determined to succeed in his daring enterprise or die trying, is portrayed as groping his way towards the dim light of his thought. The poem thus shifts from a description of the physical light of the sun whose setting submerges the earth into darkness to the mental light that exists only faintly in the mind of Columbus.

The luminous imagery continues in the next stanza in which Columbus's "small light" (luz chica) (XI.34.7) is compared to Hero's mythological lantern:

> Aquel que el Helesponto pasó a nado
> A la lumbre que puesta había en Abido,
> No tuvo menor luz, ni tan osado
> Como Colón no creo que hubiese sido. (XI.35.1–5)[28]

(That one who swam across the Hellespont by the light that was set in Abydos did not have less light nor was he as daring as I believe Columbus had been.)

Like Leander, who swam towards Hero's lamp across the Hellespont, so Columbus crosses the Atlantic guided by a small light.[29] This comparison of the Italian seafarer to Leander reinforces an earlier description of Columbus, in which the phrasing evokes Garcilaso de la Vega's portrayal of Leander in his sonnet XXIX. Zapata tells of Columbus's ardent desire to set sail, and to discover the Indies – "Thus Columbus inflamed by a great love" (Colón pues inflamado de amor grande" (XI.28.1) – much as Garcilaso describes Leander as "burning completely in amorous fire" (en amoroso fuego todo ardiendo) (XXIX.2) while he swims across the strait.

These similarities support the argument of Cacho Casal, that "Garcilaso has very often served as the artistic thread and the primary material with which he adorns his verses" (Garcilaso le ha servido muy a menudo el hilo artístico, de materia prima con la que orna sus versos).[30] Zapata also insists that Columbus's feat is more daring than that of Leander precisely because the mythological youth was strengthened by the power of love: "And since love is more vigorous, he (Leander) / did less" (Y porque es el amor más esforzado, / Hizo él [Leandro] menos) (XI.35.5–6). That is, after already having described Columbus as inflamed by love – "inflamed with great love" (inflamado de amor grande" [XI.28.1]) – the poem goes on to imply that his feat was all the more impressive because Columbus was not in love like Leander. This apparently contradictory distinction is puzzling at first, but it serves to highlight that, for Zapata, Columbus's "great love" (amor grande) (XI.28.1) was not a physical desire like Leander's, but rather a spiritual one, which required more faith and patience to fulfil. The final lines of this stanza recall accounts of other events that took place the night before the Spanish made landfall in the Indies, and comparison with these descriptions further clarifies the kind of spiritual longing that Zapata attributes to Columbus.

Accounts of Columbus's first voyage tell of the weak light that could be seen by those on the ship as it approached the shores of the New World. According to several versions, the first crew member to see land itself was a sailor named Rodrigo de Triana, who was therefore due to receive a promised financial reward, but instead, the Spanish monarchs later presented it to Columbus. Las Casas argues that this reveals the justness and beneficence of God, because only Columbus "had firm faith and steadfast perseverance in divine Providence that he would not be thwarted from his goal" (tuvo fe firme y perseverante constancia de la divinal Providencia, que no había de ser de su fin defraudado) and therefore God ordained that Columbus "achieve this favour and that having first seen land be credited for having first seen this light on it, in the spiritual sense, that by his sweat, Christ would infuse those peoples who lived in such deep darkness" (alcanzase este favor, y se le atribuyese haber primero visto la tierra, por ver primero la lumbre en ella, en figura de la espiritual, que, por sus sudores, había Cristo de infundir a aquestas gentes que vivían en tan profundas tinieblas).[31] In his view, Columbus had suffered constant hardships in gaining support, and then in executing his voyage, and it was his faithful perseverance in the providential plan entrusted to him that opened the New World to the evangelization of which Las Casas so heartily approved. Las Casas contends that seeing the light on the shore was tantamount to sighting land, and that glimmer, moreover, was symbolic of the spiritual light that Columbus was bringing to the Indigenous peoples, who supposedly lived in spiritual darkness. Las Casas's description of the determination of Columbus to succeed and of the spiritual light that dispelled the gloom recalls Zapata's portrayal of the resoluteness of Columbus and the light of his thought that guided his voyage. In both texts, Columbus comes across as an exceptionally determined individual, guided by a spiritual light that he alone is granted by God to perceive.

The divine guidance and protection of Columbus continues when growing anxieties among his crew nearly lead to mutiny. Exaggerating the travails and duration of the transatlantic crossing, the poem asserts that Columbus's ships sailed for six months during the summer, fall, and winter, and that they faced more storms than could be described (XI.36.1–8). In the midst of such a long and arduous journey, the crew becomes increasingly worried that Columbus may have deceived them, and they revolt:

> Y todos con enojo furibundo
> Después que contra él juntos conjuraron,
> Para echar a Colón en el profundo,
> Como otro tiempo a Jonas le tomaron. (Zapata XI.40.1–4)

> (And everyone, with furious anger, after they had all conspired against him to throw Columbus into the depths, just as they took Jonah in a different time.)

Thus, Columbus was about to be thrown overboard like the Jewish prophet Jonah, and the New World was at risk of never being discovered (In such danger was the New World" ["En tal peligro estuvo el Nuevo Mundo"]) (Zapata XI.40.5) until God intervened. Miraculously, the crew was temporarily pacified by Columbus's pleas, and they granted him three days (the same duration of time that Jonah spent inside a whale) to make landfall. Columbus then dutifully devoted himself to prayer and, at the end of his grace period, land was finally sighted. The radical change of attitude among the crew elicits the narrator's moralizing critique of human fickleness:

> O de los hombres seso instable, y vano
> ¿Cómo se muda presto y fácilmente?
> Poco ha que echar allí en el Océano
> con furor, a Colón quería su gente,
> y ahora vista tierra, ellos la mano

van todos a besarle encontinente,
a sus pies se echan con su barco y redes,
y le piden perdón, honra, y mercedes. (XI.43.1–8)

(Oh men of shifting and vain minds: How do you change so fast and easily? A little while ago, his men angrily wanted to throw Columbus into the ocean, and now that land is seen, they all rush to kiss his hand, and throw themselves with their nets at his feet on the boat, and ask him for forgiveness, honours, and graces.)

The reversal in Columbus's fortune is captured in the use of the verb "echar." The narrator notes that, only a short while before, the crew was prepared to throw Columbus overboard (echar allí en el Oceano" [XI.43.3]), but after land was sighted, they throw themselves at his feet (A sus pies se echan" [XI.43.7]) to beg for forgiveness and for rewards. Columbus thus goes from being despised to honoured, from impotent to powerful. Oviedo describes the moment in a similar fashion, writing:

y así, dando gracias a Nuestro Señor con todos los que con él iban, fue inestimable el gozo que los unos y los otros hacían. Tomábanle unos en brazos, otros le besaban las manos, e otros le demandaban perdón de la poca constancia que habían mostrado. Algunos le pedían mercedes e se ofrecían por suyos.[32]

(and thus, giving thanks to Our Lord with all those that went with him, the joy that it gave everyone was incalculable. Some took him into their arms, others kissed his hands, and others demanded forgiveness for the little steadfastness that they had shown. Some others asked him for rewards and offered themselves to him.)

The subject of the mutiny became intensely controversial later when legal battles raged over the legitimacy of the rights claimed by Columbus's descendants. Descriptions like Zapata's and the preceding passage from Oviedo present the Spanish crew as earnestly repentant, but therefore guilty of being incredulous, suspicious, and hostile towards Columbus. Another competing narrative emerged, however, when the Council of the Indies sought to curtail the benefits originally granted to Columbus and his heirs by the *Capitulaciones*. The crown attorney recorded many depositions that contested these accounts of the mutiny, insisting, much to the contrary, that it was actually Columbus who wanted to return prematurely to Spain. According to them, the Indies would never have been discovered if it had not been for the perseverance and insistence of Martín Alonso Pinzón, who persisted despite Columbus's fears. This version of events could be used to justify denying Columbus's heirs certain financial rewards and offices. While Oviedo's words cited above strongly suggest he was partisan of the claims of Columbus's family, he does also acknowledge in passing the counterclaims of the Spanish crew.[33] Zapata's text, like Las Casas's *Historia*, leaves no doubt, however: his portrayal of the mutiny wholeheartedly supports the side of the Columbus family, and does not hesitate to impugn the Spanish crew as cowardly and disobedient.[34]

Planting Christianity in the New World

With the mutiny quelled, the fortunes of Columbus continue to improve as he makes contact with the Indigenous peoples. When they see the Spaniards disembark, they are said to be amazed by European technology, namely, their ships and arms. They take the gleaming Spanish weapons to be an omen:

> Atónitos quedaron, tal mirando,
> Y por nuevos portentos lo tuvieron
> Como los que en las nubes peleando
> En la muerte de César armas vieron. (XI.46.3–6)

(They were speechless as they looked at such things and took them for new omens, like those who saw arms in the clouds while they were fighting at the death of Caesar.)

The simile in this passage alludes to the portents that purportedly foreshadowed Julius Caesar's death, as recounted by many sources. For example, Ovid writes in the *Metamorphoses*: "They say that arms clashing between black clouds / and fearsome trumpets and horns heard in heaven / had forewarned of the sin" (arma ferunt inter nigras crepitantia nubes / terribilesque tubas auditaque cornua caelo / praemonuisse nefas) (XV.783–5).[35] Such signs of impending demise frighten the Indigenous peoples, and they flee from the invaders. Nevertheless, the Spanish do manage to seize a woman, and after plying her with food, she acts as an intermediary and initiates commerce between the two sides:

> De los cuales los nuestros no alcanzaron
> sino a tan sola una india que huía,
> que con comer como ave la amansaron,
> y tornaron el miedo en alegría:

y a llamar a los otros la enviaron,
que vinieron allí luego aquel día,
con plata, perlas y oro en sus fardeles,
que trocaban por vidrio y cascabeles. (XI.47.1–8)

(Of whom our men did not reach anyone except a single Indian woman
who fled; and they tamed her with food, like a bird, and turned her fear
into joy: And they sent her to call for the others, who then came there that
day with silver, pearls, and gold in their bags, which they traded for glass
and bells.)

Las Casas relates a similar story in much greater detail,[36] but for his
version of the incident Zapata seems to have drawn from López de
Gómara's account, in which he writes:

Corrieron los nuestros tras ellos, y alcanzaron una sola mujer. Diéronle
pan y vino y confites, y una camisa y otros vestidos, que venía desnuda en
carnes, y enviáronla a llamar la otra gente. […] Traían aves, pan, fruta, oro
y otras cosas, a trocar por cascabeles, cuentas de vidrio, agujas, bolsas y
otras cosillas así, que no fue pequeño el gozo para Colón.[37]

(Our men ran after them and reached a single woman. They gave her
bread, wine, and sweets, and a shirt and other clothes, for she came naked,
and they sent her to call the other people. […] They brought fowl, bread,
fruit, and other things to trade for bells, glass beads, needles, bags, and
other such trifles, all to the great joy of Columbus.)

Both Zapata's and Gómara's accounts make clear how unequal trade
ensued between the Spanish and the Indigenous peoples, and from
which Columbus and his men benefited.

In the above stanza, Zapata portrays the Indies as a rich and fertile
place populated by accommodating inhabitants eager to give of their
abundant natural resources and to serve the Spanish: "And the Indians who had humbly come there served our men in everything" (Y
los indios allí humildes venidos / A los nuestros en todo les servían)
(XI.48.3–4). It depicts a peaceful coexistence, but one in which there
emerges a hierarchy tacitly accepted by the Indigenous peoples to the
advantage of the Spanish. Furthermore, unlike other epics that do fore-
shadow such events, it gives no hint of the violent conflicts that would
later result, first from Columbus's brutal demands of the Indigenous
peoples, and later from the Spanish colonists. For example, in Juan
de Castellanos's portrayal of the contact between the Spanish and the

Indigenous woman in *Elegies of Illustrious Men of the Indies*, the poet seizes the opportunity to admonish the woman and blame her mediation for the ensuing upheaval:

> Verás incendios grandes de ciudades
> En las partes que menos convenía:
> Verás abuso grande de crueldades
> En el que mal ninguno merecía;
> Verás talar labranzas y heredades
> Que el bárbaro sincero poseía,
> Y en su reinado y propio señorío
> Guardarse de decir es esto mío.[38]

(You will see great conflagrations of cities in the worst places; you will see great abuses of cruelty on those who deserved no harm; you will see cut down the fields and property possessed by the sincere barbarian who never claims something as his own.)

The similarity of this passage from Castellanos to the language of Las Casas's *Brevísima relación de la destruición de las Indias* is especially surprising given Castellanos's later mocking of Las Casas in his poem.[39] Nor does there appear in *Carlo famoso* any indication of the economic disappointments of the islands that soon were felt by the Crown and colonists alike.

Instead, in *Carlo famoso* Columbus and his men are depicted to be offering spiritual freedom and salvation to the Indigenous peoples as the divinely inspired mission reaches its culmination. In the final stanza of his narrative, Zapata relates a story that becomes commonplace in the providential version of the Columbus narrative. The narrator asserts:

> Y una cruz que en las Indias fue plantada,
> por Colón donde está hasta hoy en día,
> que de los indios ser nunca arrancada
> no ha podido jamás por su porfía;
> por solo el palo de ella (en quien cortada,
> la madera otra vez reverdecía)
> sanó copia de enfermos, cojos, tuertos,
> y así resuscitó a infinitos muertos. (XI.52.1–8)

(And a cross was planted by Columbus in the Indies, where it remains to this day, for it was never uprooted by the Indians for all their effort; only a stick from it [when it was cut, the wood grew green again] healed copious sick, lame and blind people and brought back to life an infinite number of dead.)

Columbus, it is said, erects a cross that performs a number of miracles, one of which is that it cannot be removed from the ground despite attempts by the Indigenous peoples to do so. In fact, it supposedly remained intact at the time of Zapata's writing. Moreover, it can regenerate itself when branches are broken off, and these same pieces of wood heal the sick, the lame, and the blind, but most incredibly of all, the cross resurrects countless dead. This story likely comes from Oviedo's *Historia*, according to which the cross was erected in Concepción de la Vega, on Hispaniola, at the time of Columbus's second voyage. Oviedo writes:

> Afirman muchos e tienen por cosa pública e cierta que ha hecho milagros después acá, y que el palo de esta cruz ha sanado a muchos enfermos; y es tanta la devoción que los cristianos en ella tienen que hurtan muchos pedazos e astillas de ella, así para llevar a España como a otras partes. Y es tenida en mucha veneración, así por sus milagros, como porque en tanto tiempo como estuvo descubierta, jamás se pudrió ni cayó, por ninguna tormenta de agua ni viento, ni jamás la pudieron mover de aquel lugar los indios, aunque la quisieron arrancar.[40]

> (Many assert and maintain as true and public knowledge that since then it has done miracles here, and that a stick from this cross has healed many sick people; and the devotion that Christians have for it is such that they steal pieces and splinters of it, to take it to Spain and other places. And it is revered as much as for its miracles as because, in all the time since its discovery, it has never rotted nor fallen due to any rain or windstorm; nor have the Indians been able to move it from that place even though they have tried to uproot it.)

Although Oviedo includes more details about the circumstances of the erection of the cross, Zapata offers more specifics about the kinds of conditions it heals, and also goes further than Oviedo in the powers he attributes to it.[41] In fact, the kinds of miracles that the cross works recalls the signs that Christ associates in the Gospels with the coming of the Messiah, thus once again reinforcing the image of Columbus as the *Christum-ferens*.[42] Moreover, as a kind of tree, planted in the ground where it is firmly rooted, the description of the cross and its associated miracles evokes both the power attributed to this Christian symbol against the influence of Satan in the New World, and the figuration of colonization as spiritual gardening, as studied by Cañizares-Esguerra.[43]

This conclusion, and its implications, are all the more significant given how they contrast with Las Casas's depiction of Columbus and his legacy in terms of spiritual gardening. Although the friar insisted that Columbus was chosen by God for the fulfilment of his plan for the Indies, he also believed that the admiral's execution of this mission was flawed, and that it actually introduced the very problems that came to plague the New World and its inhabitants. A major part of the problem, according to Las Casas, stemmed from Columbus's misguided preoccupation with delivering on his promise to the Spanish monarchs to find a source of wealth in the Indies and his disregard for the natural rights of the Indigenous peoples. As Las Casas explains in his *Historia*, Columbus

> introdujo y comenzó a asentar tales principios y sembró tales simientes, que se originó y creció dellas tan mortífera y pestilencial hierba, y que produjo de sí tan profundas raíces, que ha sido bastante a destruir y asolar todas las Indias, sin que poder humano haya bastado a tan sumos e irreparables daños impedir o atajar.[44]

> (introduced and began to lay such groundwork and sow such seeds that such a deadly and pestilential weed originated and grew from them and it produced such deep roots that is has sufficed to destroy and raze the entirety of the Indies such that no human power has been enough to thwart or impede such widespread and irreparable damage.)

Far from a miraculous, invincible tree that healed the sick and restored life as depicted in *Carlo famoso*, Las Casas writes metaphorically of a pestilential weed with deep roots that blighted the Indies and its peoples. No human authority has been able to eradicate the weed, or to control its deadly propagation. In this description, Las Casas inverts the discourse of spiritual gardening as it appears in *Carlo famoso*. It is the colonization of the Indies, as initiated by Columbus, that has such deleterious effects on the New World, and the Indigenous peoples are the victims of what the Spanish sow. This passage is particularly important for Obed Lira, who sees it as marking the start of what he calls Las Casas's "narrative of descent," in which Columbus, fashioned as a tragic hero, begins his downward spiral into suffering and disgrace as ordained by God.[45] Lira writes:

> Columbus's tragic flaw, formulated by Las Casas as ignorance of the laws of peoples, makes him introduce a violent form of colonization, as opposed to what the friar interprets to be Columbus's divine mission, namely, spiritual colonization. Columbus sets the precedent of colonial violence, on both bodies and lands, making him the first one to plant the seed out of which grows a deadly and pestilential weed, and which will lay down roots to such depths that it will be impossible to weed out.[46]

In Zapata, it is Columbus's cross, symbol of the life-giving benefits of Christianity, that cannot be removed, but in Las Casas, it is his weed, metaphor for the virulence of his colonization, that cannot be eradicated. For Las Casas, argues Lira, Columbus's continuous hardships and eventual death were justified punishments by God for "initiating the worst practices of Conquest."[47] His fall from favour into divine wrath, however, was not only a personal peripeteia; Columbus also served as "a synecdochical figure for Spain as a whole," and therefore as a warning.[48] Yet, unlike Las Casas, Zapata assiduously avoids any characterization of Columbus that would make him appear guilty of any wrongdoing whatsoever. Contrary to Las Casas's disappointment and ultimate condemnation of Columbus, Zapata asserts only the best of what Las Casas writes of him, and thus presents him as a virtuous apostle of Christ. Zapata does effectively follow Las Casas's example, however, by singling out a character in the story to serve as a "synecdochical figure for Spain,"[49] by which means he can affirm that something in the Indies did indeed go awry, yet still deny that Columbus deserves any of the blame.

The Anonymous Pilot as Perillus

For all the praise it lavishes on Columbus, the poem harbours only reproach and condemnation for the anonymous pilot. This is unexpected since the unlucky sailor was treated as a friend by Columbus (XI.23.7–8), and he was the primary source of Columbus's knowledge about the Indies. The most negative characterization of the anonymous pilot is expressed in a stanza-long simile that compares him to Perillus, an ancient sculptor and inventor, who became synonymous with the bronze bull that he fashioned as a torture device for the Sicilian tyrant, Phalaris. As the first person to die in his own contraption, the story of Perillus became a warning of the dangers of a wicked imagination and talents put to evil uses. Many writers would invoke his name in this sense, as will be discussed below, and Zapata writes:

> Así Perillo el inventor primero
> de la nueva manera de tormento,
> fue él que en lo que él halló murió el primero,
> donde después murieron otros ciento:
> Y así murió antes que otro el marinero
> que halló en este su descubrimiento,
> nueva manera de morir la gente,
> sin saberse aun su nombre solamente. (XI.26.1–8)

(Thus Perillus, the first inventor of a new manner of torture, was the first to die in what he found, and in which later many hundreds died. And thus the sailor, who found in his discovery a new manner of killing people, was the first to die without even his name being known.)

In the stanza preceeding this one, the narrator emphasizes the pilot's anonymity, remarking that only his Spanish nationality was known; likewise, the final lines quoted above also stress his unknown identity. The premise of the simile is that both Perillus, who devised a torture device for Phalaris, and the anonymous mariner, who stumbled upon the transatlantic route to the Indies, found new ways of killing. They are both inventors in the broad Latin sense of the word, which covered the modern notions of both discovery (as in the case of the anonymous pilot) and invention (as with Perillus). Both men were thus the first to die as a result of their deadly inventions, but there is a significant difference in intentionality that would seem to make the comparison unjustified if not downright strange. The anonymous pilot never intended to kill anyone, but Perillus deliberately set out to inflict death and torture by means of his invention, the bronze bull. Nevertheless, Zapata reinforces the culpability implied in the simile by asserting that God ordained him to die (God willed him to die" ["Dios quiso que muriese"]) (XI.24.6). This contradicts the sympathetic treatment of the pilot by Gómara, Zapata's primary source on the legendary sailor. Gómara insists that the pilot did not deserve to die without enjoying the benefits of his discovery and without recognition for it:

He aquí cómo se descubrieron las Indias por desdicha de quien primero las vio, pues acabó la vida sin gozar de ellas y sin dejar, a lo menos sin haber memoria de cómo se llamaba, ni de dónde era, ni qué año las halló. Buen que no fue culpa suya, sino malicia de otros o envidia de la que llaman fortuna.[50]

(Behold how the Indies were discovered much to the misfortune of the one who first saw them, since he reached the end of his life without enjoying them and without leaving a trace, or at least without there being any memory of his name, where he was from, or in which year he found them. Though it was not his fault, but the malice of others, or the envy of what they call fortune.)

According to Gómara, if anyone was guilty of malice, it was the ones who made a concerted effort to suppress the identity of the pilot, and this group presumably included Columbus. Significantly, Gómara's text laments the pilot's anonymity, and portrays his undeserved death as a stroke of bad luck, not a righteous act of God's justice. Zapata's condemnation of the pilot, which contrasts so strikingly with Gómara's view, leaves readers to wonder what crime the sailor committed to warrant the comparison with Perillus and the wrath of God. In short, the poem imbues the discovery of the New World with an unmistakable, but undefined, sense of guilt, and the anonymous pilot is made to pay for future sufferings for which he seems to bear no direct responsibility.

One way to reconcile the pilot's implied guilt and his ostensible innocence is to read his function in the text as akin to that of a scapegoat. In such a case, the pilot's anonymity becomes a crucial aspect of his characterization because along with a scapegoat's innocence, Terry Eagleton considers anonymity to be the "whole point of the scapegoat."[51] As with a scapegoat, moreover, the poem presents the pilot's death as propitiating a god: "God willed that he die" (Dios quiso que muriese) (XI.24.6). Eagleton explains that the scapegoat

> is a substitute for the people, and thus stands in a metaphorical relation to them; but it also acts as a displacement for their sins, and is in this sense metonymic. In burdening it with their guilt, the people at once acknowledge their frailty and disavow it, project it violently outside themselves in the slaying of the sacrificial victim. [...] The victim is thus both themselves and not themselves, both a thing of darkness they acknowledge as their own as well as a convenient object on which to off-load and disown their criminality.[52]

The scapegoat is made to assume the collective guilt of a community for some common transgression, which can only be absolved with sacrificial death or ritual banishment.[53] In *Carlo famoso*, the burdening of the anonymous pilot with the blame for subsequent, unspecified deaths also continues an epic tradition of treating an ostensibly innocent pilot as a scapegoat, or sacrificial offering, to gods for some vague, ill-defined transgression. In the *Aeneid*, for example, Neptune demands the life of the Trojan pilot, Palinurus: "One only shall there be whom, lost in the flood, you will seek in vain; one life shall be given for many" (unus erit tantum, amissum quem gurgite quaeres; / unum pro multis dabitur caput) (5.814–15). Understanding the anonymous pilot as a scapegoat thus seems plausible, but if he was symbolically blamed for devising a new way to torture and kill people, who were his victims?

The poem suggests that some of the victims of the anonymous pilot were the Spanish sailors who subsequently followed the pilot's route and suffered hardships and death in doing so. Later in the poem, for example, the difficulties of sailors who came after Columbus are described:

> Después de él otros muchos descubrieron
> lo que hoy se sabe, y llega a nuestras puertas,
> hasta llegar con sed, hambre y afanes,
> al estrecho cruel de Magallanes. (XI.49.5–8)

> (After him, many others discovered what is today known, and they arrive at our doors until they reach the cruel Strait of Magellan, thirsty, hungry, and in trouble.)

Transatlantic seafaring did certainly have a reputation for being deadly, as seen in Oviedo's *Historia*, whose final book is devoted solely to shipwreck narratives and to the perils of the sea. And the widespread perception of seafaring as a socially dishonourable occupation of last resort for men desperate to escape from poverty only enhances their appearance as victims of an unjust economic system.[54] Besides the sailors themselves, however, those who especially suffered as a consequence of Spanish navigation quite evidently included the Indigenous peoples with whom the Spanish came into contact. The victimization of both seamen and Indigenous peoples is recalled, for example, in Luis de Góngora's famous repudiation of seafaring in the *Soledades* (I.366–502). As Mercedes Blanco observes, in this portion of Góngora's poem, "one is invited to ponder the colossal price of death and suffering that these enterprises demand, a price that the sailors […] and the remote people that receive the invading seafarers also pay without any guilt" (se invita a ponderar el precio colosal de muerte y sufrimiento que exigen estas empresas, un precio que pagan los navegantes […] y que pagan también, sin culpa, los pueblos remotos que reciben a los navegantes invasores).[55] Likewise, Zapata recalls the suffering of Spanish sailors in the process of empire building, but his poem also symbolically evokes the devastation that Spanish colonization inflicted on Indigenous people.

Attending to details from the story of Perillus and his invention allows readers to appreciate Zapata's denunciation of colonial abuses of Indigenous peoples. Zapata's simile does not provide any details about the invention of Perillus, but the intended readers would have been familiar with it from authors like Pliny, who writes:

> No one should praise Perillus, who was more cruel than the tyrant Phalaris, for whom he made a bull, guaranteeing that if a man were shut up inside it and a fire lit underneath, the man would do the bellowing; and he

was himself the first to experience this torture – a cruelty more just than the one he proposed.[56]

The hollow statue of the Sicilian bull – so called by Dante in the *Inferno* (XVII.6–12) because it was commissioned by Phalaris, the iniquitous ruler of Sicily – was designed to roast people alive over a fire, and to imitate the sound of a bovine's bellowing when the victims shrieked out in excruciating pain. The horrible invention was contrived both to torture its victims and entertain sadistic persecutors with its sounds. The heinousness of the device repulsed even the tyrant Phalaris so much that he felt compelled by justice to initiate the use of the contraption on its inventor. Pliny's description of Perillus helps readers to perceive an offence that may be deliberately evoked, and then symbolically cast upon the anonymous pilot as scapegoat. Crucially, it also recalls crimes of similar cruelty publicized in a text that garnered a wide readership and enduring legacy.

Fray Bartolomé de las Casas's best-known and most widely disseminated work, *Brevísima relación de la destruición de las Indias*, was published in 1552, fourteen years before *Carlo famoso*. Like Zapata's text, it was dedicated to Philip II, who was at the time crown prince. It is well known that Las Casas's text is a compendium of atrocities committed by the conquistadors against the Indians of Spanish America during the first fifty years of the Conquest. In the prologue, the author implores the prince to bring an end to the injustices perpetrated by his subjects in lands under his control. He writes to Philip:

> Considerando, pues, yo (muy poderoso señor), los males y daños [...] he visto cometer [...] no podría de contenerse de suplicar a su Majestad con instancia importuna que no conceda ni permita las que los tiranos inventaron, prosiguieron y han cometido que llaman conquistas [...] contra aquellas indianas gentes, pacíficas, humildes y mansas que a nadie ofenden.[57]

> (Considering, then, very powerful lord, the evils and harm [...] that I have seen committed [...], I could not restrain myself from beseeching your Majesty with importunate insistence not to allow or permit the so-called conquests that the tyrants invented, continued and have committed [...] against those peaceful, humble, and meek Indian peoples who have not offended anyone.)

His words portray the conquistadors as tyrants and inventors of cruel persecutions of innocent victims, and later, in one of the most frequently quoted portions of his text, he reinforces the notion of the newness of their methods. Of the Indigenous victims he writes that the Spanish "have not done anything else [to them] in forty years [...] and continue doing it today, but tear them apart, kill them, cause them distress, afflict them, torture them and destroy them with the strangest, most novel, varied and never-before-seen, nor read-of, nor heard-of manners of cruelty" ([y] otra cosa no han hecho de cuarenta años [...] y hoy en día lo hacen, sino despedazallas, matallas, angustiallas, afligillas, atormentallas y destruillas por las estrañas y nuevas y varias y nunca otras tales vistas ni leídas ni oídas maneras de crueldad).[58] Thus, like Perillus and his bronze bull, the conquistadors invented new, barbaric methods of torture, but some of the atrocities share even more specific similarities. Las Casas describes several tortures involving fire; one in particular occurred on the island of Hispaniola. He describes that the conquistadors commonly "put a gridiron of sticks on top of tree forks and tied them [the Indigenous peoples] down and put a small fire underneath so that little by little, emitting desperate shrieks amidst that torture, their souls would leave them" (hacían unas parillas de varas sobre horquetas y atábanlos en ellas y poníanles por debajo fuego manso, para que poco a poco, dando alaridos, en aquellos tormentos, desesperados, se les salían las ánimas).[59] From the use of fire placed beneath the victims, and the description of their painful cries and death, this horrifying practice evokes vividly the infamous bronze bull. Thus, if anyone resembles Perillus, it is the conquistadors described by Las Casas, who deliberately invent and inflict the cruellest of tortures on what he describes as docile Indians, and not Zapata's anonymous mariner. The cruel and inventive conquistadors as portrayed by Las Casas are the true heirs to Perillus. Yet, through the simile, the text symbolically charges the unknown pilot with a crime reminiscent of the horrors recounted in the *Brevísima*. As a Spaniard, he is positioned to assume all the guilt of his nation to expiate the sins of an indignant God; he dies justly, not because of his own malicious acts, but because of those future ones he is made to represent. In *Carlo famoso*, then, the anonymous pilot may thus be read as symbolically taking on the blame that Las Casas imputes to Columbus in his *Historia* and that he ascribes to the conquistadors in the *Brevísima*. It is a guilt that is shared by the entire nation of Spain, and he bears the divine punishment for the nation's collective crimes.

Conclusion

And yet, of course, no symbolic sacrifice of a character in a poem could possibly rectify the transgressions committed during the Conquest. Rather, this scapegoating of the anonymous pilot would serve only to subtly acknowledge the abuses perpetrated against the Indigenous peoples and to indicate the need for some form of justice. Why Zapata would be interested in doing this could relate to historical circumstances, and his own intellectual disposition. Márquez Villanueva has convincingly shown from his analysis of *Carlo famoso* and his other writings that Zapata was familiar with the ideas of Erasmus and that he had pacifist inclinations.[60] Work by Sánchez Jiménez reinforces this view and reveals that Zapata's sensitivity to wanton violence led him, in effect, to condemn the reckless behaviour of García de Paredes, the war hero from Extremadura.[61] Thus, when Las Casas published his *Brevísima relación* in the same year that Zapata began writing *Carlo famoso*, the scathing treatise would likely have made a strong impression on him. Zapata may have felt a moral duty to call attention to the problems in the Indies. Symbolically atoning for the sins with which he may have felt in some way complicit might have assuaged his conscience. However, if this is true, readers should also expect to see some sign of sympathy towards the Indigenous peoples in Zapata's account of Hernán Cortés's capture of Tenochtitlán, or at least a criticism of the excesses of the Conquest. Otherwise, arguing that he criticized the unjust treatment of the Indigenous peoples in the Columbus narrative would be admittedly unconvincing. A more comprehensive study of that part of the poem remains to be done, but there are indications that Zapata did, indeed, intend to call attention to problems of Cortés's invasion.[62] Even so, Zapata's subtle denunciation of Spanish violence in the Indies should not be conflated with cultural respect, or an assertion of essential equality, between Indigenous peoples and Europeans. He may symbolically oppose the worst abuses of power, but he also portrays the Indigenous peoples with whom Columbus interacts as simple, naive, and ultimately inferior to the Spanish.

Wanting to distance Columbus from any wrongdoing, and instead symbolically choosing to blame the anonymous pilot, may also be comprehensible given Zapata's background and personal experience in the court of Philip II. He was the son of a noble family from Extremadura, served as a page to the crown prince, Philip, and was inducted into the Order of Santiago when he was thirteen.[63] He accompanied the prince on his famous European tour (1548–51), during which Zapata won acclaim for his outstanding performance in the chivalric games staged in Binche.[64] And yet, in 1556, after twenty-one years of companionship, Philip II summarily dismissed Zapata from the court in one of his first acts as king. The fair treatment of faithful subjects by their sovereigns was thus a matter of personal interest for Zapata, and not surprisingly it was a persistent theme in his writings. In fact, Márquez Villanueva discusses several of many passages from *Carlo famoso* that rather emphatically attest to Zapata's preoccupation with the ingratitude of princes. In such a context, then, Zapata's insistence on the debt owed to Columbus for the economic and political benefits that resulted from his voyages (XI.27.1–8) takes on special significance. These lines may very well be read as a denouncement of the Council of the Indies and Charles V for changing the terms of the original contract and not granting to Columbus's descendants all that is rightfully theirs (XI.27.8). Columbus's experience may have represented for Zapata another instance of the ingratitude with which a loyal servant of the Crown was treated, and in this regard, he even may have felt a certain kinship with the Italian seafarer. His account of Columbus, which presents Columbus to be without fault, effectively enhances this perception of being unjustly treated.

Despite these criticisms and his invectives against war, however, Zapata does certainly praise Charles V throughout the poem, and his professed desire to regain the favour of Philip II has been taken to be sincere. If Zapata really did want to return to the good graces of Philip II while also drawing his attention to Spanish abuses of power, he would have had to strike a delicate balance. It would have been foolish for Zapata to expect to achieve both objectives by employing the openly condemnatory tone used by Las Casas, especially since he had already offended the king in some way. Therefore, acknowledging Spanish transgressions in the Indies symbolically through the sacrifice of the anonymous pilot may very well have provided a workable strategy. It appears general, without singling out any guilty party other than a lowly anonymous pilot, and certainly without directly implicating any Spanish monarch. To this extent, it had the potential to be a successfully restrained admonishment.

Nevertheless, due to his naiveté, or perhaps more likely to a lack of self-restraint, Zapata does not always write like someone interested in ingratiating himself with his sovereign and erstwhile companion.[65] Zapata opens his narrative of the Columbian voyages by apostrophizing his dedicatee:

> Creo que os será historia muy amada
> Ver su descubrimiento entre renglones
> Pues particularmente yo sospecho
> Que de ello sabidor no os habrán hecho. (XI.16.5–8)

> (I think it will be a beloved story for you to see the discovery put down in writing since I particularly suspect that you have not been made aware of it.)

His assertion that Philip is unaware of the story of the discovery of the Indies can only be taken as an ironic acknowledgment that the monarch does, of course, know very well about it. This may be an example of a conventional rhetorical strategy to justify his inclusion of the otherwise extraneous story about Columbus, but it is hard to take seriously an assertion purporting to inform Philip II about the first voyage to a continent previously unknown to Europeans. He is not, after all, informing the monarch of some unknown acts of service in a remote part of the empire. Moreover, the apostrophe continues with more irony and a decidedly irreverent tone. He implores Philip to listen to his story, and not to dismiss the Indies:

> Ni de las Indias sea poco estimado
> Su gran trecho y sus campos despoblados
> Que cierto, no será el peor bocado
> De vuestros grandes reinos y ditados. (XI.17.1–4)

> (Nor should the great expanse and the depopulated fields of the Indies be underestimated for it certainly will not be the smallest piece of your grand kingdoms and titles.)

However, his flippant assurances that the Indies are not the worst bite, or piece of Philip II's far-flung imperial pie, obscure the potentially serious dimension of his comments. His reference to the depopulated lands of the Indies recalls what Las Casas writes in the prologue of the *Brevísima*, addressed to the same monarch: "y el ansia temeraria e irracional de los que tienen por nada indebidamente derramar tan inmensa copia de humana sangre, y *despoblar sus naturales moradores y poseedores*, matando mil cuentos de gentes, aquellas tierras grandísimas, y robar incomparables tesoros, crece cada día"[66] (and the reckless and irrational eagerness of those who think nothing of arbitrarily spilling such an immense quantity of human blood and *depopulating the original inhabitants and owners* by killing a billion people, their extensive lands and robbing incomparable treasures, increases by the day). Zapata's claim that Philip does not know about the history of the Spanish in the Indies along with his urging of the king not to despise the New World despite its being depopulated ends up giving these stanzas an ominous tone reminiscent of Las Casas's presentation of the devastation of the Indies. Read in light of the *Brevísima*, these preliminary remarks could be seen as portraying the monarch as wilfully ignorant and unconcerned with the kind of mass destruction and indiscriminate slaughter of innocent victims, the king's own subjects. If Philip, whom

Noel Fallows characterizes as "a devoted bibliophile quite capable of reading between the lines,"[67] proceeded beyond these incisive opening lines, the symbolic depiction of the anonymous mariner may have only confirmed his initial perception of a criticism reminiscent of Las Casas.

This would have also been intensified by the portrayal of a faultless Columbus to whom Spain owed all the territory, wealth, and power that was ultimately tainted by a cruel disregard for justice and peace. The monarch would have understood the full message, and readers are left to speculate if Zapata was so disingenuous as to believe that Philip would have received it magnanimously without taking personal offence or responding defensively. If Zapata's professed desire for reconciliation is to be believed, then he must have thought that his king possessed a truly noble spirit. However, if Fallows is correct, and Zapata sought to take revenge on Philip after being dismissed from his court, then perhaps the poet was just as happy to anger his former friend.[68] This ambiguity and ambivalence of Zapata's stance with regard to the Spanish involvement and legacy in the Indies later came to typify subsequent epic poems, most notably Ercilla's *La Araucana*, which has provoked a number of contradictory interpretations. As for the king, we may never know how he reacted to this very short account of the perfect, providential Columbus and the hapless, doomed pilot, but there is no doubt about what happened the year that *Carlo famoso* was published. Zapata was expelled quite ceremoniously from the Order of Santiago and imprisoned for nearly the remainder of his life, and the poet lamented that his epic was not received with the gratitude befitting his intentions.

NOTES

1 Posse, *The Dogs of Paradise*, 29.
2 My references are to the facsimile edition of *Carlo famoso* edited by Manuel Terrón Albarrán and published in 1981, and they appear in the text. This edition contains an extensive introduction and appendices.
3 Three years after the 1981 facsimile edition of the full text, Winston A. Reynolds expanded and republished the parts of *Carlo famoso* pertaining to the New World, which José Torribio Medina had originally excerpted and edited in 1916.
4 In chapter VII of the first part of *Don Quixote*, the priest and barber burn a book on the exploits of Charles V attributed to a certain Luis de Ávila. However, it is generally agreed that this text actually refers to Zapata's epic, *Carlo famoso*. See Sánchez Jiménez, "Cervantes y el césar Carlos de Habsburgo," for more details.

5 Cacho Casal, "Luis Zapata y el poema heroico," examines the influence of Virgil and Ariosto on Zapata's encomiastic program, and Nicolopulos, "Cortés's Shark Meets Orlando's Orca," focuses on Zapata's imitation of Ariosto in his portrayal of Cortés. For his part, Martínez argues that, despite sharing some characteristics of historical epics, such as *La Araucana*, *Carlo famoso* is much more representative of chivalric texts and courtly games than of sixteenth-century conflicts waged by professional soldiers with firearms. (Género, imprenta y espacio social," 169–74.)

6 In *Don Luis Zapata o el sentido de una fuente cervantina*, Márquez Villanueva highlights the influence of Erasmus on Zapata's anti-imperial and pacifist comments, his criticisms of Charles V and Philip II, and especially his denunciation of their ingratitude. Building on this analysis, Sánchez Jiménez argues that Zapata portrays the renowned soldier from Extremadura, García Paredes, as recklessly violent, and that this negatively influences readers' perceptions of his general, Charles V. Sánchez Jiménez also contends that Cervantes recognizes this effect and that the allusion to *Carlo famoso* in *Don Quixote* serves to reinforce the criticisms already present in Zapata's epic. (Cervantes y el césar Carlos de Habsburgo.)

7 Following Márquez Villanueva's interpretation, Fallows also identifies indiscreet criticisms in Zapata's poem as the cause of his incarceration, not his supposed unbecoming conduct and egregious debts as professed by Philip II. *Jousting in Medieval and Renaissance Iberia*, 57–68.

8 Las Casas, *Historia de las Indias*, 74. Unless otherwise indicated, all translations of sixteenth-century texts originally in Spanish are my own. This problem of Columbus's claims to have reached Asia, and the contrary explanation promoted by the legend of the anonymous pilot, is the starting point for O'Gorman's classic study. See O'Gorman, *The Invention of America*, 11.

9 Lupher, *Romans in a New World*, 214.

10 Hester, "Failed New World Epics in Baroque Italy," 204–5.

11 Roa-de-la-Carrera, *Histories of Infamy*, 142.

12 See O'Gorman, *The Invention of America*, 19–22.

13 See footnote 16 of Toribio Medina's re-edition of this portion of Zapata de Chaves,*Carlo famoso*, 26. See also Terrón Albarrán's introduction. Zapata de Chaves, *Carlo famoso*, xxv–xxix.

14 López de Gómara, *Historia general de las Indias*, 43.

15 Spelling has been modernized, and citations refer to book (Roman numerals), stanza, and lines (Arabic numerals) and appear in the text.

16 López de Gómara, *Historia general de las Indias*, 43–4.

17 Oviedo asserts that at least some people thought that Columbus was "docto" [learned] and "leído" [well-read] in cosmography, an opinion that Zapata appears to share. *Historia general y natural de las Indias*, 15.

18 He claims to have read written accounts of Columbus: "Columbus (who had been married there before) resided on the island of Madeira, Columbus of the Ligurians (*according to what I read*), a native of Nervi or Sigurella" (Colón [que se había allí antes casado] / De la Madera en la isla, residía, / Colón de los Ligures [*según leo*] / De Nervi natural, o Cigureo") (XI.19.5–8; italics mine).

19 See Barrera-Osorio, *Experiencing Nature*, ch. 2, and especially 49–55.

20 This is also similar to Las Casas's conception of Columbus in his *Historia*. Roa-de-la-Carrera, 143.

21 Upon his death in 1566, Las Casas's *Historia* was deposited in the monastery of San Gregorio in Valladolid, where it was supposed to remain unpublished until at least the end of the sixteenth century. Contrary to Las Casas's desire, officials removed the manuscript only five years after his death, and Antonio de Herrera used it to write his *Historia general*. Las Casas, *Historia*, xlv–xlvi. However, even before his death Las Casas had made more than one copy of the manuscript, on which he was incessantly labouring, and he was in frequent contact with the courts of Charles V and Philip II, where Zapata also found himself from 1535 until 1556. It is, therefore, possible that Zapata read a draft of Las Casas's work, or conversed with him in person about the Indies. After all, Zapata's grandfather, who was not entirely convinced by Las Casas's arguments, had met the friar on more than one occasion, and is said to have admired his eloquence and conviction. Thomas, *Rivers of Gold*, 398. At the very least, Las Casas's *Historia* provides a useful comparison to gauge the implications of Zapata's account of Columbus. Moreover, there can be no doubt that Zapata knew of Las Casas's *Brevísima relación de la destruición de las Indias*, and the possible influence of this text is important to my reading of *Carlo famoso*.

22 Las Casas, *Historia de las Indias*, 71.

23 Cañizares-Esguerra, *Puritan Conquistadors*, 51.

24 Cañizares-Esguerra, *Puritan Conquistadors*, 53.

25 Roa-de-la-Carrera, *Histories of Infamy*, 145–6.

26 Fernández de Oviedo, *Historia general y natural de las Indias*, 15.

27 Lupher, *Romans in a New World*, 214.

28 It should be mentioned that Zapata appears to have confused where Hero and her light were posted. She lived on the European shore of the Hellespont in Sestos, while Leander lived in Abydos. Ovid gives an account of Hero's love affair with Leander in epistles 18 and 19 of the *Heroides*. Musaeus, a fifth-century Hellenistic poet, wrote an epyllion about Hero and Leander, which was adapted by Bernardo Tasso and Juan Boscán in the sixteenth century.

29 For more on the parallels between Leander and Columbus, which appear to have been recognized by Juan Boscán in his poem *Leandro*, see McCloskey, "'Navegaba Leandro el Helesponto.'"

30 Cacho Casal, "Luis Zapata y el poema heroico," 74. I would like to thank Emiro Martínez-Osorio, who brought these similarities to my attention.

31 Las Casas, *Historia de las Indias*, 203.

32 Fernández de Oviedo, *Historia general y natural de las Indias*, 26.

33 See Fernández de Oviedo, *Historia general y natural de las Indias*, 26.

34 See Las Casas, *Historia de las Indias*, 304–7. Furthermore, contrary to the claims made in testimonies given to the crown attorney, *Carlo famoso* asserts unequivocally that Columbus was responsible for the discovery of not only the islands of the Caribbean, such as Hispaniola and Cuba, but also the continental mainland: "the islands of Hispaniola and Cuba and the Spanish Main were discovered by him] "(por él las islas fueron / Española y de Cuba descubiertas, / Y las tierras que el pie firme tuvieron) (XI.49.1–3).

35 I would like to thank Mercedes Blanco for bringing Ovid's account of this legend to my attention.

36 See Las Casas, *Historia de las Indias*, 264–6.

37 López de Gómara, *Historia general de las Indias*, 47.

38 Castellanos, *Elegías de varones ilustres de Indias*, 101.

39 Martínez-Osorio, *Authority, Piracy, and Captivity in Colonial Spanish American Writing*, 42–59.

40 Fernández de Oviedo, *Historia general y natural de las Indias*, 65.

41 See also Cañizares-Esguerra, who discusses portrayals of the cross at Concepción de la Vega in Lope de Vega's *comedia, El nuevo mundo descubierto por Cristóbal Colón* and in Antonio de Herrera's *Historia general. Puritan Conquistadors*, 113–15.

42 For example, to the question about his being the Messiah, Christ responds that prophecies of Isaiah are being fulfilled: "The blind will see again and the lame walk, The lepers are made clean and the deaf hear, The dead are raised and the poor hear the good news" (*The Revised New Testament*, Matthew 11:5).

43 For the importance of the cross in the struggle against Satan in the New World, see Cañizares-Esguerra, *Puritan Conquistadors*, ch. 3, and especially 110–14. For more on the discourse of spiritual gardening and the symbolic fruition of Christianity in fertile soil, see *Puritan Conquistadors*, ch. 5, especially 194–5.

44 Las Casas, *Historia de las Indias*, 212.

45 I would like thank Obed Lira for kindly sharing his work and information about Las Casas's texts with me.

46 Lira, "Bartolomé de Las Casas and the Passions of Language," 159.

47 Lira, "Bartolomé de Las Casas and the Passions of Language," 177.

48 Lira, "Bartolomé de Las Casas and the Passions of Language," 181–2. As Lira puts it, "[t]he Columbian narrative, however, is also the story of

Spain's original sin. Columbus is blamed for initiating the worst practices
of Conquest: the military strategy of fear-inducing preemptive strikes, the
abhorrent use of extraordinary violence and cruelty (exemplified by the
use of war dogs), and the unjust imposition of tributes, which would pave
the way for the systematic slavery and exploitation of the Amerindians."
"Bartolomé de Las Casas and the Passions of Language," 177.

49 Lira, "Bartolomé de Las Casas and the Passions of Language," 182.

50 López de Gómara, *Historia general de las Indias*, 42.

51 Eagleton, *Sweet Violence*, 278.

52 Eagleton, *Sweet Violence*, 279.

53 Eagleton, *Sweet Violence*, 278–9.

54 As Pérez-Mallaína writes, "The sixteenth-century writers who concerned
themselves with life at sea generally agreed about one thing: sailing was
a 'desperate and fearsome business,' which is to say that going to sea can
only be understood as a product of desperation," *Spain's Men of the Seas*, 23.
He goes on to assert that "[a] man might go to sea because he was driven
out by the poverty of his homeland. That is perhaps the most obvious reason and possibly the easiest to understand." *Spain's Men of the Seas*, 24.

55 Blanco, *Góngora heroico*, 327.

56 Pliny, *Natural History*, 193.

57 Las Casas, *Brevísima relación de la destruición de las Indias*, 72.

58 Las Casas, *Brevísima relación de la destruición de las Indias*, 77.

59 Las Casas, *Brevísima relación de la destruición de las Indias*, 81.

60 Márquez Villanueva notes, for example, the following stanza: "Que plaga
grande es ésta de la gente, / No dada a otro animal de otra relea, / Un león
no anda con otro diferente, / El oso con el oso no pelea: / No muerde una
culebra a otra serpiente, / Ni una víbora a otra adentellea, / Al solo hombre,
el hombre como extraños, / Le vemos proceder mortales daños" ("What a
great plague this on people, not present in any other sort of animal, a lion
does not consort with others, a bear does not fight with bears, a snake does
not bite another serpent, nor does a viper sink its teeth into another; from
man alone do we see mortal harm come to other men) (XX.1.1–8).

61 Sánchez Jiménez writes that "(a)s the good courtier that he was, Zapata is
inclined to a combination of arms and letters and despises feats of arms if
they are not accompanied by intelligence and reflection. Zapata chooses
García de Paredes as a model of thoughtless strength" ([c]omo buen cortesano que era, Zapata se inclina por una combinación entre armas y letras
y desprecia las hazañas de armas si no van acompañadas de inteligencia y
reflexión. Zapata elige a García de Paredes como modelo de fortaleza irre-
flexiva). ("Cervantes y el césar Carlos de Habsburgo," 644.)

62 For example, Zapata's nostalgia for traditional modes of combat, his
critiques of excessive violence, and the conventionally bad reputation of

firearms in the sixteenth century should influence readings of Zapata's portrayal of the devastation caused by Spanish firearms in Cortés's invasion (XIII.13.1–14.8). His depiction of Cortés's battle against a sea monster and giant eagle based on Ariosto's *Orlando furioso*, moreover, seems to border on satire. However, there are problems even if readers assume, like Nicolopulos, that Zapata treats Cortés as a hero: "We are even led to ask why Zapata makes such a great hero out of Cortés at all." (Cortés's Shark Meets Orlando's Orca," 6.)

63 For information on Zapata's biography, see the studies by Cacho Casal ("Luis Zapata y el poema heroico"), Fallows (*Jousting in Medieval and Renaissance Iberia*), Márquez Villanueva (*Don Luis Zapata o el sentido de una fuente cervantina*), Martínez ("Género, imprenta y espacio social," 170–1) and the facsimile edition of *Carlo famoso* overseen by Terrón Albarrán.

64 See Martínez, "Género, imprenta y espacio social," 170–1.

65 For example, Márquez Villanueva accepts Zapata's asserted commitment to serve Philip II in the writing of his poem, and marvels at how the poet undermines his own stated interest: "(w)hat does surprise us is the enormous naiveté of his [i.e., Zapata] hoping to restore his favour after those allusions, which as much as they are counterbalanced by rhetorical praises, must have been the last straw for the king's displeasure" ([l]o que sí nos sorprende es la enorme ingenuidad de éste [i.e., Zapata], esperando recuperar la gracia después de aquellas alusiones que, por más que se contrapesasen con elogios retóricos, debieron colmar el vaso del desagrado regio). *Don Luis Zapata o el sentido de una fuente cervantina*, 43.

66 Las Casas, *Brevísima relación de la destruición de las Indias*, 73. My italics.

67 Fallows, *Jousting in Medieval and Renaissance Iberia*, 66.

68 Of Zapata's dismissal from Philip II's court, Fallows writes that "[i]t would not be forgotten by Zapata, who would in subsequent years petulantly – perhaps also foolishly – seek vengeance through the medium of print." *Jousting in Medieval and Renaissance Iberia*, 63.

WORKS CITED

Alighieri, Dante. *Inferno*. Edited and translated by Michael Palma. New York: W.W. Norton, 2002.

Barrera-Osorio, Antonio. *Experiencing Nature: Empire and the Early Scientific Revolution*. Austin: University of Texas Press, 2006.

Blanco, Mercedes. *Góngora heroico: Las "Soledades" y la tradición épica*. Madrid: Centro de Estudios Europa Hispánica, 2012.

Boscán, Juan. *Obra completa*. Edited by Pedro Ruiz Pérez. Madrid: Akal, 1999.

Cacho Casal, Rodrigo. "Luis Zapata y el poema heroico: historia, entretenimiento y parodia." *Criticón* 115 (2012): 67–83.

Cañizares-Esguerra, Jorge. *Puritan Conquistadors: Iberianizing the Atlantic 1550–1700*. Stanford, CA: Stanford University Press, 2006.

Castellanos, Juan de. *Elegías de varones ilustres de Indias*. Vol. 1. Introduction by Miguel Antonio Caro. Bogotá: ABC, 1955.

Cervantes, Miguel de. *El ingenioso hidalgo Don Quijote de la Mancha*. Edited by Luis Andrés Murillo. Vol. 1. Madrid: Castalia, 1978.

Eagleton, Terry. *Sweet Violence: The Idea of the Tragic*. Malden, MA: Blackwell, 2003.

Ercilla, Alonso de. *La Araucana*. Edited by Isaías Lerner. 4th ed. Madrid: Cátedra, 2005.

Fallows, Noel. *Jousting in Medieval and Renaissance Iberia*. Rochester, NY: Boydell, 2010.

Fernández de Oviedo, Gonzalo. *Historia general y natural de las Indias*. Edited by Juan Pérez de Tudela Bueso. Biblioteca de autores españoles 117. Madrid: Atlas, 1959.

Góngora, Luis de. *Soledades*. Edited by Robert Jammes. Madrid: Castalia, 1994.

Hester, Nathalie. "Failed New World Epics in Baroque Italy." In *Poesis and Modernity in the Old and New Worlds*, edited by Anthony J. Cascardi and Leah Middlebrook, 201–23. Nashville: Vanderbilt University Press, 2012.

Las Casas, Bartolomé de. *Brevísima relación de la destruición de las Indias*,.ed. André Saint-Lu. Madrid: Cátedra, 2013.

– *Historia de las Indias*. Edited by André Saint-Lu. Caracas: Ayacucho, 1986.

Lira, Obed Omar. "Bartolomé de Las Casas and the Passions of Language." PhD diss., Harvard University, 2017.

López de Gómara, Francisco. *Historia general de las Indias*. 1552. Barcelona: Linkgua, 2008.

Lupher, David A. *Romans in a New World: Classical Models in Sixteenth-Century Spanish America*. Ann Arbor: University of Michigan Press, 2003.

Márquez Villanueva, Francisco. *Don Luis Zapata o el sentido de una fuente cervantina*. Badajoz: Diputación Provincial, 1966.

Martínez, Miguel. "Género, imprenta y espacio social: una 'poética de la pólvora' para la épica quinientista." *Hispanic Review* 79, no. 2 (2011): 163–87.

Martínez-Osorio, Emiro. *Authority, Piracy, and Captivity in Colonial Spanish American Writing: Juan de Castellanos's "Elegies of Illustrious Men of the Indies."* Lewisburg, PA: Bucknell University Press, 2016.

McCloskey, Jason. "'Navegaba Leandro el Helesponto': Love and Early Modern Navigation in Juan Boscán's *Leandro*." *Revista de Estudios Hispánicos* 47, no. 1 (2013): 3–27.

Musaeus. *Hero and Leander*. Edited by Thomas Gelzer. Translated by Cedrick Whitman. Cambridge, MA: Harvard University Press, 1975.

Nicolopulos, James. "Cortés's Shark Meets Orlando's Orca: The Transformation of History and Poetic Imitation in the First Golden Age Epic Treatment of the New World." *Lucero* 1 (1990): 1–9.

O'Gorman, Edmundo. *The Invention of America: An Inquiry into the Historical Nature of the New World and Meaning of Its History.* Bloomington: Indiana University Press, 1961.

Ovid. *Heroides and Amores.* Edited by G.P. Goold. Translated by Grant Showerman. Cambridge, MA: Harvard University Press, 1977.

– *Metamorphoses XIII–XV.* Edited and translated by D.E. Hill. Liverpool: Liverpool University Press, 2000.

Pérez-Mallaína, Pablo E. *Spain's Men of the Seas: Daily Life on the Indies Fleets in the Sixteenth Century.* Translated by Carla Rahn Phillips. Baltimore: Johns Hopkins University Press, 1998.

Pliny. *Natural History.* Translated by H. Rackham. Vol. 9. Cambridge, MA: Harvard UP, 1952.

Posse, Abel. *The Dogs of Paradise.* Translated by Margaret Sayers Peden. New York: Atheneum, 1989.

The Restored New Testament: A New Translation with Commentary, Including the Gnostic Gospels Thomas, Mary and Judas. Edited and translatred by Willis Barnstone. New York: W.W. Norton, 2009.

Roa-de-la-Carrera, Cristián A. *Histories of Infamy: Francisco López de Gómara and the Ethics of Spanish Imperialism.* Translated by Scott Sessions. Boulder: UP of Colorado, 2005.

Sánchez Jiménez, Antonio. "Cervantes y el césar Carlos de Habsburgo: *Don Quijote* I, 32 y el *Carlo famoso* (1566), de Luis Zapata de Chaves." In *En buena compañía: estudios en honor de Luciano García Lorenzo,* edited by J. Álvarez Barrientos et al., 639–48. Madrid: Consejo Superior de Investigaciones Científicas, 2009.

Tasso, Bernardo. *Rime.* Edited by Domenico Chiodo. Vol. 1. Turin: Res, 1995.

Thomas, Hugh. *Rivers of Gold: The Rise of the Spanish Empire from Columbus to Magellan.* New York: Random House, 2003.

Toribio Medina, José, and Winston A. Reynolds, eds. *El primer poema que trata del Descubrimiento y Conquista del Nuevo Mundo.* Madrid: José Porrúa Turanzas, 1984.

Vega, Garcilaso de la. *Poesía completa.* Edited by Juan Francisco Alcina. 7th ed. Madrid: Austral, 2000.

Virgil. *Eclogues, Georgics, Aeneid I–VI.* Edited by G.P. Goold. Translated by H. Rushton Fairclough. Cambridge, MA: Harvard University Press, 2001.

Zapata de Chaves, Luis. *Carlo famoso.* Edited by Manuel Terrón Albarrán. Facsimile ed. Badajoz: Institución Pedro de Valencia, 1981.

9 Cartography in Bernardo de Balbuena's *El Bernardo o victoria de Roncesvalles*[1]

MARTÍN ZULAICA LÓPEZ

In the past twenty-five years, scholars have grown increasingly interested in the influence that the burgeoning cartographic sciences had on literary texts of the early modern period.[2] This criticism has particularly focused on the epic genre: since classical antiquity it has been the pre-eminent repository for cosmographical and geographical knowledge. (Let us recall that Strabo described Homer as "the founder of the science of geography.")[3] The epic poets of the time, guided on the one hand by their imitation of classical authors and on the other by the development of modern cartography, included in their poems descriptions *more Homerico* based on contemporary wisdom, giving readers the satisfaction of admiring the imitation of the classics while also delighting in the discovery of the new.[4] This chapter contributes to current academic debates, with consideration given to the essential role this knowledge played in a notable example of the Iberian epic: *El Bernardo o victoria de Roncesvalles* (1624) by Bernardo de Balbuena (1563–1627).[5] The three sections of this analysis examine the following: first, how the reading and writing of epic works were affected by the emergence of a new cartographic mentality (cartodoxy) and, in particular, the generic innovation represented by the geographical charting of fantasy in the chivalric romance; second, the importance of *kataskopia* or "view from above" as a rhetorical device for introducing geographical and cartographic content, such as associating specific regions of the globe with certain shapes; and, third, a detailed study of a brief passage from Balbuena's work (*El Bernardo*, I.42–54) that drew on maps from Abraham Ortelius's *Theatrum Orbis Terratum* (1570) (see figs. 9.1 and 9.2). This approach will facilitate an understanding of the striking difference between Balbuena's ambitious poetic agenda and those of the predecessors he emulated.

Bernardo de Balbuena was born an illegitimate child in Valdepeñas, Spain. In 1584 he joined his father in New Spain, where he completed his university studies and was ordained as a priest. His most important work was composed entirely in the New World and, in accordance with the *rota Vergilii*, consists of a trio: *Grandeza mexicana* (1604), an epistle written in tercets of didascalic content, comparable to the *Georgics*, that describes and celebrates Mexico City; the pastoral novel *Siglo de oro en las selvas de Erífile* (1608); and *El Bernardo* (1624), an epic poem about Bernardo del Carpio.[6] Balbuena was among those writers who were committed to pure or noble literary production and whose texts were intended for *learned* or *select* audiences within the literary sphere of the Spanish Golden Age.[7] His works, which garnered him considerable symbolic capital at the time, were rewarded by his primary dedicatee, the Great Count of Lemos Pedro Fernández de Castro, earning him noble favours (*mercedes*) that were initially beyond his reach given his illegitimate birth: namely, his appointment as Abbot of Jamaica in 1608 and later, in 1619, as Bishop of Puerto Rico. In recognition of his profound relationship with the continent, Balbuena has been called the "true patriarch of [Spanish] American poetry."[8]

El Bernardo, an expansive poem completed between 1595 and 1600 and whose future publication was touted by the author in his two previous works, recounts Roland's disastrous end at the hands of Bernardo del Carpio at Roncevaux. This legendary hero was the illegitimate son of Count Sancho Saldaña and Doña Jimena, the sister of Alfonso II. Bernardo del Carpio first appeared in the ballads (*romances*) and chronicles of the Spanish Middle Ages.[9] Separated from his parents at birth because the king did not approve of the relationship of which he was a result, he attempted to win the favour of meeting them through daring service to the Crown, most notably his command of the Leonese troops at Roncevaux and his extraordinary victory over Roland, the primary conflict in *El Bernardo*. Balbuena may not have been the first chronologically to compose a continuation of the Italian *romanzi* with his adaptation of this medieval legend – prior to him, during what some refer to as the "Bernardo period" (*momento bernárdico*), Nicolás Espinosa, Francisco Garrido de Villena, Francisco Núñez de Oria (in New Latin), Agustín Alonso, and Luis Barahona de Soto (in the intended second part of his *Angélica*) had done the same.[10] However, *El Bernardo* can, without doubt, be considered the foremost of these continuations due to its literary merits.

The action of the poem revolves around the famous Battle of Roncevaux (778) in which Roland was defeated as leader of the twelve peers of France.[11] While the French tradition, as recounted in the *Chanson de Roland*, places their defeat at Roncevaux mainly in the hands of the Saracens, a legend emerged in the medieval Hispanic kingdoms that they

Figure 9.1. Abraham Ortelius, "Europa" from *Theatrum Orbis Terrarum* (1570). Courtesy of the Library of Congress, G1006.T5 1570.

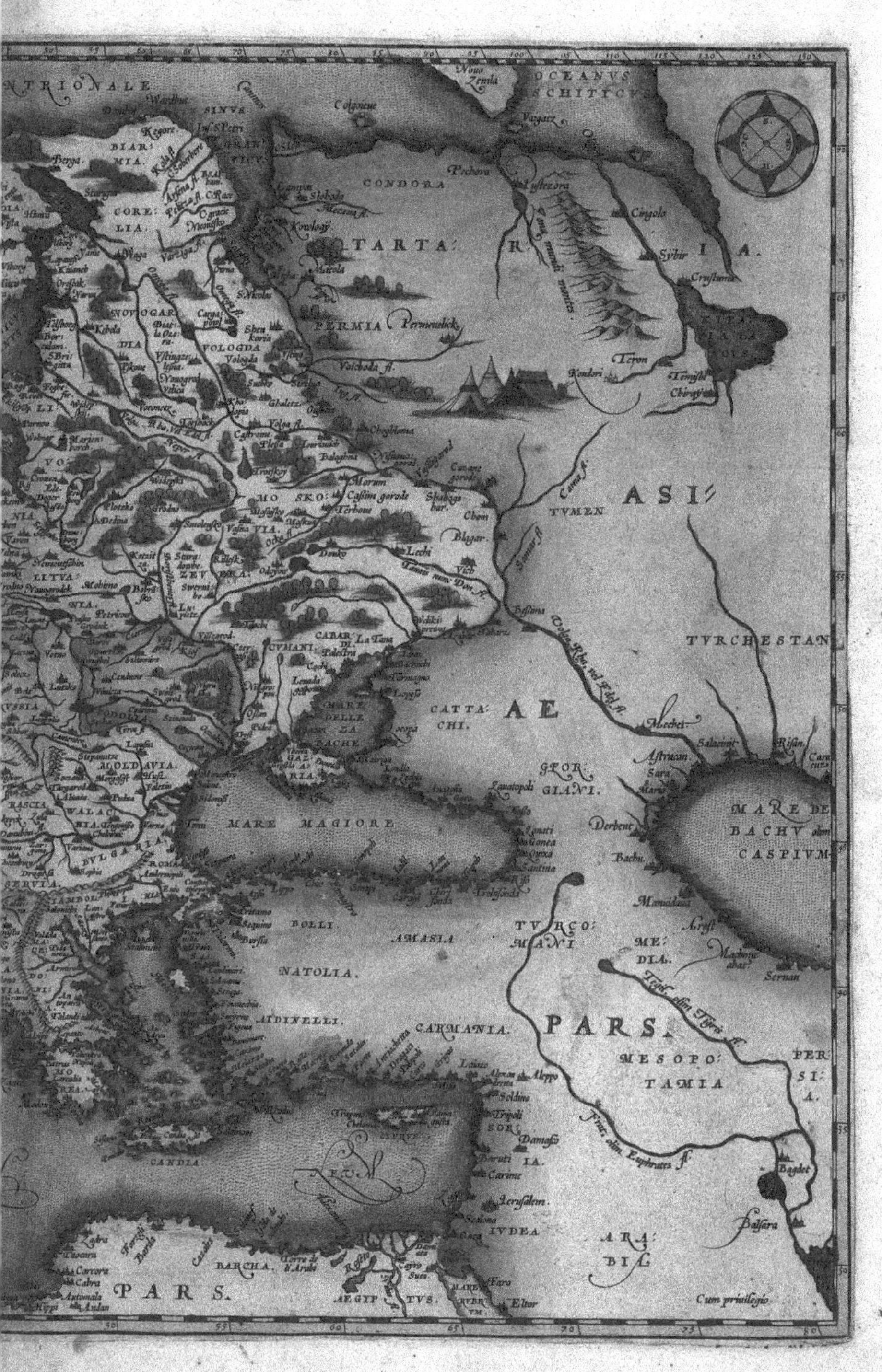

Figure 9.1. (*Continued*)

Figure 9.2. Abraham Ortelius, "Septentrionalium regionum descriptio" from *Theatrum Orbis Terrarum* (1570). Courtesy of the Library of Congress, G1006.T5 1570.

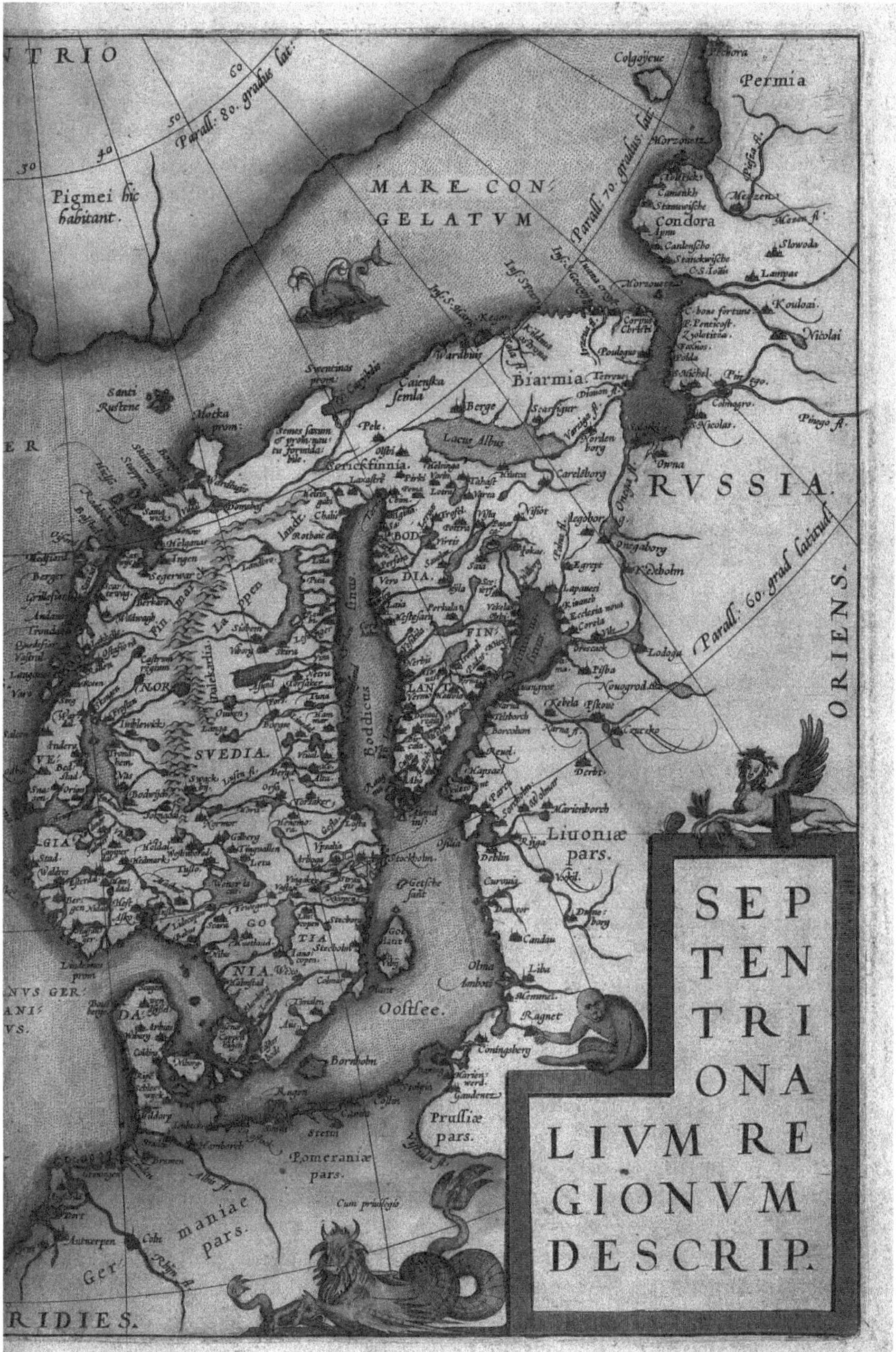

Figure 9.2. (*Continued*)

had in fact been defeated by Bernardo del Carpio, a commander from the Kingdom of Asturias, preventing what would have been an unjust invasion by the Carolingian Empire.[12] Balbuena conceived *El Bernardo* as "the fulfillment [of], last line [in], and key [to]" (el cumplimiento, la última línea y la clave) the *Matière de France*, in its final Renaissance phase. In other words, since Roland and most of the peers of France had died at Roncevaux, it represented the final episode in their heroic feats, about which Boiardo and Ariosto had written in their *romanzi*. Ariosto had also attempted to lead his narrative to this battle in the *Cinque canti*, which, as we know, he was never able to conclude or conveniently interweave with the rest of his poem.

In these *romanzi*, the group of sorceresses, which included the notable sisters Alcina and Morgana, appeared as the antagonists of the twelve peers of Charlemagne in response to various offences they had suffered.[13] Taking this as his point of departure, in his poem Balbuena presents the sorceresses as defenders of Bernardo del Carpio, whom they will help throughout his knightly training. Imperceptibly to the hero, they provide him with the best instruction (II.71–8; III.181), the best weapons (II,95–8; IX,156–8; XIX,118 and 131), knight him (IV.123–31), and lead him into battle where he kills Roland. In a sense, Balbuena blends the chivalric tradition of the Italian poems with that of Spanish chivalric books, such as *Amadís*, in which the enchantress Urganda the Unknown is the constant protector of the hero. In this chapter, the main passage that I will analyse, which presents Alcina's aerial journey to Morgana's palace to conspire against the French heroes, is inscribed within this context.

Cartodoxy and Charting Fantasy

Nowadays images of the Earth via satellite are commonplace, and representations of its distinct regions have been firmly integrated into our minds. Our perception of the world includes these global-scale reproductions. Since the sixteenth century and the development of new representational models, from which the Mercator projection would eventually emerge as the standard, these images became a part of European visual culture as new tools for understanding the world. This standardized way of conceiving geographic regions in the imagination through reference to maps, termed in English-speaking circles as *map-mindedness*, but which I will refer to as *cartodoxy*, is an essential element in the comprehension of any geographical discourse from the early modern period onward.[14] These changes in the apprehension of space, whose material basis are found in the development of maps, came to be reflected in literature as well.[15] It was then that the phenomenon of cartodoxy, a particular form of spatial intellection produced by recurrent exposure to maps, also appeared. (The term *cartography* would not emerge until the first part of the nineteenth century.)[16]

In terms of geographical subject matter, *El Bernardo*'s model is also Ariosto's *Orlando furioso*, a work that introduces fantasy into a cartographical space. Ariosto's new geography has been meticulously studied by Alexandre Doroszlai in relation to extant maps located in the library of the noble House of Este.[17] In *Orlando furioso*, the characteristic geography of chivalric romances, filled with wondrous locations, is interwoven with actual cartography. Thus, for example, it tells us that during their return journey from Alcina's fictional island, the heroes "had from Ind[ia] to England rounded all / The right-hand side of the terrestrial ball"[18] (girato da l'India all'Inghilterra / tutto avea il latto destro della terra) (*Orlando furioso*, XXII.24.7–8). These verses have led some traditional criticism about *Orlando furioso* to associate the sorceress's island with Marco Polo's Cipango (modern-day Japan).[19] Every place in Ariosto's poem corresponds to a concrete location in the spherical earth, whether the reader is aware of it or not, including those extraordinary places associated with the fantastic world. That is, through distance and a medieval conception of geography, space was made in regions like Catay or Mangi in China to hold the wonders that Marco Polo described. Such was also the case with those northern territories of which Europe learned thanks to Olaus Magnus, or with the remote Trabzon and Hyrcania from chivalric romances like *Claris de Trapisonda*, or *Felixmarte de Hircania* (1556) written by Melchor Ortega and parodied by Miguel de Cervantes. However, once they had been given such descriptions, these lands would not easily relinquish the wonders with which they had been associated, regardless of how much modern cartography enabled sixteenth-century Europeans to attribute them with real, concrete locations and an outline in their imagination. Not without some contradiction (undoubtedly more for us than for those of the time), fantasy had become part of the map.

A case similar to Ariosto is that of Edmund Spenser, who in a well-known passage from *The Faerie Queene* omits information about the location of Faerieland. In the prologue to Book 2, Spencer slyly declares that just as other regions were not known to the Ancients but have gradually been discovered over time, citing the examples of Peru, the Amazon, and Virginia, so would the same occur with Faerieland, a territory not yet located on the map.[20] Based on the following stanza, Ramachandran has argued that "Spenser's epic takes shape in the fecund space of unknown possibility opened up by the European voyages of exploration."[21]

> But let that man with better sence advize,
> That of the world least part to vs is red:
> And daily how through hardy enterprize,
> Many great Regions are discovered,
> Which to late age were never mentioned.
> Who ever Heard of th'Indian Peru?
> Or who in venturous vessell measured
> The Amazonas huge river now found trew?
> Or fruitfullest Virginia who did ever vew? (*The Faerie Queene*, II.2)

While writing *El Bernardo*, Balbuena faced a dilemma similar to that of Ariosto or Spenser. Throughout his twenty-four cantos and forty thousand verses, he prolifically deploys his cosmographical and cartographical knowledge within a narrative framework that incorporates fantasy into the cartography of the known world, while at the same time describing many places of wonder. An emblematic example occurs at the beginning of the poem when Alcina visits Morgana. The territories travelled by the sorceress in stanzas 49 to 54 are portrayed in dynamic descriptions founded on cartographical realities. There, in a distant place, but with a definite location inside the world's geometry, Morgana's imposing palace is found, whose wonders Balbuena recounts in great detail (*El Bernardo*, I.53–64, 208–33; II.8–9).[22] Then again, in *El Bernardo* this is the norm rather than the exception. Other examples where wondrous places have been located on the map include the sumptuous tent of the sorceress Arleta, located on the banks of the Tagus in a forest near the town of Fuentidueña (VII.104–5, 113–15); the hermitage of San Vicente, erected by divine work in the Promontorium Sacrum – today Cape of San Vicente – (XII.105–6, 115–37); or the cave of the Indigenous enchanter Tlascalán, located inside the Tlalocatepetl volcano (XVIII.124–34, 147–59).

Kataskopia and Its Symbolic Dimension: The Dragon and the Queen

The disruption of the traditional chronotope of the fantastic tale to result from its hybridization with modern cartodoxy is especially palpable in the passages that include geographical descriptions. These are constructed through the abstraction of a privileged point of view that was characteristic of the classical tradition. In Book XIV of Balbuena's

El Bernardo, the reader is told how Mars, pierced by Cupid's arrow, has fallen hopelessly in love with Angelica. When he rises into the air above the island of Cyprus to search for the object of his desire, he observes:

> Los ojos tiende por el bajo suelo,
> de diversas naciones ocupado;
> a Europa mira y su benigno cielo,
> su rico asiento, su vivir templado. (XIV.97.1–4)

(His eyes turned toward the ground below, / covered with diverse nations; / he beholds Europe and its kind skies, / its rich location, its tranquil lifestyle.)

Over the course of the next twenty stanzas, the poet offers a description of inland Asia interlaced with glimpses of Europe and Africa.[23] This privileged, bird's-eye view afforded to the gods is already present in Homer; for example, it can be seen with both Zeus and Poseidon at the beginning of canto XIII of the *Iliad* (XIII.1–14). Likewise, the Muses, whom the poet invokes when initiating the famous catalogue of ships, witness everything from their palaces atop Mount Olympus (Homer, *Iliad*, II.484). From above one can see the world in a single gaze, making this vantage point the necessary key to render geography knowable. These descriptions from a panoramic point of view are a mainstay of epic works and are referred to in rhetoric as *kataskopia*. For example, in *Orlando furioso*, Ariosto lifts Astolfo onto the back of the hippogriff in order to present the geography that lies between Europe and Prester John's kingdom in Ethiopia (XXXIII.96–106); in *O segundo cerco de Diu*, Corte-Real places Alecto among the peaks of the Appenine Mountains in order to describe the tripartite globe;[24] in *La Araucana*, Ercilla is taken to a mountain by the goddess Bellona, who appears to him in a vision, so that he can witness the Battle of Saint-Quentin (XVII.51); and in *Paradise Lost*, Milton recounts how Saint Michael the Archangel carries Adam to the highest promontory in Eden so that he can gaze down upon it (11381–6). In Balbuena's *El Bernardo*, similar ascents occur: during the voyage from Alcina (alluded to earlier), making the description of northern Europe possible; or to enhance Mars's field of vision; or during the flight of Malgesí's enchanted ship, an occurrence which gives rise to the majority of the poem's geographical descriptions, including his depiction of the West Indies (XVIII.100–14), an element to which I will return later. A variation of this device entails gaining access to the panoramic perspective using a scientific or magical artefact.

Such is the case in Camões's *Os Lusíadas* when Tethys uses the globe to offer Vasco de Gama a description of the heavens and a geographical description of the new worlds while on the Isle of Love (X.80–91and X.91–141); or in Ercilla's *La Araucana* when Fitón's all-seeing orb (poma milagrosa) divides the world into two parts: one within Castilla's rule and the other without (XXIII & XXVII), much like the maps by Fernández de Enciso or López de Velasco.

The political implications of global domination conveyed by this rhetorical tool are obvious, as Ramachandran sums up with reference to Camões and Spenser: "The very mastery of worldly knowledge that permits the *kataskopos* can become the basis of a claim to global, imperial control. As Camões and Spenser reflect on their own location as exiles writing from the colonial margins (Goa, Mozambique, Ireland), they observe and chronicle the emerging, twinned discourses of modern imperialism and globalism."[25]

To a lesser degree, an anecdote involving Charles V is particularly revealing as it demonstrates how the imagination's perception of mapped territory can induce a powerful trick within the cartodoxic mind. According to a coetaneous French source, Martin Du Bellay's *Mémoires*, during Charles V's invasion of Provence in 1536, he studied the maps of the region so carefully that he became convinced that it was already in his possession before ever entering into battle. The ironic conclusion was, of course, that in the end he lost the fight for its control: "normally [Charles V] had in his hand or before his eyes a map of the Alps and Lower Provence, which the marquis of Saluzzo had given him. He studied it so often and so intensely, using it to further his designs and his desires, that he began to think he had the country in his grasp instead of just the maps."[26] Using this same abstraction of the overhead kataskopic view, ancient geographers referred to different regions of the globe by comparing the outline they would display if seen from the sky with the shape of familiar objects found in our everyday field of vision. Strabo, for example, compared the shape of the Iberian Peninsula with the oxhide and the Peloponnese with a leaf of a plane tree so that readers could better imagine them.[27] This classical practice substituted or complemented cartographic knowledge and, to a certain extent, continues to be valid in such paradigmatic examples as the identification of Italy with a boot; that comparison first arose during the seventeenth century and is internationally recognized today.[28] As for Bernardo de Balbuena, he includes two of these idealized sketches of the outline of Europe: "Europe in the shape of a dragon" (*Europa in forma draconis*) and "Europe in the shape of a queen/virgin" (*Europa in forma regina/ virginis*).

Europa in forma draconis

In *El Bernardo*, the first of these images is pronounced by the wizard Malgesí, who crosses the seas in his enchanted vessel together with three knights to whom he offers a comprehensive description of the world:

> ved esta breve mancha que torcida
> la forma hace de un dragón hermosa,
> y es de Europa la tierra, en quien ceñida
> del mundo está la parte más preciosa. (XV.165)

> (see this slight stain that twisted / takes the shape of a beautiful dragon, / and is the land of Europe, wherein on / earth is found the loveliest part.)

As indicated in the stanza above, the outline of Europe is compared to that of a dragon. Rather than the result of Balbuena's own imagination, it was likely humanist Petrus Apianus, mathematician to Charles V, who initially conceived it. The first instance of this emblematic representation that I have encountered is found in Apianus's *Libro de la cosmographia*, a text that enjoyed unrivalled success in its field with numerous editions and translations:

> en el medio se estiende hacia el norte y mediodía a manera de alas, en forma de dragón, y allí es su mayor anchura. […] En Europa la primera región hacia el occidente es España, a la cual los griegos decían Iberia, y es la cabeza de la forma de dragón que representa Europa. (*Libro de la cosmographia*, fol. 32r)

> (in the centre it [Europe] extends towards the north and south like wings, in the shape of a dragon, and there it has its greatest width. […] In Europe the first region to the west is Spain, which the Greeks called Iberia, and it is the head of the dragon shape that Europe represents.)[29]

Unfortunately, there is no graphic representation of Europe in Apianus's highly illustrated manual matching this description, and I have not located any other text that does.[30] Furthermore, Apianus does not indicate any classical or modern source for this model. Everything suggests that the image was his, a hypothesis I believe to be strengthened by his predilection for dragons in his masterpiece, *Astronomicum Caesareum* (1540). I am convinced that Apianus is Balbuena's source because this visualization of Europe was not very widespread; I have only been able to document it in the works of Magini (1596), Cluverius (1624), and

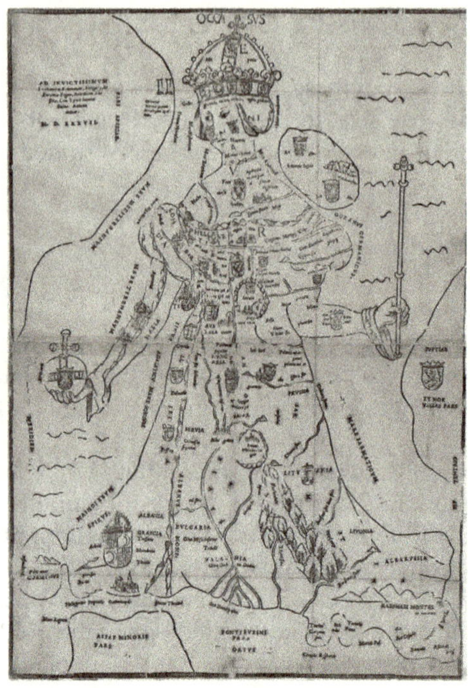

Figure 9.3. Ioannes Buccius, "AD INVICTISSIMVM / Ferdinandum Romanorum, Hungariae, et / Bohaemiae Regem, Archiducem Au-/striae, Cum Tyrolis Ionnes / Bucius Aenicola/ dedicat. / M. D. XXXVII" (1537). Courtesy of the Tyrolean Provincial Museum (Tiroler Landesmuseum Ferdinandeum), Innsbruck.

Knittel (1674).[31] All three derive from Apianus, and only Magini's work (it falsely claims to have taken it from Strabo, most likely to give it a more classical air) appeared prior to *El Bernardo*.[32]

Europa in forma regina/virginis

The second of the two depictions, the popular gynomorphic representation of Europe as a maiden and queen where the Iberian Peninsula is her head, enjoyed much greater renown. It seems that Ioannes Buccius, its creator, first presented it to Charles V in Italy in 1535,[33] but no examples of this early image have survived. The earliest extant testimony of this tradition is a xylograph engraved for Ferdinand I of Hapsburg, King of the Romans, Hungary, and Bohemia, and the future successor of his brother Charles V as Emperor of the Holy Roman Empire (see fig. 9.3).[34]

The engraving, a celebration of the House of Hapsburg, was accompanied by a Neo-Latin poem composed by Buccius titled "Europa lamentans" in which the future of the continent was entrusted to Providence through the work of these two fraternal monarchs. Unsurprisingly, the pre-eminence that this image granted the Iberian Peninsula caused it to be quickly adopted by intellectuals serving the Spanish and Portuguese Crowns, and, in particular, by cosmographers with the Portuguese Casa da Índia (India House) and the Spanish Casa de Contratación (House of Trade). Based on my research, the earliest testimony of its acceptance is from Pedro de Medina, who was associated with the latter of the two aforementioned institutions. In his *Libro de las grandezas y cosas memorables de España* (1548) he remarked that in the "body" of Europe, Spain (in a geographical sense, that is, ancient Hispania) is the head:

> La región de España, de quien en este libro se ha de tratar, es principio y cabeça de todas las otras regiones del mundo. Esto muestran algunos autores entre los cuales uno es Plinio Veronense, que en el libro que hizo de la discreción [*sic*] del mundo dice: la redondez de la tierra se divide en tres partes, que son: Europa, África, Asia. Y para decir destas comiença de España así como principio y cabeça dellas. También se muestra ser España principio y cabeça de todas las otras regiones por demostración en su asiento y figura.[35]

> (The region of Spain, the subject of this book, is the beginning and the head of all other regions of the world. This is demonstrated by several authors, one of whom is Plinio Veronense, who in the book he wrote on the world's description says: The roundness of the earth is divided into three parts, which are: Europe, Africa, Asia. And regarding these, we must start with Spain as their beginning and head. Spain also appears to be the beginning and head of all other regions as demonstrated by its position and shape.)

This widely disseminated work was composed in Seville, the centre of Spain's overseas operations and, at the same time, an important site of Spanish Renaissance humanism.[36] Several researchers have studied Camões's use of this same image in *Os Lusíadas* to symbolize Iberian power, and even to elevate Portugal amongst the Iberian territories.[37] Two examples of note are "Behold here appears noble Spain, / As the head of all Europe" (Eis aqui se descobre a nobre Espanha, / Como cabeça ali de Europa toda) (III.17.1–2); and "Behold here, almost like the head / Of all Europe, the Lusitanian kingdom" (Eis aqui, quasi cume da cabeça / De Europa toda, o Reino Lusitano) (III.20.1–2). However, the inclusion of this design in the Spanish epic during the same period, something previously explained as an homage to Charles V, has gone largely unnoticed. The first transference of this design from cosmographic treatises or maps into literature was carried out by Juan de Mal Lara in his work *Hércules animoso* (completed around 1565 with little circulation at the time and remaining unpublished until recently).[38] The image appears once again in *El Bernardo* and is introduced by the wizard Malgesí during the flight of his enchanted ship. In the text, the Persian King Orimandro asks him to describe the Spanish lands, a territory he considers to be "the great palace of Mars" (de Marte el gran palacio) (*El Bernardo*, XVI.48). The wizard complies with a detailed chorography of the peninsula that begins:

> En lo mejor del habitable mundo
> como cabeza de él la asentó el cielo
> combatida de un crespo mar profundo,
> que por tres partes ciñe el fértil suelo;
> no en el clima tercero, ni el segundo,
> ni en el sexto, ni sétimo en que el velo
> con tal rigor sobre sus golfos baja
> que en roscas de cristal los trepa y cuaja. (XVI.52)

(In the best of the inhabitable world / the heavens placed it as the head / battled by a deep agitated sea, / which borders on three sides the fertile ground; / it is neither in the third climate, nor the second, / nor the sixth, nor the seventh where the veil / descends with such force upon its gulfs / covering and crystallizing them in crystal rings.)

In addition to Spain being imagined as the head of the world, this passage offers other specifics concerning its location inside an inhabitable climate (the *temperata borealis* zone). For this information, Balbuena was also able to draw on Apianus's *Libro de la cosmographia*:

> Los antiguos astrólogos partieron la tierra según la anchura, solamente en siete partes. Y a cada cual dellas llamaron clima. Nosotros, por lo que en nuestros tiempos se ha descubierto, la dividimos en nueve climas. Clima se dice espacio de tierra entre dos paralelos, en el cual hay diferencia de media hora en el mayor día del año, del principio al fin de dicho espacio.[39]

(Ancient astrologers divided the land by width into but seven parts. And each one of them they called climates. Based on what we have discovered in our time, we divide them into nine climates. Climate refers to the stretch

Figure 9.4. Petrus Apianus, *Libro de la cosmographia* (1548), fol. 5r. Image courtesy of the Thomas Fisher Rare Book Library, University of Toronto.

of land between two parallels in which there is a difference of half an hour
on the longest day of the year, from the beginning to the end of this space.)

The text goes on to provide more details regarding the classifications of
the nine climates mentioned, each identified primarily by city names. The
following figures (see figs. 9.4 and 9.5) from Apianus's book facilitate understanding of the previous stanza, and reconstruct some aspects of the
material culture for readers contemporary to Balbuena. Figure 9.4 identifies the world's zones by their inhabitability, and details the nine climates
in each of the *zonae temperatae*, the only ones that were inhabitable according to ancient beliefs. In Balbuena's text, it is evident that Spain is positioned between the fourth and fifth climates, although this is determined
by rejecting those of which it is not a part and discarding those located at

Figure 9.5. Petrus Apianus, *Libro de la cosmographia* (1548), fol.7r. Image courtesy of the Thomas Fisher Rare Book Library, University of Toronto.

the far ends: that is, the first, eighth, and ninth. The climates associated with Spain are those of the cities of Rhodes (fourth) and Rome (fifth); in effect, they approximately demarcate the meridional and septentrional limits of the Iberian Peninsula.

Cartography and Epic Writing

Beginning with its frontispiece, Balbuena's *El Bernardo* highlights the assimilatín of geográphical content: "Work woven from […] geographical descriptions of the most florid parts of the world" (Obra toda tejida de […] geográficas descripciones de las más floridas partes del mundo);

and then later in its preface "descriptions of places […] with an almost universal geography that the world has artfully cultivated" (descripciones de lugares […] con una casi universal geografía del mundo, sembrada artificiosamente por él) (75).[40] These early announcements are not unjustified as the "geographical" descriptions span almost 350 stanzas of the poem, and occur at the three levels identified by sixteenth-century cosmographers, that is, cosmographical, geographical, and chorographical or topographical.[41] The first of these levels is highlighted by Malgesí's astronomical description (Balbuena, *El Bernardo*, XVII.1–32), which is a complete portrait of the cosmos: "Malgesí resumes his journey pointing out every image and sign in the sky" (Prosigue Malgesí su viaje mostrando todas las imágenes y signos del cielo) (Balbuena, *El Bernardo*, XVII, Synopsis); and even more so by the American wizard Tlascalán's astronomical declarations in the subsequent book:

> Tiénese por sospechas que esta lumbre,
> que es de todas las lumbres la primera,
> no como el mundo juzga está en la cumbre,
> mas en el fijo centro de la esfera;
> y la demás inmensa muchedumbre
> de estrellas rubias con su rueda entera
> en torno rueda de él y también rueda
> la Tierra aunque parece estarse queda.
>
> Que él, como silla y soberano asiento
> de los dioses, se está inmudable y fijo,
> de cuya eterna luz toma sustento
> la suya, y de ella el mundo regocijo.
> Vosotros, que en los páramos del viento
> recodo y vuelo disteis tan prolijo,
> sabréis quizá lo que ahora se desea,
> si se anda el sol o el mundo le rodea. (Balbuena, *El Bernardo*, XVIII.163–4)

(Have no doubt that this flame, / which is of all flames the first, / is not at the summit as everyone suggests, / but firmly in the centre of the sphere; / and the rest of the enormous cluster / of stars revolves around it and the Earth / also revolves though it seems to be still. / And it, as chair and sovereign seat / of the gods, is unchanging and fixed, / from whose eternal light theirs derives / its sustenance, and the world its joy. / You, who upon the wind of the treeless plains / made such an extensive detour and flight, / perhaps now know what we seek, / if the sun moves or if the world circles it.)

The author's strategy here is to demonstrate that he is knowledgeable – and perhaps an adherent – of the Copernican heliocentric solar system hypothesis in *De revolutionibus orbis* (1543) and, therefore, *au courant* with the latest research in natural philosophy. It is notable that Copernicus's text was read and taught at the University of Salamanca, the institution where Pedro Fernández de Castro, Balbuena's benefactor and the poem's implied reader, studied for several years.[42]

The geographical and chorographical levels are normally found to be interwoven given that one typically begins with geographical considerations before shifting to chorography. The most notable passage of this type in the poem is presented via *kataskopia*. In *El Bernardo*, Balbuena has the French wizard Malgesí resort to diabolical forces to cast a spell to cause a ship to fly (XV.146), following a very old tradition of aerial voyages which dates back to the myth of the Babylonian King Etana and to *A true story* of Lucian of Samosata.[43] In the presence of three other knights, he overflies the entirety of Europe (XV.165–86; XVI.7–44), carries out an extensive exploration of the Iberian Peninsula (XVI.46–186), ascends to the celestial spheres (XVII.1–32; XVIII.94–100), and lastly, introduces the lands of the New World (XVIII.101–22). The description of the American territories that were part of the Spanish Empire begins with Brazil. This circumstance allows the poet to point out the political unity that existed on the Iberian Peninsula following the Spanish Crown's annexation of Portugal in 1580.[44]

However, given the enormous complexity and length of the poem (Balbuena's intention was, in his own words, to present "an almost universal geography of the world), I will focus on one particular description that is shorter, but comparable in its narrative scheme. It is the first to appear in the poem and is a dynamic description mentioned earlier (Balbuena, *El Bernardo*, I.49–54).[45] In this section of *El Bernardo*, which imitate the travels of Astolfo and Ruggiero on the back of the hippogriff, Alcina appears riding in her enchanted carriage drawn by two griffins and flying over various regions of Europe until she reaches the meridional coasts of the White Sea (called *lago Blanco* by Balbuena and *lacus albus* in the maps of the period), ancient Bjarmaland.[46] Alcina begins her journey with the port city of Calais and the Cliffs of Dover to her left and Denmark to her right, and reaches its end after travelling over modern-day Norway, Sweden, and Finland.[47] The sources for this type of episode are diverse in nature. As will become clear, unlike the methods of such authors as Ercilla, who primarily utilized a written source for the main geographical passage in *La Araucana*, Balbuena produced his description of Alcina's flight in consultation with maps.[48]

Figure 9.6. Olaus Magnus (Olao Magno), detail from *Carta marina et descriptio septemtrionalium terrarum ac mirabilium rerum in eis contentarum diligentissime elaborata* (1539). Note in the centre, the name of the city of Calmarnia written as "Calmar."

The main cartographic source on Scandinavia for all of early modern Europe was *Carta marina* (1539)[49] by Olaus Magnus (aka Olao Magno, 1490–1557), with simplified versions of it included in his renowned *Historia de gentibus septentrionalibus* (*A Description of the Northern Peoples*) (1555). However, Balbuena did not refer to this work directly when composing his description. Several names mentioned by the poet help to identify the particular map that he used. Such is the case of Kalmar (the principal city of Gothia or Götaland, one of the three historic regions making up the south of Sweden), which Balbuena, following his source, names Colmar but which is, in fact, a corruption of "Calmarnia" and its abbreviation "Calmar." This form was already present in *Carta marina* (see fig. 9.6), and both "Calmarnia" and "Calmer" are found in Magnus's *Historia de gentibus septentrionalibus* (IX.XXI) with respect to the frequent battles for the city.

This term "Colmar" was then incorporated into the Mercator projections of Europe (1554; 1572) and of the world (1569).[50] Yet these maps, in addition to being extraordinarily rare, do not offer the geographical information presented by the poet in his descriptions.[51] Therefore, Balbuena must have used one of the inaugural collections of modern cartography. Mercator himself was the first to conceive of the idea of publishing a collection of maps, though it was his friend, Abraham Ortelius, who first realized such a project when he published his *Theatrum Orbis Terrarum* in 1570; as will be made clear, this work was used by the poet.[52] Prior to *El Bernardo*'s publication, two more significant cartographic projects appeared: *Speculum Orbis Terrarum* (1578) by Gerard de Jode and Mercator's *Atlas* (1595). Nevertheless, Jode's maps can be quickly dismissed as a possible source since they do not contain the city of Calmarnia, nor any other cities, rivers, or mountains present in Balbuena's descriptions. It is more difficult, however, to distinguish between the use of Ortelius's work and that of Mercator since Ortelius relies on Mercator's previously mentioned freestanding maps when designing his own, while Mercator, in turn, incorporates some of Ortelius's corrections when publishing his *Atlas*, as will later be seen in the case of Iceland.[53] As a result, the information offered by both is largely identical.[54]

To articulate this dynamic description, Balbuena utilized two maps from Ortelius's collections: a map of Europe and a map of the Nordic countries. Upon embarking from Paris, Alcina journeys through the "waters and forests" (aguas y florestas) of the Rhine until Holland comes into view.[55] Then, flying over the province of Zeeland, she heads out to sea in the direction of Norway, leaving behind the Cimbric Peninsula or Jutland (Denmark) to her right and England and the city of Calés (Calais) to the left. The choice of the city of Calais in the description is not by chance given that the Spanish held the strategic site for a period of two years, between 1596 and 1598, during the religious wars, around the same time as the poem's composition. Furthermore, the strait that this city controlled, today called the English Channel (La Manche), had its own map in Ortelius's "Caletensium [...] accurata descriptio." Unlike Mercator's freestanding maps, and the map of Europe created by his son and included in his *Atlas*, Ortelius's map of Europe is the only one that contains the cartographic information that Balbuena depicts. The difference between the two maps is minimal, yet there are indeed several recognizable clues in the description. For example, while Ortelius includes the names of the two regions mentioned by Balbuena (Holland and Zeeland), Mercator does not, which would indicate he consulted Ortelius's map (see figs. 9.7 and 9.8).

Figure 9.7. Abraham Ortelius, detail of "Europa" from *Theatrum Orbis Terrarum* (1570). Courtesy of the Library of Congress, G1006.T5 1570.

Figure 9.8. Gerard Mercator and Rumold Mercator, detail of "Europa" from *Atlas sive cosmographicae meditationes de fabrica mundi et fabricati figura* (1595). Courtesy of the Library of Congress, G1007.A7 1595.

Until now Balbuena had been referring to the map of Europe, but here he turns to the second of the two, that of the Nordic countries, entitled "Septentrionalium regionum descriptio."[56] Alcina makes out in the distance "the famous fortresses" (los alcázares famosos) of Colmar in Gothia (I.51); Balbuena identifies them according to the explicative text of the region found in *Theatrum*. In English translation, the Spanish version of this text reads: "Gothia means: good land. It is ruled by the king of Sweden. In it there is a large city called Calmar: it is a port and a commercial city, and it has a fortress so large as to rival that of Milan" (Gothia quiere decir: buena tierra. Está debajo del rey de Suecia. En ella hay una ciudad grande que llaman Calmar: es puerto y ciudad de comercio, y tiene una fortaleza tan grande que se puede poner con la de Milán).[57] The fact that Balbuena decides to portray this city utilizing the information available about the septentrional regions on this map – notice the mention of the fortress – indicates that this map was his source. Further confirmation arises when one considers that this is how the location appears on the map of the Nordic countries, whereas it is written as "Calmar" on the map of Europe (see figs. 9.9 and 9.10).

Here it is possible to see how material culture carries with it ecdotic consequences. When editing this passage, it is necessary to consider "Colmar" to be the official form though fully aware that it is a mistake by the author. Balbuena most likely wrote "Colmar" in accordance with his source, and this is how the text should be preserved, even when it includes an erroneous toponym. The magical carriage flies next over the coast of Sweden, where once again can be detected Balbuena's use of the explanation that Ortelius includes in his map of the Nordic countries. The poem reads: "and following the coast of the westerly wind. / In Sweden she marvels at the precious / metals that burst from its cliffs" (y siguiendo la costa del poniente. / de la Süecia goza los preciosos / metales que revientan por los riscos) (Balbuena, *El Bernardo*, I.51) while Ortelius, in the Spanish edition of his work, states: "Sweden: it is a kingdom rich in silver, copper, lead and iron" (Suecia: es reino rico de plata, cobre, plomo y hierro).[58] Balbuena then sends Alcina to the north along the coast, and adjusts her course towards the west to the region of Finnmark in Norway, rather than have her continue straight ahead to the White Sea; this adjustment facilitates mention of two further cartographic elements recorded by Ortelius. The first is a promontory that Balbuena refers to as Subentino:

Pasa a Fimarquia y sobre el cristalino
y endurecido mar que la costea,
conoce en el peñasco Subentino
el peligroso golfo que la ondea. (*El Bernardo*, I.52.1–4)

Figure 9.9. Abraham Ortelius, detail of "Septentrionalium regionum descriptio" from *Theatrum Orbis Terrarum* (1570). Courtesy of the Library of Congress, G1006.T5 1570.

Figure 9.10. Abraham Ortelius, detail of "Europa" from *Theatrum Orbis Terrarum* (1570). Courtesy of the Library of Congress, G1006.T5 1570.

(She reaches Finnmark and over the crystalline / and hardened sea that
borders it, / encounters at Subentino Bluff / the dangerous gulf that
crashes against it.)

On Ortelius's map, the name of the bluff is written as "Swentinos
prom[ontorium]" and located adjacent to a gulf off the north coast of
the Scandinavian Peninsula. These correspond with the Varangerfjord
and Varanger Peninsula, respectively. The reason that Balbuena characterizes this gulf as dangerous is again found in an annotation on
Ortelius's map: there is depicted a vortex within its waters together
with the word "Carÿbdys." Balbuena included this danger based on
the cartographic material available to him, but, as an epic poet, he rejected the inclusion of Ortelius's mythological reference, revealing his
resistance to placing Charybdis in a non-Mediterranean location. Later
in the poem (El Bernardo, XVI.12), Balbuena will place this whirlpool
off the coast of southern Italy near the Gulf of Taranto, an element he
takes from Virgil's *Aeneid* (III.551–60). Ortelius's annotation originated
in the work of Olao Magno (Olaus Magnus). In his *Carta marina*, the
Nordic bishop had recorded the traditional belief concerning a maritime zone near the region of Trøndelag where the currents swallowed
ships whole, remarking: "This is the terrible Charybdis" (Hec est horrenda Caribdis) (see fig. 9.11).[59]
In his *Historia de gentibus septentrionalibus* (II.VII, VIII), Magnus further explains this mythological addition by indicating that there is a
hole located at this point in the ocean (maris hiatus) into which ships
would plunge. Mercator, who collected new information, repositioned
this phenomenon much farther north on his map of Europe, but main-
tained the mythological annotation (see fig. 9.12).[60] Ortelius locates
Charybdis in this region based on Mercator's information, and it is
from Ortelius's map that Balbuena then learns of the dangerous gulf
that crashes against Subentino Bluff.
The second of the cartographic elements that Balbuena mentions during this deliberate detour on which he takes Alcina is the mythological
island of Thule, a place he identifies as Iceland. Although Olaus Magnus had made a distinction between the two islands in *Carta marina*,
in his *Historia de gentibus septentrionalibus* he conflates them in accordance with medieval tradition.[61] This identification is then incorporated
into Mercator's Europe and world maps, and later into Ortelius's maps
of Europe and the Nordic countries. Hence, on the "Septentrionalium
regionum descriptio" map in *Theatrum* utilized by Balbuena, there is
written over the island: "Iceland once Thule" (Islant, *olim* Thule) (see
fig. 9.11).[62] This explains the verses in which the reader is told that

Figure 9.11. Olaus Magnus (Olao Magno), detail of inscription from *Carta marina et descriptio septemtrionalium terrarum ac mirabilium rerum in eis contentarum diligentissime elaborata* (1539), which reads: "Hec est horrenda Caribdis."

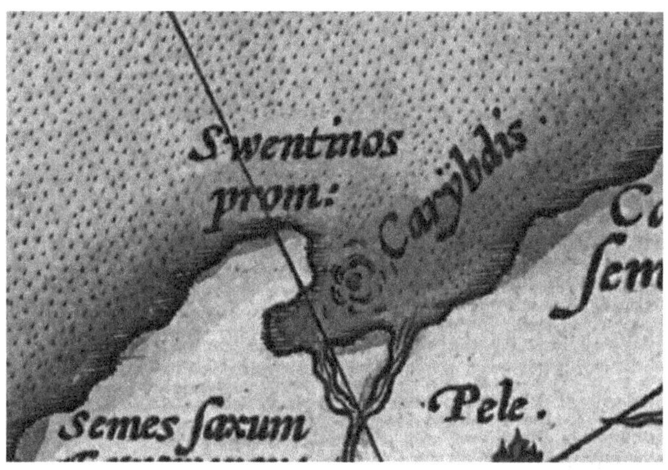

Figure 9.12. Abraham Ortelius, detail of "Septentrionalium regionum descriptio" from *Theatrum Orbis Terrarum* (1570). Courtesy of the Library of Congress, G1006.T5 1570.

Alcina leaves behind her a "continuous fire" (contino fuego) that burns on the island of Thule, when this detail does not appear anywhere in classical sources. A thorough investigation of classical texts yields no references to such a circumstance. Strabo, who gathered the most information on Thule in his comments on the texts of Pytheas of Massalia, makes no mention of the island being in flames, and even doubts its very existence, believing Pytheas to be untruthful.[63] On the other hand, in Iceland there was indeed knowledge of such a fire, as noted by Olaus Magnus: according to the Archbishop of Uppsala, the volcano Hekla brought fire from the centre of the Earth into contact with the surface snow and ice resulting in an ever-present plume of smoke.[64] And even Ortelius, Balbuena's source, somewhat belatedly alludes to these undying fires in the text that accompanies his map of Iceland, though without any reference to Thule (see figs. 9.13 and 9.14). Balbuena, therefore, maintains the identification established in Ortelius's maps of Europe and the septentrional regions, describing a smoldering Thule, rather than accept Ortelius's own refutation of this detail in his map of Iceland and the accompanying text. The corresponding passage in *El Bernardo* reads:

> y dando a las espaldas el contino
> fuego que en la encubierta Tile humea
> a las alturas de Biarmia sube,
> y allí se baja de su hueca nube. (I.52.5–8)

> (and turning her back on the continuous
> fire smoldering on the enshrouded Thule
> she ascends to the heights of Bjarmaland,
> and there descends from its empty cloud.)

Moreover, in this particular case, by confirming the toponym mentioned by Balbuena based on the physical maps he used, there is now the opportunity to amend a deformation in the text, one found in all of its editions: an erroneous union of words in the first edition resulted in the mysterious location of Tyleumea.[65] With maps in hand, we are able to correct it as "Tyle-umea," modernized to read "Tile humea" (Thule smolders): when Alcina changes course over Finnmark towards the White Sea, she leaves behind her the smoldering and enshrouded island of Thule.

Once Alcina's airborne voyage reaches its final destination, there are further indications that Ortelius's maps were Balbuena's cartographic sources for this description, and not those of Mercator. Upon arriving in

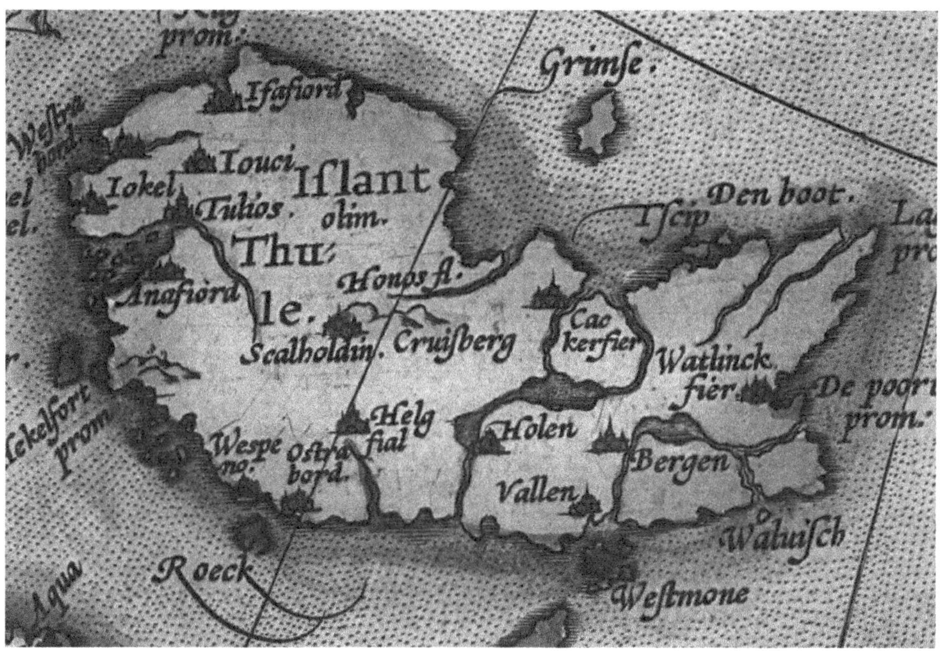

Figure 9.13. Abraham Ortelius, detail of "Septentrionalium regionum descriptio" from *Theatrum Orbis Terrarum* (1570). Courtesy of the Library of Congress, G1006.T5 1570.

Figure 9.14. Abraham Ortelius, detail of "Islandia" from *Theatrum Orbis Terrarum* (1570). Courtesy of the National Library of Spain, GMG/1147.

Figure 9.15. Abraham Ortelius, detail of "Septentrionalium regionum descriptio" from *Theatrum Orbis Terrarum* (1570). Courtesy of the Library of Congress, G1006.T5 1570.

Bjarmaland, the poem informs the reader that Alcina lands in the Elsingue Meadow: "She sets the moldings of the wheels down/ in the delightful Elsingue meadow" (Estampa de las ruedas las molduras/ en la vega de Elsingue placentera) (*El Bernardo*, I.53.1–2), and crosses the groves to the shore of the lake.[66] Ortelius's map indeed places the toponym "Helsinga" amid a meadow on the shore of the White Sea (see fig. 9.15), while on Mercator's map the toponym "Helsingavat" is situated beside a mountain range and far removed from the lakefront (see fig. 9.16). Furthermore, here the poem states that the lake loses some of its volume and fish because the Varziga (now Varzuga) River empties into the sea:

> [...] y la corriente
> de Varciga [da] a la mar nuevos pescados,
> que de sus revoltosos y anchos senos
> por secretos caminos le hace menos. (Balbuena, *El Bernardo*, I.54.5–8)

> ([...] and the current / of the Varciga [gives] new fish to the sea, / which from its broad and turbulent inlets / along secret paths makes it less.)

This element again confirms Balbuena's use of Ortelius's map as opposed to Mercator's, given that only the former indicates the name of

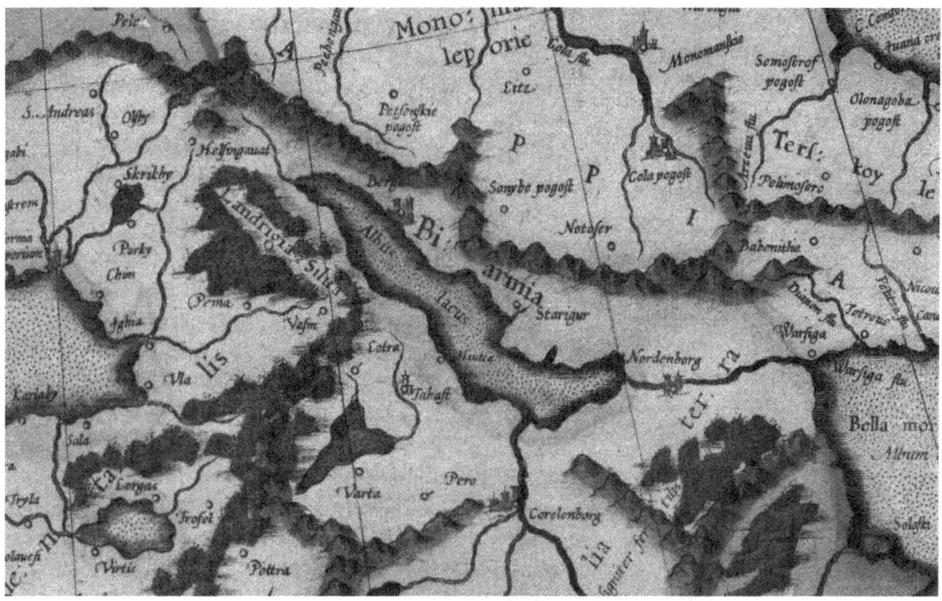

Figure 9.16. Gerard Mercator and Rumold Mercator, detail of "Svecia et Norvegia" from *Atlas sive cosmographicae meditationes de fabrica mundi et fabricati figura* (1595). Image courtesy of the Thomas Fisher Rare Book Library, University of Toronto.

this river with the inscription "Varziga fl[uvius]" and, thus, only from there could Balbuena have derived such information. Alternatively, Mercator's map depicts the city whose name it shares with the river and at whose mouth it is located: Warsiga. Together, these examples demonstrate how cartography can act as an intertext, strictly speaking, in epic literature, in that it provides a specific onomastic collection that poets incorporate into their works.

Conclusion

Bernardo de Balbuena was an erudite ecclesiastic with vast knowledge of classical texts from Virgil, Ovid, and Lucan, among others,[67] and modern literature from Spain (his work contains imitations of Garcilaso de la Vega, Fray Luis de León, and Alonso de Ercilla, among others) and Italy, particularly Petrarch, Boiardo, and Ariosto. As was typical with his contemporaries, one of the principal pillars of his work was the *imitatio* of *auctoritates*.[68] As a result, his writing is markedly literary. Balbuena lived surrounded by books. It is known, for example, that in 1610 he acquired a licence to take with him to New Spain an enormous amount of "books from his study"[69] and that, as Lope de Vega recounts in *Laurel de Apolo* (1630), his library was stolen during a pirate attack on the island of Puerto Rico, where he was bishop:

Tenías tú el cayado
de Puerto Rico cuando el fiero Enrique,
holandés rebelado,
robó tu librería,
pero tu ingenio no, que no podía. (Silva II, 114–28)

(You held the crosier / of Puerto Rico when the fierce Hendrik, / rebellious Dutchman, / stole your library, / but not your brillance, which he could not.)

Unlike soldier-poets of previous generations, such as Garcilaso de la Vega or Alonso de Ercilla, Balbuena only embodied the heroic ideal of *sapientia*, just one of two qualities traditionally associated with the classical Virgilian hero. However, he does so with pleasure, something he insists on pointing out in *El Bernardo*, because he concedes the second quality, *fortitudo*, to the heroic Bernado del Carpio, with whom he shares his name and illegitimate birth. This same ideal was modernized in Iberian literature with the also-paired ideas of "arms and letters" (las armas y las letras) and "the sword and the pen" (la espada y la pluma). However, in this essay I have shown how his *sapientia* and his letters are not only the result of his education and literary-mindedness when writing, but also of his cartographic culture, which made him the possessor and transmitter of a cartodoxic mentality. One can therefore affirm that if his poem's hero triumphed in his adeptness with the sword, Balbuena did as well in his adeptness with the pen and with maps.

NOTES

1 Translated from the Spanish by Sean Manning and Emiro Martínez-Osorio.
2 The research conducted for this essay is part of Proyecto de I+D del Programa Estatal de Generación de Conocimiento (MCIU/FEDER) PGC2018–095757-B-I00: *Magia, Épica e Historiografía Hispánicas: Relaciones Literarias y Nomológicas II*. In this essay, I revise two articles published earlier (Zulaica

López 2018 and 2019). I am grateful to the editors of this volume for their generous suggestions.

3 Strabo, *Geography*, I.I.2.

4 The most authoritative work on the development of cartography in Renaissance Europe is Harley and Woodward, *The History of Cartography*, vol. 3; for their consideration of Spain, see chapters 39 to 41. For more on Spanish cartography, see Hernando, "The Spanish Contribution to the History of Cartography"; Portuondo, *Ciencia secreta*; and Crespo, *Los grandes proyectos cartográficos nacionales*.

5 Hereafter *El Bernardo*. Citations that follow will draw on the 2017 edition of Balbuena's work edited by Zulaica López and appear in the text.

6 Herreros Tabernero pointed out Balbuena's goal to imitate Virgil. (Las *Geórgicas* de Virgilio," 113, 235–6, 358, and 401). Cacho Casal expanded the comparison between the *Georgics* and *Grandeza mexicana* in "Balbuena's *Grandeza mexicana* and the American Georgic."

7 Gutiérrez, *La espada, el rayo y la pluma*, 59 and 81.

8 In the original Spanish, "verdadero patriarca de la poesía americana." See Menéndez y Pelayo, *Antología de poetas hispanoamericanos*, I.LVII–LVIII.

9 He was also the likely protagonist of a now lost *cantar de gesta*.

10 For more on these authors and works, see Vilà, "De Roncesvalles a Pavía."

11 Van Horne offers a detailed, stanza-by-stanza summary of each book. Van Horne, *El Bernardo of Bernardo de Balbuena*, 45–102.

12 Rattcliffe, "Honor y legitimidad: Bernardo del Carpio en el Siglo de Oro," 521–6.

13 For example, Roland had robbed the avaricious Morgana's treasure room (*Orlando Innamorato*, II, viii, 24–35), freed her prisoners (*Orlando Innamorato*, II, ix, 26–7), and destroyed Falerina's garden (*Orlando Innamorato*, II, iv, 14–15, 39, 42–5, 54, 58–61, 70–3). In addition, Ruggiero escaped from the lustful Alcina, who had bewitched him (*Orlando furioso*, VII, 16–79).

14 I propose the use of the term *cartodoxy* in place of *map-mindedness*, coined by Harvey, due to the fact that the latter does not easily translate into Romance languages. A literal translation in Spanish, for example, would be *mapamentalidad*. However, I believe that this term will, for lexicological reasons, not be easily accepted in the academic world. In Romance languages compound formations are considerably less common than in Germanic languages. There are even numerous cases where compound words in English can only find their place in Romance languages through circumlocutionary expressions. For a more comprehensive explanation of the advantages of using the term *cartodoxy* instead of *map-mindedness*, see my essay "Sobre cartografía y cartodoxia en textos literarios altomodernos."

15 For an introduction about the evolution of spatial representation in Spanish literature throughout the sixteenth century and dating back to the

medieval T and O maps, portolan charts, and navigation itineraries, as well as for a chronological account of the progress of cartographic sciences and the discoveries of America, see Padrón, *The Spacious Word*.

16 Van der Krogt, "The Origin of the Word 'Cartography.'"

17 Doroszlai, "Les sources cartographiques et le *Roland furieux*" and *Ptolémée et l'hippogriffe*.

18 Ariosto, *The Orlando Furioso*, 433. English translation by W.S. Rose. References are to this edition and appear in the text.

19 A discussion on the accuracy of this identification with respect to the maps of the time can be found in Doroszlai, *Ptolémée et l'hippogriffe*, ch. 3.

20 Ariosto and Spencer were preceded by Thomas More, who placed the fictional island of Utopia (work of 1516) somewhere in the Pacific and attributed its discovery to a Portuguese sailor.

21 Ramachandran, *The Worldmakers*, 126.

22 For a study on the "wondrous architecture" (*arquitecturas maravillosas*) of *El Bernardo*, see Zulaica López, "'Sobre cimientos de alabastro.' Las arquitecturas maravillosas en *El Bernardo* de Balbuena."

23 This is not the only geographical description of Asia found in the poem. Earlier in the same book 14, Balbuena provides an account of its other regions (*El Bernardo*, XIV.46–58).

24 Corte-Real, *O segundo cerco de Diu*, 216–23.

25 Ramachandran, *The Worldmakers*, 112.

26 Quoted in Parker, "Maps and Ministers," 135. English translation by Geoffrey Parker.

27 Strabo, *Geography*, II.30 and III.1.

28 The poet Giuseppe Giusti popularized this image in his poem "Stivale" in 1836, prior to the country's unification process, but its origin is much earlier. Fumagalli, *Chi l'ha detto?*, 273. Already in the fourteenth century, Benvenuto da Imola compared the shape of Italy with a leg (*similis tibiae hominis*) in his commentary on Dante's *Commedia*; and, in 1651 Antonio Abati da Gubbio deemed it a boot in several of his poems: for example, in his satire *Il viaggio*: "gia che l'Italia ha d'un Stival la forma." Abati da Gubbio, *Delle frascherie*, 281.

29 The 1548 edition cited here is the first in Spanish. This passage differs slightly from the original Latin from 1524: "nisi ubi circa mediam sui partem (quo magnis frontibus tam versus meridiem quam versus aquilonem in altum procurrit) duabus alis, quibus draconis speciem reddit, maxime extenta est. […] In ea prima ab occidente est Hispania tripartita (a graecis Iberia dicta) draconis caput, quem supra retulimus representans." Apianus, *Cosmographicus liber*, 1524, fol. 65.

30 I have examined more than thirty editions of this work. The fact that it has been translated into over ten languages, and exists in an estimated sixty

editions (Bagrow and Skelton, *History of Cartography*, 130), complicates a comprehensive investigation.

31 See Magini, *Geographiae Cl. Prolomaei Pars Secunda*, 33v; Cluverius, *Introductionis in universam geographiam, tam veterem quam novam, libri VI*, 31; and Knitl, *Cosmographia Elementaris*, II, 3.

32 I am not aware of any research concerning this representation of Europe. The only mention of it that I have found is in Walser-Bürgler, "Geopolitical Instruction and the Construction of Europe in Seventeenth-Century Neo-Latin Texts," 328–9. The author seems to assume that its origin came after what has been documented here, well into the seventeenth century, and promises a forthcoming analysis of this matter.

33 Meurer, "Europa Regina," 20–4.

34 This image was first studied by Van der Heijden (*De oudste gedrukte kaarten van Europa*, 118 and ss.) who describes its later use in illustrating works like Sebastián Münster's *Cosmographia*, to which it was added beginning with the 1588 edition. It was included in ensuing adaptations. Recent studies on this cartographic tradition include Marino (The Invention of Europe); Meurer (Europa Regina), which contains the text of the poem "Europa lamentans" by Buccius; and Detering and Pulina (Rivalry of Lament).

35 Medina, *Libro de las grandezas y cosas memorables de España*, fol. 1r°.

36 With the use of the Real Academia Española's CORDE, I located the presence of this image in other texts from the seventeenth century: Juan Jerez's *Razón de corte* (ca. 1620) and Diego Sarmiento de Acuña's *Carta al Duque de Monteleón* (1622).

37 See Tavares de Pinho, "A Descriçao Camoniana Da Europa E Cartografia Ginecomórfica," and Piechocki, *Cartographic Humanism*.

38 *Hércules animoso*, III, "Breve declaración," 1630.

39 *Libro de la cosmographia*, fol. 6v.

40 Friedlein has taken an interest in the allegorical significance of the "geographical" episodes included in the poem, and the modernization of classical clerical discourse on the ambition for knowledge that they present. Friedlein, *Kosmovisionen*, 326.

41 Apianus opens *Cosmographicus liber* (1524, I.I) with a study of this tripartite distinction. At the same time, his treatise was guided by Ptolemy's *Almagest* and *Geography*. The first work was a cosmographical study, while the second was dedicated to the other two mentioned levels: the first book in *Geography* begins with the differentiation between geography, which involves the graphic representation of the outlines of lands and seas (limited to the ecumene, or the inhabited areas of the globe), and chorography, which focuses only on a particular region or place. Hernando, *El mapa de España*, 98.

42 Copernicus's text was included in the Roman Catholic *Index* of forbidden
    books from 1616, demanding the bowdlerization of certain passages. On
    the circulation of his treatise in the Hispanic world, see Alatorre, *El helio-
    centrismo en el mundo de habla española.*

43 The literary tradition that gives rise to this magical flight has its origin in
    the myth of the Babylonian King Etana, who traversed the skies on the
    back of an eagle in order to acquire divine vision. This character is the
    basis for the biblical Nimrod or the fictional Alexander (Wallis Budge,
    The Alexander Book in Ethiopia, VIII–IX; 248–9). Pulci was inspired by these
    sources for his narration of the aerial voyage of Renaud, Richardet, and the
    demon Astaroth in *Morgante* (XXV.200–8), which Chevalier considers to
    be one of Balbuena's sources (*L'Arioste en Espagne*, 368). Similarly, Ariosto
    was influenced by this when writing about Astolfo and Ruggiero's aerial
    voyages. Nevertheless, I find the most significant source for Balbuena's
    text is found in Lucian of Samosata's *A True Story* (I.9–29), in which a ship
    is lofted into the sky by a typhoon and sails through the stars (treated like
    islands), a detail also found in Balbuena's text (*El Bernardo*, XVI.210). The
    event from *A True Story* begins: "a typhoon suddenly arose that spun the
    ship about and, raising it some three hundred furlongs, it could no longer
    reach down to the sea below, but instead, finding itself suspended among
    the heavens, the wind blew upon its canvas and carried it forth at full sail"
    (sobrevino de repente un tifón que hizo girar la nave y, elevándola por el
    aire unos trescientos estadios, ya no la dejó descender al mar, sino que,
    hallándose en las alturas, sopló viento sobre su velamen y la arrastraba a
    vela hinchada) (I.9.184).

44 For more on the dual (metapoetic and political) dimension of this passage,
    see Friedlein, "El vuelo mágico por los Andes en *El Bernardo* de Bernardo
    de Balbuena entre dos funcionalidades."

45 In his study on Ariosto, Doroszlai establishes this distinction between
    static descriptions, expressed from a fixed point, and *dynamic* descriptions,
    which detail regions as the character, who may or may not be the speaker,
    advances through them (*Ptolémée et l'hippogriffe*, 9).

46 Olaus Magnus (aka Olao Magno) writes about the folklore related to this
    lake. Magno, *Historia de gentibus septentrionalibus*, XIX.XLV.689.

47 The name Albion, formerly given to the largest of the British islands, was
    due to the white colour of the "cliffs" of Dover (*peñascos*" ["crags"]). Ac-
    cording to Covarrubias's *Tesoro de la lengua castellana o española*, s. v. *"peña,"*
    they were: "Crags, large rock faces in the mountains or beside the sea"
    (Peñascos, peñas grandes en los montes y en las riberas del mar), located
    facing Calais. Ariosto errs slightly when he attributes the origin of this
    toponym to the colour of the sand on the beaches rather than to the cliffs:
    "And then directs its course towards the white sand, / whence England

was named Albion" (e poi si drizza invêr l'arena bianca, / onde Ingleterra si nomò Albïone) (*Orlando Furioso*, IX.16.3–4). The idea was also recorded by Zapata: "To their left they saw and looked at / the tall white mountains and land, / from which England was called Albion" (Que a su siniestra vieron y miraron / los altos montes blancos y la tierra, / de donde Albión, se dijo Inglaterra) (*Carlo Famoso*, I.38.6–8); and later in a mythological passage in Spenser's *The Faerie Queene* in which the Roman Brutus claims to be the discoverer of Britannia Major according to medieval tradition: "Ne did it then deserve a name to have, / Till that the venturous Mariner that way / Learning his ship from those white rocks to save, / Which all along the Southerne sea-coast lay, / Threatning unheedie wrecke and rash decay, / For safety that same his sea-marke made, / And namd it *Albion*" (II.x.6).

48 See Gómez Canseco, "Ercilla, Giovio et la geographie du globe." In other descriptive passages in *El Bernardo*, it is evident that Balbuena also made use of written sources. In particular, I believe that the description of Spain (XVI.46–186) should be compared with the High Medieval tradition of the "Praise to Hispania" (*laus Hispaniae*) and, specifically, with Lucio Marineo Siculo's *De las cosas memorables de España* (1539) and Pedro de Medina's *Libro de las grandezas y cosas memorables de España* (1548); as we can read in the opening argument to Book XVI, at the Orimandro's behest, Malgesí delivers "a famous epilogue on the great deeds of Spain and its antiquities" (un famoso epílogo de las grandezas de España y sus antigüedades).

49 A second edition of this map by Magnus was printed in Rome by Antonio Lafreri Seguani in 1572: http://umedia.lib.umn.edu/node/89541. The images from *Carta marina* included here are taken from a facsimile created in 1949, and housed in the James Ford Bell Library, University of Minnesota.

50 Before Mercator, the work of Olaus Magnus had already served as a source for the Italian cartographer Johannes Dominicus Zorzi, who registers this city as "Calmur" in his "Vera descriptio totius Europe" (1545). A reproduction of this map can be found in Van der Heijden, "Gedrukte kaarten van Europa vóór Ortelius," 9, fig. 8.

51 It is highly improbable that these freestanding maps reached Balbuena. The last complete surviving copy of Mercator's 1554 map of Europe was destroyed in Breslauer Stadtbibliothek in 1945 (Dürst, "Die Europa-Karten von Gerard Mercator, 1554–1595," 3). We only know of it today thanks to old facsimile editions like the one from the Gesellschaft für Erdkunde in 1891. Indeed, several fragments from various copies of this map make up the so-called "Mercator Atlas" at the British Library (http://www.bl.uk/turning-the-pages/?id=223c7af8-bad6–4282-a684–17bf45bd0311&type=book).

52 According to Gualtero Ghymmio (Walter Ghim) in *Vita (…) Gerardi Mercatoris Rupelmundani*, included as a preface to the Mercartor *Atlas* (fol.1v), this was Mercator's idea. However, while Mercator was still compiling materials,

his friend Ortelius published *Theatrum*. As a result, Mercator temporarily abandoned his project and Ortelius managed to sell numerous copies and earn a considerable amount of money. Publishing a collection of maps was nothing new; they were already included in Renaissance printings of Ptolemy's *Geografia*, a geographic work that contributed to the relaunching of cartographic sciences. Furthermore, there were very successful modern authors who followed this model, like Sebastian Munster's *Cosmographia* (1544), which enjoyed a total of twenty-four editions. Ortelius's collection was the first to be based on meticulous revisions of cartographic measurements, and the development of new representational projections. Marino's "The Invention of Europe" and Van der Heijden's "Gedrukte kaarten van Europa vóór Ortelius" explore the origins of this new cartographic tradition in terms of the evolution in the representation of Europe throughout the sixteenth century until the creation of Ortelius's map of Europe in 1570.

53 For details about how Ortelius utilized Mercator's maps to develop his own, see Marino, "The Invention of Europe," 150; and Van der Heijden, "Gedrukte kaarten van Europa vóór Ortelius," §7.

54 It is important not to lose sight of the fact that Ortelius, as well as his heirs, worked in Antwerp, the economic and printing capital of the Spanish Netherlands (Catholic at the time), and that his work is dedicated to Philip II and Philip III of Spain. On the other hand, Jodocus Hondius, or Joost de Hondt, who is the one who published and progressively expanded Mercator's *Atlas*, lived and worked in the Protestant environments of England and Holland, contributed through his publication to the bolstering of the cultural and economic rise of the Calvinist north of the Flemish complex to the detriment of the meridional Netherlands (Antwerp in particular), and dedicated his work to Louis XIII of France. It is logical to believe this to be one of the reasons that Ortelius's work enjoyed greater circulation in Spain.

55 In verse I, 49, 6 of *El Bernardo*, Balbuena states that Alcina "passes the Rhine, its waters and glades" (pasa el Reno, sus aguas y florestas). Here the verb "pasar" (to pass) does not mean to cross the river, but rather to move along it, to travel its length.

56 For more about the changes to Ortelius's atlas throughout the subsequent editions, and his inclusion of new maps or modifications to existing maps, see Van den Broecke, *Ortelius Atlas Maps*. The two maps of interest (Europe" and "Septentrionalium regionum description) were present in every edition of *Theatrum* from the first (1570) to the last (1641).

57 Ortelius, *Theatro d'el orbe de la tierra*.

58 Ortelius, *Theatro d'el orbe de la tierra*.

59 Magno, *Carta marina*.

60 Mercator includes this information in his maps of Europe, both in the freestanding maps from 1554 and 1572, as well as the one included in his 1595 *Atlas*. However, he does not include it in the map of the Nordic countries.

61 See Magno, *Historia de gentibus septentrionalibus*, II.III.
62 Ortelius takes this from Mercator's 1569 world map, which contains this exact phrase. A very similar text can also be found on Mercator's maps of Europe (1554 and 1572): (Iceland, ancient Thule" (Islandia, veteribus Thule), and on Ortelius's map of Europe: "Islandia, olim Thule." However, despite the fact that Ortelius includes this description when copying from Mercator's works, he later rejects it in the text that accompanies his map of Iceland, citing numerous authorities, and it does not appear on the 1585 Icelandic map itself. Mercator also eliminates it from the maps he produced after Ortelius's work appeared, and which he included in his own *Atlas* (1595) – that is, his maps of Europe and Iceland. This is a very unique case in which two noteworthy cartographers feed off the advances of one another in a dueling evolution that lasted decades.
63 Strabo, *Geography*, I.IV.
64 Magno, *Historia de gentibus septentrionalibus*, II.II.
65 This error is present in the nineteenth-century editions from Sancha (1808), Rosell (1851), and Gaspar y Roig (1852), as well as in Viader's 1914 edition. See the critical apparatus in my edition of Balbuena's *El Bernardo*.
66 The city that Balbuena uses to identify the meadow corresponds to Helsingaval, Helsingavat, and Helsinga in Magno's *Carta marina*, Mercator's "Svecia et Norvegia Cum Confinys," and Ortelius's "Septentrionalium regionum descriptio," respectively. Of the three, Ortelius's is observably the name that most closely resembles what appears in Balbuena's text. I have been unable to locate the equivalent modern-day toponym, if there is one. However, ancient maps place it in the region of Finnish Lapland (Österbotten), and due to its position on these maps with respect to the cities of Chim (now Kemi) and Pele (now Pello), we can locate it near the city of Rovaniemi.
67 For an extensive exploration of Balbuena's knowledge in this area, see Goñi Echeverría, "Tradición clásica en *el Bernardo* de Bernardo de Balbuena."
68 See Ponce Cárdenas, *La imitación áurea*.
69 "libros de su estudio." Permit issued to Bernardo de Balbuena, Archivo General de Indias, 53.2.10.

WORKS CITED

Manuscript Sources

Permit issued to Bernardo del Balbuena to take collection of books to New Spain. *AGI* (Archivo General de Indias), 53.2.10.

Printed Sources

Abati da Gubbio, Antonio. *Delle frascherie di Antonio Abati fasci tre.* Venice: Matteo Leni, 1651.

Alatorre, Antonio. *El heliocentrismo en el mundo de habla española.* Mexico City: Fondo de Cultura Económica, 2011.

Apianus, Petrus. *Astronomicum caesareum.* Ingolstadt: In Aedibus nostri, 1540.

– *Cosmographicus liber Petri Apiani mathematici studiose collectus.* Excusum Landshutae: Typis ac formulis D. Ioannis Weyssenburgers, impensis Petri Apiani, 1524.

Apianus, Petrus, and Gemma Frisio. *Libro de la Cosmographia de Pedro Apiano.* Antwerp: Gregorio Bontio, 1548.

Ariosto, Ludovico. *Cinque Canti.* In *Opere minori,* by Ludovico Ariosto, edited by Cesare Segre, 581–754. Milan-Naples: Riccardo Riccardi Editore, 1954.

– *Orlando furioso.* Edited by Gioacchino Paparrelli. 2 vols. BUR classici. Milan: Rizzoli, 2006.

– *The Orlando furioso.* Translated by W.S. Rose. London: Bohn's Illustrated Library, 1858.

Bagrow, Leo, and R.A. Skelton. *History of Cartography.* Enlarged 2nd ed. New Brunswick, NJ: Transaction Publishers, 2010.

Balbuena, Bernardo de. *El Bernardo, o victoria de Roncesvalles.* Edited by Martín Zulaica López. Preface by Alberto Montaner Frutos. Madrid: Ars Poetica, 2017.

Cacho Casal, Rodrigo. "Balbuena's *Grandeza mexicana* and the American Georgic." *Colonial Latin American Review* 24, no. 2 (2015): 190–214.

Camões, Luís Vaz de. *Os Lusíadas.* Lisbon: Antonio Gõçalvez, 1572.

Chevalier, Maxime, *L'Arioste en Espagne (1530–1650): recherches sur l'influence du "Roland furieux."* Bordeaux: Institut d'Études Ibériques et Ibéro-Américaines, 1966.

Cluverius, Philippus. *Introductionis in universam geographiam, tam veterem quam novam, libri VI.* Lugduni Batavorum: Elzeviriana, 1624.

Corte-Real, Jerónimo. *Sucesso do segundo cerco de Diu (…).* Lisbon: António Gonçalves, 1574.

Covarrubias, Sebastián de. *Tesoro de la lengua castellana o española.* Edited by Ignacio Arellano Ayuso and Rafael Zafra Molina. Madrid: Iberoamericana; Frankfurt am Main: Vervuert, 2006.

Crespo, Antonio. *Los grandes proyectos cartográficos nacionales. La representación del territorio en Castilla y León.* Madrid: CNIG, 2013.

Detering, Nicolas, and Dennis Pulina. "Rivalry of Lament: Early Personifications of Europe in Neo-Latin Panegyrics for Charles V and Francis I." In *Contesting Europe: Comparative Perspectives on Early Modern*

Discourses of Europe, 1400–1800, edited by Nicolas Detering, Clementina Marsico, and Isabella Walser-Bürgler, 13–98. Leiden: Brill, 2019.

Doroszlaï, Alexandre. "Les sources cartographiques et le *Roland furieux*: quelques hypothèses autor de l'"espace réel' chez l'Arioste." In *Espaces réels et espaces imaginaires dans le Roland furieux*, 11–46. Paris: Université de la Sorbonne Nouvelle, 1991.

– *Ptolémée et l'hippogriffe: la géographie de l'Arioste soumise à l'épreuve des cartes.* Alessandria: Edizioni dell'Orso, 1998.

Dürst, Arthur. "Die Europa-Karten von Gerard Mercator, 1554–1595." *Cartographica Helvetica* 10 (1994): 3–19.

Ercilla, Alonso de. *La Araucana*. Editred by Isaías Lerner. Madrid: Cátedra, 1993.

Friedlein, Roger. "El vuelo mágico por los Andes en *El Bernardo* de Bernardo de Balbuena entre dos funcionalidades." *Revista iberoamericana* 253 (2015): 1077–94.

– *Kosmovisionen: Inszenierungen von Wissen und Dichtung im Epos der Renaissance in Frankreich, Portugal und Spanien.* Stuttgart: Franz Steiner Verlag, 2014.

Fumagalli, Giuseppe. *Chi l'ha detto?: tesoro di citazioni italiane e straniere, di origine letteraria e storica, ordinate e annotate.* Milan: Ulrico Hoepli, 1989.

Gómez Canseco, Luis. "Ercilla, Giovio et la geographie du globe." *Les Langues Néo-Latines* 394 (2020): 11–26.

Goñi Echeverría, Íñigo de. "Tradición clásica en el *Bernardo* de Bernardo de Balbuena." PhD thesis, Universidad Complutense de Madrid, 2020.

Gutiérrez, Carlos M. *La espada, el rayo y la pluma: Quevedo y los campos literario y de poder.* Purdue Studies in Romance Literatures 32. West Lafayette, LA: Purdue University Press, 2005.

Harley, John Brian, and David Woodward. *The History of Cartography: Cartograhy in the European Renaissance (vol. 3), (Parts I and II).* Chicago: University of Chicago Press, 2007.

Harvey, P.D.A. *The History of Topographical Maps: Symbols, Pictures and Surveys.* London: Thames-Hudson, 1980.

Hernando, Agustín. *El mapa de España: siglos XV–XVIII.* Madrid: Centro Nacional de Información Geográfica, 1996.

– "The Spanish Contribution to the History of Cartography." *Cartographic Journal* 36 (1999): 111–23.

Herreros Tabernero, Elena. "Las *Geórgicas* de Virgilio en la poesía española." Madrid: Universidad Complutense de Madrid, 1998. https://eprints.ucm.es/id/eprint/3938/.

Homer. *Iliad*. Chicago: University of Chicago Press, 1971.

Jode, Gerard de. *Speculum Orbis Terrarum.* Antwerp: A. Coninx, 1578.

Knitl, Casparo. *Cosmographia Elementaris: Propositionibus Physico-Mathematicis Proposita* ... Prague: Typis Universitatis Carolo-Ferdinandae in Collegium Soc: Jesu ad S. Clementem, 1673.

Luciano de Samosata, "Relatos verídicos." In *Obras*, translated by Andrés Espinosa Alarcón, 176–227. Vol. 1. Madrid: Gredos, 2002.

Magini, Giovanni Antonio. *Geographiae Cl. Prolomaei Pars Secunda*. Venice: Apud Haeredes Simonis Galignani de Karera, 1596.

Magno, Olao. *Carta marina*. Rome: Antonij Lafreri, 1572. http://umedia.lib .umn.edu/node/89541.

– *Carta marina et descriptio septemtrionalium terrarum ac mirabilium rerum in eis contentarum diligentissime elaborata*. Venice: Thome de Rubis, 1539. Facsimile edition. Stockholm: Thulins Antquariat, 1949. https://www.lib.umn.edu /apps/bell/map/OLAUS/TOUR/indext.html.

– *Historia de gentibus septentrionalibus*. Rome: Ioannem Mariam de Viottis Parmensem, 1555.

Mal Lara, Juan de. *Hércules animoso*. Edited by Francisco Javier Escobar Borrego. 3 vols. Mexico City: Frente de Afirmación Hispanista, 2015.

Marineo Siculo, Lucio. *De las cosas memorables de España*. Alcalá de Henares: Juan de Brocar, 1539.

Marino, John A. "The Invention of Europe." In *The Renaissance World*, edited by John Jeffries Martin, 140–65. New York: Routledge, 2007.

Medina, Pedro de. *Libro de las grandezas y cosas memorables de España*. Seville: Dominico de Robertis, 1548.

Menéndez y Pelayo, Marcelino. *Antología de poetas hispanoamericanos*. 4 vols. Madrid: Sucesores de Ribadeneyra, 1893.

Mercator, Gerard. *Drei Karten von Gerhard Mercator: Europa, Britische Inseln, Weltkarte: Fac-simile Lichtdruck nach den Originalen der Statdbibliothek zu Breslau hergestellt von der Reichsdruckerei*. Gesellschaft für Erdkunde. London: Sampson Low & Co., 1891.

Mercator, Gerard, and Rumold Mercator. *Atlas sive cosmographicae meditationes de fabrica mundi et fabricati figura*. Duisburg: Albertus Busius, 1595. https:// www.loc.gov/item/map55000728/.

Meurer, Pete. "Europa Regina: 16th Century Maps of Europe in the Form of a Queen." *Belgeo* 3–4 (2008): 355–70.

Milton, John. *Paradise Lost*. Edited by David Scott Kastan. Cambridge: Hackett Publishing Company, 2005.

Ortelius, Abraham. *Theatro d'el orbe de la tierra*. Antwerp: Plantino, 1602.

– *Theatrum orbis terrarum*. Antwerp: Plantino, 1570. https://www.loc.gov /item/2003683482/.

Padrón, Ricardo. *The Spacious Word: Cartography, Literature, and Empire in Early Modern Spain*. Chicago: University of Chicago Press, 2004.

Parker, Geoffrey. "Maps and Ministers: The Spanish Hapsburgs." In *Monarchs, Ministers, and Maps: The Emergence of Cartography as a Tool of Government in Early Modern Europe*, edited by David Buisseret, 124–52. Chicago: University of Chicago Press, 1992.

Piechocki, Katharina N. *Cartographic Humanism: The Making of Early Modern Europe*. Chicago: University of Chicago Press, 2019.

Ponce Cárdenas, Jesús. *La imitación áurea: Cervantes, Quevedo, Góngora*. Paris: Éditions hispaniques, 2016.

Portuondo, María M. *Ciencia secreta: la cosmografía española y el Nuevo Mundo*. Madrid: Iberoamericana, 2013.

Pulci, Luigi. *Morgante*. Edited by Franca Ageno. Milan-Naples: Riccardo Riccardi Editore, 1955.

Raisz, E. "Introduction." *The Professional Geographer* 2, no. 6 (1950): 9–11.

Ramachandran, Ayesha. *The Worldmakers: Global Imagining in Early Modern Europe*. Chicago: University of Chicago Press, 2015.

Ratcliffe, Marjorie. "Honor y legitimidad: Bernardo del Carpio en el Siglo de Oro." in *Edad de oro cantabrigense: Actas del VII Congreso de la Asociación Internacional de Hispanistas del Siglo de Oro*, edited by Anthony J. Close, 521–6. Madrid: Asociación Internacional del Siglo de Oro, 2006.

Real Academia Española. *Banco de datos (CORDE) [online]. Corpus diacrónico del español*. http://www.rae.es.

Spenser, Edmund. *The Faerie Queene*. Edited by Carol V. Kaske. 5 vols. Indianapolis: Hackett Publishing Company, 2006–7.

Strabo, *Geography*. Translated and edited by Horace L. Jones. 8 vols. London: William Heinemann; New York: G.P. Putnam's Sons, 1917–32.

Tavares de Pinho, Sebastião. "A Descriçao Camoniana Da Europa E Cartografia Ginecomórfica." In *Actas da VI Reunião Internacional de Camonistas*, edited by Seabra Pereira and Manuel Ferro, 251–79. Coimbra: Imprensa da Universidade de Coimbra, 2012.

Van den Broecke, Marcel. *Ortelius Atlas Maps: An Illustrated Guide*. 2nd ed. Houten: HES & de Graaf, 2011.

Van der Heijden, H. a. M. *De oudste gedrukte kaarten van Europa*. Alphen aan den Rijn: Canaletto, 1992.

– "Gedrukte kaarten van Europa vóór Ortelius. Een toevoegsel." *Belgeo. Revue belge de géographie* 3–4 (2008): 269–86.

Van der Krogt, Peter C.J. "The Origin of the Word 'Cartography.'" *e-Perimetron* 140, no. 3 (2015): 124–42.

Van Horne, John. *El Bernardo of Bernardo de Balbuena. A Study of the Poem with Particular Attention to its Relations to the Epics of Boiardo and Ariosto and to its Significance in the Spanish Renaissance*. Urbana: University of Illinois Studies in Language and Literature, vol. 12, no. 1 (1927).

Vega, Lope de. *Laurel de Apolo*. Edited by Antonio Carreño. Madrid: Cátedra, 2007.

Vilà, Lara. "De Roncesvalles a Pavía: Ariosto, la épica española y los poemas sobre Bernardo del Carpio." *Criticón* 115 (2012): 45–65.

Wallis Budge, Ernest Alfred. *The Alexander Book in Ethiopia*. Oxford: Oxford University Press, 1933.

Walser-Bürgler, Isabella. "Geopolitical Instruction and the Construction of Europe in Seventeenth-Century Neo-Latin Texts." In *Contesting Europe: Comparative Perspectives on Early Modern Discourses of Europe, 1400–1800*, edited by Nicolas Detering, Clementina Marsico, and Isabella Walser-Bürgler, 317–46. Leiden: Brill, 2019.

Zapata, Luis. *Carlo famoso*. Valencia: Ioan Mey, 1566.

Zulaica López, Martín. "El espacio en la épica del Siglo de Oro: concepción y concreción en *El Bernardo* de Balbuena." In *Espacios en la Edad Media y el Renacimiento*, compiled by María Morrás, 547–62. Salamanca: SEMYR, 2018.

– "La cartografía como fuente para la redacción épica. El viaje de Alcina a los palacios de Morgana en *El Bernardo* de Balbuena." *Bulletin Hispanique* 121.1 (2019): 227–42.

– "'Obra toda tejida de una admirable variedad de cosas': La écfrasis en *El Bernardo* de Balbuena." *Hipogrifo: Revista de Literatura y Cultura del Siglo de Oro* 4, no. 1 (2016): 171–81.

– "Sobre cartografía y cartodoxia en textos literarios altomodernos. Una propuesta terminológica interlingüística para la historia de las mentalidades." *Avisos de Viena* 3 (2022): 109–13.

– "'Sobre cimientos de alabastro.' Las arquitecturas maravillosas en *El Bernardo* de Balbuena." *Hipogrifo: Revista de Literatura y Cultura del Siglo de Oro* 5, no. 2 (2017): 295–306.

Afterword

MERCEDES BLANCO

Verse made the long narratives of epic poetry pleasing to the Iberian readers of the sixteenth and seventeenth centuries whereas prose tended to tire them, which explains the almost systematic insertion of verse tirades into the prose fictions of that time. For present-day readers, it is rather an obstacle. Almost inaudible for the majority of us, and thus devoid of the pleasures of rhythm, it imposes, especially when it is rhymed, a sought-after vocabulary, circumlocutions, and a style rich in tropes and other ornaments which makes even more obscure the natural opacity of an archaic language. It is not rare, while leafing through these large volumes, to come across a captivating narrative, an impressive description and, from time to time, a line of striking beauty, but this is not enough to overcome the apprehension of those who remain at the door of these vast mazes, for which one generally lacks both a plan and a guide. These barriers to reading remain mostly unspoken because they presuppose, in the person who admits them, a certain lack of courage and curiosity. However, they have always existed, even if they have been aggravated by the passage of time. It was in anticipation of such reluctance that Lope de Vega, so eager to please and so well aware of the resistance of the reader to anything that requires sustained effort, placed on the title page of his *Jerusalén conquistada* (1609) a sentence from the preface of Saint Jerome to his translation of Isaiah: "Let them first read and then despise, so as not to seem to condemn by hateful prejudice things they do not know" (Legant prius et postea despiciant, ne videantur non ex iudicio, sed ex odii presumptione ignorata damnare).

Now the hostile prejudice, which Lope de Vega sensed in his rivals and perhaps especially in Luis de Góngora, is not entirely unfounded. At first glance, there is enough in this literature to justify a principled dislike: several of these epic poems, and among the most renowned, are about the colonial expansion of the Spaniards and Portuguese. Their authors seek to clothe with grandeur and splendour the battles waged against the dangers of the sea, then against the Indigenous peoples, or against the "pirates," emissaries of the rival European powers, without ignoring the civil and internal wars between the Crown and the conquistadors or their descendants, or between the colonists of the first and subsequent generations. Luis de Camões's poem *Os Lusíadas*, a jewel of Portuguese literature (discussed in two of the essays in this volume), celebrates a founding episode of this expansion, Vasco da Gama's expedition of 1497–9. The most famous Spanish-language epic of the sixteenth century, Alonso de Ercilla's *La Araucana* (topic of three of the essays in this volume) focuses on a minor episode of American conquest that will gradually reveal its real and symbolic importance: the armed revolt of Indigenous groups of Chile against European domination, which broke out shortly after the arrival of the Spaniards and which the punitive "pacification" campaigns failed to extinguish in the long term. At first glance, these poems glorify acts of violence responsible for the destruction of millions of people and entire cultures, and they legitimize them in the name of warrior virtues and self-assertion at the expense of others. They express a political allegiance to their nation that degenerates into nationalism, racism, and intolerance. Not to mention the bloodthirsty brutality often shown by the historical heroes of these aggressive operations of expansion: thus, the acts of extreme cruelty committed in the guise of reprisals by Vasco da Gama[1] or by Don García Hurtado de Mendoza, main characters of Camões and Ercilla. The poet usually omits such acts or attributes responsibility for them to subordinates, so that the character in the narrative departs from the man that emerges from the historical sources and appears idealized; in the eyes of readers, contamination of the hero by what is known of the historical character is, however, inevitable. In sum, attaching to such subjects the sublime accents of the epic "song" appears, in the post-colonial era, an unpleasant beautification of crimes against humanity, and a shocking inversion of what should be a cause for shame into a reason for pride.

Of course, all this may seem both too simple and too well known, but we do not fear to hammer home the point that these two very different reasons have been intertwined in the neglect with which Renaissance epics have been long treated. A few canonical works are exceptions: Luis Vaz de Camões'*Os Lusíadas*, Torquato Tasso's *Gerusalemme liberata*, Edmund Spenser's *The Fairie Queen*, and John Milton's *Paradise Lost*, and to a lesser degree *La Araucana*. But it is worth noting that it is as patrimonial monuments of their respective literatures, Portuguese,

Italian, or English, that these reputedly brilliant works have received from the scholars and the most cultured readers of their respective countries a respectful attention. It is not certain yet that this attention has been equal to the stakes: Camões's poem, so praised in Portugal and so well known elsewhere, is still awaiting a critical and commented edition equal to its fame, so much so that it is the lengthy commentary, in Spanish, by Manuel de Faria e Sousa, published in Madrid in 1639, which remains, according to some specialists, the richest sum of information and reflections on the text. *La Araucana* (1569–89), the work of a noble military man, raised in the entourage of Prince Philip, has a particularly unstable position. Around the Centenary of Independence, at the beginning of the twentieth century, it was treated as a literary monument of the young Chilean republic: that earned it a very careful edition – oversized to the point of being almost unusable – from José Toribio Medina (1910–18). However, Ercilla did not spend more than a year and a half in the territory of present-day Chile, and only stayed in America for eight years in all, as a soldier serving his king. Juan de Castellanos's *Elegías de varones ilustres de Indias* had a similar fate in Colombian literature, which is a less surprising case if we take into account the personality of the author. Born of Andalusian peasants, Castellanos emigrated at a very young age in 1539, and having made his fortune as a merchant and priest in New Granada, ended his life as a notable of the city of Tunja, located in present-day Colombia. However, it is the perspective of the conquerors that he adopts in his huge and fragmented account of the beginnings of the colonization of New Granada and the adjacent territories (from the first voyage of Christopher Columbus in 1492 to the capture of Cartagena by Francis Drake in 1586). According to Martínez-Osorio, the long poem is neither triumphalist nor typical of a creole: it consistently adopts the feelings and ideas of a Spanish military caste that was about to be defeated in its fight for the administrative and economic control of the colony.[2]

These poems, written from the viewpoint of the actors of the conquest, could not keep the costume of national founders in which they were sometimes dressed without postulating a form of continuity between the era of the conquests (by the "illustrious men of Indies") and the rise of modern homelands, Chilean or Colombian. This role of fathers of the nation could only be bestowed on them at the cost of a reconciliation of the original antagonisms of colonial America in a viable and original synthesis. Some believed it was possible in the first half of the twentieth century, when the indigenous pride of certain intellectuals was easily combined with a culture and a mentality of European bourgeois. The citizens of Chile, white or mestizo, could imagine themselves heirs to the indomitable Araucanian warriors glimpsed or imagined by Ercilla. Such a position today is much more difficult, even if for the second centenary of Chilean independence, in 2010, some modest tributes were paid to the memory of Ercilla as father of the nation.[3] In addition to the decline of nationalism and its naiveté, the transformation of a Spanish courtier like Ercilla, a Spanish captain like Villagrá, or a Spanish priest like Castellanos into the great official bard respectively of Chile, New Mexico, and Colombia encounters a powerful obstacle in the presence, even today, of Indigenous communities hardly less hostile to the states by which they feel oppressed than their remote ancestors were to the Spanish colonizers. Very distant from us by its idealism, by its language, and by the medieval and humanist roots of the culture it handles, the Iberian epic poem nevertheless highlights sometimes issues that are still burning.

In any case, a little more than one hundred years after José Toribio Medina's edition, it is Spain, through an official institution, the Real Academia de España, that has taken on the task of confirming *La Araucana*'s status as a classic of the Spanish language. Francisco Rico, creator and director of the collection Biblioteca Clásica, now under the aegis of the Royal Academy, entrusted a leading scholar, Luis Gómez Canseco, with the task of producing a compact, materially beautiful edition endowed with a critical apparatus and an annotation commensurate with the fame of the work. This edition, currently in press, will represent a big step forward in our knowledge of the poem.[4] The least we can say, though, is that the path of *La Araucana* to a canonical position has been long and full of pitfalls, due to, among other things, its constitutive division between Spain and Chile, between Spanish and Araucan heroes.

Tasso's *Gerusalemme* and Milton's *Paradise Lost* present the clearest examples of early modern epics that enjoy the rank of great classics. Without denying the dazzling beauty that set them apart, this distinction can be explained by their respective subject matters, which have more to do with Christian myth than with history, and which are free of overt political or national implications. They are therefore relatively safe from a reception conditioned by the vagaries of ideological recovery or rejection. It is true that they do not escape the confessional fracture lines between the atmosphere of the Catholic Counter-Reformation which surrounded the painful delivery of the poem of Tasso and that of the Protestant puritanism affecting Milton's mind. In any case, they are literary monuments solid enough to survive the thorny questions of "genre" posed by *Paradise Lost* and the explosive charge attached to the idea of crusade, and to the memory of the bloody capture of Jerusalem that *Gerusalemme liberata* sings. Epic seems to need changes of era before its eminently political character is defused. This consideration is particularly true of the Iberian epic, whose most famous examples are related, as we have seen, to the prominence of the Spanish and Portuguese in the early phases of European colonial expansion. The appreciation of this enterprise has not yet lost, five centuries later, its capacity to divide by virtue of partisan affiliations.

Yet, far from reinforcing each other, the two reasons for disaffection with this epic that we have recalled cast some discredit on each other: moral disapproval may seem, to those who refrain from looking more closely, a mere alibi for laziness. The number, extent, and complexity of the texts, which discourage reading, also allow us to suppose that it is reductive to see in them simple celebratory or propaganda undertakings. Even before reading them, it would be fair to conjecture that there must be in these so long, so stylistically elaborate accounts, which for their authors were often the work of a lifetime, something other than a purpose of flattering the powerful, and exalting victories and conquests. On the other hand, the pure and simple ignorance of what the poems have to tell us is not an adequate response to the unsavoury character of the actions they report. This kind of response, carried to its final consequences, would involve burying most of the narratives and representations of our cultures' past and present. The poems we have just named, *Os Lusíadas* and *La Araucana*, as well as others, are related to the models of the ancient epic, and also to the chivalric literature, to the Petrarchanism, to the eclogue, and to the amorous lyric, genres that had formed in the cradle the medieval courts and transformed in the Renaissance. The aim of imitating Virgil's *Aeneid*, which is the common base of many of these works, is not only to get closer to a model of incomparable authority, but also to use the most refined and ingenious poetic devices to ask political questions that have an obvious analogy with those which were posed in Augustan Rome. For epic poetry is indeed about open questions, submitting to a subtle elaboration and to a dialectic full of detours and not admitting to simple answers. The loves and the enchantments of the knightly world, of which our poets try to do without sometimes, but to which they return by a kind of invincible gravitation, show well the difficulty of detaching the heroic story from the courtly universe, on the side of arms as well as of that of love. This remains true when the purpose is to praise the prowess of a nation since the chivalrous spirit introduces into the narrative a strongly subjective bias, implying criticism and a half-suppressed revolt.

Regardless of any moral or even aesthetic judgment, one should not ignore such a strenuous effort to put into narrative events whose meaning and significance were crucial for their contemporaries, and which initiated a history in which we remain immersed. If a good part of these poems speak of wars and perilous journeys, ones which had a traumatic effect on those who experienced them, they can be seen as attempts to heal from these traumas. They aim to re-establish continuity beyond the rupture, and to integrate the new into a tradition. If it is permissible to spend some effort on a literature that is difficult to recuperate in terms of comfortable consumption for today's readers and even students, one is therefore justified in rigorously studying these epic texts from Portugal and Spain of the early modern era.

This book is a progress report in the path towards the realization of this aim, demonstrating where the academic communities of Europe and America are currently engaged on the topic. During the last decades, the publications have multiplied and the ways of approaching the problems have become diversified and refined. Recently some scholars have taken note of this new departure. Thus, Karl Kohut, in the first lines of a 2014 paper (limited to literature in the Spanish language), observed: "Después de un olvido prolongado de más de tres siglos, la épica hispana de los siglos XVI y XVII ha despertado nuevo interés, lo que atestigua el número de estudios aparecidos a partir de los años 90 del siglo pasado, y de varias reediciones de poemas épicos que habían sobrevivido solo en los manuales de literatura."[5] Two years earlier, in an essay titled "Volver a un género olvidado, la poesía épica del Siglo de Oro," Rodrigo Cacho Casal wrote: "La llamada épica culta o literaria recibió, en cambio, menos favores y la mayoría de estos textos permanecen sin estudiar o editar ... las cosas comenzaron a tomar un nuevo rumbo a partir de 1999."[6] These two very different scholars, without the benefit of any consultation, coincide in their diagnosis of a new start of the research that they situate at the beginning of the third millennium. They illustrate this statement by citing a cluster of books published around 2000: José Lara Garrido's *Los mejores plectros. Teoría y práctica de la epica culta en el siglo XVI* (1999), Elizabeth Davis's *Myth and Identity in the Epic of Imperial Spain* (2000), and Lara Vilà's thesis, *Épica e imperio. Imitación virgiliana y propaganda política en la epica española del siglo XVI* (2001).

Kohut also cites James Nicolopulos's book, *The Poetics of Empire in the Indies. Prophecy and Imitation in "La Araucana" and "Os Lusíadas"* (2001). Neither of them mentions a work that deserves it more than any other, but whose language, Portuguese, and publication by a Portuguese university press, did not facilitate its diffusion: *Camões, Corte-Real e o sistema da epopeia quinientista* (2001) by Hélio Alves, an author who honoured us with a contribution to this volume. Neither Kohut nor Cacho Casal mention Ricardo Padrón's book, very influential in the United States, *The Spacious World: Cartography, Literature and Empire in Early Modern*

Spain (2004), which bases its most original theses on daring interpretations of *La Araucana*. This book derives, after significant reworking, from a thesis defended at Harvard in 1997: *Travels without a Hippogriff. Cartography and Literature in Early Modern Spain*. It too belongs therefore to this extended year 2000, which was apparently an *annus mirabilis* for the study of Iberian epics. In a field almost deserted until then, the almost simultaneous publication of this handful of books of some scope seems surprising. In their retrospective review, Cacho Casal and Kohut note this sudden eruption without attempting to explain it. In any case, it will serve as a milestone or a pretext, in the brief considerations that follow, to outline some questions that emerge after reading this book, without doing again what Emiro Martínez-Osorio's introduction does so well: to show the topicality of the approach of the papers gathered here and the relevance of their collection.

We will ask ourselves, first of all, what can explain this cluster of publications around the year 2000, given that their authors conducted their investigations in ignorance of each other and with profoundly dissimilar methods and conceptual tools. We will see that despite their disparate character and their unequal diffusion, these works have been fruitful in several respects and have contributed to the expansion of research on the field that has characterized the last twenty years. Finally, we will ask the questions: what is happening now? what points seem to have been generally admitted that were not in 2000? and in what directions do we seem to be moving today?

With regard to the first point, the aforementioned publications produced at the turns of the twentieth and twenty-first centuries lead us to observe the emphasis placed by their authors on the concept of imitation (Vilà, Nicolopulos, Lara Garrido, Alves) and on the notion of empire (Vilà, Nicolopulos, Davis, Padrón). The epics, in the Iberian Peninsula as elsewhere, are imitations-emulations of the *Aeneid* and *Orlando furioso*, sometimes with the supplement of Lucan and Homer, and punctual resonances of the later Latin epic (from Stace to Claudian). On the other hand, some earlier epics that were particularly successful were a model for the subsequent ones: so, Camões's for Iberian poets, Ercilla's for a number of Spaniards, and Tasso's for the European epics written after 1590. At the same time, ignoring or minimizing the divorce of poetry and history posed by Aristotle, many authors (not all of them) see themselves as historians. Consequently, they draw part of their tools, features of style, and method, often the facts they report, from ancient and modern historiography. In the cluster of papers and books around 2000, the reflection on the Spanish and Portuguese epics takes for the first time fully into account their non-linear connection to the classical tradition. To sum up, the Virgilian epic was reborn in the sixteenth century in light of *Orlando furioso*, thus combining the highest classical authority with the seductiveness of a poem that met with immense success among courtiers, soldiers, women, and all sorts of moderately literate people. Ariosto's poem, nourished by classical culture and the great vernacular poetry of Dante and Petrarch, was understood to belong to the genre of the *romanzo*, in which some saw a modulation of the ancient epic, while others postulated an entirely different and modern genre, not subject to Aristotelian precepts.

Now the field of forces induced by this polarity between epic and *romanzo*, between Virgil and Ariosto, between the rigour of the ancient and the freedom of the modern, complicated still by the aspiration to tell the truth and to do justice to historical feats, generates in the Iberian epic a formal complexity and a multitude of technical problems that make their study highly rewarding. In order to be fully aware of this, we needed a perspective acquired through the analysis of the path that goes from Ariosto to Tasso. In other words, the first step had to be an accurate knowledge of the rebirth of epics in the Renaissance by means of an intense discussion carried out throughout the sixteenth century in the Italy of courts, academies, and universities. Two generations of scholars at least ought to make visible the efforts of Renaissance humanists, poets, thinkers, and publicists in their quest for the so-called *poema eroico*, the reasons of their hopes, their successes, and their failures. The task was achieved in the last decades of the twentieth century: we owe a clear and articulate view of it to the efforts of Bowra, Bruscagli, Burrow, Caretti, Chevalier, Durling, Fichter, Greene, Javitch, Jossa, Meletinskij, and Zatti (among other scholars).

On the other hand, we notice with more or less intensity in this small group of publications around 2000 a putting forward of the notion of empire. The idea of empire incites a reading of the poems in phase with the New Historicism, more powerful and more pugnacious in America than in Europe. Following this movement, literature participates in the construction of ideas and symbolic forms by means of which human beings seek to configure the history that shapes them, especially in its turning points and crises. From this point of view, it cooperates in its own way in an enterprise to which other discourses, considered as non-literary, and other practices of representation and regulation, contribute with the same claims for consideration, among them painting, architecture, theology, but also pharmacopoeia, festivals, or cartography. It is in this spirit that we can decline, as far as Spain and Portugal are concerned, the question of epic and empire: by what rhetoric of legitimization and praise or, on the contrary, by what admission of doubts and anxieties, by what negotiation of the impulsive and social forces at play in them and around them, do Portuguese and Spanish poets accompany with their epics the construction of their respective empires? In other words: the construction of territories and cities, of centres and marginalities; of hierarchies and values; of dominants and dominated.

The idea of interrogating the empire after the epic, or the epic as empire builder – something which stands out neatly in Davis's monograph, in Vilà's thesis, and in Nicolopulos's and Padrón's works – received a strong impulse from David Quint's slightly earlier book, *Epic and Empire. Politics and Generic form From Virgil to Milton* (1993), and to a lesser extent from Michael Murrin's *History and Warfare in Renaissance Epic* (1994). Quint succeeded in the risky challenge of rereading the main milestones of the epic tradition, from Virgil to Eisenstein, as the conflict and combined influence of two ways and two attitudes, derived respectively from Virgil and Lucan (the latter strangely put in the same category of "romance" as Ariosto). What is particularly interesting, from my point of view, is that these brilliant books, in their sweeping picture of the epic genre in Europe between antiquity and the Renaissance, gave a prominent place to the Portuguese epic of Camões and to epics in the Spanish language: for Quint, those of Alonso de Ercilla and Gaspar de Villagrá; for Murrin, these as well, but also those of Pedro de Oña and Juan Rufo.

The ideas agitated and put to the test around 2000 animated the discussion in the two decades that followed. The opposition of an epic of the victors and another of the vanquished, or the confrontation between questions of military technology and poetic choices,[7] has been rich in developments for Spanish and Portuguese epics. It is clear that the epic that sings of the "victors" of the colonial enterprise often casts doubt on the legitimacy of their actions and puts into the mouths of the "vanquished," who sometimes win, eloquent pleadings and indictments that reveal flaws in the consciousness of the actors of the conquest. The political and ideological field is much too unstable and complex to make possible a monolithically official poetry, especially when it is a question of a narrative about conflicts and calamities that bring into play various levels of responsibility, merit, and fault: the subjective bias and the particular interests of each poet largely counterbalance the great collective enterprise of "propaganda" or of "building the empire." The concept of propaganda is, moreover, obviously inadequate because, contrary to Augustus, builder of the Ara Pacis or sponsor of the Secular Games, the kings of Portugal and Spain never led concerted actions to encourage literary or other monuments to the glory of their monarchy, and even less so of their "empire," since the mere notion is absent from their vocabulary. If they approved or rewarded these initiatives, it was rarely, weakly, and always after the fact – something about which the poets regularly complained.

Many critics consider that the admiration or compassion for the defeated Indigenous peoples (and also Indians, Ottomans, and other "barbarians" and "infidels") displayed by poets like Corte-Real, Ercilla, Castellanos, or Rufo only serves – following in the footsteps of Virgil – in a roundabout way their royal and imperial propaganda purpose. This is how Lara Vilà sees things, without any nuance; in a more sophisticated way, but restricting his field to the confrontation-rivalry of Camões and Ercilla, Nicolopulos sustains the same view, in spite of taking into account the book of Quint, who himself thought Ercilla an anti-imperialist poet. Some even go so far as to attribute to the poets perfidious strategies of allusion in order to lower the subjugated natives, or even to sexually humiliate and emasculate them: thus Ricardo Padrón, followed by several others, reads Ercilla's cartographic imaginary a bit like a dream decipherer, through an erotic symbolism of a somewhat sadistic kind.

Nevertheless, the awareness of the complexity of the works and of the genre as a whole seems to be more and more widespread. Scholars have become sensitive to the need for editions that fix the texts, that solve their many difficulties of detail, that describe their architecture and style, that gather sufficient information about their authors, their circumstances, and their sources. Such editions have appeared in the last two decades in perhaps equal or greater numbers than in the entire preceding century. Without pretending to be exhaustive, we will mention *Alteraciones del Dariel* (Orjuela, 1994); *Poema del asalto y conquista de Antequera* (Martínez Iniesta, 2000); *La hermosura de Angélica* (Trambaioli, 2005); *De Cortés valeroso y Mexicana* (Pullés-Linares, 2005); *Armas antárticas* (Firbas, 2006); *La Dragontea* (Sánchez Jiménez, 2007); *El peregrino indiano* (Rodilla León, 2008); *Historia de la Nueva México* (Martín Rodríguez, 2010); *Espejo de paciencia* (Marrero-Fente, 2010); *Segundo cerco de Diu* (Labrador & Di Franco, 2011); *Austríada* (Cichetti, 2011); *Sepúlveda e Lianor, canto I* (Alves, 2014); *Arauco domado* (Gianesin, 2014); *Austrias carmen* (Wright, 2014); *Hércules animoso* (Escobar Borrego, 2015); and *Bernardo o victoria de Roncesvalles* (Zulaica López, 2019). Collecting these books, despite the dispersed nature of their places of publication and their restricted distribution, is today within the reach of any public or private library. We hope that these publishing activities will continue, providing a more solid foundation for the critical and historical research enterprise on the Iberian epic.

If one had to characterize in a simple way the new orientations of this enterprise in the last twenty years, perhaps the notion of decompartmentalization would be expedient and encompassing. Epic poetry can no longer be isolated from the literary field as a whole; if the sixteenth-century epic constitutes "a system," to use the term of Hélio Alves, it is a flexible system, in permanent communication with the other genres and with the entire literature. The variety of the episodes that the poems contain transforms them in hybrid and quasi-encyclopedic productions, permeable to the integration of allogeneous elements: from the tragedy to the pastoral and to the elegy, from lyric poetry to the panegyric and to the satire, from history to allegory and to the pagan and Christian marvellous. The very diversity of the classical models that came to nourish epic poetry, and the complexity of these models, from Homer to Claudian passing by Virgil and Lucan, but also by Lucretius, by Ovid, and by Stace, support a remarkable capacity of dynamism and metamorphosis. In the seventeenth century, the notion of heroic style developed by Torquato Tasso, and that of the sublime, which emerges from the rediscovery of the treaty of the Pseudo-Longinus, blur the borders still further, and move certain elements of the epic tradition towards the panegyric, towards the "fable," derivation of the Alexandrian and Ovidian epyllion, as well as towards sacred, hagiographic, or biblical poetry. The authors of the latter were often defectors forced to negotiate between a Judaism in crisis and divided, and a Christianity no less problematic. All this without counting the derived, but no less refined, forms of the heroic-comic and burlesque poem, with their animal wars or travesties of myths.

This unifying character of the epic, insofar as it blurs borders and annexes territories, is particularly noticeable in America. It emerges in the fine collection devoted by Rodrigo Cacho Casal and Imogen Choi to Spanish poetry produced across the Atlantic, *The Rise of Spanish American Poetry (1500–1700)* (2019). Only the third and final section of the book, under the title "Epic Poetry and the New Frontier," discusses openly epic poetry, but the problematic of the genre permeates other contributions. In order to take this into account, we decided to mark the chronological boundaries of *The War Trumpet* with two dates that are not those of epic poems: 1543, the year when *Obras de Boscán y algunas de Garcilaso de la Vega* was published in Barcelona, and 1639, the year when Manuel de Faria e Sousa's extensive commentary on *Os Lusíadas* appeared in Madrid. Emiro Martínez-Osorio has perfectly explained this chronology in the introduction to this volume. In addition to the reasons he gives, I could add that Garcilaso de la Vega and Boscán, through the apparently purely technical importation of Italian metrics brought to the Peninsula a poetry that naturalized the language of humanism. Spanish poetry thus became able to integrate the classical models, and among them were those of Virgil and the epic. Without the hendecasyllabic, so well handled by Garcilaso, without the *octava real*, as a close transposition of the ottava rima, the vast majority of epic poems written in the Iberian world for two centuries would have been unthinkable. Many would hardly be possible without Garcilaso's self-fashioning as a poet who holds both sword and pen. It is this same humanistic conception of a learned, encyclopedic poetry, but marked by the authority of a singular personality and endowed with military freedom and frankness, that leads, almost a century later, to a commentary as copious as that of Manuel de Faria e Sousa.

On the other hand, it has become clear that Iberian poets, on both sides of the Spanish-Portuguese border, had a great deal in common, in the period of the Union of the Crowns (1580–1640), but also before and after. A close network of links was established between these two Iberian powers, bringing together and opposing men and texts. It is probably much more accurate and promising to consider their belonging to a "peninsular literary field," as Galbarro and Plagnard have proposed,[8] than to confine them to national literatures, and this regardless of the thorny, and perhaps poorly posed, question of their imperialist or anti-imperialist design. This issue is one of the focuses of Aude Plagnard's insightful book, *Une épopée ibérique* (2019), which reads a small group of epics published around 1570, two by the Portuguese Corte-Real (in Portuguese and Spanish) and one, in three parts, by the Spanish Ercilla. At the end of reading her analysis, one tends to agree with her and to think that it is relevant to look at the whole set as a single epic, of course Iberian.

This epic, rooted in the ancient past and especially in the memory of Rome, links its fate to the uprooting of these many men and women from Portugal and Spain, who flee the peninsula or who return to it, as a result of the fragmentation of a monarchy torn apart in the four corners of Europe and that had to keep open the routes crossing the oceans. Their dispersion responds to the dissemination of the subjects of this Iberian monarchy, which sends its nobles, its merchants, its soldiers, its lawyers, its monks, its heretics, and its Judeao-Christians all over the world. This reality of the object seems to call for a transnational and transoceanic framework for literary studies, and particularly for the epic genre, which is often nomadic given its authors and its subject matter.

For the members of this population on the move, faced with experiences that are variously exhilarating or trying, the homeland is no longer bounded by the walls of a city. They tend to inhabit a language, often Castilian, even when they were born in Portugal or Guatemala, and to let themselves be rocked by the rhythms of Castilian and Portuguese verse, octosyllabic or hendecasyllabic. Sometimes they choose the prestigious but malleable form of the long narrative poem, to tell a story of wars or travels, of victorious or slaughtered peoples, of holiness or wandering, chosen for a purpose often very different from that announced in the ritual "proposition." The poem, while pretending to sing great men and founding enterprises, tries to put forward a cause which is often that of the author himself, or of the more or less dissident and marginal group to which he belongs. This group may be that of the military, which in its incessant displacements, shares the soil of a common culture and a Republic of Letters all its own, in which writing serves as an entertainment, an outlet, and a distinction. Miguel Martínez has dedicated a book and some papers to these soldiers, and to the way they practise certain forms of epic poetry; they are among the most stimulating research carried out in this field in the last years.

The one who takes the challenge of wearing the prestigious costume of the epic poet pours into his work, often written and rewritten over many years, the memory of all his reading, all his knowledge of language and world, all his rhetorical skill, all his talent as a storyteller and his power to depict men and things. By means of different stories that he incorporates into his narration, of arms and loves, of victories and defeats, stories in which fiction always has its place, he tries to conduct a mental experiment, and he puts to the test the political and ethical notions and principles that he has at his disposal, whether he has drawn them from conversations or from literature. Taking this circumstance into account, Imogen Choi, in published papers and in a coming book derived from her thesis, conducts a close reading of *La Araucana* as the pursuit of an argument around some of Machiavelli's ideas about the art of war and the reasons of success and failure in the practice of government.

In other "Peruvian" epics, those of Pedro de Oña and Juan de Miramontes Zuázola, she discovers, by the same method of close reading and the confrontation with a political culture, a polemical knot, an affair of parties and interests precisely situated in the actuality of the writing. One understands, therefore, that the epic poem can become an instrument for a political reading of the world, led from historically precise circumstances. This reading, always partial and tendentious, is also always open to complexity and contradiction. In short, the research of Aude Plagnard, who participates in this volume, of Miguel Martínez and Imogen Choi, whom the contributors know well, emanating from youthful personalities and full of originality, discreetly mark some of the most promising directions in which the study of the epic could engage in the immediate future.

NOTES

1 During his second voyage, not narrated in the Camões's poem, he burnt alive several hundreds of passengers of an Arabian vessel he had captured.
2 Martínez-Osorio, *Authority, Piracy and Captivity in Colonial Spanish American Writing*, xii.
3 See Martínez and Huenún, *Memoria poética*.
4 In the last forty years, the most widely used critical editions of *La Araucana* were the ones produced by Marcos A. Morínigo and Isaías Lerner.
5 Kohut, "La teoría de la épica en el Renacimiento y el Barroco hispanos y la épica Indiana."
6 Cacho Casal, "Volver a un género olvidado, la poesía épica del Siglo de Oro."
7 See Murrin, *History and Warfare in Renaissance Epic*.
8 Galbarro and Plagnard, "Literatura áurea ibérica. La construcción de un campo literario peninsular en los siglos XVI y XVII."

WORKS CITED

Alves, Hélio J.S. *Camões, Corte-Real e o sistema da epopeia quinhentista*. Coimbra: Centro Interuniversitário de Estudos Camonianos, 2001.
– *Sepúlveda e Lianor. Canto primeiro* [de Jerónimo de Corte-Real]. Lisbon: Centro Interuniversitario de Estudos Camonianos, 2014.
Bowra, Cecil M. *From Virgil to Milton*. London: Macmillan, 1945.
Bruscagli, Riccardo. *Stagioni della civiltà estense*. Pisa: Nistri-Lischi, 1983.
Burrow, Colin J. *Epic Romance: Homer to Milton*. Oxford: Clarendon Press, 1988.
Cacho Casal, Rodrigo. "Volver a un género olvidado: la poesía épica del Siglo de Oro." *Criticón* 115 (2012): 5–10.
Cacho Casal, Rodrigo, and Imogen Choi, eds. *The Rise of Spanish American Poetry 1500–1700: Literary and Cultural Transmission in the New World*. Oxford: Legenda, 2019.
Camões, Luís de. *Lusíadas de Luis de Camões comentadas por Manuel de Faria i Sousa*. Madrid: Ivan Sanchez a costa de Pedro Coello, 1639.
Caretti, Lanfranco. *Ariosto e Tasso*. Turin: Einaudi, 1961.
Castellanos, Juan de. *Primera parte de las elegías de varones ilustres de Indias*. Madrid: En casa de la viuda de Alonso Gómez, 1589.
Chevalier, Maxime. *L'Arioste et l'Espagne (1530–1650). Recherches sur l'influence du "Roland furieux."* Bordeaux: Université de Bordeaux, 1966.
Choi, Imogen (née Sutton). "'De gente que a ningún rey obedecen': Republicanism and Empire in Alonso de Ercilla's *La Araucana*." *Bulletin Hispanic Studies* 91, no. 4 (2014): 417–35.
Choi, Imogen. "¿'Adonde falta el rey, sobran agravios' (IV.5)? The Battle of Saint-Quentin and Two Worlds of War in Alonso de Ercilla's *La Araucana*."

In *Artifice and Invention in the Spanish Golden Age*, edited by Stephen Boyd and Terence O'Reilly, 173–84. London: Legenda, 2014.

Cichetti, Ester, ed. *La Austríada*. By Juan Rufo. Pavia: Ibis, 2011.

Davis, Elizabeth B. *Myth and Identity in the Epic of Imperial Spain*. Columbia: University of Missouri Press, 2000.

Durling, Robert M. *The Figure of the Poet in Renaissance Epic*. Cambridge, MA: Harvard University Press, 1965.

Escobar Borrego, Francisco Javier, ed. *Hércules animoso*. By Juan de Mal Lara. 3 vols. México: Frente de afirmación hispanista, 2015.

Fichter, Andrew. *Poets Historical: Dynastic Epic in the Renaissance*. New Haven, CT: Yale University Press, 1982.

Firbas, Paul, ed. *Armas antárticas*. By Juan de Miramontes Zuázola. Lima: Pontificia Universidad Católica del Perú, 2006.

Galbarro, Jaime, and Aude Plagnard. "Literatura áurea ibérica. La construcción de un campo literario peninsular en los siglos XVI y XVII." *e-Spania* 27 (2017). http://journals.openedition.org.janus.bis-sorbonne.fr/e-spania/26636.

Gianesin, Ornella, ed. *Arauco domado*. By Pedro de Oña. Pavia: Ibis, 2014.

Greene, Thomas M. *The Descent from Heaven: A Study in Epic Continuity*. New Haven, CT: Yale University Press, 1963.

Javitch, Daniel. *Proclaiming a Classic: The Canonization of "Orlando furioso."* Princeton, NJ: Princeton University Press, 1991.

Jossa, Stefano. *La fondazione di un genere. Il poema eroico tra Ariosto e Tasso*. Rome: Carocci, 2002.

Kohut, Karl. "La teoría de la épica en el Renacimiento y el Barroco hispanos y la épica Indiana." *Nueva Revista de Filología Hispánica* 62 (2014): 33–66.

Labrador Herraiz, José J., and Ralph A. DiFranco. *La verdadera historia y admirable suceso del Segundo Cerco de Diu*. Translation of a poem of Jerónimo Corte-Real by Pedro de Padilla. Mexico: Frente de Afirmación hispanista, 2011.

Lara Garrido, José. *Los mejores plectros. Teoría y práctica de la épica culta en el Siglo de oro*. Málaga: Analecta Malacitana, 1999.

Latino, Juan. *Austrias carmen*. In *The Battle of Lepanto*, edited by Elizabeth Wright, Sarah Spence, and Andrew Lemons. Cambridge, MA: Harvard University Press, 2014.

Marrero-Fente, Raúl, ed. *Espejo de paciencia*. By Silvestre de Balboa. Madrid: Cátedra, 2010.

Martín Rodríguez, Manuel M., ed. *Historia de la Nueva México*. By Gaspar de Villagrá. Alcalá: Universidad de Alcalá, 2010.

Martínez, Luz Ángela, and Jaime Huenún. *Memoria poética. Reescrituras de "La Araucana."* Santiago: Editorial Cuarto Propio, 2010.

Martínez, Miguel. *Front Lines: Soldiers Writing in the Early Modern Hispanic World*. Philadelphia: University of Pennsylvania Press, 2016.

Martínez Iniesta, Bautist. *Poema del asalto y conquista de Antequera*. By Rodrigo de Carvajal y Robles. Málaga: Universidad de Málaga, 2000.

Martínez-Osorio, Emiro. *Authority, Piracy and Captivity in Colonial Spanish American Writing: Juan de Castellanos' Elegies of Illustrious Men of the Indies*. Lewisburg, PA: Bucknell University Press, 2016.

Medina, José Toribio. *La Araucana*. 5 vols. Santiago: Imprenta Elzaviriana, 1910–18.

Melentinjski, Eleazar M. *Introduzione alla poetica storica dell'Epos e del Romanzo*. Bologna: Il Mulino, 1993.

Murrin, Michael. *History and Warfare in Renaissance Epic*. Chicago: University of Chicago Press, 1994.

Nicolopulos, James. *The Poetics of Empire in the Indies: Prophecy and Imitation in "La Araucana" and "Os Lusíadas."* University Park: Pennsylvania State University Press, 2000.

Orjuela, Hector H., ed. *Alteraciones del Dariel*. By Juan Francisco de Páramo y Cepeda. Bogotá: Editorial Kelly, 1994.

Plagnard, Aude. *Une épopée ibérique: Alonso de Ercilla et Jerónimo Corte-Real (1569–1589)*. Madrid: Casa de Velázquez, 2019.

Pullés-Linares, Nidia, ed. *De Cortés valeroso y Mexicana*. By Gabriel Lasso de la Vega. Frankfurt-Madrid: Iberoamericana-Vervuert, 2005.

Quint, David. *Epic and Empire: Politics and Generic Form from Virgil to Milton*. Princeton, NJ: Princeton University Press, 1993.

Rodilla León, María José, ed. *El peregrino indiano*. By Antonio de Saavedra y Guzmán. Madrid: Iberoamericana, 2008.

Sánchez Jiménez, Antonio, ed. *La Dragontea*. By Lope de Vega. Madrid: Cátedra, 2007.

Segas, Lise, ed. "La épica en el mundo hispano (Siglo de Oro)." Monographic issue of *Bulletin Hispanique* 121, no. 1 (2019).

Trambaioli, Marcella, ed. *La hermosura de Angélica. Poema de Lope de Vega Carpio*. Madrid-Frankfurt: Universidad de Navarra-Iberoamericana-Vervuert, 2005.

Vilà, Lara. *Épica e imperio. Imitación virgiliana y propaganda política en la épica española del siglo XVI*. Barcelona: Universitat Autònoma de Barcelona. Serveix de Publicacions, 2001.

Zatti, Sergio. *L'ombra del Tasso. Epica e romanzo nel Cinquecento*. Milan: Mondadori, 1996.

– *The Quest for Epic: From Ariosto to Tasso*. Toronto: University of Toronto Press, 2006.

Zulaica López, Martín, ed. *El Bernardo o victoria de Roncesvalles*. By Bernardo Balbuena. 2 vols. Madrid: Ars poética, 2017.

Contributors

Hélio J.S. Alves is Professor of Portuguese Literature at the University of Lisbon. His field of research is European Renaissance literature, with special reference to Portuguese. He is the author of *Camões, Corte-Real e o Sistema da Epopeia Quinhentista* (2001). In English, his research has appeared in the journals *Modern Philology* and *Bulletin of Hispanic Studies*, among others; in the volumes *The Reinvention of Theatre in Sixteenth-Century Europe* (2015) and *Milton in Translation* (2017); and in reference works (*Princeton Encyclopedia of Poetry and Poetics*; *Oxford Bibliographies*). His most recent book is a bilingual anthology (Portuguese and English) co-authored with Landeg White: *Poetas Que Não Eram Camões/Poets Who Weren't Camões* (2018).

Mercedes Blanco is *Professeur des Universités, classe exceptionnelle* at Sorbonne Université and a membre of the Institut de France. A scholar of sixteenth- and seventeenth-century Spanish literature, she has published many articles and book chapters on the subject, in addition to several on early modern Italian authors and Jorge Luis Borges. She is the author of *Les rhétoriques de la pointe: Baltasar Gracián et le conceptisme en Europe* (1992), *Introducción al comentario de la poesía amorosa de Quevedo* (1998), *Góngora heroico: Las "Soledades" y la tradición épica* (2012), and *Góngora o la invención de una lengua* (2012). She has also edited several collections of essays, among them *Tres momentos de cambio en la creación literaria del Siglo de Oro* (2014), *Villes à la croisée des langues (XVIᵉ–XVIIᵉ siècles): Anvers, Hambourg, Milan, Naples et Palerme* (2018, with Roland Béhar), *Controversias y poesía (de Garcilaso a Góngora)* (2019, with Juan Montero), and *El universo de una polémica. Góngora y la cultura española del siglo XVII* (with Aude Plagnard). She is also the founder, editor, and a contributor to the *Góngora et les querelles littéraires de la Renaissance*, which makes available at no cost critical and annotated editions of almost thirty texts written in the seventeenth century in Spain and Spanish America as part of the controversy surrounding Góngora's major poems.

Nicole Delia Legnani is assistant professor of Spanish at Princeton University. She is the translator of *Titu Cusi: A 16th-Century Inca Account of the Conquest* (2006) and author of *The Business of Conquest: Empire, Love and Law in the Atlantic World* (2020). Her work on Juana Inés de la Cruz has appeared in *Bulletin of Hispanic Studies* and *Romance Notes*. Her essays on the imbrication of capitalism with the category of the *natural*, as articulated in the works of Christopher Columbus and Bartolomé de Las Casas, are available in *Latin American Culture and the Limits of the Human* (2020) and *The Routledge Hispanic Studies Companion to Colonial Latin America and the Caribbean* (2020).

Emiro Martínez-Osorio is associate professor of Spanish at York University. He is the author of *Authority, Piracy and Captivity in Colonial Spanish America: Juan de Castellanos' "Elegies of Illustrious Men of the Indies"* (2016). His scholarly articles have appeared in *Calíope: Journal of the Society for Renaissance and Baroque Hispanic Poetry*, *Revista Canadiense de Estudios Hispánicos*, and *Cuadernos de Literatura*. In 2013, he collaborated with Emelie Chhangur, Assistant Director of the Art Gallery of York University, in preparing a bilingual (Spanish/English) catalogue of the art exhibit *Imaginary Homelands* (2015). With Paul Firbas, he co-edited *La Araucana (1569–2019)*, a special issue of *Revista Canadiense de Estudios Hispánicos*.

Jason McCloskey is associate professor of Spanish at Bucknell University and co-editor of the book series *Campos Ibéricos* (Bucknell UP). His teaching and research draws on the visual arts and historiography to examine the representation of seafaring and piracy in the epics depicting the conquest of the New World. He is the co-editor of *Signs of Power in Habsburg Spain and the New World*. His work has appeared in *Hispanic Review*, *Revista de Estudios Hispánicos*, *Bulletin of Hispanic Studies*, and *Calíope: Journal of the Society for Renaissance and Baroque Hispanic Poetry*.

Matthew Da Mota is a doctoral candidate at the University of Toronto, Centre for Comparative Literature. He works on early modern Iberian literature and history in Portuguese, Spanish, and Latin, with a focus on epic poetry, historical narratives, shipwreck narratives, and soldiers' chronicles. Taking Luís de Camões's life and the different editions and translations of *Os Lusíadas* as a starting point, his current research interrogates the complex relationship between narrative, literature, and history in the Iberian Peninsula.

Aude Plagnard is *Maîtresse de Conférences* in Comparative Studies at the University Paul-Valéry (Montpellier, France). She is the author of *Une épopée ibérique. Alonso de Ercilla y Jerónimo Corte-Real 1569–1589* (2019) and of several articles on sixteenth-century Iberian epic poetry, focusing on the relationship between epic, historiography, and politics. Her research also addresses the relationship and circulation of epic and lyric poetry between Spain and Portugal in the seventeenth century and the connection between the debates about epic poetry in Portugal and the controversy surrounding the poetry by Luis de Góngora.

Luis Rodriguez Rincon is assistant professor of Spanish at Haverford College. His research focuses on early modern Iberian poetry as it intersects with the History of Science and outlines a framework for interpreting the pagan maritime gods and grottos as veiled natural history in sixteenth- and early seventeenth-century literature and art. His recent article on the early modern grotto, "The Aesthetics of the Early Modern Grotto and the Advent of an Empirical Nature," appears in the volume, *The Aesthetics of the Undersea*, edited by Margaret Cohen and Killian Quigley. His research has been supported by the Lane Fellowship in the History of Science at Stanford University as well as the Huntington Library.

Martín Zulaica López is assistant professor in the area of Literary Theory and Comparative Literature at the Universidad Rey Juan Carlos (Madrid, Spain). He is a member of the research project "Narremes and Myhemes: Units for Epic and Historiographical Elaboration" (NYMUEEH, PID2021-127063NB-100) based at the Universidad de Zaragoza. He is finishing a monograph on the reception of Bernardo de Balbuena's *El Bernardo, o victoria de Roncesvalles*, as well as a critical edition of the same poem.

Index

Page numbers in italics indicate figures or information in their captions.

Toronto Iberic